TERENCE
ANDRIA

EDITED BY

SANDER M. GOLDBERG

University of California, Los Angeles

CAMBRIDGE
UNIVERSITY PRESS

University Printing House, Cambridge CB2 8BS, United Kingdom

One Liberty Plaza, 20th Floor, New York, NY 10006, USA

477 Williamstown Road, Port Melbourne, VIC 3207, Australia

314–321, 3rd Floor, Plot 3, Splendor Forum, Jasola District Centre,
New Delhi – 110025, India

103 Penang Road, #05-06/07, Visioncrest Commercial, Singapore 238467

Cambridge University Press is part of the University of Cambridge.

It furthers the University's mission by disseminating knowledge in the pursuit of
education, learning, and research at the highest international levels of excellence.

www.cambridge.org
Information on this title: www.cambridge.org/9781009200653
DOI: 10.1017/9781009200639

© Cambridge University Press 2022

First published 2022

Printed in the United Kingdom by TJ Books Limited, Padstow Cornwall

A catalogue record for this publication is available from the British Library.

ISBN 978-1-009-20065-3 Hardback
ISBN 978-1-009-20066-0 Paperback

CONTENTS

PREFACE

We do not know the name given at birth to the man who wrote *Andria*. We know only the name of the man who once owned him, for Publius Terentius Afer appears to be a freedman's name. If so, our author was a man who entered the Roman world by force as a slave from North Africa. This mattered very little to the Romans, for whom enslavement was no impediment to literary distinction. Terence's great predecessor Caecilius Statius also bore a freedman's name, and Lucius Accius, who would dominate literary life in the later second century, was a freedman's son. The hint of slave origin matters much more to us, especially when combined with the report that Terence was "dark-complexioned" (*colore fusco*). Could one of the first great dramatists in the western tradition have been a black African and his plays a form of slave literature? That intriguing possibility, which has a long and checkered history in the modern discourse of letters, poses a particular challenge to students of the plays, which offer biographical criticism all too little purchase. Almost without exception, the characters, actions, and attitudes found in these six comedies can be traced not to the personal experience of their author but directly to the well-documented themes and conventions of their genre. Did Terence so thoroughly remove himself from his creation that only his name endures in the text? The best a commentary can do is remain alive to the possibility of biographical resonances, taking care neither to ignore nor to invent them.

What about the genre itself? We have made great progress in appreciating its dramatic brilliance, but for those taking the long view, that greater understanding does not make *palliata* comedy any less problematic. Terence's version may lack Plautus' hard-bitten edge, but his plots still turn on violence toward slaves, callousness toward women, and the self-satisfied arrogance of powerful men. What does that inherent brutality say about the genre, about the society that produced it, and about us, who still find ample reason to enjoy it? Plautine scholarship has begun, albeit slowly, to acknowledge these sensibilities and to address these concerns. Terentian scholarship has lagged behind, so that to modern ears, much in the traditional bibliography can sound tedious, pedantic, or somehow beside the point. Yet that work still has things to teach, and a commentary has a duty to profit from and give credit to all its lessons. Grammar and syntax, vocabulary and meter, textual transmission and textual criticism are as much its business as ever, and in commenting on a dramatic text, discussions of dramaturgy and performance naturally join the mix. We need to see (at least in the mind's eye) what characters do as well as what they say and to imagine how audiences might respond to their actions as well as to their words. After all that, there may nevertheless remain a sense that something is missing, some acknowledgment of an underlying unpleasantness in the drama that neither philological commentary nor literary analysis addresses squarely. That is a legitimate concern, and here too, the best a commentary can do without compromising its primary objectives or distorting its results is to alert users to its own potential shortcomings and empower them to improve upon it.

Commentators invariably accrue debts, and I am no exception. Mine are especially keen and heartfelt: to scholars of the past from Aelius Donatus to Anne Dacier to Peter Brown, who have taught me a great deal and from whom (in the long tradition of commentators everywhere) I have stolen a great deal; to present colleagues unstinting in their advice and generous in their critiques, notably Fred Franko, Toph Marshall, Denise McCoskey, Tim Moore, and especially Amy Richlin, who has compelled me to think about Roman life as well as Roman literature; to the best editors any author could have, Philip Hardie and Stephen Oakley, for so often saving me from myself; and above all to my students over the years, avid Terentians and amused skeptics alike, not just for showing me so earnestly what they wanted to know but for wanting to know such interesting things.

ABBREVIATIONS

The abbreviated titles of plays by Plautus (Pl.) and Terence (T.) follow the practice of the *OLD*, those of Menander (Men.) those of *LSJ*. Other works cited by abbreviation are:

Ashmore   S. G. Ashmore, ed. *The Comedies of Terence*. New York: 1908
Barsby   J. Barsby, ed. *Terence*, 2 vols. Loeb Classical Library. Cambridge, MA: 2001
Bentley   R. Bentley, ed. *Publii Terentii Afri, Comoediae*. Cambridge: 1726
Brown   P. Brown, ed. *Terence. The Girl from Andros*. Aris and Phillips Classical Texts. Liverpool: 2019
Dacier   A. Dacier, ed. *Les Comedies de Terence, avec la Traduction et les Remarques de Madame Dacier*, 2 vols. Paris: 1688
GLK   H. Keil, ed. *Grammatici latini*, 8 vols. Leipzig: 1857–1870
J   S. Jäkel, ed. *Menandri Sententiae; Comparatio Menandri et Philistionis*. Leipzig: 1964
K–T   A. Körte and A. Thierfelder, eds. *Menandri, quae supersunt. Pars altera*. Bibliotheca Teubneriana. Leipzig: 1959
NLS   E. C. Woodcock, *A New Latin Syntax*. Cambridge, MA: 1959
OCT   R. Kauer and W. M. Lindsay, eds. *P. Terenti Afri Comoedia*, rev. ed. Oxford Classical Texts. Oxford: 1958
OLD   P. G. W. Glare, ed. *Oxford Latin Dictionary*. Oxford: 1982
PA   J. Kirchner, ed. *Prosopographica Attica*, 2 ed. Berlin: 1966
PCG   R. Kassel and C. Austin, eds. *Poetae comici graeci*. Berlin: 1991–
R   O. Ribbeck, ed. *Scaenicae Romanorum Poesis Fragmenta*, 3 ed. Leipzig: 1897
SEL   C. E. Bennet, *Syntax of Early Latin*, 2 vols. Boston: 1910, 1914
Shipp   G. P. Shipp, ed. *P. Terenti Afri*, Andria *with Introduction and Commentary*. Oxford: 1960

INTRODUCTION

1 COMEDY AT ROME

In 240 BCE, following their victory over Carthage in the First Punic War, the Romans expanded a traditional fall celebration honoring Jupiter, the *ludi Romani*, into an international festival in the Greek style. Since that meant, among other things, adding formal dramatic productions to the scheduled entertainments, the Senate commissioned a Greek from Tarentum named Andronicus to produce a tragedy and a comedy in Latin for the occasion.[1] The experiment proved so successful that by the early second century plays of various kinds had become regular features at three additional festivals, the *ludi plebeii* (November), *Apollinares* (July), and *Megalenses* (April), and also began appearing on the bill at votive games, triumphs, and the more elaborate aristocratic funerals. Plays were created on Greek topics and Roman ones, ranging from the serious to the comic, from myth to history to the foibles of daily life, and whether by accident or design, their growing popularity made them a significant medium for popularizing Roman traditions and fostering Roman civic identity.[2] Yet of the many different types of play performed on these occasions, only Latin comedies performed in Greek dress, the so-called *comoedia palliata*, survive in more than fragments, and of the two hundred or so plays written for the *palliata* stage in the third and second centuries by a dozen or more different playwrights, only the six of Terence and twenty by Plautus survive intact.[3] The history of this *palliata* comedy is well treated

---

[1] The tradition regarding this initiative in 240 BCE is reasonably sound: Cic. *Brut.* 72–3, *Sen.* 50, *Tusc.* 1.3, Gell. 17.21.42–3. See Gruen 1990: 80–92, Bernstein 1998: 234–51. Its significance, however, is far less certain. Though Varro saw in Andronicus' scripts the true beginning of Latin literature, his predecessors Accius and Porcius Licinus championed rival narratives based on rival chronologies (Welsh 2011). Nor is the history of stage entertainment (*ludi scaenici*) before Andronicus at all clear, e.g. Oakley 1998: 40–72 and Feldherr 1998: 178–87 on the notoriously problematic excursus at Liv. 7.2. See the extensive bibliography in Suerbaum 2002: 51–7, and for a good summary of the problem, Manuwald 2011: 30–40.

[2] The classic study of the performance schedule is Taylor 1937. Duckworth 1952: 76–9 is also helpful. For the financing of games, a combination of state allocations and private resources, see Shatzman 1975: 84–7, and for drama's role in the formation of civic identity, Wiseman 1995: 129–41, 1998: 1–16, controversial in detail but surely correct in outline.

[3] Ribbeck 1897: 388–90 provides a list. Gell. 3.3.11 reports that in his day (second century CE) 130 plays still circulated under the name Plautus, though Varro had identified only twenty-one as indisputably authentic. These (including the

elsewhere and requires no repetition here,[4] but three overarching factors
in our understanding of the genre are particularly important to acknowledge when assessing the construction of any individual play and the way a
Roman audience would have responded to it.

1.1 Conditions of Performance

Large-scale formal support for drama, the kind of institutional support
found in the Greek world, was alien to the Roman experience. There
was no equivalent in Republican Rome to the Athenians' heavy public
investment in theatrical entertainment, which included a formal civic
mechanism for selecting plays and funding productions, and an increasingly elaborate permanent home for them in the precinct of Dionysus.
Occasions like the Greater Dionysia soon became highpoints of the
liturgical and civic calendar: immense prestige attached to the dramatic
competitions at Athens, which even in the fifth century could turn producers, playwrights, and actors into celebrities.[5] In later times, itinerant
professional companies performed their own versions of Athenian plays
throughout the Hellenistic world. These companies also enjoyed considerable, though less political prestige and enjoyed the use of elaborate
public facilities in the cities they visited.[6] That renown makes the comparative informality of the corresponding Roman arrangements especially striking.

Though the Senate authorized the staging of plays and made a financial
contribution to their production, it persistently refused to sanction construction of a permanent theater in the city. Arrangements were left largely
to the discretion and personal resources of the magistrates responsible for

fragmentary *Vidularia*) are probably the ones that survive. Much less is known of
the plays on Roman themes in Roman dress, the so-called *praetextae* and *togatae*.
See Wiseman 2008, and for full discussion of the Republican genres, Manuwald
2011: 129–86.

[4] Gratwick 1982 provides an excellent, brief introduction; a full account is provided by Manuwald 2011: 144–56. Duckworth 1952 and Hunter 1985 remain val-
uable. Manuwald 2010 offers a rich assortment of ancient testimonia.

[5] Pericles, e.g., first attracted notice as *choregos*, backing productions of Aeschylus
that included *Persians*. Sophocles held several important offices, including election
as *strategos* at the time of the Samian crisis of 441/440. By 449 BCE there were separate prizes for actors. Dramatists and actors were commonly citizens in the fifth
century, and their talents tended to run in families (Sutton 1987). *Choregoi* at the
Dionysia, though not the Lenaia, were also citizens (Wilson 2000: 27–32, 51–7).

[6] On the Greek dramatic festivals, see Goldhill 1997 and Rehm 2007, and for
the later acting troupes, Lightfoot 2002. Documentary evidence for all these issues
is available in Csapo and Slater 1995: 103–206, 239–55.

the games, who would contract for a temporary stage to be built on each occasion before the temple of the god being honored.[7] That structure included a backdrop (*scaenae frons*) usually presenting two or three house doors and an acting platform before it representing the street (*platea*, 796n.). A small altar was also visible (726n.). Thus in *An.*, one door represented the house of Simo and a second that of Chrysis and Glycerium. (Whether a third door was used for Charinus' house is unclear.) In addition to these functional doors, entrances and exits could be made from the two sides of the stage. At Athens, where New Comedy's conventions were developed, the orientation of the Theater of Dionysus suggests that the wing to the spectators' right would appear to lead to the agora and harbor and that to their left toward the country, but this convention may not have been consistently employed. At Rome, dramatists continued to represent forum and country (or harbor) in opposite directions, but since the orientation of Roman stages is unknown (and was probably variable), no consistent representation of left and right can be established.[8]

Limited seating may have been provided immediately before this stage structure in the area Greek theaters reserved for choral performances, but most spectators would have had to find their own places on or around the temple or in the adjacent area.[9] Roman actors, instead of performing in an enclosed building that by its very nature committed actors and spectators to the shared endeavor of creating a play, therefore had to work much harder to attract and hold the attention of their audiences, who were subject to distraction by rival entertainments in the vicinity or by the discomforts of whatever vantage points they had secured. A kernel of

---

[7] For the festivals at which T. offered plays, these magistrates were the aediles. Their precise role in the production process and the value of these shows for furthering their careers is obscure. See Gruen 1992: 188–95.

[8] Thus Vitr. 5.6.8 notes *una a foro altera a peregre aditus in scaenam.* See Beare 1964: 248–55, and for Athenian practice, Taplin 1977: 449–51. The porters' entrance at *An.* 28 would have established one direction as to the forum, with the opposite then leading abroad, as for Crito's arrival from Andros at 796. Access to the stage through the orchestra, as shown on so many phlyax vases (n. 18), is not indicated one way or the other in the extant texts.

[9] This is most clearly the arrangement at the Megalensia, where the space on the Palatine hill before the temple of the Magna Mater was especially restricted (Goldberg 1998). Conditions in the forum, where funeral games were celebrated, would have been somewhat different (Goldberg 2018, Hanses 2020a). See more generally Marshall 2006: 31–56, Sear 2006: 54–7, Manuwald 2011: 55–68, and for the temporary stages themselves, Beacham 2007. The first set of plays performed at Augustus' *Ludi Saeculares* in 17 BCE deliberately recalled the archaic style by being offered *in scaena quoi theatrum adiectum non fuit nullis positis sedilibus* (*CIL* VI.32323 = *ILS* 5050, lines 100–101). Cf. the tradition dimly recalled by Tac. *Ann.* 14.20 *si uetustiora repetas, stantem populum spectauisse.*

truth may thus underlie T.'s complaint in the *Hec.* prologues of performances disrupted by the prospect of acrobats (4–5), boxers (33–6), and
gladiators (39–42).

The improvisational quality of the Roman venues had further consequences. A purpose-built stage necessarily limited rehearsal time on site,
with an especially narrow window in the case of the Megalensia, since the
aediles responsible did not assume office until mid-March and the festival
was held at the beginning of April.[10] The resulting time constraints may
have encouraged what became some of Roman comedy's most striking features, e.g. its passion for stock scenes and routines, its opportunities for
improvisation, and the occasional traces in our texts of places to expand
or shorten, elaborate or simplify performances as time and circumstances
required.[11] Such flexibility was facilitated by the high degree of profes-
sionalism that characterized Roman drama from the time the Senate first
charged Andronicus with the task of producing plays. How he created those
first scripts in Latin and recruited actors capable of performing them are
among the many mysteries of early Roman theatrical history, but it is clear
that by the end of the third century, a community of actors and writers was
officially established at Rome as a professional guild under the patronage
of Minerva.[12] Contracts for producing plays were awarded to these companies of professional actors, not to individual playwrights, and the heads
of the companies assumed responsibility for the success of the shows.

This at least is the role that T.'s impresario, Ambivius Turpio, claims
for himself in the prologues to *Hau.* and *Hec.*[13] Turpio was a *senex* by the
160s and speaks to T.'s audiences with the authority of age: he identifies
himself as the young playwright's patron (*Hec.* 52 *in tutelam meam*), as he

---

[10] Thus Ritschl 1845a: 348 took Pl.'s joke at *Trin.* 990 *uapulabis meo arbitratu et
nouorum aedilium* ("You'll be beaten on my order and that of the new aediles") to
indicate performance at the Megalensia. Contracts might possibly have been ne-
gotiated in the interval between the aediles' election and installation – the story at
Eun. 19–24 assumes sufficient time for the aediles to award a contract and Luscius
to challenge it – but physical preparation on site could only have come later.
[11] Plautine texts sometimes contain "doublets" that likely represent alternative
ways to play a scene, e.g. with more or less elaborate music (Goldberg 2004), or
preserve the remains of successive variations (Jocelyn 1995). For the role of stock
scenes and improvisations, see the essays in Benz et al. 1995 and Marshall 2006:
260–79.
[12] Festus 333M, though the details of this so-called *Collegium poetarum* are debated. See Jory 1970, Horsfall 1976, Gruen 1990: 87–90. The theatrical community at Rome consisted largely of freedmen and slaves.
[13] Turpio of course speaks the words and plays the part T. wrote for him, but
the part is consistent with other testimony regarding Roman actor-managers. See
Duckworth 1952: 73–6, Beare 1964: 164–70, Leppin 1992: 49–59, Lebek 1996,
Brown 2002, Goldberg 2005: 72–3.

had been a generation earlier for the great Caecilius (*Hec.* 14–15). A curious anecdote about Turpio in rehearsal tells us a little more about their partnership. Turpio, says Don., played the parasite Phormio while yawning, tipsy, and scratching his ear, and T., though initially annoyed by the actor's apparent inebriation, eventually had to admit that this insouciance was exactly what he had imagined for the character.[14] The playwright's active engagement in the rehearsal is as striking as the actor's condition. Turpio's company produced all six of T.'s plays, and the scripts may well have been tailored to the capabilities of the troupe. That kind of customization has long been suspected for Plautus: among the more obvious signs of a similar process in the Terentian corpus is the variety of musical effects in the recitatives, which may reflect the special talents of Turpio's resident musician, Flaccus. The contributions of people like Turpio and Flaccus remind us that success on the Roman stage required considerably more than just a good script.[15]

1.2 The Audience

The improvisational quality of Roman venues also facilitated contact, or at least the illusion of contact, between actors and audience. The inevitable commotion as a play gets under way is evoked in various Plautine prologues, such as this moment in *Poenulus*.[16]

> scortum exoletum ne quis in proscaenio
> sedeat, neu lictor uerbum aut uirgae muttiant,
> neu dissignator praeter os obambulet
> neu sessum ducat, dum histrio in scaena siet.

---

[14] Don. ad *Ph.* 315 *quibus auditis exclamauit poeta se talem eum scriberet cogitasse parasitum.* What few details of original performance survived the six centuries between T. and Don. probably entered the scholarly tradition through Varro. The comment on Ambivius' acting style at Cic. *Sen.* 48 may simply be Cicero's own experience of Roscius projected back on an earlier generation.

[15] For the importance of the company (*grex*) in the collaborative effort of play-production, see Marshall 2006: 83–94, Kruschwitz 2016. Flaccus is credited in the didascaliae with the music for each of the six plays, a striking distinction. Cf. Fraenkel 2007 (1960): 416, "In general one must never forget that a writer like Plautus who wrote all his comedies for performance by a particular company on a particular occasion, had to take account of the aptitudes of the actors who composed the troupe." Gilula 1989: 104–105 makes a similar point about T. Similarly, the Shakespearean corpus reflects the changing strengths over time of the Chamberlains' and King's Men and the different requirements of the (outdoor) Globe and (indoor) Blackfriars. See Shapiro 2010: 228–31, 245–51.

[16] Pl. *Poen.* 17–20, though all of 1–45 contributes to the picture. Additional vignettes of the Roman audience appear at *Amph.* 64–95 and *As.* 4–5.

Let's have no worn-out tart sitting on the
stage or lictor bandying words or rods waving
or an usher getting in someone's face or
seating anyone while an actor is on the stage.   (17–20)

At *Captivi* 10–14, the prologue-speaker interrupts his own exposition to
single out an individual in the crowd for abuse, confirming in the process
how indistinct the boundaries of improvised theatrical space can be.

iam hoc tenetis? optumest.
negat hercle illic ultumus. accedito.
si non ubi sedeas locus est, est ubi ambules,
quando histrionem cogis mendicarier.
ego me tua caussa, ne erres, non rupturus sum.

Have you got this then? Great.
That man far in the back says no. Come forward.
If there's no place to sit, take a hike,
since you're forcing an actor into beggary.
I won't rupture myself for your sake, so you don't miss anything.

Still more striking is a similar interaction *during* the performance, as
Euclio in *Aulularia* desperately seeks to recover his stolen treasure.[17]

obsecro uos ego, mi auxilio,
oro, obtestor, sitis et hominem demonstretis, quis eam abstulerit.
quid est? quid ridetis? noui omnes, scio fures esse hic
complures,
qui uestitu et creta occultant sese atque sedent quasi sint frugi.
quid ais tu? tibi credere certum est, nam esse bonum ex uoltu
cognosco.
hem, nemo habet horum? occidisti. dic igitur, quis habet?
nescis?

Please help me, all of you!
I beg, I implore you to point out the man who took it.
What's that? You laugh? I know you all. I know there are plenty
of thieves here,
who disguise themselves in fancy clothes and sit about like
honest men.

---

[17] Pl. *Aul.* 715–20. Direct address to the audience in Greek comedy tends to
be more generic. See the examples in Bain 1977: 190–4. Dionysus' appeal to his
priest at Aristoph. *Ra.* 297 is a closer, though more fleeting, parallel.

What do *you* say? I'll surely believe *you*, since I see from your face
   you're upright.
What? None of these has it? You've done me in. Say then, who
   has it? You don't know?

His first, sweeping appeal seems generic, but the switch to the singular
at 719 (*quid ais tu?*) means that Euclio has singled out an individual, and
the follow-up (*hem . . . ?*) means he waits for a response and does not
immediately let go of his victim. Seating that brought spectators close to
the stage platform would have facilitated such immediacy, allowing actors
to acknowledge and perhaps even to mingle with them in the course of
the performance, especially if the action spilled beyond the confines of
the *scaena*.[18]
   Euclio's address is also striking because those men in their fancy clothes
may have included members of the senatorial elite: after 194 BCE, senators in attendance at the shows could claim special places for themselves
that later practice suggests were immediately before the stage.[19] If Euclio's
jibe reflects the widespread resentment this new privilege generated, it
may also suggest greater license for social comment than is often envisioned in Roman contexts. The fact that senators could claim this right
does not necessarily mean, of course, that they ever attended in large
numbers or that the shows were staged primarily for their benefit: other
sources allude to women, children, slaves and the urban poor among the
crowd.[20] What united them all was their passion for *palliata* comedy. The
very strength of the tradition and the enthusiasm with which dramatists
embraced and exploited its conventions suggest an audience well versed
in its devices and deeply appreciative of its effects. Thus John Wright, after
documenting the enduring appeal of its traditionality, concludes: "Widely

[18] The so-called phlyax vases of southern Italy, e.g. the Cheiron vase and New
York Goose Play (figs. 12.6 and 10.2 in Taplin 1993), often show action in what
would notionally be the audience's space, and while this material predates the *palliata* by as much as two centuries, it is hard to imagine Roman producers ignoring
such easy opportunities to enrich their action.
[19] So Cic. *Har. resp.* 24 *ante populi consessum senatui locum.* Liv. 34.44 and 54, Val.
Max. 2.4.3, Ascon. 70C are less specific. The motives and effects of this development remain unclear, though the resentment it aroused is well attested. See Gruen
1992: 202–205, Gilula 1996. The joke at *Capt.* 15–16 expands to acknowledge
wealthier spectators, though not necessarily senators, in their seats. On the whole
vexed question of seating by class, see Rawson 1987, and for Roman seating more
generally, Moore 1995, Beare 1964: 241–7. The practice is easier to envision – and
enforce – in the formal theaters of later times than at the temporary venues of the
second century.
[20] Beare 1964: 173–5 assembles the evidence. See also Chalmers 1965, Moore
1998: 8–23, Marshall 2006: 79–81, Manuwald 2011: 98–108.

travelled (many would have seen some of the best Greek theater of the day during military service in Sicily and South Italy), self-confident, sophisticated, thoroughly accustomed, thanks to their experiences in forum, court, and comitium, to every facet of artistic verbal ritual, the Romans clearly made up one of the great theatrical audiences of all time."[21] The details are probably exaggerated: not all were widely travelled or could claim active experience of forum, court, and comitium, but a significant majority surely knew what they wanted and insisted upon getting it. And they were almost certainly demonstrative in making known their pleasure or disappointment. Notoriously animated in Cicero's day, there is no reason to think Roman audiences were any more restrained a century and more earlier.[22]

1.3 Greek Models

In saying that his *Andria* re-works two plays by Menander (9–14), T. alludes to a basic fact of contemporary practice: Roman dramatists did not create *palliata* scripts out of nothing. Their characters, plots, and settings all originated in the New Comedy of fourth- and third-century Athens. Pl., too, may freely and even proudly admit as much.

> Clerumenoe uocatur haec comoedia
> graece, latine Sortientes. Diphilus
> hanc graece scripsit, postid rursum denuo
> latine Plautus cum latranti nomine.

> This comedy is called *Clerumenoi*
> in Greek, in Latin *The Lottery*. Diphilus
> wrote it in Greek; the eventual Latin remake
> was done by Plautus, of the barking name.   (Pl. *Cas.* 31–4)

> graece haec uocatur Emporos Philemonis,
> eadem latine Mercator Macci Titi.

> In Greek this play of Philemon is called *Emporos*,
> the Latin version is *The Merchant* of Titus Maccius.   (Pl. *Merc.* 9–10)

---

[21] Wright 1974: 191. The old stereotype of the obtuse Roman audience, e.g. Norwood 1923: 2 "the immense majority of Romans did not appreciate good art," has largely vanished from scholarship.

[22] Cic. often notes the animation of audiences for both tragedies and comedies, e.g. *Amic.* 40, *Parad.* 3.26, *Q. Rosc.* 30, and with a specifically political turn, *Att.* 2.19.3, *Sest.* 118–23. Greek audiences were famously demonstrative in all periods: Csapo and Slater 1995: 301–305.

Fidelity to these models was not a priority. Simply preserving the original Greek dress and settings for characters who then proceeded to speak and act like Romans inevitably turned Athenian comedies of daily life into Roman domestic fantasies. Plautus went even further. His musical extravaganzas may owe nearly as much to native Italian traditions of stage entertainment as to what he found in Diphilus or Menander, and he sometimes stretched his models well beyond the point of recognition.[23] T.'s more restrained style of adaptation created plays that are easier to reconcile with scholarly preconceptions about Greek comic art, but the difference between the two dramatists does not obviate a central issue common to all discussions of Roman comedy: What counts as "original" or "creative" in a tradition so shamelessly derived from another?

That question has a long, problematic history in the study of Roman comedy. By the late nineteenth century, scholars anxious to see through the Latin plays to the lost Greek ones behind them were not always kind to the Roman authors whose techniques of adaptation often obscured their view. Even the great Friedrich Leo, a particularly astute and appreciative reader of Plautus, treated him as a stepping-stone to something else.[24] The subsequent rediscovery of much original New Comedy, which began in earnest with publication of the Cairo codex of Menander in 1907 and continues to the present day, has gradually relieved this pressure on the Latin texts. Hellenists with genuine New Comedy to read increasingly leave the Latin "copies" to Latinists and allow the Roman plays to stand on their own merits. Pl.'s reputation has risen accordingly. His passion for the stock characters and situations of the *palliata*, his mastery of lyric rhythms (rivaled only by Horace nearly two centuries later), and the easy rapport he established with his audience evoke widespread admiration: we have learned to judge his achievement not by how well he escapes, but by how brilliantly he exploits his traditional material.[25] With Roman stage practice now a legitimate focus of attention in its own right, the question

[23] At *Cas.* 60–6, 1012–14, Pl. proudly claims responsibility for what must have been a significant change in the action and emphasis of the original, and *Epid.* has been so radically reworked that the contours of its putative model have long defied recognition (Fantham 1981). On the general problem of "models," see Manuwald 2011: 282–92. Fraenkel 2007 (1922): 275–86 on how Pl. "dismembered" Greek drama remains basic.

[24] So in the words of his student Fraenkel 2007 (1922): 2, "Leo loved Plautus, but he loved Greek comedy even more, and if he could gain access to the Greek forms through the Roman plays, this gave him complete satisfaction, and sometimes he did not go any further." See Goldberg 1986: 61–6, Halporn 1993: 191–6, and Goldberg 2011: 206–10.

[25] This is the great lesson of Wright 1974: 195–6. Few today would agree with Norwood 1923: 1 that Pl. "wrote like a blacksmith mending a watch."

that so preoccupied Fraenkel's generation, "How did Plautus translate?",
no longer seems pressing. As Erich Segal noted at the very start of this
shift in the scholarly paradigm, "once the play begins, everything becomes
'Plautus'."[26]

T. nevertheless speaks of rendering a scene from Diphilus "word for
word" (*Ad.* 11 *uerbum de uerbo expressum extulit*), a suggestion of fidelity
only strengthened by the ancient exegetical tradition, which occasionally
encourages comparison with his Greek models. Don. sometimes quotes
phrases that suggest direct translation, as at *An.* 204, where T.'s *nil me
fallis* clearly renders Men.'s νῦν δ' οὐ λέληθάς με, while Men.'s version of
the midwife's instruction at *An.* 484 preserved in the Byzantine anthology
of Photius, καὶ τεττάρων | ᾠῶν μετὰ τοῦτο, φιλτάτε, τὸ νεόττιον ("and after-
wards, dear, the yolk of four eggs") has prompted considerable discussion
of T.'s departure from its greater specificity.[27] Fidelity on this verbal level,
however, is regularly eclipsed by more radical changes. Eliminating an
expository prologue, interpolating scenes or characters from a second
play, turning dialogue to monologue (or monologue to dialogue), and
eliminating act divisions inevitably produce significant alterations in the
way a play works on its audience. The one case where an extant Roman
play can now be set against a continuous fragment of its original, Pl.'s
Bacchides and Men.'s *Dis Exapaton*, clearly shows the Roman dramatist
altering not only the sequence of his action, but the psychology of his
actors.[28] Equally significant changes in T. can be harder to evaluate since
our knowledge of them comes largely through the filter of Don.'s commentary (Introduction 6); a comparative approach working from that
sort of evidence may in the end leave us suspecting rather more than we
can know about what was a complex creative process. If what we really

---

[26] Segal 1987: 6. On the earlier question, cf. Fraenkel 2007 (1922): 3-4 and the
new Preface to the English edition, xi-xxii. By 1960, Fraenkel had acknowledged
the futility of reconstructing lost originals: "Perhaps it will be necessary to make
do, more often than Leo, Jachmann, and I did, with the finding that the course
of the action which we find in Plautus could not have been the same in a Greek
comedy, and it will be necessary to give up the attempt to reconstruct the action or
essential elements of the action of lost Greek plays" (416).

[27] See commentary ad loc. and Appendix II for a full list of Greek quotations.
Close translation is not unique to T. The correspondence of what is now Men. fr.
111 K–T ὅν οἱ θεοὶ φιλοῦσιν ἀποθνῄσκει νέος to Pl. *Bacch.* 816–17 *quem di diligunt/
adulescens moritur* helped Ritschl 1845b: 406 identify *Dis Exapaton* as Pl.'s model.

[28] The papyrus, officially published in 1997 as P. Oxy. 4407, has been known
and discussed since 1968. See Handley 2001, and for analysis from a Roman perspective, Damen 1992, Batstone 2005. The structural comparison is unique in the
record, though an extended stylistic comparison is also provided by Gell. 2.23,
setting excerpts from Caecilius' *Plocium* against its Menandrean model. See Wright
1974: 120–6.

care about is a *Roman* comedy, why, then, should we pay more than token attention to the fact that it was based on a Greek one?

Modern scholarship has increasingly responded to the fact of models by assimilating them, whether known directly or indirectly, into the larger body of "intertexts" that comprise the literary milieu in which Roman dramatists operated. This approach, which engages not exclusively with dramatic texts but encourages us to extend our analysis to the influence of oratory, polemic, and even to Callimachean poetics, vastly enriches the field of scholarly inquiry while avoiding the old pitfalls of a source criticism too inclined to fault Roman comedy for not being Greek comedy.[29] Its potential weakness is that in privileging a meditative, text-based style of analysis, it brushes aside the possibility that scripts created for second-century theater audiences, who favored broad strokes, immediate effects, and rapid pace, might require different critical methods from texts created for private enjoyment.[30] A more traditional alternative draws analogues and parallels from the Greek material without necessarily positing direct relationships as sources or targets of allusion. This can make the critic's task a little easier. Where Athenian audiences, for example, would very likely have recognized an allusion to Euripides' Electra in the entrance of Knemon's daughter to fetch water from her well and Diphilus probably parodied such tragic scenes with a water jar in the original of *Rudens*, Romans watching the antics of Pl.'s Sceparnio and Ampelisca were less surely attuned to the full range of their scene's dramatic antecedents.[31] By recognizing the tradition's capabilities, which is what parallels represent, we can appreciate the choices Pl. made in writing the scene as he did (and not in some other, equally possible way) without needing first to reconstruct specifically what he found in Diphilus or to consider whether his audience had a comparable grasp of the tradition's history.[32]

---

[29] For these intertexts, Sharrock 2009: 75–83, and as applied to *Eun.*, 219–32. The possibility of allusions to Callimachus in Roman drama, still highly controversial, is well argued by Sharrock, less well by Fontaine 2010: 197–200. A more narrowly constructed intertextuality is discussed by Manuwald 2011: 309–20.

[30] Sharrock 2009: 79 n. 140 observes in response that "it is worth remembering that dramatic works also have a textual life outside the performance," though whether second-century scripts enjoyed any "textual life" among contemporaries is uncertain. It is not even clear that whole scripts existed, much less circulated outside the troupes in the dramatists' lifetime. See Deufert 2002: 44–57, Goldberg 2005: 48–50.

[31] Men. *Dysk.* 189–217, Pl. *Rud.* 331–457. The correspondences and "intertexts" of these two scenes are approached in interestingly different ways by Handley 2002: 106–16 and Fontaine 2010: 42–9.

[32] Though effect and intention are not the same, dramatists certainly produced the former and began with the latter, and while authorial intent need not be the sole object of critical inquiry, it remains a legitimate one. See Hinds 1998: 47–51.

2 THE CAREER OF TERENCE

Nothing is known for certain about the life of T., although much was said about it in antiquity. A biography ascribed to Suetonius records that P. Terentius Afer was born at Carthage, came to Rome as the slave of an (otherwise unknown) senator named Terentius Lucanus, and secured his freedom by virtue of intellectual talent and good looks. His dramatic career, which consisted of six comedies produced in the course of the 160s, was supported by his great predecessor Caecilius Statius and by leading Romans later identified with Scipio Aemilianus and Gaius Laelius. Then, still in his mid-twenties, he drowned in a shipwreck on his way back from Greece with a fresh collection of Greek plays adapted for the Roman stage, leaving behind a small estate on the Appian Way and sufficient money for his daughter to marry an equestrian. In spinning this tale, Suetonius cites numerous authorities, who all disagree with each other. As so often with literary biography in antiquity, the author's life has largely been deduced – and probably embellished – from the author's work. Not even a birth at Carthage and early death at sea are necessarily true: Afer "the African" is not a cognomen restricted to those of North African origin, and the fatal trip to Greece may simply have been deduced from the undeniable fact of the small corpus and too literal an interpretation of T.'s complaint (*Eun.* 41–3) about the limited amount of material at his disposal.[33]

The possibility of African origin, and in particular of black African origin, has long attracted the interest of modern readers,[34] though the plays are so thoroughly deracinated that not even the appearance of a freedman in *An.* (28–171) or a black slave in *Eun.* (471) directs any special attention to matters of race or social status. Ancient readers cared much more about questions of patronage. T.'s own prologues hint at aristocratic connections (*Hau.* 22–4, *Ad.* 15–21), hints strengthened by the fact that

---

[33] Though T.'s name certainly suggests a freedman from Africa, it is worth recalling that Quint.'s teacher, the famous orator and consul Gn. Domitius Afer, was neither a freedman nor an African. The ancient life is preserved in MSS of Don. Text and commentary are provided by Rostagni 1954 and Carney 1963: 5–17; for critical explication see Beare 1942, Courtney 1993: 87–90, Fantham 2004, Davis 2014.

[34] Suet. *VitaT* 6 *fuisse dicitur mediocri statura, gracili corpore, colore fusco.* Interest in T.'s race was first articulated in the Renaissance and becomes significant by the eighteenth century. Phillis Wheatley, the first published African-American poet, proudly identified him with "Afric's sable race" in "To Maecenas," introducing her *Poems on Various Subjects, Religious and Moral* (1773), while Thomas Jefferson, "Query XIV: Laws," *Notes on the State of Virginia* (1785), was no less emphatic in claiming him for "the race of whites." For the Renaissance reception of the biography, see Teramura 2018: 878–91. The history of its later reception has yet to be written.

Hec. and *Ad.* were produced at the funeral games for Aemilius Paullus. That information derives from the so-called didascaliae, production notes included in the MSS, which together with occasional notes in Don.'s commentary permit reconstruction of a likely chronology for T.'s career.[35] The plays, occasions, and dates seem to be these:

> *Andria*, at the Ludi Megalenses of 166 BCE
> *Hecyra*, at the Ludi Megalenses of 165 BCE (aborted)
> *Heauton timorumenos*, at the Ludi Megalenses of 163 BCE
> *Eunuchus*, at the Ludi Megalenses of 161 BCE
> *Phormio*, at the Ludi Romani of 161 BCE
> *Hecyra*, at the funeral games of Aemilius Paullus in 160 BCE
> (aborted)
> *Adelphoe*, at the funeral games of Aemilius Paullus in 160 BCE
> *Hecyra*, at the Ludi Romani of 160 BCE

Since plays by the early second century were regularly commissioned for four of Rome's great festivals, the apparent predilection for the Megalensia is perhaps significant: it may have been an easier venue to manage, smaller in size and scale than the others.[36] It is also clear that his taste ran toward the New Comedy style of Menander, since four of the six plays are based on Menandrean originals and the other two, *Ph.* and *Hec.*, are based on plays by Apollodorus of Carystos, whose own style of play-making is sometimes said to have been modeled on Menander's.[37]

That interest in the character-driven comedy of Menander ultimately distinguishes T.'s plays from those of Pl., whose comedies tend to be louder and broader in their effects even when, as in *Amphitruo* and *Aulularia*, character not only drives the plot, but is a major center of dramatic interest. T. seems in comparison quieter and more thoughtful, and, given the

---

[35] For the didascaliae, see Klose 1966, Goldberg 2005: 69–75, and the commentary ad loc. The antiquarian research of Varro and his teacher Aelius Stilo is thought to stand behind the information recorded by such later sources as Suet. and Don. (Schmidt 1989). The attack on the accuracy of the didascalic record by Mattingly 1959 rests on too credulous a reading of the highly rhetorical prologues, as does the largely political interpretation of T.'s career by Umbrico 2010: 59–111.

[36] The space available on the Palatine was physically smaller than venues for the other games, and the date at the beginning of April provided little time to prepare. Weather may also have been a factor. Since the mid-Republican calendar was out of rhythm with the sun, Roman "April" was still mid-winter, which might have discouraged attendance. See Goldberg 1998.

[37] What little is known about Apollodorus is gathered at *PCG* II 485–6. Belief in a close association of Apollodorus and Menander, a modern idea, is encouraged by the thematic similarity of Men.'s *Epitrepontes* and T.'s *Hec.*, which was based on an Apollodoran *Hekyra*.

Romans' growing experience and deepening appreciation of Hellenism in this period, it has long been common to imagine T. as standing somehow apart from the other authors of *palliatae*, a playwright more interested in giving Romans a close Latin equivalent of what Greek art had achieved than feeding them more of the old Roman comic stereotypes (Introduction 3.3). The polemical prologues he created to introduce his plays encourage this idea by suggesting the ongoing struggle of a young innovator against older rivals eager to sabotage his efforts (e.g. *An.* 5–7, *Ad.* 1–5) while ridiculing the absurdities of their own cliché-ridden stage devices (*Hau.* 30–4, *Eun.* 35–40, *Ph.* 6–12).[38] That view has not been altogether good for T.'s reputation. His admirers, even at their most lyrical, hasten to acknowledge a certain limitation of vision. So, for example, the famous Italian philosopher-critic Benedetto Croce: "In the plays of Terence there is a unity of feeling, a steady and coherent personality, an artistic chastity and nobility, a shyness about leaving his own range and breaking or straying into those of others."[39] On the other side stands a whole school of criticism so impressed by the semblance of Atticism in T. that they mistake it for the real thing: "Terence found in the Attic comedies such a completely formed tradition of the well-made play that he knew his own attempts could not, as a rule, compete with it. As long as this reservoir was not exhausted, it probably seemed to him pointless to offer necessarily weaker creations of his own . . . Where he found occasion to alter his models with inventions of his own, the result was normally not an essentially new creation."[40] T.'s very artistry then deprives him of art.

Scholars of all persuasions really ought to have known better. The prologues are not accurate witnesses to anything except T.'s gift for literary invention. Deeply rhetorical, and thus inevitably artificial, they are no more reliable in their testimony than the *parabaseis* of Old Comedy, to which they have been reasonably compared. Having stripped them of any overt expository function – itself a bold move reflecting confidence in his plays' ability to introduce their own action – T. turns the prologues into a new kind of entertainment to do the traditional work of winning

---

[38] So Wright 1974: 183–5 imagines T. struggling against the monopoly of the contemporary Collegium poetarum, though the prologues also cite the example of Naevius, Plautus, and Ennius (all safely dead) to justify his own practice (*An.* 18–21, *Hau.* 20–21).

[39] Croce 1966 [1936]: 784–5. So too Norwood 1923: 3–4, "these six works show a serious failing . . . That is to say, his subject matter is amazingly limited."

[40] Ludwig 1968: 180–1, echoed in respect to *An.* by Shipp 1960: 23: "T. is essentially a translator, or, if one prefers, an adapter of Greek plays, not a creator." The German approach shaping Ludwig's judgment is surveyed by Gaiser 1972. See in particular his comparison of Pl. and T. at 1107–9.

the audience's attention and fueling their interest in the play to come.[41] The character created for this purpose, the old theatrical hand wise in the ways of plays and audiences, is not, strictly speaking, T.'s producer Ambivius Turpio, but Turpio playing a part (*orator ... ornatu prologi, Hec.* 9, cf. *Hau.* 1–2). Given such explicit role-playing, not even the fact of a quarrel with contemporary dramatists is entirely certain, much less the aesthetic grounds for it.[42] As a practical matter, it is hard to believe that T., with the unwavering support of a leading impresario and the sympathy of influential aristocrats to guarantee his contracts, was in any meaningful sense an outsider, nor did he ever deny exploiting Roman comic conventions or claim any greater fidelity to his models than his predecessors showed. Friedrich Leo, at the very beginning of modern scholarly interest in T., noticed the artificiality of his Atticism: he was no mere translator and no truer to his models than Pl. was. He simply altered them in a different way.[43]

The truth of that insight is clear on inspection. Though mocking dramatic convention in his prologues, T. does not abandon it. He certainly ridicules a rival by hinting at the absurdity of a stock device:

> qui nuper fecit seruo currenti in uia
> decesse populum: quor insano seruiat?
>
> who recently had a crowd yield to a slave running
> in the street: why indulge a madman?   (*Hau.* 31–2)

Yet the running slave, so intent on delivering his message that he fails to see the person he seeks and so exhausted by his efforts that he is unable to speak when contact is eventually made, was a great favorite of the Roman stage, and T. makes full use of him. There are four running-slave routines in his six plays, the first here in *An.* when the slave Davos rushes onstage

---

[41] The move is not entirely unprecedented. Pl. *Curc.* and *Epid.*, e.g., lack prologues entirely, though these may possibly have been lost in the course of transmission. *Asin.* has a minimal prologue, and that of *Trin.* introduces themes rather than details of plot. Expository prologues are delayed in *Cist.* and *Mil.* Fuller discussion in Duckworth 1952: 211–18, Hunter 1985: 24–35, Moore 1998: 12–17.

[42] *Ph.* 12–17 may itself hint at the artificiality of the quarrel. The uniformly combative tone of all seven prologues suggests the same speaker throughout, though Turpio is only identified twice. Young men, says T. (*Hau.* 2), normally played these parts, but the generalization may not apply to his own practice.

[43] Leo 1913: 246–7, "One readily feels that T. is simpler, clearer, and more Attic than Pl. It is not the case, however, that he on principle translated more faithfully; we have observed that he handled his models as freely in his own way as Pl. did. It is because he developed his own art, in which, as was the case with Pl., he reveals his own nature."

with news for his young master (338–51). It is comparatively restrained in its stage business, but T. would go on to develop the stock scene in various ways, perhaps none more brilliantly effective than when the over-wrought Geta in *Ad.* actually wishes to find people in his way and proceeds to act out in frenzied mime the punishment he would inflict upon meeting them.[44]

Stock characters of the sort T. dismisses (*Hau.* 37–9) also appear to great effect in his own plays. There is a greedy pimp in *Ad.*, a soldier and parasite in *Eun.*, and in *Hau.* and *Ph.* formidable wives able to hold their own against even the magnificent Cleostrata of Pl.'s *Casina* or Menaechmus' ferocious wife in Epidamnus. Yet here, too, T. is especially good at inverting roles: the clever Davos of *An.* succeeds in his scheme only because the tale he spins turns out to be true, and Parmeno in *Hec.*, initially so proud of his abilities, is eventually left confused and uncertain about what, if anything, he has achieved for his young master. The humor for T., as for Pl., works most effectively by embracing convention, not denying it. Audiences get their best laughs precisely because they come to the play with expectations and see those expectations brilliantly realized or ingeniously overturned. And finally, it is important to remember that T.'s passion for rhythmic variation even within scenes is very much in the Roman musical tradition and not, so far as we know, in the Greek one.[45] The significant differences in tone between Pl. and T. should not obscure the fundamental fact that, with the one notorious exception of *Hec.*, T.'s plays had no difficulty finding and keeping audiences. Indeed, *Eun.* was so popular it garnered an immediate encore and a record fee (Suet. *VitaT* 3), and even after T.'s death, his plays almost certainly remained in the active repertory through at least the 140s.[46]

---

[44] *Ad.* 299–329. The other two such scenes are *Ph.* 179–99 and 841–60. See Duckworth 1936, Lowe 2009. The *currens* was such a stage favorite that he left his mark on the material record with pictures and figurines reflecting the character-istic mannerisms of his routine, the many Greek illustrations strengthening claims of a Greek origin for this familiar Roman figure (Csapo 1989, 1993). A variant on the device sends someone off on a fool's errand, from which he returns exhausted and frustrated: *Hec.* 430–43, 799–815 (Parmeno), *Ad.* 570–86, 713–18 (Demea).

[45] Moore 2007, 2012: 182–4. T.'s *tibicen* Flaccus probably both composed and played the score, which would account for his prominence in the didascaliae.

[46] The didascalia to *Ph.* in the Bembine codex (A) garbles names that may be the consuls of 106 BCE (so Tansey 2001), which would be the last attested produc-tion of T., though a similar set of consuls appears in the *fasti* for 141. The reference in Var. *R.* 2.11.11 to the *senex* of *Hau.* wearing a leather smock is not unequivocal evidence that Var. saw the play in performance: his context is standard rustic dress, and the other example cited (Caecilius' *Hypobolimaeus*) was certainly best known as a book (cf. Cic. *Rosc. Am.* 46). For T.'s popularity in his time, see Parker 1996.

3 ANDRIA

Before the aediles would buy his first play (or so the story goes), T. was told to win the approval of Caecilius Statius. Having made his approach at dinner, the poor and unknown neophyte began reciting *An.* from a stool at the great man's feet but did not get very far before an admiring Caecilius invited him up to share the meal. Like so many good stories, this one is probably apocryphal: Caecilius was almost certainly dead by the early 160s.[47] T.'s opening scene, though, was in fact widely admired, and as the first play in the corpus, *An.* has always received particular attention. Ancient rhetoricians cite it more than any of the other five; it was the first Roman comedy translated into a vernacular language; Richard Steele turned it into a sentimental comedy in the eighteenth century and Thornton Wilder into a sentimental novella in the twentieth. Critics note in particular its original treatment of the traditional master-slave rivalry, its sly allusions to the artificialities of the *palliata* genre, and especially its shift in emphasis from a play of intrigue to one of character as T. explores with great sensitivity the fraught relationship of a well-intentioned but imperious father unwilling to confront his son and an honest but overwhelmed son afraid to confide in his overbearing father. As with all drama, taking stock of this achievement requires reconciling the insights of text-based exegesis that clarify what the words on the page say and the action they demand with what the material evidence encourages us to imagine when that text was brought to life in performance.

3.1 Some Technical Issues

However imaginative in conception and deft in language, *An.* remains a beginner's play with a roughness around the edges that hints at a dramatist still learning his craft. Not every ostensible flaw is significant: *palliata* comedy readily tolerated a certain vagueness in detail. It should not unduly trouble us that the interval between Chrysis' funeral and the dramatic present goes unspecified, or that T. leaves unclear whether Glycerium's pregnancy is the result of a consensual liaison or a rape.[48] Where Charinus lives or how and when word of Chrysis' death reached

---

Whether the spurious final scene of *An.* was written for a later revival is unknown. See Appendix I.

[47] Suet. *VitaT* 3. The fact that Ambivius Turpio was also Caecilius' producer probably lies behind the anecdote (*Hec.* 4–15). Gell. 13.2 records a similar story about Accius and the aged Pacuvius.

[48] Contrast *Ad.*, where Philumena's condition is explicitly described as the result of rape (466–73), with the off-stage birth the culmination of a full-term pregnancy

Andros are not matters of interest. Other apparent anomalies of structure and characterization, however, do repay attention. Arising directly
from additions T. made to his core model, they provide important insight
into the mechanics and priorities of his dramaturgy.

3.1.1 The Character of Sosia

Sosia is T.'s creation. He appears only in the expository dialogue T.
imported to *An.* from Men.'s *Perinthia*, where the part was played by the old
man's wife (Don. ad 14). He is Simo's freedman, singled out for his *fides
et taciturnitas* (33–4) to keep an eye on Pamphilus and Davos (168–70).
Loyalty and discretion are traits well suited to a *libertus* and will assume
thematic significance as we come to see Pamphilus torn by conflicting
obligations to his father, to Glycerium, and to Charinus, so we could say
that Sosia is appropriately cast for his role. He nevertheless remains a curi-
ously problematic character.

   Don. identifies him as a cook, glossing his initial question *nempe ut
curentur recte haec?* as *diligenter coquantur* (ad 30) and his eventual acceptance of Simo's instructions (*curabo*) as *ut coquus* (ad 171). The MSS's illustration for this scene appears to agree: Sosia in the miniature holds a ladle
in his left hand, and his dark-complexioned mask with three braids recalls
what Pollux calls the "cicada" (*tettix*) mask associated by Athenaeus with
non-citizen cooks.[49] On that reading, Sosia believes he has been hired to
supervise the preparation of a wedding feast. That makes some sense, for
the professional cook (*mageiros*) was a familiar figure of New Comedy with
a well-established set of stock jokes and farcical routines. He is invariably
bombastic and vain, with a propensity to steal from his employers, and
like pimps and parasites, he delights in his very outrageousness. Several
such cooks appear in Pl., and even the minor walk-on of *Cur.* 251–73, an
otherwise anonymous *cocus*, is unable to resist a boast or two. T. avoids the

---

(475). *An.* hints at a more equal partnership between a couple unambiguously
represented as lovers (215–24, 945–6).

[49] Clearly shown on leaf 4v of *An.* in Vat. lat. 3868 (digi.vatlib.it/view/MSS_Vat.
lat.3868), the oldest and most detailed of the many copies. The slave mask Pollux
4.148 describes as "bald and dark-skinned, with two or three black braids on his
head, his beard also black; he has a squint" (ὁ δὲ θεράπων τέττιξ φαλακρὸς μέλας, δύο
ἢ τρία βοστρύχια μέλανα ἐπικείμενος, καὶ ὅμοια ἐν τῷ γενείῳ, διάστροφος τὴν ὄψιν) is
identified with Webster 1995: no. 26. Cf. Athen. 14.659a, and for its associations,
Dohm 1964: 11–22. The figure labeled "Mageiros" in the famous Mytilene mosaic
of Menander's *Samia* seems to be wearing this mask. Though dark-complexioned
masks are well documented, their cultural connotations are not well understood.
See Richlin 2019.

type, though the slave Syrus of *Ad.*, who at one point supervises a procession of porters bearing foodstuffs and instructs them on their preparation, affects some of the cook's traditional mannerisms (*Ad.* 364–81).[50]
The problem here is that nothing in this well-established character type
could be further from the *taciturnitas* and *fides* of the obsequious Sosia,
and to say with Simo that *nil istac opus est arte* (32) would in effect be to
dismiss the entire complex of motifs that gives the comic cook his raison
d'être. Why, then, would T. introduce a cook but not have him *be* a cook?[51]

Nor is this the only anomaly. Freedmen are rare figures in Roman
comedy, in part no doubt because the Greek models would have lacked
equivalent figures, but probably also because *palliata* dramatists found
insufficient comic potential in the distinctly Roman freedman/patron
relationship.[52] So why is Sosia a freedman? It is particularly tempting
in this case to think biographically. Neither his African origin nor early
enslavement attracted much interest in antiquity, but since T. was said
to be *non institutus modo liberaliter sed et mature manu missus* (*Vita T* 1), a
close reader like Don. might easily have made the obvious association
and thought that with Sosia, whose freedom came *propterea quod seruibas
liberaliter* (38), T. had written himself into his play. Simo's claim of having
provided a *iusta et clemens seruitus* (36) could then be T.'s oblique acknowledgment of his debt to Terentius Lucanus. The well-established association of food with comedy and by extension of poets with cooks – the
particularly voluble cook of *Ps.* 790–904 has been called a "metatheatrical double for the playwright" – might then have encouraged the further
identification of this surrogate T., however mild his tone, with cookery.[53]

3.1.2 What Does Simo Do at 171?

Exits and entrances are for the most part clearly indicated in Roman comedy: characters state explicitly when and where they are going or why they
have come. T.'s reconstruction of *An.*'s expository scene, however, ends

---

[50] For cooks in Greek comedy, see Dohm 1964: 203–11, Wilkins 2000: 387–414;
for Pl.'s cooks, Fraenkel 2007 (1922): 398–401, Lowe 1985, Gowers 1993: 87–107.

[51] Another stereotype evoked but abandoned in *An.* involves the midwife Lesbia, described in prospect as *temulenta et temeraria* (229), but who appears in practice to be a perfectly competent professional (481–8).

[52] The *aduocati* who enter with Agorastocles at Pl. *Poen.* 504 and identify themselves as *liberti* (519–20) are the only other surviving example, though references
to freedmen and their condition are found at Pl. *Pers.* 838–40, his *Faeneratrix* fragment, and T. *Eun.* 539. See Rawson 1993, and for Sosia, Anderson 2004.

[53] Feeney 2010: 284. For the association of cooks with poets, see Frangoulidis
1996 and Gowers 1993: 78–87 and on *Ps.*, 93–107.

with an ambiguity, for while Sosia's exit into Simo's house is clearly indicated, when and to where Simo leaves the stage is not. There are two possibilities. Taking his *i prae, sequar* (171) at face value makes it an exit line
for Simo, as it is for Thais at *Eun.* 908, responding to Chaerea's *abeamus
intro* (906).[54] On this interpretation, Simo turns and follows Sosia into
his house, leaving the stage momentarily empty. Since the following line
(172) is also spoken by Simo, this means he must then almost immediately
reappear. There are indeed occasions in Roman comedy when a character exits and the script indicates an almost immediate return, though a
notional interval is then usually signaled by a musical interlude, explicitly
so at Pl. *Ps.* 573a (*tibicen uos interibi hic delectauerit*), by implication at *Cist.*
630–1, where Melaenis exits speaking and returns to music.[55] Here, however, the music begins only with Davos' entry at 175: nothing between 171
and 172 indicates a passage of time. We would have to imagine a notional
interval during which Simo encountered Davos inside and decided his
son's reluctance to marry was confirmed by Davos' behavior: *modo* at 173
with the sense "just now" (*OLD* 5) would then be the only hint that some
time has passed. It is hard to see any dramatic value in this "discovery,"
however, which leaves Simo's re-entry unmotivated and requires Davos to
follow closely, but unexpectedly on his heels.[56] What would be gained by
such an awkward sequence?

An alternative staging holds Simo back after Sosia's exit. He then turns
to the audience, and in the brief monologue of 172–4 takes the spectators
into his confidence. On that interpretation, he has made no new discovery, but is simply being franker about his son's behavior with them than he
had been with Sosia. The reference to Davos' fear looks back to his slave's
initial response to the proposed marriage, which is what had originally
put Simo on his guard against possible plots (159–63, 196–8): *modo* on
this reading means "then" (*OLD* 6b). Simo's train of thought is at that
point interrupted by Davos' appearance. When he does eventually exit at

---

[54] The attribution of parts in our MSS is not authoritative. Here it is thought
unlikely that, as the MSS say, *eumus nunciam intro* belongs to Sosia, an initiative
that seems ill-suited to the obsequious freedman, but *i prae* could be understood
as deferential and assigned to him (so Brown, also reading *sequor*). Either way, the
problem of Simo's exit remains.

[55] So too T. *Ad.* 854–5. For the role of music in marking such intervals, see
Moore 2012: 17–20. The exit and immediate return of Chremes, still speaking,
at *Hau.* 170–1 remains an intractable exception to all the apparent norms. The
regular patterns of exit and re-entry are reviewed by Johnston 1933: 114–19.

[56] The scene at Men. *Dys.* 906–8 adduced by Shipp, p. 134, is not directly comparable: there the exit and prompt return of Sikon and Getas is driven by their
determination to bring Knemon outside and is accompanied by appropriate stage
business.

205, it must be not into his house but in the direction of the forum, since that is where Pamphilus will say he encountered his father (253–4). T. leaves the motive for that change of direction unexpressed: the exchange with Davos presumably led Simo to abandon his original intention, and he instead retraces his footsteps to the forum in search of his son.

3.1.3 The Addition of Charinus and Byrria

Charinus, frustrated in his love of Chremes' daughter, and his slave Byrria were not characters found in Men.'s *Andria*, though whether T. created them himself or introduced them from the Greek *Perinthia* remains unknown.[57] They make a natural entrance at 301 that seems well integrated into the developing action, although nothing in the initial exposition prepared for their appearance. Their addition is explained in various ways. Don., somewhat sentimentally, claimed T.'s purpose was to ensure that Philumena, the girl initially betrothed to Pamphilus, would not be left without a husband when Pamphilus became free to marry Glycerium, but T. makes no effort to develop her character, and when her father seeks to break off the proposed match with Pamphilus, he expresses no concern over finding a substitute. She is thus never much more than a name. More to the point (and more dramatically significant) is how the assurances made to Charinus represent one more strand in the web of conflicting obligations that enmeshes and threatens to overwhelm Pamphilus, and the scene where Byrria overhears Pamphilus seeming to acquiesce to the proposed marriage is a masterpiece of comic misunderstanding and misdirection (412–31). A scene of dialogue framed by double asides, it requires four speakers and must in this form therefore be T.'s original creation. As for Charinus, though largely colorless and ineffectual – Davos will casually dismiss his appeal for help (709–14) and his eventual betrothal to Philumena comes almost as an afterthought (977–8) – he has one of the few genuinely lyric passages in T. (625–41), a short aria largely in old-fashioned cretics that stands in pointed contrast to the parallel expression of despair by Pamphilus in the iambo-trochaic rhythms of T.'s new musical style (237–64).[58] Performance may thus have

---

[57] Don. ad 301.2 and 977 (Appendix II.3) is explicit on the first point, frustratingly vague on the second, which has consequently engendered much, largely futile, discussion. Good summary by Lefèvre 2008: 58–63.

[58] Welsh 2014 notes T.'s use of the older comic style. Both Pamphilus and Charinus sing not of love frustrated but of obligations dishonored. For Charinus' thematic contribution to the play, see Goldberg 1986: 126–35.

brought more color to Charinus and Byrria (and almost certainly made them more memorable) than the text alone would suggest.

There is, however, an undeniable awkwardness or inconcinnity surrounding their movements: Pamphilus urges Charinus to take action that never happens (334), Byrria is sent off in no clear direction for no clear reason (337) and on his return announces a task assigned for no discernible purpose (412–15). At 431 he unceremoniously disappears for good. Although Charinus professes love for Philumena, the fact that Chremes initially proposed a union with Pamphilus (99–101) seems to leave him out of everyone's calculation: it is never clear whether he is an undeclared suitor or a previously unsuccessful one. Helpless and hapless, he eventually goes home in momentary despair (714), only to return when the action is effectively over, pinning his renewed hopes on Pamphilus' intervention (974–8). He is no more effective a foil for Pamphilus than Byrria is for Davos. Though ancient critics praised T.'s addition of this second lover, Charinus' situation never achieves the level of integration, complexity, or prominence that will generate the doubled love interests of *Hau.* and *Eun.*, much less the kind of fully formed sub-plot we find in *The Conscious Lovers* when Richard Steele turned Charinus into the fully formed Myrtle (Introduction 3.4.1). Small wonder that a later reader of *An.* provided Charinus some closure by adding the betrothal scene that T. had explicitly denied him.[59]

3.2 Metatheater

In opening his play with a mixture of theater history and theatrical polemic, T. reminds his audience from the outset that *palliata* comedy is a genre replete with traditions and conventions, a self-awareness his characters carry over into the body of the play. Simo describes Davos using vocabulary characteristic of the *seruus callidus* (159–64), and his skeptical response to the sudden onset of Glycerium's labor (474–7), to the midwife's instructions delivered from the street (490–4), and to Crito's opportune arrival (916–17) calls attention to the artificiality of these devices. Dismissing true accounts as *fabulae*, as both Davos and then Simo do, exploits the word's semantic range from "story" to "nonsense" and, in a dramatic context, from "plot" to "play" (224, 925), and every time a character turns to the audience or comments unheard by others on

---

[59] Appendix I. Contrast *An.* 977 and Don. ad loc. At *Ph. praef.* 1.9 he rightly observes that all of T.'s plays save *Hec.* have a double love interest, but the contribution each doubling makes to the *argumentum* varies considerably. The table of putative doublings in T. (and Pl.) compiled by Sharrock 2014: 183–5 makes this clear.

the stage, the artificiality of the situation is at least tacitly acknowledged. So too with the role-playing when Davos orchestrates discovery of a baby on Simo's doorstep (730–95), a scene that draws an added laugh as a fiction recognized within a fiction. Such scenes and such comments are frequently flagged as "metatheatrical," which in discussions of Roman comedy has come to mean "theatrically self-conscious."[60] At moments like this, the play seems to turn its humor on itself, its characters recognizing their roles *as* characters, its conventions and its stereotypes openly acknowledged for what they are. Self-awareness of this kind is hardly unique to *palliata* comedy, of course. The set of practices that makes it possible can be found employed for varying purposes and with varying effects in tragedy as in comedy throughout the history of western drama. The concept of "metatheater" has thus with some reason been criticized as "overloaded": by embracing too much, it runs the risk of revealing too little. What do we mean – and what do we gain – by saying that Simo shows "an extraordinary understanding of the conventions of Roman comedy," that "the source of his knowledge is the comic tradition," or that the competing interests of *An.* are "a constant battle for authorial control," a battle in which T. himself is but one of the warring parties?[61]

When Simo calls his slave *sceleratus* and full of *dolus* or doubts the reality of a plot-driven coincidence, he is using language the audience has heard before or reminds them of an action they have seen before. His comments depend for their effect upon a bond between actors and audience, since the character is drawing attention to knowledge held in common and alluding to shared experience. As a critical concept, metatheater encourages us to identify these devices and consider their cumulative power, but there is more to this recognition than simply an exercise in close reading. Rather than distancing the audience from the play's world, these devices draw the audience into it, and bringing the audience into the analysis this way encourages us to align what we find in the text with the consequences of what we know about its performance (Introduction 1.1). This is, however, where the terminology, if not necessarily the underlying concept, starts to break down.

---

[60] Thus Slater 1985: 13–15, who popularized the concept in Plautine criticism by directing toward aspects of technique a term coined by Abel 1963 to define a genre he identified as the modern successor to tragedy. Current views are summarized in Manuwald 2011: 302–9 and specifically for T., Knorr 2007.

[61] So, respectively, Moodie 2009: 145, McCarthy 2004: 104, Sharrock 2009: 140–1. By this measure, Pamphilus, too, seems capable of a metatheatrical awareness (607–9). For metatheater as an overloaded concept, see Rosenmeyer 2002 and the long survey of metatheatrical devices in Thumiger 2009.

In the Roman world before there were permanent theaters, little in the way of either conceptual or physical space separated those on the stage from those gathered before it: actors and audiences were joined together in the open air, in daylight, united in a shared enterprise, and there was scant distance or physical boundary to be found between those engaged in and by the performance and the surrounding bustle of festival or forum. The improvised venues would thus have made spectators as self-aware as the performers were. Under such conditions, it would be natural for Simo and Davos not only to spar in direct confrontation but to carry their rivalry by proxy to the audience through asides and monologues designed to gain their confidence and secure their sympathy and support (e.g. 489–532). Acting style, too, would have facilitated this sense of closeness. Because masks limit the actors' vision, masked performance encourages lines to be spoken out front, making any distinction between self-address and audience-address difficult to maintain: an actor thinking aloud is inevitably speaking to the audience, and to be heard, comments notionally "aside" are still directed toward them. Illusion in the modern sense is impossible under such conditions, where artifice and artificiality are not only inseparable, but made integral to the action and to the genre itself.[62] Since Roman comedy is consistently self-conscious, the "meta-" of "metatheater" is something of a misnomer: there was no theater separable from the theater being commented upon.[63] Since the *palliata* tradition drew much of its power from playing to crowds wise in its ways and delighting in its effects, its audiences were not just witnesses to but complicit in the creation of its fictions.

3.3 Terence v. Plautus?

T. had good reason to count Pl. among his *auctores* (18–19). Come to *An.* with expectations honed by the experience of Pl. and the world of *palliata*

---

[62] On masked delivery, see Marshall 2006: 166–7. Though the expository function of monologue and its structural role in marking entrances, exits, and scene changes has long dominated scholarship, e.g. Denzler 1968, more theoretically aware discussion has begun to shift attention toward monologue's effects on dramatic pace and characterization, e.g. Stürner 2011. The role of solo performance, whether spoken or sung, in creating bonds between individual characters and audience continues to demand attention.

[63] So for Rosenmeyer 2002: 91, "there is no need of a prefix. The traits Abel recognizes in his new genre clearly function *within* theatrical practice." Batstone 2005 defends the concept by looking not for "traits" but by returning to Abel's idea of metatheater as a genre reflecting a particular way of thinking about (and then representing) the world. Contrast his analysis of Pl. *Bac.* along these lines with the more conventional "metatheatrical" discussion of Barsby 2001: 55–61.

comedy is instantly recognizable. The plays are still musical and the stage still populated by familiar characters in familiar situations, who still speak (and sing) in language peppered with the alliterations, archaisms, and pleonasms typical of the genre. Familiar routines are found throughout the corpus, e.g. the running slave of *An.* 338–45, and the charade played out for Chremes' benefit at 739–95 is as brilliant an exploitation of the stage space as anything in Pl. An occasional awkwardness may be found (Introduction 3.1), but it is not true, as a first reading of T. might suggest, that "his plays show the marks of his lack of practical theatre experience."[64] Yet *something* of substance does lie behind the widely felt discomfort with his dramaturgy: T.'s debt to his tradition also underscores the extent of his difference. The music, though no less essential to the play's effect, is not music in the Plautine style. Davos may be a clever slave, but he is not clever enough to maintain the upper hand for long. Language is not exploited for its own sake, the "what" of Terentian dialogue always taking precedent over the "how." Nor do the twists and turns of circumstance have the familiar Plautine edge. The equanimity with which Chremes recounts the loss of his brother and daughter (935–7) stands in sharp contrast to the agony of a Hanno or a Sosicles, whose quests for a lost relative drive the plots of Pl.'s *Poenulus* and *Menaechmi.* Slavery, too, loses much of its viciousness.[65] The freedman Sosia's obsequious gratitude to his former master sets the new tone at the outset.

> gaudeo
> si tibi quid feci aut facio quod placeat, Simo,
> et id gratum fuisse aduorsum te habeo gratiam.   (40–2)

The gift of manumission culminates what Simo calls, as if such a thing were possible, a *iusta et clemens seruitus* (36). Davos, too, freely and with comparable lack of irony accepts as a matter of course his duty to his young master.

> ego, Pamphile, hoc tibi pro seruitio debeo,
> conari manibus pedibus noctesque et dies,
> capitis periclum adire, dum prosim tibi.
> tuomst, si quid praeter spem euenit, mi ignoscere.   (675–8)

The fact that he does this by frustrating his *old* master is secondary. Contrast the world of Pl., where trickery is an end in itself, the master

---

[64] Slater 1985: 169
[65] The exception that proves the rule is Simo's sudden resort to violence against Davos, which earns a prompt rebuke from Chremes (865–8).

is ultimately the one seeking forgiveness, and the slave wins his freedom
malitia sua.[66]

Something has changed, and audiences seem to have noticed. The
uetus poeta of the Terentian prologues was not alone in his complaints.
The prologue of *Casina*, rewritten for a post-Plautine revival, says as much.

> qui utuntur uino uetere sapientis puto
> et qui lubenter ueteres spectant fabulas.
> antiqua opera et uerba quom uobis placent,
> aequomst placere ante alias ueteres fabulas,
> nam nunc nouae quae prodeunt comoediae
> multo sunt nequiores quam nummi noui.

> Those who choose old wine I deem discerning
> and those who enjoy watching old plays.
> Since traditional workmanship and words please you,
> it's right that old plays please above others,
> since now the new comedies they produce
> are even more worthless than new coins.   (5–10)

Those worthless new coins are almost certainly the plays of T., whose own
prologues emphasize their newness.[67]

> date crescendi copiam
> nouarum qui spectandi faciunt copiam
> sine uitiis.

> give a chance to flourish
> to those who create a chance to see new plays
> without faults.   (*Hau.* 28–30)

The complaint is easy enough to understand: the richness of Pl.'s language and broadness of his humor even today maintain their appeal. The
impetus for change, the deliberate departure from what was evidently a
winning formula, is what requires explanation.

A purely literary line might ascribe the palpable differences between Pl.
and T. to the fact of different personalities working in the same tradition,

---

[66] *Epid.* 722–33 and *Ps.* 1326–31 are notable examples. Trickery in T. "operates
more as a characterizing device than as a plot device" (McCarthy 2004: 103).

[67] So too *Hau.* 7, *Ph.* 24, *Ad.* 12, and throughout the two prologues to *Hec.* The
revival of *Cas.* is undated, but even if it is as late as the 150s (so Mattingly 1960),
T. remains its likely target, his own polemical style being turned against him. This
recollection of T. is noted by Leo 1913: 214–17. For revival performances in the
Republic generally, see Manuwald 2011: 108–19, Hanses 2020b: 40-63.

but that would be to reckon without the no less palpable differences between the third-century world that shaped Plautine comedy and conditions in the 160s. Rome's ascendancy in this period brought not just vast wealth and cheap labor to Italy but significant cultural change, a process that accelerated noticeably after 168 with Aemilius Paullus' victory over Macedonia at Pydna. Paullus was a notable philhellene, though hardly the first distinguished Roman to immerse himself in Greek culture. In 205, Scipio Africanus was observed wearing Greek dress in Syracuse and reading Greek books as he planned the invasion of Africa; T. Quinctius Flamininus, the self-styled liberator of Greece, was fluent in the language and composed Greek verses to adorn his dedications at Delphi. Yet Paullus' commitment to Greek culture stands out even in that company, and not only because he was also bilingual: he capped his military success with a tour of Greece that was as much a declaration of cultural respect as political domination, and among the spoils that found their way to Rome after Pydna were the Macedonian royal library and, as Polybius would wryly observe, a flood of learned Greeks.[68] Under those conditions, it becomes possible to imagine an audience increasingly attuned to Greek patterns of thought and as receptive to Latin versions of Menander's more nuanced representations of domestic life as they were to Roman historic narrative set in the meter and style of Homer. Pl. had boasted of making his models "barbarian" (*As.* 11, *Trin.* 19 *uortit barbare*); T., we are told, made a final, fatal trip to Greece because he wanted to understand better the manners and institutions of the region.[69]

But was this more Hellenized comedy written for the same audience Pl. knew? The common, if tacit assumption is that while plays may always have attracted a cross-section of the Roman population, the interests, prejudices, and perspectives of the elite invariably and continually set the tone. This was, after all, the class that authorized the occasions and paid the bills. Why would the *palliata* then not have developed in tandem with their growing Hellenization and reflected their new perspective on the world at their feet? The problem with this view is that Plautine comedy can be understood on close inspection not to further aristocratic interests but to subvert aristocratic values. It represents a world where slaves win,

---

[68] Polyb. 31.24.6–8. For the philhellenic interests of elite Romans in this period, see Gruen 1992: 241–8, and for the import of Aemilius' travels after Pydna, Russell 2012.

[69] *Vita T* 5 *causa . . . percipiendi Graecorum instituta moresque, quos non perinde exprimeret in scriptis.* Comedy's development might thus be understood within the larger context of Rome's literary evolution in the course of the second century, for which see Feeney 2016: 155–69.

masters lose, and characters cope with the uglier consequences of Roman domination. That might well suggest, in Amy Richlin's formulation, "the performance art of urban slaves, displaced persons, and the free poor in central Italy," a drama by and for the lowly "playing to an audience that had a lot to be angry about."[70] Traces of such an angry Plautine world can still be found in T. – conditions for the underclasses of Rome in the 160s were hardly improved over the 190s – but it is no longer the center of comic interest. That is why Davos is no Pseudolus and the Terentian Simo becomes a more complex, interesting figure than his Plautine namesake. T.'s version of comedy no longer speaks so directly to the lowly. Why not?

A few clues may lie among the less dubious details of the Terentian biography. T. himself claimed significant aristocratic connections. A reply to one purported complaint trumpets the support of powerful friends (*Hau.* 22–7, *Ad.* 15–21), and the literary preoccupations of all six prologues, which address specific issues of content and style and advance a critical vocabulary unprecedented on the Roman stage, certainly hint at an audience more attuned than ever before to literary issues.[71] Since *Hec.* and *Ad.* were performed in 161 at the funeral games of Aemilius Paullus, the friends in question are commonly identified with Paullus' extended family. These were the Romans whose education and outlook put Polybius, like T. an initially involuntary resident of Rome, at his intellectual ease, and as Romans with little to be angry about themselves, it is easy to imagine their interests and sensibilities informing T.'s more forgiving comic style.[72] Suspicions even persisted for generations that the plays were actually ghostwritten by Paullus' son Scipio Aemilianus or by Scipio's friend C. Laelius.[73] The original complaint of aristocratic

---

[70] Richlin 2017: 2 and 478–9. Cf. 250–1 on the *palliata* as "made up of things slaves want," an idea echoed by Fitzgerald 2019: 189, pointing out that "the subversive character of the clever slave is not confined within a single role; it acts as a lightning rod for other characters who may be dissatisfied with their position." Richlin 2017: 17–20 critiques earlier interpretations of the *palliata* as consistently advancing aristocratic values.

[71] Thus Parker 1996: 603, "If T. spent the opening moments of every single play discussing literary criticism, the state of the theater, and current theatrical feuds, it is because he thought his audience was *interested* in such things," a true observation in an otherwise over-heated presentation. In arguing (rightly) for T.'s contemporary success, Parker assumes his popularity was secured by the same sort of plays appealing to the same sort of audience as Pl.

[72] Thus Momigliano 1975: 24: "Polybius could not have written his history as he did if he had not found in Rome an aristocracy which he could instinctively understand because he shared its attitude to life." For his status as a hostage at Rome, see Erskine 2012.

[73] The accusations are acknowledged by Cic. *Att.* 7.3.10, *Amic.* 89; a speech by the praetor C. Memmius (*ORF* 13); Quint. 10.1.99. This type of charge was a

influence may thus have encompassed not just the practical one of inter-
ference in the awarding of contracts, but an aesthetic one centered on
producing the sort of plays such people would like. Remnants of the old
audience, the audience thought to welcome a revival of *Casina,* no doubt
endured, but T.'s popularity strongly suggests the emergence of a new one
as aristocratic tastes and interests put their stamp on the genre.[74]

3.4 Reception

T. was a school author by the late second century BCE and remained a fixture of the curriculum for centuries thereafter, claiming a position among
poets second only to Virgil. As the first play in the corpus, *An.* continually
attracted particular attention as a text for study, as a source of inspiration,
and (to a lesser extent) as a play to perform. Ben Jonson would build slyly
on those multiple instantiations in the Induction to *The Magnetick Lady*
(1632).

> Damplee: You have heard, Boy, the ancient Poets had it in their pur-
> pose, still to please this people.
> Probee: I, their chiefe aime was –
> Damplee: *Populo ut placerent*: (if hee understands so much.)
> Boy: *Quas fecissent fabulas.* I understand that, sin' I learn'd Terence, i'
> the third forme at Westminster: go on Sir.

The full record of *An.*'s long afterlife is much discussed: a few representative examples follow.[75]

3.4.1 As a Play

If, as seems likely, the script of *An.* remained the property of Turpio's acting
company, performances subsequent to its debut at the *ludi Megalenses* of 166
BCE are likely, but the garbled reference to aediles of the 130s in Don.'s
didascalic note is the only tangible hint of a revival under Republican conditions. The significant influence of *palliata* comedy on subsequent Roman

---

well-established tool of literary invective (Fairweather 1983: 328–9). What Polybius, whose understanding of Roman *ludi* was decidedly incomplete (e.g. 30.22.1–2
on the games of Anicius Gallus), may have made of T.'s plays is anyone's guess.

[74] So Gruen 1992: 218–21. T.'s rapid acceptance as a school text and stylistic
model, a status never accorded Pl., would be congruent with such a development.
The claim by Fontaine 2010: 183–7 that Pl.'s audience was "predominately aristocratic," which has not won acceptance, might be reconsidered for this later period.

[75] For fuller descriptions, see Lefèvre 2008: 15–40, Brown 2014, Goldberg
2019: 51–77, 117–21.

literature and the documented activity of comic actors (*comoedoi*) well into
the empire nevertheless suggest a continuing tradition of performance,
though the evidence is hardly unequivocal.[76] The situation in later antiquity
is problematic in a different way. On *An.* 28.5, for example, Don. remarks,
"OFF WITH YOU should be read rather energetically, since he is hurry-
ing off those looking back and separating them from Sosia," but whether
this reflects an actual stage memory (his own or that of a source) or was
simply deduced from the text itself remains unclear. A note about Mysis,
whether played as in T.'s day by a man or *per mulierem, ut nunc uidemus* (ad
716.1), may hint at a fourth-century performance or may simply generalize
from contemporary stage practice.[77] The alternative ending, certainly post-
Terentian, that is found in some MSS may conceivably have been intended
for a revival performance (Appendix I); whether the elegant illustrations
created by Calliopius' scriptorium in the early fifth century reflect stage
practice at that time remains controversial (Introduction 7).

The ancient trail goes cold after that, but T.'s eventual return to the
modern stage began with *An.* The first documented production of any
Roman comedy since antiquity was a staged recitation of *An.* in Latin
mounted at Florence in 1476 by students of the humanist Giorgio
Antonio Vespucci (uncle of the geographer, Amerigo), first at his school,
then at the Medici palace, and then publicly in the Palazzo della Signoria.
Another followed at Ferrara in 1491, and productions have continued
ever since, albeit intermittently and most often delivered with a distinctly
academic accent. In June 1816, for example, a production at Ealing Great
School included George Adams, son and grandson of American presi-
dents, in the role of Crito.[78] Professional productions were rare. Molière's
protégé Michel Baron (1653–1729) performed a French adaptation as
L'Andrienne in 1703, and in 1777, a version that billed itself as "a modern
translation of Terence's *Andria*" was recast in German as *Die Engländerin
in Berlin* (*The English Girl in Berlin*). As manager of the court theater at
Weimar, Goethe made Terence an important part of his effort to raise by
example the quality of German drama. Standards of decency were high at
Weimar, and Goethe particularly admired the delicacy with which Terence

---

[76] The evidence and the case for continuing performance are presented by
Hanses 2020b: 49–112.
[77] The passage is discussed in detail by Kragelund 2012: 418–20, who suspects
a reference to performance.
[78] Much to the relief of his family, who had feared his appearance in a less respectable role (Rous 2020: 313–15). The production database of the Archive of
Performances of Greek and Latin Drama lists primarily school performances,
Westminster School productions prominent among them: www.apgrd.ox.ac.uk/
research-collections/performance-database/productions.

handled even morally dubious subjects. In addition to performances of
Ad., *Eun.*, and *Hau.* between 1801 and 1807, a version of *An.* by August
Hermann Niemeyer received five performances in the 1803/1804 sea-
son. Years later, Goethe commended the version of *An.* sent to him by his
young protégé Felix Mendelssohn, who had translated it into German
equivalents of the original meters. That version included stage directions,
too, though by then Goethe had left theater management behind and
performance was not Mendelssohn's objective.

The modern reclamation of *An.* for the stage went beyond revivals and
adaptations. T.'s style of polemical prologue was taken up with gusto by
English playwrights and became a fixture of the seventeenth- and eighteenth-century stage. Ben Jonson opened *Epicoene; or, The Silent Woman*
(1609) not just with a palpable echo of *An.*'s prologue, but with a similar
assault on the state of contemporary drama.

> Truth says, of old the art of making plays
> Was to content the people; and their praise
> Was to the poet money, wine, and bays.
>
> But in this age, a sect of writers are,
> That, only, for particular likings care,
> And will taste nothing that is popular.
>
> With such we mingle neither brains nor breasts;
> Our wishes, like to those make public feasts,
> Are not to please the cook's taste, but the guests'.

Half a century later, after the enforced hiatus of the Puritan Commonwealth,
John Dryden offered his own take on that passage in the prologue to *An
Evening's Love* (1668), spun out now with the slyly ribald license typical of
comedy under the restored monarchy.

> When first our Poet set himself to write,
> Like a young Bridegroom on his Wedding-night
> He laid about him, and did so bestir him,
> His Muse could never lye in quiet for him:
> But now his Honey-moon is gone and past,
> Yet the ungrateful drudgery must last:
> And he is bound, as civil Husbands do,
> To strain himself, in complaisance to you:
> To write in pain, and counterfeit a Bliss,
> Like the faint smackings of an after-Kiss.

In defending the easy morality of the Restoration stage, Dryden argued
that it was not comedy's business to champion virtue at the expense of

vice and blithely cited in support the example of Terentian comedy,
"where you perpetually see not only debauch'd young men enjoy their
Mistresses, but even the Courtezans themselves rewarded and honour'd
in the Catastrophe."[79] Yet however true, this would not be the formula for
future success.

The aims and methods of comedy, hotly debated by the late 1690s,
gave rise in the early eighteenth century to a more sentimental comedy,
"in which," as Oliver Goldsmith described it, "the virtues of private life are
exhibited, rather than the vices exposed; and the distresses rather than
the faults of mankind make our interest in the piece." Not surprisingly, T.
was a major inspiration for that new style, most notably through Richard
Steele's *The Conscious Lovers* (1722). Steele had long admired Terentian
comedy precisely because it was not, in his view, overtly funny. A 1712
essay in *The Spectator* had praised *Hau.* precisely for what it did not have:
"It is from the Beginning to the End a perfect Picture of human Life,
but I did not observe in the whole one Passage that could raise a Laugh.
How well disposed must that People be, who could be entertained with
Satisfaction by so sober and polite Mirth?"[80] In setting out to produce
such sober mirth himself, he turned to *An.*

Steele opens his play as T. does: Sir John Bevil confides to his faithful
servant Humphrey that the rich Mr. Sealand proposed the marriage of
his daughter and heiress Lucinda to Sir John's seemingly virtuous son,
but Sealand now hesitates since at a recent masked ball the young man
revealed an attachment to a mysterious orphan named Indiana, who
resides with an older woman, Isabella. Sir John will test the young man's
loyalty by insisting on an immediate marriage, charging Humphrey to
watch his son's scheming servant and divine his intentions. The expected
complication that young Bevil's friend, Myrtle, truly loves Lucinda soon
follows, along with some additional twists: a second, rakish suitor for
Lucinda (Cimberton), the servant Tom's flirtation with Lucinda's maid
(Phillis), and even the prospect of a duel between the younger Bevil
and Myrtle. As if by way of compensation, there are omissions: the dead
Chrysis is replaced by the very much alive Isabella; far from compromising
Indiana, young Bevil has been too modest even to confess his love; and
the eventual recognition is affected not by the timely arrival of a stranger

---

[79] From the preface to *An Evening's Love.* Samuel Pepys saw the play on 20 June
1668 and was not amused: "[I] do not like it, it being very smutty."
[80] Steele, *The Spectator* No. 502, for Monday, 6 October 1712. Goldsmith's "Essay
on the Theater" appeared in 1773. For the success of *The Conscious Lovers,* see
Kenny 1968. Steele's debt to Terence is discussed in detail by Brown 2014: 257–9,
Goth 2014.

but by Sealand himself, whose visit to the mysterious orphan leads to the chance discoveries that she is his long-lost daughter by a first, now deceased wife and that her protector Isabella is his sister. All can then end happily.

Unusually successful on the Drury Lane stage and promptly translated into Italian (1724), French (1736, 1778, 1784), and German (1752, 1767), *The Conscious Lovers* is today most striking for Steele's ability to do with comedy things Terence could neither do nor even imagine doing. Intertwined plotlines were so well-established a feature of play-construction by the eighteenth century that Steele easily creates a truly complex action around a fully formed Charinus in Myrtle and the rival Cimberton, and includes action below stairs through the conversations of Tom, Phillis, and Humphrey. These changes add social dimensions not found in Terence. It matters that Sir John Bevil's roots are in the landed gentry while the richer Mr. Sealand comes from the rising merchant class. It matters even more that Steele's servants have not just lives and opinions of their own, but opportunities to express them. While the play does not directly challenge distinctions of class, it does not ignore them.[81] One brother speaks as a social equal to another when T.'s easy going Micio excuses his son's brutality by telling the censorious Demea, "If neither you nor I did these things, it was because poverty didn't allow us to do them" (*Ad.* 103–105). In Steele, a similar observation becomes a function of class when Humphrey tells Sir John, "Ah sir, our manners were formed from our different fortunes, not our different age. Wealth gave a loose to your youth, and poverty put a restraint upon mine" (I.i). The obsequious Sosia could hardly have spoken this way to Simo. In this dramatic world, women are also free to speak their minds. Chrysis spoke only indirectly through the voice of a man, and Glycerium hardly speaks at all, but Steele's Phillis is as forthright as Humphrey, Lucinda is fully empowered to declare her feelings for the suitors pressed upon her, and Indiana is the agent of her own recognition. Her perspective on young Bevil's conduct toward her is significant and even moving: "The goodness and gentleness of his demeanor made me misinterpret all . . . He never made one amorous advance to me. His large heart and bestowing hand have only helped the miserable." No Glycerium would or could ever say such a thing!

---

[81] Whether the play advanced social positions is a topic of current debate. See Wilson 2012, Wolfram 2012. As an Anglo-Irishman and thus himself something of a social outsider, Steele may have felt some affinity with the *libertus* T. (Orr 2020: 54–8).

3.4.2 As a Text

The evidence for T.'s continued life and growing influence as a text is clearer and more consistent. By the later days of the Republic, the complaints of rivals like Luscius and critics like Volcacius were well behind him, and T.'s work came to be regarded as the very model of stylistic elegance and correct Latinity. Cicero consistently praised his diction, mined his text for maxims, and cited him in rhetorical contexts as a master of narration and argument. *An.*'s opening scene was a particular favorite, quoted no doubt in part for its familiarity to readers from their own school days. So, for example, in setting out the rules for what rhetoricians called "partition," the statement of topics to be discussed in a speech, the youthful handbook *De inventione* commends (and quotes) *An.* 49–50; some thirty years later, the mature Cicero was still citing that same passage for its graceful, varied, and lively narrative (Appendix III). Given the conservatism of ancient rhetorical training, it is then hardly surprising that Don.'s note on the passage includes a similar observation: "These are the divisions: 'my son's life,' 'my plan,' 'what I want you to do in this situation' ... it is a three-part distribution. ... his son's life is divided in two parts in the narrative: the good done previously and the current bad part" (ad 49.2–4).

Don.'s student Jerome often quotes *An.*, sometimes with a particular point, but at other times simply because a phrase seems to have lingered in his mind. So, for example, the Preface to his second book on Micah affects a combative stance familiar from the *An.* prologue: "si enim criminis est Graecorum benedicta transferre, accusetur Ennius et Maro, Plautus, Caecilius et Terentius, Tullius quoque ... quorum omnium aemulari exopto neglegentiam potius quam istorum obscuram diligentiam," a passage replete with Terentian echoes. (He quotes the line again at *Ep.* 49.15.1.) Augustine, too, regularly quotes T., including some twenty-seven recognizable echoes of *An.*[82]

T.'s importance as a school text continued well into early modern times, especially as a stylistic model and source of maxims and stock phrases. Among the earliest printed books in England was a collection of phrases culled from T. under the title *Vulgaria quedam abs Terencio in anglicam linguam traducta* (1483), eventually replaced by the Tudor schoolmaster Nicholas Udall's *Floures for Latine Spekynge* (1534), which reduced *An.*,

---

[82] At the heart of this familiarity again lies T.'s status as a school author (Jürgens 1972: 112–22, Hagendahl 1974: 217). For T.'s reception in antiquity, see Marti 1974 and Cain 2013, and for developments from late antiquity to the Renaissance, the essays in Torello-Hill and Turner 2015.

Eun., and *Hau.* to a sequence of phrases useful for the exercises in spoken and written Latin that dominated the Tudor curriculum. It continued as a best seller well into the next century. Students learned that *paucis te volo* means "I would speak a word or two with you" and that "*habere gratiam* is properly to thanke in hert, *agere gratias*, to thanke in wordes." It probably also served as a crib manqué: how often schoolboy conversation would otherwise require a phrase like *gravida est e Pamphilo* ("She is with childe by Pamphilus") may be difficult to imagine. By perfecting the technique of quotation without context, essentially reducing plays to a series of disjointed fragments, Udall largely avoids the more awkward implications of Terence's plots.[83] Two and a half centuries later, it was still natural for a serious student like John Quincy Adams to round off his Latin studies with *An.*, which he enjoyed more for its "sentiments" than for its plot.[84]

Those sentiments eventually took a different turn in Thornton Wilder's 1930 novella *The Woman of Andros*, which owes less to *An.* than to its back story.[85] We are on the fictional island of Brynos, not Athens, and Chrysis, not Glycerium, is the Andrian woman of the title. Though still a hetaira, she is elevated to a kind of Socratic stature, with an entourage of rich young men hanging on her every word and a dependent household of outcasts, misfits, and invalids. She dies between pages 107 and 108, with only a third of the story still to come; the only explicit point of intersection with T.'s play comes just there with the narrative of her funeral (pp. 108–12 ~ *An.* 104–46). Pamphilus must then wrestle with his obligation toward the pregnant Glycerium, while Simo (a more humane and worldly version of the Terentian figure) stresses the serious social consequences of marrying her, and Chremes frets in the background. The one decisive action comes when Simo intervenes to prevent Glycerium and Mysis from being sold into slavery to pay Chrysis' debts, after which a reconciliation seems at hand. But it is not to be: "This flowering of goodness, however, was not to be put to the trial of routine perseverance . . . for on noon of the third day Glycerium's pains began and by sunset both mother and child were dead" (p. 159).

---

[83] Brown 2015. T. was one of the earliest classical authors printed: by 1470 in Europe and 1495 in London, a two-volume quarto edition, followed in 1504 by a folio edition with commentary. Some thirty editions, largely aimed at the academic market, were available in Italy by 1500 (Gehl 2016).

[84] Adams, then eighteen, writing to his father John Adams, thought "the unravelling of the Plot is not very probable; indeed I might say it fails highly against the probability" (15 February 1786: founders.archives.gov/documents/Adams/03-01-02-0008-0002).

[85] Page references in what follows are to the first edition, New York 1930. The following summary draws on Goldberg 1977, Borgmeier 2001, and Hanses 2013.

Despite its sentimental gloss, the novel focuses tightly and sympa-
thetically on those at society's edge. Wilder makes clear the threats and
fears behind Chrysis' mask of tranquility and the vulnerability of her
dependents after her death. The bleakness of his climax is relieved only
in part by a vague promise of a more compassionate, Christian world to
come, a less than satisfying resolution, since Brynos lacks the feel of a
real place inhabited by real people. Wilder appears less interested in the
lives of individuals than in Life in general, an interest borne out by later
developments.

At one point, Chrysis offers a parable to the young men she entertains:
a dead hero is granted a return to earth to relive the least eventful day of
his life. He endures the experience for less than an hour, quickly overcome by the discovery that the living are too immersed in the mechanics
of life to appreciate its wonder (pp. 33–6). Emily Webb, of course, learns a
similar lesson when reliving her twelfth birthday. The sparse narrative that
seems only effete and affected in *The Woman of Andros* works agonizingly
well on the barebones stage that becomes the equally mythical Grover's
Corners, New Hampshire. As Wilder would himself eventually acknowledge, "The novel is pre-eminently the vehicle of the unique occasion, the
theatre of the generalized one."[86] That is the truth behind the success of
Our Town, and also behind the enduring appeal of New Comedy, which
as developed by Menander and Terence explored the vagaries of human
behavior and the fragility of human relationships within the frame of a
readily generalized occasion.

3.4.3 Translation and Commentary

An. was also the first Roman comedy translated into a vernacular language.[87]
Early in the sixteenth century, Niccolò Machiavelli (1469–1527) developed a version in Tuscan prose, though whether intended as an (aborted)
commercial venture or an exercise for self-study remains unknown. It survived in two manuscripts, a draft with corrections and a later clear copy,
which reveal something of his creative process. Reproducing Terentian
effects could come naturally, e.g. the alliteration of *verum illud verbumst*
(426) readily becomes *vero è quel proverbio,* but Machiavelli might also seek
to bring T.'s decorous, occasionally anodyne Latin closer to what he might
have heard on a Florentine street corner. So Davos' neutral *quid hoc uolt?*

---

[86] Preface to *Three Plays* (New York: Harper, 1957) iv.
[87] For T. in translation, see Barsby 2013, and for the inherent difficulty of the
task, Goldberg 2019: 79–101.

(184) becomes "What does this prick want?" ("Che vuole questo cazzo?"), though how far to move in that direction could be uncertain: Pamphilus' *metuo ut substet hospes* (914) becomes "I'm afraid this stranger will shit himself!" (*Io ho paura che questo forestiero non si cachi sotto!*) in the first version but "piss in his pants" (*si pisci sotto*) in the second.

Nearly contemporary with Machiavelli was an explicitly commercial project in England. Around 1520, a version of *An.* appeared in London as an anonymous pamphlet under the title *Terens in Englysh*. Since T. in Latin was still a mainstay of the school curriculum, the title is itself something of a provocation. An epilogue hints at a hope of stage production, but the choice of rhyme royal, the seven-line, ababbcc rhymed stanza of Chaucer's *Troilus and Criseyde*, proved ill-suited to the easy flow of Terentian speech. Thus Pamphilus at Chrysis' funeral (131–6):

> Then Pamphilus, in mind all dismayed,
> His hid-before love out showed he tho:
> He ran, and took her by the middle, and said,
> "My Glycery," quod he, "what wilt thou do?
> Thyself for to slay why dost thou go?"
> Then she (as the wont love one may well espy)
> Turned to him, weeping, familiarly.

The reasonably accurate translation was not expected to stand on its own: the original Latin, printed as prose, was crowded into its outside margins, as if to show that the goods were genuine.

A second English *An.* appeared in 1588, this one by the Welsh soldier-poet Maurice Kyffin (ca. 1555–1598). Verse, he confessed in a preface, had proved beyond him: "perceiuing what difficultie it was, to enforce the pithie and prouerbiall sayings of Terence into Rime . . . I haue thereupon somwhat altered my cours, and indeuored to turne it into prose, as a thing of lesse labour in show, and more libertie in substance." The result was T. in a more natural idiom:

> wherat my sonne Pamphilus being sore frighted, did than lo, bewray his love which hee had cunningly cloked and kept secrete all this while: he runnes unto her, and takes her about the middle: My sweete hart *Glycerie* (quoth he) what do you? why goe you about to cast away your selfe? with that, shee caste her selfe weeping, and leaning upon him so familiarly, as a man might easily perceive their old accustomed love.

Though explicitly addressed to "all young Students OF THE LATIN TONG (for whose onely help and benifit this Comoedie is published)," Kyffin did not intend solely a crib for translating Latin: each scene is introduced by a brief "Argument" and includes marginal stage notes to fix the action in the mind's eye. Ten years later, the translation was incorporated into a complete, bilingual T. by the Puritan clergyman Richard Bernard (1568–1641) that remained a popular teaching text throughout the seventeenth century.[88]

Not until the 1760s did anyone ask "how can the translator of Terence hope to catch the smallest part of his beauties by totally abandoning the road of poetry, and deviating entirely into prose?" That was the impresario and dramatist George Colman (1732–1794), whose 1765 edition of T. opened with a strikingly robust *An.* in blank verse:

> Then! there! the frighted Pamphilus betrays
> His well-dissembled and long-hidden love:
> Runs up, and takes her round the waist, and cries,
> Oh my Glycerium! what is it you do?
> Why, why endeavour to destroy yourself?
> Then she, in such a manner, that you thence
> Might easily perceive their long, long love,
> Threw herself back into his arms, and wept
> Oh how familiarly!

Colman knew very well how to write speakable verse, but his edition is no less important for its introductory essay and integrated commentary, all deeply indebted to the pioneering edition of 1688 by Anne Dacier (1647–1720), one of the foremost classical scholars of her time. Translation had emerged from the schoolroom in the course of the seventeenth century to play a central role not just in the understanding of classical authors but in larger Enlightenment debates over the direction and the aspirations of national literatures, and Mme. Dacier was a major figure in this development. She had published an edition of Plautus in 1683 and begins her companion edition of T. with an astute essay on the difference between the two dramatists, while the commentary itself, keyed to the Latin text, blends her own shrewd and sensitive observations about language and characterization with the best of the ancient source material. The work was reprinted throughout the eighteenth century and brought the explication of T. to an ever-widening readership, her bilingual, richly annotated T. doing much to shape his subsequent reception by European readers.[89]

---

[88] Brown 2015. These editions are available through Early English Books Online (eebo.chadwyck.com).

[89] For her career, see Wyles 2016: 65–76, for her edition of Terence, Farnham 1976: 117–21, and for the role of translation more generally in this period,

4 LANGUAGE AND STYLE

Change came with increasing rapidity to Latin over the last two centuries of the Republic, as ever more people found ever more reasons
to speak the Romans' language. Though the Senate never established
any official language policy or attempted to impose linguistic hegemony
on subject peoples, competence in Latin proved to be so economically
or politically advantageous by the second century BCE that non-natives
throughout the Mediterranean basin began acquiring it. In the Aegean,
for example, the international trading community on Delos had long
found bilingualism expedient, while in 180 BCE, the people of Cumae
on the Bay of Naples, proud native speakers of Greek or Oscan, nevertheless petitioned the Senate for permission to conduct their public
business in Latin.[90] And in the capital city, of course, the language was
inevitably tugged in various directions as the population grew larger and
more ethnically, socially, and economically diverse. These developments
had significant aesthetic, as well as technical, consequences for both
how T.'s characters speak and how their speech sounded to subsequent
generations.

4.1 Orthography

Though T., pursuing his career in the 160s BCE, wrote in a genre that had
by then developed a characteristic style of its own, he was hardly immune
to the forces of linguistic change around him. For that reason, he sometimes sounds more "modern" to us than Pl. a generation earlier, but he
still falls on the far side of what we perceive as a linguistic watershed. His
language looked and sounded somewhat different from the "standard"
Latin familiar to us from Cicero and Virgil two hundred and more years
later, and it is customary to preserve the most significant of those differences in our printed text of the plays.[91] Not all the old spellings are reproduced, though consistency might encourage it. Editors are unmoved by

Hayes 2009: 1–25. John Adams offered his son a copy, which was refused, fearing
his tutor might disapprove "because when I translate him he would desire that
I might do it without help" (John Quincy Adams to John Adams, 18 February
1781," *Founders Online*, National Archives, founders.archives.gov/documents/
Adams/04-04-02-0055).

[90] Liv. 40.43.1. The request was clearly an exercise in political ingratiation: the
Cumaeans had enjoyed the *ciuitas sine suffragio* since 338 BCE but were hoping
to acquire full citizen rights. See Adams 2003: 113–15, and for the situation on
Delos, 642–9.

[91] For the salient characteristics of mid-Republican Latin, see Clackson and
Horrocks 2007: 90–111, Palmer 1961: 74–94.

the fact that even Cicero and Virgil wrote *caussae* and *cassus* for *causae* and *casus*, but the accusative plural of *i*-stems was regularly -*īs* until the Augustan age, and so we consistently print *omnīs* and *fidēlīs*.[92] The genitive singular of the second declension is regularly -*ī*: thus *Terentī*, not *Terentiī*.[93] Other spellings felt to be old-fashioned or deliberately archaic when encountered in a late Republican author like Sallust probably represent the language as spoken by T.'s contemporaries and have a legitimate claim to attention. The most common such spellings that are reproduced in modern dramatic texts are these:

-*u*- instead of -*i*- before labial consonants, e.g. *maxume, lubidinem*

-*u*- instead of -*e*- in gerunds and gerundives of the third and fourth conjugations, e.g. *faciundum, experiundo*

uor- instead of *uer*-, e.g. *reuortor, aduortite*

-*uom* instead of -*uum* (e.g. *aequom, tuom*) and -*uos* instead of -*uus* (e.g. *saluos*)

In addition, dramatic texts of this period preserve a few distinctions later obscured by some of the phonological changes already underway in T.'s time. Most notable of these are forms in *quo*- that were later spelled (and pronounced) *cu*-. T.'s text thus distinguishes the conjunction *quom* from the preposition *cum* and offers *quor* where authors of Cicero's generation were beginning to write *cur*. An. prefers the pronoun forms *quoi* and *quoius*, though *cui* and *cuius* become more common in later plays, a further indication of the language in flux.[94]

---

[92] Varr. *L.* 8.67 notes the lack of standardization in his day between -*ī*/-*ē* and -*ēs*/*īs* in the abl. sg. and acc. pl. respectively. (So too Gell. 10.24.8, Macr. 1.4.20.) The grammarian Probus (ap. Gell. 13.21) reported similar inconsistency in what he took to be an autograph MS of Virgil. For -*ss*- see Quint. 1.7.20 and Allen 1978: 36. The MSS of Pl. and T. are not consistent in their preservation of original spelling, nor are modern editors. See, e.g., Redard 1956, Questa 2001: 68–73.

[93] An -*iī* genitive is not attested until the late Republic (Weiss 2020: 240).

[94] So too the old nom. prn. *hisce* (=*hī*) found in Pl. appears a generation later in T. only once (*Eun.* 269). For the difference between Latin [kʷ] and [k] see Allen 1978: 14–20. Change was naturally slow and erratic. At Cic. *Mur.* 41 *dicundi* coexists beside *decernendi* and *audiendi*. The famous papyrus of Cornelius Gallus (P. Qaṣr Ibrîm inv. 78-3-11), probably written between 50 and 25 BCE, has *quom* but *maxima*. Quint. found the change to *maximus* first in an inscription of Caesar, while Scipio Africanus popularized the spelling *uer*- over *uor*-. Quint.'s own teachers, i.e. early in the first century CE, still preferred to write nom. *ceruos* and *seruos* (1.7.21–26). For the complex forces behind the standardization of language, see Clackson and Horrocks 2007: 77–89.

4.2 Diction

T.'s diction is restrained by the traditional standards of Roman comedy. Where Pl. deliberately exaggerates features of colloquial speech, T. tends to understate them: terms of abuse, diminutives and frequentatives, extravagant catalogues and extended metaphors are rare. Puns and neologisms are also uncommon by Plautine standards, as are linguistic twists like Chremes' play on the meanings of *fero* (832). Nor do T.'s characters seem to relish the very sound of Latin words as thoroughly as Pl.'s characters do.[95] Their speech is nevertheless peppered with a variety of conversational mannerisms not commonly found in more formal Latin, e.g. emphatic particles like *pol* and *hercle* (in origin oaths by Pollux and Hercules), emotive sounds like *hem, ehem,* and *heus,* where the exact meaning depends on the context, and the emphatic *em* meaning "There you are!" or when signaling a blow, "Take that!" There are also contractions. Syncopated perfects (e.g. *amisti* = *amisisti, audisti* = *audiuisti*) are common, as are some specifically conversational forms like *sodes* (*si audes* "please") and the compression of demonstrative *-ce* and interrogative *-ne* (e.g. *hocine* = *hoc* + *-ce* + *-ne*). Requests may be softened or intensified by *obsecro* or *quaeso.* Exclamatory *ne,* which looks like a conjunction or adverb, is in fact the Greek asseverating particle νή (324, 772, 939); the adv. *quī,* in origin an archaic locative or instrumental form of the indef. prn. *quis,* must be distinguished from the rel. prn. Special care should be taken over the imperatives *cĕdo* (pl. *cette*), not from *cēdo, cēdere* but from the deictic particle *ce* + *do, dare* "Tell me!" (150, 383) or "Hand it over!" (730),[96] and *sine,* the imperative of *sino,* with a range of colloquial meanings from a neutral "allow" (153, 622) to a more peremptory "Put up with it!" (900). The connotations of all such expressions, especially the emotional charge they carry and their register (and thus the English equivalents we choose for them), must be deduced from the specific requirements of the situations in which they appear.[97]

---

[95] Barsby 1999: 19–27 offers a useful comparison. See also Fantham 1972: 3–6, Dutsch 2008: 18–30. Such stylistic differences lie behind the conclusion of Wright 1974: 151 that T. "writes, by and large, as if the comic tradition at Rome never existed."

[96] For the form, probably based on an old aor. imper., see Weiss 2020: 449, 462. The colloquialism endured: so in the fifth cent. CE, Macr. 5.3.17 *cedo igitur Vergilianum uolumen* "Let me have a text of Virgil."

[97] No generalization about meaning is thus any better than the specific interpretations on which it rests. Pioneering work in this area was done by Hofmann 1951 and Luck 1964. Müller 1997 and Barrios-Lech 2016 are especially reliable. Bagordo 2001 and Karakasis 2005 can be useful.

A representative assortment of such colloquial features appears at
350–2 as Davos assures his young master that he will not have to marry
Chremes' daughter.

DAV	atque istuc ipsum nil periclist. me uide.
PAM	obsecro te, quam primum hoc me libera miserum metu.
DAV	em
	libero. uxorem tibi non dat iam Chremes.
PAM	qui scis?
DAV	scio.

DAV	There's absolutely no danger of that. Trust me!
PAM	Please, as soon as you can, free me from this fear. I'm miserable!
DAV	There!
	I free you. Chremes won't give you a wife now.
PAM	How do you know?
DAV	I know.

The syncopated genitive *pericli*, idiomatic *uide me*, *obsecro te*, and demonstrative *em* all give the exchange a conversational feel. The instrumental adverb
qui, often found in comedy but rare elsewhere, is probably also colloquial.

Along with these recollections of everyday speech appear old-fashioned,
sometimes archaic forms and turns of phrase: thus we find *ipsus* as well
as *ipse*, *potis* + *sum* as well as *possum*, the subjunctive singulars *siem*, *sies*, *siet*
and plural *sient*, the sigmatic subjunctive *faxo*, and, especially common at
line-end, the present passive infinitive ending in *-ier*, e.g. *deludier*, *immutarier*. Metrical convenience may account for much of this variation, but the
third pl. perf. in *-ēre* (e.g. *conuenēre*, 13) seems chosen to elevate the tone,
and the reduplicated perfs. *tetulissem* (808) and *tetulit* (832) are certainly
intended as a characterizing mannerism.

4.3 Arrangement

Other manifestations of colloquial style can be more challenging for modern readers to master. A word or phrase readily inferred from the context
may be left unexpressed (**ellipsis**), a practice Don. thought characteristically Terentian.[98] So at 56–7, as Simo describes his son's pastimes, *aut
equos alere aut canes ad uenandum aut ad philosophos*, a second verbal idea

---

[98] Don. ad 57.1 *familiaris Terentio*, ad 285.1 *figurae proprie Terentianae*, ἀσύνδετον
et ἔλλειψις. For the use of ellipsis in T., see Müller 1997: 187–214, and for Don.'s
analysis of the figure, Jakobi 1996: 114–17.

(Don. suggests *audiendos* or *sectandos*) must be supplied with *ad philosophos*. At 120, *adeo modesto, adeo uenusto ut nil supra*, a verb for the *ut*-clause is required; at 231–2 *importunitatem spectate aniculae | quia compotrix eius* the link between the two ideas – Don. suggests *ideo illam uult arcessi* – is missing.

T. may also employ a flexible word order designed to recall the loose, sometimes emotional jumble of words in conversation. Several ways to create a sense of ease are apparent on inspection, though their specific effect on listeners can be more difficult to judge. Some possibilities: The key word or phrase in a sentence may simply be thrust ahead of its natural position, a figure called **hyperbaton**: *haec primum affertur iam mi ab hoc **fallacia*** (471), the explanation of *haec* being added almost as an afterthought. Sometimes an interlocking word order works in conjunction with the meter to create its effect, e.g. *bene et pudice **eius** doctum atque eductum sinam | coactum egestate **ingenium** immutarier?* (274–5), where *eius* [= Glycerium] is foremost in Pamphilus' thought and so thrust ahead of its noun (*ingenium*), both words gaining some emphasis by their position just before and then after the caesura. A common variant on this trick of word order is to add a syntactic shift, moving the emphatic word not just physically out of its expected position but also grammatically out of its logical clause, a figure called **prolepsis**, e.g. *non satis me pernosti etiam qualis sim, Simo* (503), where the subject of the dependent clause appears first as the object of the main clause. Prolepsis may even be used to create and then exploit a momentary ambiguity, as at 866–7 *si uiuo, tibi | ostendam erum quid sit pericli fallere*, where the angry Simo threatens to show what it means to be the master by his power to punish trickery.

4.4 Aesthetic Effects

Such stylistic choices, each seemingly minor in isolation, have a significant effect in aggregate. Though the plays' characters represent the same social classes and occupations we find in Pl., what passes for Terentian "street talk" sounds like the talk of a much tonier street. That represents an important shift. Other writers of *palliata* comedy, from Andronicus at the beginning to Turpilius 150 years later, universally cultivated the extravagant linguistic effects so apparent in Pl. Even T.'s esteemed predecessor Caecilius Statius, whom scholarship once cast as a kind of transitional figure between Pl. and T., actually took care to preserve the traditional style.[99] Lovers of that more robust comic diction may well have found T.'s

---

[99] T. aligns himself with Caecilius at *Hec.* 14–23, the passage that probably lies behind the later story that Caecilius was the first to recognize his talent. For the

new effects effete and bloodless, or so T. himself seems to acknowledge in the prologue to *Phormio*, when speaking of the jealous rival Don. identifies as Luscius of Lanuvium.[100]

> Postquam poeta uetus poetam non potest
> retrahere a studio et transdere hominem in otium,
> maledictis deterrere ne scribat parat:
> qui ita dictitat, quas ante hic fecit fabulas
> tenui esse oratione et scriptura leui ...

> Since the old poet cannot drive our poet
> from his work and force our man into retirement,
> he contrives slanders to keep him from writing:
> He keeps saying our playwright's previous plays
> are meager in style and light in substance ...   (*Ph.* 1–5)

Under the later influence of Callimachus, *tenuis* and *leuis* would become positive terms in the Roman aesthetic vocabulary, but here they are clearly pejorative.[101] The plays criticized would have been *An.* and *Hec.*, both of them notably short on traditional stylistic effects, though T.'s very statement of the accusation here suggests its own refutation by slyly aping the old style it replaces through the juxtaposition of *poeta uetus* and *poetam* in a line full of *p*'s (cf. Pl. *Truc.* 1 *perparuam partem postulat Plautus loci*), the teasing near-jingles of *hominem in otium* and *scribat parat*, the frequentative *dictitat*, and the line-ending alliteration of *fecit fabulas*. T.'s repudiation of Luscius – a parody of his dramaturgy follows immediately (6–8) – is thus cast in the elder poet's own terms.

Luscius' criticism did not prevail. What T. elsewhere proudly calls "good writing" (*pura oratio, Hau.* 46) led Romans in succeeding generations to value the plays as stylistic models: T. was praised for his *lectus sermo* (Cicero) and as *puri sermonis amator* (Caesar), and long after the

---

fundamental traditionality of Caecilius, see Wright 1974: 105–26, and for T.'s stylistic innovations, Haffter 1953: 80–93, Goldberg 1986: 170–202.

[100] Don. ad *An.* 1. He is T.'s strawman throughout the prologues, e.g. *An.* 5–7, *Hau.* 22–6, *Ad.* 15–17. See Duckworth 1952: 62–5, Garton 1972: 41–51, Manuwald 2011: 242–4. There is no evidence that Luscius was in any official sense a spokesman for the *Collegium poetarum*, as suggested by Wright 1974: 183–6 and now Umbrico 2010: 85–90.

[101] "Small" and "insignificant" are the values commonly associated with the words throughout their history. So Cic., ironically, of Fannius' accounts: *leue et tenue hoc nomen est? HS* cccↃↃↃ *sunt* (*Q.Rosc.* 4) and two centuries later, Gell. 2.6.2 *uerbum esse leue et tenuis*. The mode and timing of their aesthetic revaluation (and T.'s role in it, if any) are problematic. See Sharrock 2009: 80–3, and for doubts about Callimachean influence as early as Pl., Hunter 2006: 81–4.

plays ceased to be mainstays of the commercial stage, they endured as mainstays of the school curriculum.[102] Their virtue in that role was *elegantia* (Cic. *Att.* 7.3.10, Quint. 10.1.99), the very term Quintilian famously applied to Tibullus (*tersus atque elegans*, 10.1.93), and that proved to be a quality with staying power. In tenth-century Saxony, the pious Hrotsvit of Gandersheim still found inspiration in T.'s "sweetness of style" (*dulcedine sermonis*), the very trait Cicero had praised a millennium earlier (*omnia dulcia dicens*). That stylistic achievement, however, had two unexpected consequences. First, T.'s growing prestige in antiquity eventually motivated some readers to question not the quality of the plays but their authorship. By the later second century, his association with the family of Aemilius Paullus took a sinister turn when it was swept up in a rising tide of anti-Scipionic propaganda: accusations of sexual exploitation joined the rumors of ghost-writing by Laelius or Scipio or some other suitably aristocratic Roman.[103] Those reluctant to praise an ex-slave from North Africa as a stylistic model could instead look to a more worthy figure, much as some modern readers periodically convince themselves that only a more august personage could possibly have written the plays attributed to that glover's son from Stratford.[104]

Not even the most scurrilous of rumors, however, did any lasting harm to T.'s reputation. Cicero and Quintilian made a point of brushing them aside. The old ghost-writing slander makes an appearance in Montaigne,[105] but the authorship question afterwards lost its urgency. Modern critics nevertheless found a new way to turn a virtue into a defect. Those more sympathetic to Greek aesthetic achievements than to Roman ones identified the elegance of T.'s understated Latinity so closely with the "Attic" style of his models that it became one more reason to regard him not as an innovator in a Roman context but as faithful copyist, even translator

---

[102] The epigrams of Cicero and Caesar are preserved in Suet. *VitaT* 7. From the famous lightness of T.'s style may derive the eventual statement that he was himself *mediocri statura, gracili corpore* (*VitaT* 6). So, we are told, the Hellenistic poet Philitas of Cos was so thin (λεπτός) he weighted his shoes with lead to keep from blowing away (Ath. 12.552B, Ael. *VH* 9.14). For *An.*'s enduring influence as a school text, see Introduction 3.4.2.

[103] Suet. *VitaT* 2, 4. For the roots of these rumors in anti-Scipionic propaganda, see Umbrico 2010: 14–39. The relative youth of Scipio and Laelius in the 160s makes them chronologically improbable (Gruen 1992: 197–202).

[104] Candidates in the modern debate over "Shakespeare" come and go, with the Earl of Oxford currently in favor. Shapiro 2010: 17–69 shows how eighteenth-century "bardolatry" precipitated and fueled the resulting controversy. As with T., class-consciousness plays a significant role in resisting the historical reality.

[105] Montaigne I.40 "Considération sur Cicéron." The praise of T. in the more famous essay "Des livres" makes no similar mention of Scipio and Laelius.

of a Greek one. There are indeed, as we have seen, times when T. can be observed following his Greek original closely, but the apparent Atticism of his style rests on thoroughly Latin foundations, as close inspection shows. His writing is many things, but it is not Greek verse in translation.[106]

5 METER

Roman drama was verse drama. Traditional metrics, which seeks to describe its rhythmic phenomena as fully and precisely as possible, developed a rich, complex, and sometimes daunting set of technical terms, categories, and "laws" for doing so. Laidlaw 1938 describes T.'s metrical practice in these traditional terms; a fuller, more authoritative analysis of all Roman comic verse is provided by Questa 2007. Other recent approaches to metrics strive for greater explanatory power by identifying the organizing principles behind the poets' metrical practice, a mode of analysis that emphasizes the structures that ostensibly distinct metrical patterns share rather than the differences observed between and among them. This new metrical sensibility is cogently surveyed by Deufert 2014 and applied especially well to T. by Barsby 1999: 290–304, building on Gratwick 1993: 40–63, 251–6. Another contemporary approach treats meter more explicitly as a function of language, recognizing that metrical practice is rooted in linguistic practice and, as is especially clear in the case of drama, represents both evidence for and a response to the rhythms of natural speech. Allen 1973 provides an essential introduction to this approach, carried now to a new level of sophistication by Fortson 2008.

A basic sketch of the principles at work in Terentian metrics is provided here. T. J. Moore's website The Meters of Roman Comedy (romancomedy.wulib.wustl.edu) allows users to analyze verse type by character and function through the entire corpus of *palliatae*; the Hypotactic site of David Chamberlain provides scansion for a wide variety of Greek and Latin texts, including full scansion of *An.* at hypotactic.com/latin/index. html?Use_Id=andria.

5.1 Syllables

Spoken Latin employed a stress accent, giving acoustic prominence to one syllable of a word by delivering it with greater force. Words of two syllables

---

[106] Jachmann 1934: 613–18 provides a useful compilation of the Greek evidence for T.'s "translation," encouraging the condescension of his conclusion, "Auch Übersetzen ist eine Kunstleistung" (625). See also Traina 1968, and for the superficiality of T.'s Atticism, Goldberg 1986: 187–92.

regularly received this stress on the first syllable, e.g. *ámor*, *cánō*.[107] In poly-syllabic words, the stress depended on whether the next-to-last ("penul-timate") syllable was heavy or light. If it was heavy, i.e. contained a long vowel or diphthong or was "closed" by a consonant, it received the stress, e.g. *amóris*, *canámus* and also *habéntur*, *patérnus*. Otherwise the syllable was light and the stress moved back to the preceding syllable, e.g. *hábeō*, *cécinī*. Any Latin utterance, whether prose or verse, thus presents a sequence of stressed and unstressed syllables: *senátus hǽc intéllegit*, *cónsul uídet*. Since heavy syllables were felt to take twice as long to pronounce as light ones, an utterance also has a characteristic rhythm, a function of time as well as stress.

When poets began writing in Latin for the Roman stage, they exploited the phonological properties of the spoken language to create sequences of light and heavy syllables that recalled the quantitative patterns found in their Greek models.[108] So, for example, the string of syllables that con-stitutes *An.* 2 forms the following pattern:

id-si-bi-ne-gō-tī-crē-di-dit-sō-lum-da-rī
— ◡ ◡ ◡ — — — ◡ — — — ◡ —

The rhythmic sequences of *An.* are all produced by similar strings. Most of these are notionally either light–heavy (i.e. iambic, ◡ —) or heavy–light (i.e. trochaic, — ◡), but because actual speech is rarely so regular, these strings are not normally composed exclusively of iambs or trochees. The iambic or trochaic character of a line will almost always reveal itself at the end, but dramatists allowed themselves considerable flexibility in allocat-ing heavy and light syllables at most other positions. Syllables that a rigid metrical scheme would require to be light might in practice be either light or heavy (*anceps* "two-headed"), and two light syllables could often be substituted for a single heavy one ("resolution") even where an anceps syllable was being treated as heavy. This system of substitution meant that a notional iamb (◡ —) could in practice be not only a spondee (— —), but

---

[107] Apparent exceptions like *ēdúc* and *illíc* have actually lost a final syllable, viz. *ēdúce*, *illíce*. Latin avoided pairs like Eng. cóntent (n.) and contén(adj.), présent (n.) and presént (v.). For fuller discussion of Latin accentuation, see Allen 1978: 83–8, Weiss 2020: 118–22. For purposes of syllabification, a single consonant be-tween vowels begins the following syllable (e.g. *pau-cōs*). Two or more consonants in succession will end one syllable and begin the next, except where a consonant cluster can itself begin a word (e.g. *nūl-la* but *me-re-trīx*). See Weiss 2020: 75–9.

[108] Since there are significant phonological differences between Greek and Latin, doing so required considerable ingenuity. See West 1982: 186–8. To avoid confusion in what follows, vowel quantities are marked *above* the vowel and syllable weight is indicated by marks *below* the syllable.

a dactyl (— ‿‿), an anapest (‿‿ —), a tribrach (‿ ‿‿), or a proceleus-
matic (‿‿ ‿‿).[109] Such flexibility enables the sequence of syllables at *An.*
2 to be perceived, despite its rhythmic variations, as a six-foot iambic line:

$$— \, ‿ \, ‿ \, | \, ‿ \, — \, | \, — \, — \, | \, ‿ \, — \, | \, — \, — \, | \, ‿ \, —$$

T. greatly preferred these iambo-trochaic patterns, which he employed in
a variety of ways to produce a variety of musical effects.[110] Though he was
never as spectacular a writer of polymetric lyric as Pl., *An.* is one of only
two plays that also employ lyric meters. At 481, the maid Lesbia enters
singing four lines of bacchiacs (‿ — —), and at 625 Charinus gives vent to
his despair in a polymetric song (*canticum*) that opens with a line of four
dactyls unique in Roman comedy and continues in a mix of cretics (— ‿
—) and trochees that seems deliberately to recall the older, traditional
comic style of T.'s predecessors.[111]

5.2 *Prosody*

No Roman ever carried on a conversation in the cadences of Virgil or
Horace or Ovid, but poetry written for the comic stage clearly sought to
capture the rhythms of ordinary speech.[112] This tendency of dramatic
verse to recall, if not always to duplicate, the phonology of the spoken
language distinguishes its prosody from the more formal Latin verse of
later times. Beside a more liberal use of anceps and resolution to vary the

---

[109] The rules of Latin phonology, however, did normally restrict resolution in
two ways. First, the two light syllables are generally found either in the same word
(e.g. *rĕ-pĕ-rĭ-ās*) or in two closely connected words (e.g. *inter eas,* i.e. *in-tĕ-rĕ-ās*). Second, the two light syllables will not be the final two syllables of a polysyllabic word.
The first of these restrictions, "Ritschl's law," avoids splitting a resolution between
words (i.e. ‿ | ‿). The second, "Hermann's law," avoids creating an anapestic
rhythm split between two words (i.e. ‿‿ | —). See Fortson 2008: 7–8. Bibliography
and discussion in Ceccarelli 1991: 350–3.

[110] This reliance on iambo-trochaic forms distinguishes T.'s metrical practice
from that of Pl., though music remains essential to his dramaturgy. T. was in his
own way a highly skilled manipulator of metrical and musical effects, with *An.,*
his first play, noteworthy for its frequent metrical shifts and other signs of musical
experimentation. See Moore 2013, and more generally Braun 1970, Moore 2007.

[111] Welsh 2014: 65–8. T.'s only other experiment with lyric meter comes at *Ad.*
610–17, another song of despair, but that one built primarily of dactyls (– ‿ ‿) and
choriambs (– ‿ ‿ –).

[112] So for Fortson 2008, "Plautus's poetry therefore is invaluable for the light it
can shed on the phonology-syntax interface of the spoken Latin of his time" (10).
Despite individual variations in metrical practice, the basic rules for creating the
desired rhythms remained constant among authors working in the *palliata* tradition.

arrangement of light and heavy syllables within the line, certain habits of pronunciation could alter the very recognition of syllables or perception of their weight. A few of these habits, like elision, manifest themselves in Latin verse of all periods, but others are much more frequent in drama. The most noteworthy practices affecting the scansion of Terentian verse are these:

Apocope, "cutting off" the final -*e* of *ne* produces such forms as *egon* (*ego* + *ne*), *tun* (*tu* + *ne*), and *satin* (*satis* + *ne*). The final -*s* that would otherwise close a light syllable may also be discounted for metrical purposes, e.g. *simul sceleratu' Dauo' si quid consili* (159).[113]

Breuis in longo. A light syllable readily occupies the final position in a line, since the strong metrical boundary there makes that syllable feel heavy. Substitution of a light for a heavy syllable is also permitted at the end of half-lines, notably at the diaeresis of the iambic septenarius and octonarius.[114]

Elision and **Prodelision**. When a word ends with a vowel or a vowel + *m* (indicating nasalization) and the following word begins with a vowel or an *h* (indicating aspiration), the first vowel in that sequence normally has no metrical value. Elision is common and may occur even across changes of speaker, where it can have dramatic value, e.g. *An.* 838–9, as Chremes hastens to overcome Simo's skepticism: *erras. cum Dauo egomet uidi iurgant(em) ancillam.* :: *sci(o).* :: *at | uero uoltu* . . . How elision was treated in delivery nevertheless remains problematic.[115]

A subtype of elision, common even in later, more formal types of verse, involves *es* and *est*. These regularly lose their opening vowel (aphaeresis) and elide with what precedes, producing what our text prints as a single word, e.g. *nemost, Glyceriumst.* This is called **prodelision.** When prodelision either alone or combined with apocope

---

[113] This license is not universally applied. Thus, scansion requires *ipsu' tristis* (360) and *nullu' sum* (599), but *libertus mihi* (37) and *senis sententiam* (207). The weak articulation of this final -*s* ("sigmatic ecthlipsis") in early Latin, analogous to the treatment of final -*m*, is discussed in detail by Pezzini 2015: 193–205.

[114] In Pl., *breuis in longo* is also found at other colon boundaries within the line, notably at the end of the fourth foot of the senarius and the corresponding place in the septenarius, the so-called *loci Jacobsohniani*, but T. appears to have resisted this license (Questa 2007: 293–6, and for Pl., Fortson 2008: 76–97).

[115] Strategies for handling elision are reviewed by Gratwick 1993: 251–3, but see below §5.4.

generates a potentially ambiguous form, its presence is indicated by
an apostrophe, e.g. *quid meritu's?* (621), *dictura's quod rogo?* (751).

Hiatus. Lack of an expected elision is fairly common in Pl. but
used sparingly by T., usually for special emphasis, e.g. at a change
of speaker (593, 895). It is indicated in the text by a long mark
over the non-elided vowel or diphthong, e.g. 957: *prouiso quid agat
Pamphilūs. atque eccum.* Elision may also be avoided by a related
phenomenon called **Prosodic Hiatus**, where a syllable is lightened
instead of elided, e.g. *sed uĭm ŭt queas ferre* (277). Emphatic monosyl-
lables, which might otherwise disappear in pronunciation, are often
treated this way, e.g. *mĭ homo* (721), *dŭm id efficias* (825).

Iambic shortening, sometimes called *breuis breuians* ("the shortening short [syllable]"). A word of iambic shape (e.g. *ămō, bŏnīs*) may
have its second vowel shortened, turning ˘ – into ˘˘ (technically,
a "pyrrhic"). *ămō* then becomes *ămŏ* and *bŏnīs* becomes *bŏnĭs*. This
shortening is primarily a result of word accent since the second,
unaccented syllable of an iambic word naturally lightens. The process may extend to polysyllabic words, e.g. *nescĭŏ* (734), and across
word boundaries: in phrases of the shape ˘ – ×, an accent on the
third syllable will lighten the middle one, e.g. *ĭn ĭncértas* (830), and
where the light syllable of an iambic sequence precedes a two syllable word, its heavy syllable may be lightened, especially in the first
part of a line, e.g. *quid ĭllud est?* (237), *apŭd forum* (254).

Synizesis. Two vowels in succession may blend to form a single heavy
syllable, an especially common occurrence with oblique forms of
the pronoun *is*, e.g. *ēās, ēum*, genitive singular of the demonstrative
pronoun, e.g. *illŭus, huŭus*, possessive adjectives, e.g. *suām*, but also
occasionally with other words, e.g. *fŭisse, dĭe, spĕi*. Words of iambic
shape like *ēās* could instead be scanned as two lights by iambic shortening, but synizesis is generally preferred by editors. See Soubiran
1988: 179–84.

To summarize the diacritical marks used to indicate these prosodic
features:

> ‒ over a non-elided vowel or diphthong (**hiatus**)
> > e.g. *quid dixtī? :: optume inquam factum.* (593)
> over a short vowel lengthened at the end of a colon (**breuis
> in longo**)
> > e.g. *Mysis, salue. :: o salue, Pamphilē.* (267)

⌣   over a non-elided vowel in **prosodic hiatus**
     e.g. *et mĕ ĕt tĕ ĭmprudens* (642)
   over a vowel affected by **iambic shortening**
     e.g. *sciăs posse habere* (95)

’   indicating an otherwise ambiguous result of **prodelision**
     e.g. *ita aperte ipsam rem modo locutu's* (202)

⌢   indicating vowels merged by **synizesis**
     e.g. *e͡o pacto* (49)

5.3 Verse Patterns

Iambo-trochaic verse is traditionally said to be structured in "feet," i.e. iambs or trochees, and described by the number of feet in the line. A verse composed of six iambic feet is thus called an iambic senarius.[116]

Verses are commonly divided into two (rarely more) metrical phrases or *cola* by a break called a *caesura* if it falls within a foot or a *diaeresis* if it falls between feet, though such breaks do not necessarily coincide with a pause in sense. The normal place for this break in the following schemata is indicated by a double line (‖).

The final syllable of a colon within a line is often permitted to be either heavy or light, but not "resolved" into two lights. That position is then *indifferens*. Substitution of a light for a heavy syllable (*breuis in longo*) is found at the end of lines and half-lines.

Verses with a strong sense-pause at the end, commonly marked in modern texts by a period, colon, or semicolon, are said to be end-stopped. When the sense continues on from one line to the next without significant pause, the lines are said to be enjambed.

The meters of *Andria* are schematized below using the following symbols to denote the constituent syllables:

⌣   =   breuis
—   =   longum, i.e. — or ⌣⌣
×   =   anceps, i.e. ⌣ or — or, with a "resolved" longum, ⌣⌣
⌃   =   breuis in longo, i.e. — or ⌣
▽   =   indifferens, i.e. ⌣ or — (but *not* ⌣⌣)

---

[116] The conventional term implies a contrast with the corresponding Greek verse, also composed of six iambs but structured as three units (metra) of the shape × — ⌣ — and therefore called a trimeter. In fact, however, Roman dramatists also treated the odd and even feet of the iambic line differently, thus producing a closer Latin equivalent to the Greek trimeter than later grammarians recognized. So Hor. *S.* 1.10.43 (on Pollio's tragedies) *canit pede ter percusso*. See Morgan 2010: 130–2.

I Iambic Patterns

A. The *iambic senarius* (ia⁶)

$$\times - \times - \times \parallel - \times - \times - \cup \overline{\wedge}$$

Add two iambs to the front of a senarius and the result is an eight-foot line,

B. The *iambic octonarius* (ia⁸)

$$\times - \times - \times - \times - \times \parallel - \times - \times - \cup \overline{\wedge}$$

If, instead of the usual caesura in the fifth foot of an octonarius, the line includes a colon boundary after the fourth foot (diaeresis), the two cola are treated as metrically identical, i.e.

$$\times - \times - \times - \cup \overline{\wedge} \parallel \times - \times - \times - \cup \overline{\wedge}$$

A "catalectic" (lit. "stopping short") version of this line, i.e. an octonarius lacking its final syllable, is,

C. The *iambic septenarius* (ia⁷)

$$\times - \times - \times - \cup \overline{\wedge} \parallel \times - \times - \times - \overline{\cup}$$

In this pattern, a colon boundary after the fourth foot is the norm and the final syllable becomes *indifferens*.

In addition to these regular iambic patterns, *An.* has iambic dimeters, i.e. two units of two iambs each, at 176, 244, 252 and 537, which scan like the last four feet of the iambic octonarius.

II Trochaic Patterns

A. The *trochaic octonarius* (tr⁸)

$$- \times - \times - \times - \overline{\cup} \parallel - \times - \times - \times - \overline{\cup}$$

In this pattern, diaeresis after the fourth foot normally creates two metrically identical cola. Eliminating the final syllable creates a catalectic version of this verse that is the most common trochaic pattern in comedy, namely,

B. The *trochaic septenarius* (tr⁷)

$$- \times - \times - \times - \overline{\cup} \parallel - \times - \times - \cup \overline{\wedge}$$

Here the first colon is identical to the octonarius, but the seventh foot must be a pure trochee and the final heavy syllable can be replaced by a *breuis in longo*.

III Lyric Meters

A. The *bacchiac tetrameter* (ba⁴)

T.'s one passage of bacchiacs (481–4) can be quite regular,

> adhuc, Archylis, q(uae) adsolent quaeq(ue) oportent   (481)
> ◡ − − | ◡ − − − | ◡ − − | ◡ − −

or can vary the rhythm by substituting a molossus (− − −) for a bacchiac and/or resolving a heavy syllable into two light ones,

> sign(a) ess(e) ad salut(em), omni(a) huic esse uideo.   (482)
> − − − | ◡ − − | ◡ − − | ◡ ◡ ◡ −

B. The *cretic tetrameter* (cr⁴)

After a short opening run of four regular dactyls (− ◡ ◡) at 625, cretics establish the rhythm of Charinus' song at 626–38. The cretics can be regular,

> tanta uecordi(a) innata quoiq(uam) ut siet   (626)
> − ◡ − | − ◡ − | − ◡ − | − ◡ −

or, since the second element is anceps, the rhythm can be varied through substitution of a molossus,

> ut malis gaudeant atq(ue) ex incommodis   (627)
> − ◡ − | − ◡ − | − − − | − ◡ −

and/or with the resolution of heavy syllables,

> idnest uer(um)? im(mo) id est genus hominum pessum(um), in
> − − − | −   ◡ − | ◡ ◡ ◡ ◡ − | − ◡   −
>
>   (629)

Diaeresis is commonly found after the second cretic.

5.4 Interpretive Challenges

Characterizing verse in terms of its feet is a practice deeply rooted in antiquity, as Ovid attests with his famous joke about Cupid turning the poet's hexameters to elegiacs by stealing a foot.[117] Yet metricians since antiquity have also recognized that no fundamental difference distinguishes iambic

---

[117] Ov. *Am.* 1.1.4 [Cupido] *dicitur atque unum surripuisse pedem.* The joke is all the more striking since no metrician would describe the resulting pentameter as a catalectic hexameter. A similar reference to feet as the characterizing unit of verse

from trochaic sequences. The great eighteenth-century scholar Richard
Bentley, whose essay "De metris Terentianis ΣΧΕΔΙΑΣΜΑ" provided the
first coherent modern account of Latin dramatic meter, illustrated this
fact with an English example of what in Latin terms would be called a
trochaic septenarius:[118]

> Háppy is the Coúntry life, blest wíth content, good heálth an'
> ease.

Add a single syllable to the front, Bentley notes, and the line becomes an
iambic octonarius:[119]

> Thrice háppy is the Coúntry life, blest wíth content, good heálth
> an' ease.

Division into feet also distracts attention from the characteristic cretic
rhythm ($-\cup-$) that ends not only the iambic senarius and octonarius, but
the trochaic septenarius, too. The pattern is so well established that when
one of these lines ends with an iambic word, dramatists regularly avoided
preceding that word with another pure iamb, since the resulting cadence
($x-\cup-\mid\cup-$) would produce a cretic rhythm one foot too soon.[120]

Clearly, a system of analysis that obscures such basic facts of metrical
practice will not tell us all we might like to know about dramatic verse.
Modern scholars thus increasingly prefer an algebraic notation for verse
structure that focuses on syllables rather than feet. Under this scheme, the
iambic senarius and trochaic septenarius are represented by the sequences

$$A\ B\ C\ D\ A\ /\ B\ C\ D\ A\ B\ c\ D$$
$$B\ C\ D\ A\ B\ C\ D\ A\ /\ B\ C\ D\ A\ B\ c\ D$$

where A's and C's are the *ancipitia* of traditional analysis, B's and D's the
longa, lower case letters indicate light syllables (and resolutions), and a

---

informs Cicero's discussions of meter, e.g. *Orat.* 173, 218; *Tusc.* 2.37. So too Hor.
Ars 251–62.

[118] The English stress marks, following Bentley's example, indicate the start of
every second trochee. The essay introduced his groundbreaking 1726 edition of
Terence. This essential fact of iambo-trochaic verse was well known to imperial
grammarians like Caesius Bassus (*GLK* VI.250). It is a reason Terentian scenes can
slip so easily between iambic and trochaic rhythms and why ambiguities in scansion can lead to ambiguities in meter (e.g. 237).

[119] T. does something similar at *An.* 863–5, where elimination of a syllable momentarily changes a passage in octonarii to a trochaic septenarius at 864, before reverting
to iambs at 865, after which the music stops and the scene continues in senarii.

[120] The practice is known as "Luchs' Law." The linguistic basis for this and related practices is examined by Fortson 2008: 34–53. See also Gratwick 1993: 56–7,
Barsby 1999: 302–3.

forward slash marks significant word divisions.[121] The iambic sequence of
An. 2 would then be represented as

A bb c D A / B c D A B c D

and the trochaic sequence of *An.* 338 as

B c D a B C D A / bb C dd A B c D

The structural similarity and final cretic cadence of the two meters then
become obvious at a glance.

Yet even this approach obscures something important. Bentley's example of metrical flexibility is especially telling because he probably knew
"Happy is the Country Life" not as a poem but as a song.[122] Behind all
metrical questions lies the presence (or absence) of music: from the audience's standpoint, the most obvious defining fact of Roman dramatic verse
is not apparent from scansion alone. The iambic senarius was a spoken
verse. Everything else was performed to the tibia, either sung or in recitative. Texts we read in those meters were, in effect, song lyrics, and that
makes a difference.[123] On a purely textual level, lyrics seem to behave like
any other verse. Consider, for example, W. S. Gilbert's Duke of Plaza Toro:

> In enterprise of martial kind, when there was any fighting,
> He led his regiment from behind, he found it less exciting.

The English stress accents form the equivalent of an iambic septenarius,
with diaeresis after the fourth foot and one strategic resolution in the
second line:

$$\cup\ -|\cup\ -|\cup\ -|\cup\ -\|\cup\ -|\cup\ -|\cup\ -\times$$
$$\cup\ -|\cup\ \cup\cup|\cup\ -|\cup\ -\|\cup\ -|\cup\ -|\cup\ -\times$$

Reading these lines "metrically," however, creates a very distorted view of
what an audience actually hears. Sullivan's melody, in 2/4 time, actually
spreads the opening monosyllable of each verse over two sixteenth-notes

---

[121] The system first gained currency in the analysis of Greek dramatic meters by
Handley 1965: 56–62 and was carried into discussion of Latin by Gratwick 1993:
52–4. See also Barsby 1999: 303–4, Fortson 2008: 25–30. Deufert 2014: 492–3
illustrates its application in a variety of verse forms.

[122] The lyric by John Playford (1623–1686) was widely distributed together with
a musical setting in vol. 4 of the popular anthology, *Wit and Mirth: or Pills to purge
Melancholy* (1719). For the influence of English lyric on Bentley's metrical analysis,
see Haugen 2011: 178–81.

[123] For the distinction between spoken and accompanied verse, see Moore
2008, and for the difference music makes between even such structurally close
forms as septenarius and senarius, see Moore 2012: 172–7.

(semiquavers) sung a third apart, "any" in the first line is sung as four sixteenth-notes, with two notes for each syllable, and the rhythm is not in fact dotted (the musical equivalent of iambs or trochees) but a long string of unaccented eighth-notes (quavers). And at the finale, nothing in the lyric when printed as text indicates that the culminating praise of that "celebrated, cultivated, underrated nobleman" is in double time. Gilbert, working in partnership with Sullivan, doubtless knew what the music would do, but his words alone do not give an entirely accurate idea of how the verse is performed.

How, then, should we understand Terentian verse and the role of music in creating its effects? Though not as spectacular a writer of lyric as Pl., T. was in his own way a highly skilled exploiter of the genre's metrical and musical capabilities, which meant he worked in close partnership with his actors and with Flaccus, his tibicen.[124] Even here in *An.*, his first play, prominent use of the iambic octonarius and effortless transitions between iambic and trochaic patterns already indicate a high level of musical experimentation.[125]

Metrical and dramatic effects often work together, as at 592–3, when Davos is momentarily taken aback by Simo's claim that Pamphilus' marriage is again in prospect. Their dialogue plays out in octonarii.

Dav	quidnam audio?			
Sim		gnatam ut det oro uixque id exoro.		
Dav				occidi!
Sim				hem!
	quid dixtī?			
Dav		optume inquam factum.		
Sim			nunc per hunc nullast mora.	

---

[124] Cic. *De or.* 3.102, using examples from tragedy, notes how actor and musician together control the tone and pace of performance. Moore 2012: 135–9 and Marshall 2006: 234–44 discuss that partnership. How fully our texts reflect the actual rhythms of performance is unclear. Moore 2012: 144–70 analyzes the possibilities. For a more optimistic view, at least in the Greek context, of the relationship of text to accompaniment, see Dale 1969: 160–4, West 1982: 20–2.

[125] Moore 2013. The fact that a single anceps element added to the front of a trochaic septenarius produces an iambic octonarius facilitates such alternations. See Questa 2007: 348–55, Moore 2012: 180–4. Nearly half of *An.* is in accompanied verse, the precise figure varying with the metrical scheme adopted. The only more musical play in the corpus is *Hec.*, which is 56 percent accompanied. (According to Moore 2007: 93 n. 1–2, the corresponding figure for accompanied verse in the entire Plautine corpus is 68 percent, with a high of 79 percent for *Epid.*)

Elisions in 592 enhance the shock of Davos' distress as *occidi!* tumbles out over Simo's *exoro*, itself cut short as Simo, with *hem!*, catches something of Davos' exclamation aside. Davos then needs a moment to think his way out of the problem, a moment provided by the hiatus after *dixtī* as he turns *occidi* into *optume*.

The fact remains, though, that much of *An.* is spoken, not sung, and while a Gilbert and Sullivan libretto might slip into prose to move the plot along, T.'s play is entirely in verse. Reconciling the persistent, discernible pulse of that verse with the starts and stops required by comic action and comic delivery raises the further question of how metrical principles align with dramatic needs. Here, for example, Davos instructs Mysis in what he wants her to say in Chremes' hearing (751–3).

> dictura's quod rog(o)? :: au! :: conced(e) ad dexteram.
> ⏤ ⏤|⏤ ⏑ ⏑ | ⏑   ⏤ | ⏑ ⏑ | ⏤ ⏑ |⏑ ⏢

> deliras. non tut(e) ipse—? :: uerbum si mihi
> ⏤⏤|⏤ ⏑ ⏑ |⏤ ⏑ |⏑   ⏤ |⏤ ⏑ |⏑ ⏢

> unum praeterquam quod te rogŏ faxis, caue!
> ⏤ ⏤| ⏤ ⏑ ⏤ |⏤   ⏑ ⏤ |⏤ ⏑⏑|⏤⏤ |⏑ ⏢

Scansion requires the second vowel of *rogo* to elide, but Mysis' pained exclamation responds to some action by Davos – a shake of the shoulder, a yank of the arm, a shove in the back? – that takes place at the caesura between his *rogo?* and her *au!* Since that movement must take at least a moment, what happens to the elision that otherwise dissolves the boundary between the two utterances? There is probably also a small interval between this line and the next to cover the time while Davos draws her to one side. Contrast the more dramatically comprehensible elision in the second line, where *tutipse* forms one emphatic unit of sense, while *uerbum* is spoken in haste to prevent Mysis from saying too much.

Davos is still speaking in senarii at 784–6 as he wrests the initiative from Chremes, who insists (wrongly) that he knows everything.

> auscult(a). :: audiui iam omni(a). :: ann(e) haec t(u) omnia? ::
> ⏤ ⏤| ⏤ ⏤|⏤ ⏑ ⏑ |⏑   ⏤ | ⏤ ⏑ ⏤ |⏑⏢

> audiu(i), inqu(am,) a principi(o). :: audistin, obsecr(o)? em
> ⏤ ⏤| ⏤   ⏤ |⏤ ⏑⏑ | ⏤ ⏤|⏑ ⏤ |⏑ ⏢

> sceler(a)! hanc i(am) oportet in cruciat(um) hinc abripi.
> ⏑ ⏑   ⏤| ⏑⏤| ⏑⏤| ⏑⏑ ⏤ | ⏤ ⏑ ⏤|⏑⏢

Elisions at each change of speaker in 784–5 again reflect the effort of each character to dominate the other. A pause, however, seems necessary after *scelera!* in 786 as Davos turns to gesture toward Mysis (*hanc*), and while the second foot requires the collapse (synaloepha) of *iam* into *oportet*, something of the adverb must be heard for its presence to be recognized. These are dramatic requirements not so readily aligned with the conventions of metrical analysis. Yet action must claim a place beside meter and syntax in discussions of dramatic verse.[126]

Noteworthy points of prosody are discussed in the commentary, as are some of the more obvious examples of metrical manipulation for dramatic effect. More of these remain to be discovered, though much is of necessity unknown and probably unknowable.

6 DONATUS

In addition to the *Ars grammatica* that became a standard text of the Middle Ages, the famous fourth-century grammarian Aelius Donatus wrote extensive commentaries on the two most important poets of the Latin curriculum, Virgil and Terence.[127] Neither commentary survives in its original form. That on Virgil was eclipsed within a century by the work of Servius, who appropriated much of its content. The T. commentary suffered a different fate. Extracts from it were over time copied into the margins of the dramatist's MSS and eventually replaced the continuous commentary from which they were drawn; only some centuries later was an effort made to reconstitute those marginalia once again as a separate book. The *Commentum Terenti* we know today is thus not the work as Don. wrote it but an anonymous, undated compilation of disparate fragments and presumed fragments of the lost original, with extraneous material from other sources quite possibly added to the mix. Yet for all the resulting inconsistencies, repetitions, contradictions, and frustrations, what remains of this great work has shaped the course of Terentian studies for centuries, copied and re-copied by fifteenth-century humanists, in print by 1472, and included with editions of T. by 1476.[128] As a result, many of

---

[126] Music ought by right to be a fourth component, but unlike action, pitch and (to a lesser extent) tempo cannot be clearly reconstructed from clues in the text.

[127] His student Jerome set Don.'s *floruit* at 353 CE. For his career, see Kaster 1988: 275–8, Zetzel 2018: 296–7, and for his style of exegesis, Zetzel 1981: 148–67, Jakobi 1996, Brown 2012. Material from the lost commentary on Virgil may survive in the augmented version of Servius known as Servius Danielis (Cameron 2011: 408–13).

[128] Reconstitution of the text is unlikely to have occurred before the seventh century, with its two earliest (partial) witnesses dating from the eleventh and thirteenth centuries. Rediscovered in 1433 and then the 1440s, these were then frequently recopied as a continuous commentary on five of the six plays (*Hau.* is

its insights have long since passed into the vast realm of received opinion, but commentaries – including this one – continue to be in its debt. It is therefore important to understand what information ascribed to "Don." in the following notes does and does not represent.

Don. did not teach or write in a vacuum. The original work was a massive variorum commentary that routinely borrowed from predecessors ranging as far back as the antiquarian P. Nigidius Figulus, a contemporary of Varro (ad *Ph.* 233). A question of attribution in *Ad.*, for example, thus easily compresses the exegetical tradition of two centuries: "Probus assigns this to the character of Sostrata; Asper does not want the slave to respond to everything, but thinks the nurse says this."[129] Probus may in fact have been a major source for Don., although his name appears only twice in the *An.* commentary, in notes on the punctuation at 720 and on whether Simo's *ain* at 875 is simply an expression of doubt ("What's that you say?" *OLD* 2) or introduces a genuine question ("Are you saying that . . . ?" *OLD* 3). Don. was also heir to a comparative method that sought elucidation of diction, characterization, plot construction, and dramaturgy through reference to T.'s Greek models. Though he does not appear to have consulted texts of Menander or Apollodorus himself, the commentary preserves lines (often garbled in transmission) of the Greek originals and notes where T. departs from his models in matters of plot construction and characterization.[130]

Like any good teacher, Don. takes pains to clarify basic points of grammar for his students, e.g. explaining an apparent Grecism (ad 204, 543.1), simplifying a difficult prolepsis (ad 401), reminding students that negative clauses of fear are introduced by *ut*, not *ne* (ad 705). He discusses textual variants, sometimes quoting from a text somewhat different from

missing). For the complexities of the resulting text history, see Reeve 1983a; for Don.'s earliest appearances in print, Torello-Hill and Turner 2020: 53–60; for the significance of the commentary, Victor 2013: 353–8, Demetriou 2014. The standard edition remains Wessner 1902–1908; Cioffi 2017 provides a new edition of the *An.* commentary. Hyperdonat, an online critical edition of the complete commentary with an annotated bilingual text (Latin and French) has been produced by a team at the University of Lyon (hyperdonat.tge-adonis.fr/).

[129] Don. ad *Ad.* 323, *Probus personae assignat hoc Sostratae, Asper non uult ad omnia seruum respondere, sed nutricem putat hoc loqui.* Aemilius Asper commented astutely on T., Sallust, and Virgil in the second century CE. M. Valerius Probus, the great scholar of Flavian Rome, made a special study of (then unfashionable) Republican authors (Suet. *Gram.* 24, with Kaster 1995: 242–66, Zetzel 2018: 312–16).

[130] The point of the ancient comparative exercise does not appear to have been a measure of T.'s originality, though modern critics have used Don.'s reports for that purpose. See Barsby 2002, Goldberg 2020, and for Don.'s comments on the models for *An.*, Appendix II.3. Don.'s use of Greek is on many levels problematic. See most recently Maltby 2019.

ours.[131] He is consistently helpful in pointing out nuances of word choice, e.g. the difference between *oro* and *supplico* (ad 312), *coram* and *palam* (ad 490), or tense usage (ad 38), and he notes when an expression seems proverbial (190, 214, 248, 305). The rhetorical aims of Roman education lie behind his readiness to break a narrative into parts (ad 49), to identify figures of speech (ad 51, 624), to note a faulty syllogism (ad 372). Since speeches culled from plays were often turned into oratorical exercises, Don. included numerous pointers about delivery, e.g. voice (ad 667.3 *cum odio hoc pronuntiandum est*), gesture (ad 184.4 *more seruili et uernili gestu*), or facial expression (ad 380.3 *hoc uultuose pronuntiandum est*).[132] He remains well aware that the text is the record of a performance: *haec scaena actuosa est, magis enim in gestu quam in oratione est constituta* (ad 722). Dramatically complex scenes, where what characters say may make little sense without also understanding what they are doing, thus receive especially close attention. The charade staged for Chremes' benefit at 740, for example, is built of interrogations, instructions heard, unheard, and misheard, exclamations of outrage and surprise, and considerable stage business centered on an infant left conspicuously at Simo's house door. To make sense of it all requires detailed explanation, which Don. proceeds to offer.

> ad 750: He [Davos] cleverly asserts that he has not seen Chremes, although he both did see him coming and now sees him present.

> ad 759: This line is spoken aloud, the following line spoken softly so the old man doesn't hear.

> ad 760: Davos needs to restrain Mysis, since Chremes has not yet heard everything, has not yet learned where the woman is from and about the infant she has picked up.

He thus fills his commentary with the stage directions absent from his text.[133] Bringing these plays to some kind of life was itself part of Don.'s own tradition of explication.

---

[131] Close analysis has shown that the text he used must have been independent of the two surviving manuscript families that form the modern text of T., but although an independent witness to what T. wrote, it was not for that reason necessarily a better one (Grant 1986: 77–96, Jakobi 1996: 18–46).

[132] The three components of delivery (*actio*) as defined by *Rhet. Her.* 3.20–7, Cic. *De or.* 3.216–23, Quint. *Inst.* 11.3. Cf. Quint. *Inst.* 1.11 on the utility of employing a comic actor to coach students. For practice speeches, see Bonner 1977: 267–70, Fantham 1982: 258–62, and for the overlap between acting and oratory, Fantham 2002. Jakobi 1996: 8–14, 133–43 traces the rhetorical underpinnings of the commentary.

[133] Whether such observations derive from a memory of stage performance or dramatic reading, a classroom exercise, or simply his own active imagination is im-

Behind all this lies a real power of imagination and a lively intellect, which should not surprise us. Jerome never forgot the dry wit his teacher brought to the classroom, as when he glossed T.'s observation *nullumst iam dictum quod non dictum sit prius* (*Eun.* 41) with the remark, *pereant qui ante nos nostra dixerunt*, precisely the kind of comment to stick in the mind of a precocious student.[134] Similarly shrewd observations of all kinds are found in the commentary.

7 TEXT AND TRANSMISSION

The text of T. followed two discernible routes to the modern world. Our sole witness to the first of these is itself ancient, the so-called Codex Bembinus, a MS of the fourth or fifth century CE now in the Vatican library and conventionally identified as A in a critical apparatus.[135] This venerable parchment book, in rustic capitals, preserves T. in the form that Don., Servius, and Macrobius would have known and remains the single best witness to what T. wrote. Because its initial leaves have been lost, however, its utility for establishing the text of *An.* is limited: a coherent text of our play only begins at line 889. A second route to survival, independent of A, is much better attested. As many as 700 medieval MSS of T., all written in minuscule script, share a common ancestor now lost (Σ) and are known collectively as the Calliopian family because several of them acknowledge in a subscript the editorial intervention of an otherwise unknown scholar they call Calliopius.[136] We take A and Σ to represent different branches of the tradition because A preserves readings not found in any descendant of Σ and presents the plays in a different order, but the MSS of the extensive

possible to determine. See Barsby 2000: 511–13 with examples drawn from *Eun.*, and more broadly Thomadaki 1989: 368–72, Jakobi 1996: 8–14.

[134] Jer. *In Eccles.* 1. The comment does not appear in the extant commentary: the anecdote as told clearly suggests an informal moment. So, rightly, Kaster 1988: 277.

[135] Scholarly convention identifies extant MSS by Roman letters and lost MSS from which they are believed to descend by Greek ones. The Bembinus (Vat. lat. 3226) takes its name from the Bembo family of Venetian humanists, who owned it from some time in the fifteenth century until 1579. It was willed to the Vatican library by Fulvio Orsini in 1600. A facsimile is available (Prete 1970), but the MS is most easily consulted online, digi.vatlib.it/view/MSS_Vat.lat.3226.

[136] The subscription reads *Calliopius recensui(t)* or *feliciter Calliopio bono scholastico*. No. 194 in the prosopography of Kaster 1988: 388–9, his activity is tentatively dated to the early fifth century, though the surviving Calliopian MSS are all significantly later. There was no ancient authority for the early medieval tradition that recast Calliopius as the producer or public reciter of T.'s plays (Torello-Hill and Turner 2020: 33–7).

Calliopian family are not themselves all closely related. Σ had two (also lost) descendants, Γ and Δ, each of which produced a sub-group in the Calliopian line.[137] Surviving MSS either derive directly from one or the other of these two groups or are judged to form a third, "mixed" group representing a contamination of the two traditions. The readings in this large family of MSS vary in quality – no Calliopian MS is as consistently good a witness as A – but they include another noteworthy feature: several of those descended from Γ contain lively illustrations at the head of each scene that depict the plays' characters and occasionally the stage action.[138]

Editors of *An.* can draw on two additional ancient witnesses. Remnants of a fourth-century papyrus codex now in Vienna preserve fragments of *An.* 489–99, 513–21, 540–54, 575–82, and from Oxyrhynchus come two largely intact, though non-consecutive leaves of a codex produced perhaps a century later containing *An.* 602–68, 925–50, 957–79. These papyrus texts appear to be independent of both A and Σ, reflecting a time before editorial intervention imposed some uniformity on the tradition. The Oxyrhynchus codex is particularly interesting as a document in the history of Terentian reception, since it is punctuated and annotated for the use of Greek-speaking students.[139]

As a group, all the MSS of T. share two striking features. First, they do not uniformly recognize that the plays are in verse, much less indicate the various kinds of verse. The Bembinus distinguishes accurately between senarii and accompanied meters, while the roughly contemporary Oxyrhynchus codex is internally inconsistent in its colometry. The Calliopian family is variable. Some MSS get things right or largely right, but the ninth-century C (Vat. lat. 3868), which is in other respects among the finest of them, treats the text largely as prose. In another important

---

[137] A preserves the plays in the order *An.*, *Eun.*, *Hau.*, *Ph.*, *Hec.*, *Ad.* The Γ-subgroup of the Calliopian family reverses *Ph.* and *Ad.*, while the Δ-subgroup presents them in alphabetical order, with *Ph.* = F.

[138] The most beautifully illustrated of the Calliopian MSS, the ninth-century Vat. lat. 3868, is available in facsimile (Jachmann 1929) and online, digi.vatlib.it/view/MSS_Vat.lat.3868. A twelfth-century MS in Oxford (Bodleian MS. Auct. F.2.13) first published as a DVD (Bodleian Digital Texts 2, edited by B. J. Muir and A. J. Turner) is now also online, digital.bodleian.ox.ac.uk/objects/odf0371f-bofb-4cb7-9c4d-8d108c06a694. The miniatures as a group are reproduced by Jones and Morey 1930–1931, their analysis now superseded by Wright 2006. The origin of the miniatures, their relation to one another, and especially their relation to any tradition of stage performance remain controversial. See Dodwell 2000, Lateiner 2004, Dutsch 2007, Keefe 2015.

[139] P. Vindob. inv. L 103 is available at digital.onb.ac.at and P. Oxy. 2401 at www.papyrology.ox.ac.uk/POxy. For discussion, see respectively, Danese 1989 and Macedo 2018.

way, though, all MSS of T. accurately reflect an original Roman practice: they lack act divisions. The act structure often found in our printed texts was imposed by Renaissance editors, who knew on Horace's authority that a play should have five acts, though they must also have known – as ancient commentators like Don. certainly knew – that no five-act structure suits these plays very well.[140] Their Greek models were certainly organized in acts punctuated by independent choral interludes, but the Roman preference for continuous action led authors of *palliata* comedies to work around the resulting breaks in the original action.[141] The structural unit that mattered to them was instead the scene as defined by the characters' entrances, and our MSS consistently mark scene divisions by setting out before each one the names and roles of the characters to appear in it.

Constructing a modern text from this material can be complex. The exact relation of individual Calliopian MSS to each other and to their ancestors remains controversial, as does the quality of their testimony and the degree of credence a modern editor should give it.[142] Though fewer than one hundred lines of *An.* survive in the Bembinus, for example, they contain two unique and significant variant readings, the deliberative subjunctive *feras* at 921 for Calliopian *feres* and *ad Andrum* at 923 for *apud Andrum*, both of which would have gone unsuspected. Don., too, preserves otherwise unattested readings that command respect, notably the colorful phrase *mihi conflauit sollicitudines* "he sparked my concerns" where the MSS all read *confecit* (650) and the idiomatic indicative *respondes* for MSS *responde* at 849. Unmetrical lines in the MSS require correction. Some such corrections, e.g. removing an otiose *tuo* at the end of 307, are easy. Solutions may differ for others, e.g. the MSS reading *ubi illic est scelus qui me perdidit* at 607, which does not scan as the first half of a trochaic octonarius, is corrected in our text to *ubi ille est scelus qui perdidit*

[140] Hor. *Ep.* 2.3.189–90 *neu minor neu sit quinto productior actu/ fabula*, a case where Hellenistic literary theory was at odds with Roman literary practice. Thus Don. Praef. ad *An.* II.3 *difficile est diuisionem actuum in Latinis fabulis internoscere obscure editam* (cf. Praef. ad *Eun.* I.5). See Duckworth 1952: 98–101, Brink 1971: 248–50, Hunter 1985: 35–42, and for the Renaissance imposition of act divisions, Torello-Hill and Turner 2020: 109–14.

[141] The clearest example is the scene at Pl. *Bac.* 494–562, which smooths over the choral interlude at Men. *Dis Exapaton* 59–63. See Introduction 1.3. Traces of the original act divisions discernible in Latin texts furnish important clues for reconstructing their lost models, e.g. Gaiser 1972: 1038–41. The one clear example of such a break in *An.* occurs after Davos' exit at 819.

[142] The MS tradition is surveyed by Reeve 1983b, with a significant update by Victor 2014.

me, which does.[143] Editorial intervention may also be required to identify speakers, since attributions in the MSS have no authorial value, and to explain stage action that must be deduced from what characters say, since ancient scripts lacked stage directions.

The need to pass judgment on each discrepancy or inadequacy in the sources raises one final question, viz. to what end? What is the text an edition aspires to establish for modern readers? Some perspective may help. The origins of our surviving witnesses, A and Σ, can at best be traced back no further than Flavian times, i.e. still nearly three hundred years after the playwright's death.[144] Nor were these the only witnesses to what T. wrote that were available to readers of late antiquity, as the additional variants in the papyri and attested by Don. show. The process of transmission from the original creation of a script in the 160s BCE for (and by) Ambivius Turpio's acting troupe to what Flavian scholars may have found under T.'s name to what Donatus knew to what we know today as the text of *An.* is thus nearly as problematic in outline as in detail. That should not surprise us. Editors of Shakespeare continue to debate whether Hamlet's flesh was too solid, sallied, or sullied, and we will never be able to say with any more certainty whether T. initially wrote *respondes* or *responde*, much less what his actor may have said on the stage at any one time or what members of his audience thought they heard. Behind the eventual text lies, ultimately, the record of performance, and "if," as current thinking runs, "it is a performing text we are dealing with, it is a mistake to think that in our editorial work what we are doing is getting back to the author's original manuscript: the very notion of 'the author's original manuscript' is in such cases a figment."[145] Getting as close as possible to what subsequent

---

[143] This is the emendation of Karl Dziatzko (1884). Other solutions include the aposiopesis Bentley created by omitting *perdidit* and *ubi illic est scelus qui me perdit* in Andreas Spengel's 1888 edition.

[144] Even this assumption is problematic. Jachmann claimed a common ancestor for A and Σ, which he called Φ and believed to derive from an "edition" of T. by the late first-century grammarian Valerius Probus (Jachmann 1924: 87–90, Grant 1986. 5–10), but the hypothesis has been seriously challenged, e.g. Victor 1996a. Significant exegetical work only became common in the century after Probus (Zetzel 2018: 88–94).

[145] Orgel 1991: 84, in the context of Renaissance drama. Thus Kruschwitz 2016 recognizes that the script of a Terentian play was always in some sense a collaborative effort. See also Marshall 2006: 257–61 and Lucarini 2016, though Vickers 2002: 18–43 points with some truth to scripts as "the single most important thing in mounting a play." As for the famous crux at *Hamlet* 1.2, the earlier quartos (1603, 1604) read "sallied." i.e. either "assailed" or the equivalent of "sullied," while the magisterial folio of 1623 reads "solid." No editorial choice is universally accepted. Questa 1965: 33–4 n. 31 notes similar, performance-based variations in the history of opera librettos.

Roman readers eventually knew as "Terence" is about the best we can do, though, as will emerge, that will be an entirely adequate approximation.

The text presented here is essentially what John Barsby prepared for his Loeb edition of T. and is reproduced with kind permission of the Loeb Foundation and Harvard University Press. Punctuation, often problematic when Latin syntax aligns poorly with English conventions, is sometimes altered. More significant changes include:

> 434 *aegre* for *aeque*
> 728 *iurato* for *iurandum*
> 781 *au* for *eho*
> 817 change of speaker within the line
> 849 *respondes* for *responde*
> 893 *licetne* for *liceatne*

These variations, along with other interpretive questions rooted in problems of text and meter, are discussed in the commentary. To encourage attention to meter, verse forms are identified in the left margin, with diacritical aids to scansion derived from Lindsay's OCT. The traditional act and scene numbers are included as marginalia for ease of reference. Line numbering, however, is continuous.

P. TERENTI AFRI ANDRIA

Don. *Andria* Praefatio I.6

Haec prima facta est, acta ludis Megalensibus M. Fuluio M.' Glabrione [Q. Minucio Thermo L. Valerio] aedil. curul. egerunt L. Atilius [Latinus] Praenestinus et L. Ambiuius Turpio. modos fecit Flaccus Claudi [filius] tibiis paribus [dextris uel sinistris]. et est tota Graeca, edita M. Marcello C. Sulpicio consulibus.

Personae

SIMO senex

SOSIA libertus

DAVOS seruus

MYSIS ancilla

PAMPHILVS adulescens

CHARINVS adulescens

BYRRIA seruus

LESBIA obstetrix

GLYCERIVM uirgo

CHREMES senex

CRITO senex

DROMO lorarius

Scaena: Athenis

Argumentum

[C. Sulpici Apollinaris Periocha]

ia⁶

Sororem falso creditam meretriculae
genere Andriae, Glycerium, uitiat Pamphilus,
grauidaque facta dat fidem uxorem sibi
fore hanc. nam aliam pater ei desponderat,
gnatam Chremetis, atque ut amorem comperit   5
simulat futuras nuptias, cupiens suus
quid haberet animi filius cognoscere.
Daui suasu non repugnat Pamphilus.
sed ex Glycerio natum ut uidit puerulum
Chremes recusat nuptias, generum abdicat.   10
mox filiam Glycerium insperato adgnitam
hanc Pamphilo, aliam dat Charino coniugem.

Prologvs

a⁶

Poeta quom primum animum ad scribendum appulit,
id sibi negoti credidit solum dari,
populo ut placerent quas fecisset fabulas.
uerum aliter euenire multo intellegit.
nam in prologis scribundis operam abutitur,   5
non qui argumentum narret sed qui maleuoli
ueteris poetae maledictis respondeat.
nunc quam rem uitio dent, quaeso, animum aduortite.
Menander fecit Andriam et Perinthiam.
qui utramuis recte norit ambas nouerit,   10
non ita dissimili sunt argumento, et tamen
dissimili oratione sunt factae ac stilo.
quae conuenere in Andriam ex Perinthia
fatetur transtulisse atque usum pro suis.
id īsti uituperant factum atque in eo disputant   15
contaminari non decere fabulas.
faciuntne intellegendo ut nil intellegant?
qui quom hunc accusant, Naeuium, Plautum, Ennium
accusant, quos hic noster auctores habet,
quorum aemulari exoptat neglegentiam   20
potius quam istorum obscuram diligentiam.
dehinc ut quiescant porro moneo et desinant
maledicere, malefacta ne noscant sua.
fauete, adeste aequo animo, et rem cognoscite,
ut pernoscatis ecquid spēi sit relicuom,   25
posthac quas faciet de integro comoedias
spectandae an exigendae sint uobis prius.

Simo Sosia

a⁶

Sim   uos istaec intro auferte. abite! Sosia,
     ades dum. paucis te uolo.
Sos   dictum puta:
     nempe ut curentur recte haec?
Sim   immo aliud.
Sos   quid est   30
     quod tibi mea ars efficere hoc possit amplius?
Sim   nil istac opus est arte ad hanc rem quam paro,
     sed eis quas semper in te intellexi sitas,
     fide et taciturnitate.
Sos   exspecto quid uelis.

Sim	ego postquam te emi, a paruolo ut semper tibi 35
	apud me iusta et clemens fuerit seruitus
	scis. feci ex seruo ut esses libertus mihi,
	propterea quod seruibas liberaliter.
	quod habui summum pretium persolui tibi.
Sos	in memoria habeo.
Sim	haud muto factum.
Sos	gaudeo 40
	si tibi quid feci aut facio quod placeat, Simo,
	et īd gratum fuisse aduorsum te habeo gratiam.
	sed hōc mihi molestumst, nam istaec commemoratio
	quasi exprobratiost immemori benefici.
	quin tu uno uerbo dic quid est quod me uelis. 45
Sim	ita faciam. hoc primum in hac re praedico tibi:
	quas credis esse has non sunt uerae nuptiae.
Sos	quor simulas igitur?
Sim	rem omnem a principio audies.
	ēō pacto et gnati uitam et consilium meum
	cognosces et quid facere in hac re te uelim. 50
	nam is postquam excessit ex ephebis, Sosia, et
	liberius uiuendi erat potestas (nam antea
	qui scire posses aut ingenium noscere,
	dum aetas, metus, magister prohibebant?)—
Sos	itast.
Sim	—quod plerique omnes faciunt adulescentuli, 55
	ut animum ad aliquod studium adiungant, aut equos
	alere aut canes ad uenandum aut ad philosophos,
	horum ille nil egregie praeter cetera
	studebat et tamen omnia haec mediocriter.
	gaudebam.
Sos	non iniuria. nam id arbitror 60
	apprime in uita esse utile, ut ne quid nimis.
Sim	sic uita erat: facile omnis perferre ac pati;
	cum quibus erat quomque una eis se dedere;
	ēōrum obsequi studiis, aduorsus nemini,
	numquam praeponens se illis; ita ŭt facillume 65
	sine īnuidia laudem inuenias et amicos pares.
Sos	sapienter uitam instituit. namque hoc tempore
	obsequium amicos, ueritas odium parit.
Sim	interea mulier quaedam abhinc triennium
	ex Andro commigrauit huc uiciniae, 70
	inopia et cognatorum neglegentia

  coacta, egregia forma atque aetate integra.
Sos ei! uereor ne quid Andria apportet mali.
Sim primo haec pudice uitam parce ac duriter
  agebat, lana et tela uictum quaeritans.   75
  sed postquam amans accessit pretium pollicens
  unus et item alter, ita ut ingeniumst omnium
  hominum ab labore procliue ad lubidinem,
  accepit condicionem, dehinc quaestum occipit.
  qui tum illam amabant forte, ita ut fit, filium   80
  perduxere illuc secum ut una esset meum.
  egomet continuo mecum: "certe captus est,
  habet." obseruabam mane illorum seruolos
  uenientis aut abeuntis. rogitabam: "heus, puer,
  dic sodes, quis heri Chrysidem habuit?"; nam Andriae 85
  illi id erat nomen.
Sos   teneo.
Sim   Phaedrum aut Cliniam
  dicebant aut Niceratum, nam hi tres tum simul
  amabant. "eho! quid Pamphilus?" "quid? symbolam
  dedit, cenauit." gaudebam. item alio die
  quaerebam. comperibam nil ad Pamphilum   90
  quicquam attinere. enĭmuero spectatum satis
  putabam et magnum exemplum continentiae.
  nam qui cum ingeniis conflictatur eĭusmodi
  neque commouetur animus in ea re tamen,
  sciăs posse habere iam ipsum sūae uitae modum. 95
  quom id mihi placebat tum uno ore omnes omnia
  bona dicere et laudare fortunas meas,
  qui gnatum haberem tali ingenio praeditum.
  quid uerbis opus est? hac fama impulsus Chremes
  ultro ad me uenit, unicam gnatam suam   100
  cum dote summa filio uxorem ut daret.
  placuit, despondi. hic nuptiis dictust dies.
Sos quid obstat quor non uerae fiant?
Sim   audies.
  fere in diebus paucis quibus haec acta sunt
  Chrysis uicina haec moritur.   105
Sos   o factum bene!
  beasti. eī metui a Chryside.
Sim   ibi tum filius
  cum illis qui amabant Chrysidem una aderat frequens.
  curabat una funus. tristis interim,

nonnumquam collacrumabat. placuit tum id mihi.
sic cogitabam: "hic paruae consuetudinis   110
causa huius mortem tam fert familiariter:
quid si ipse amasset? quid hĭc mihi faciet patri?"
haec ego putabam esse omnia humani ingeni
mansuetique animi officia. quid multis moror?
egomet quoque eius causa in funus prodeo,   115
nil suspicans etiam mali.

Sos   hem! quid id est?

Sim   scies.
ecfertur, imus. interea inter mulieres
quae ibi aderant forte unam aspicio adulescentulam
forma—

Sos   bona fortasse.

Sim   —et uoltu, Sosia,
adeo modesto, adeo uenusto ut nil supra.   120
quae tum mihi lamentari praeter ceteras
uisast et quia erat forma praeter ceteras
honesta ac liberali, accedo ad pedisequas,
quae sit rogo. sororem esse aiunt Chrysidis.
percussit ilico animum. attat! hoc illud est,   125
hinc illae lacrimae, haec illast misericordia.

Sos   quam timeo quorsum euadas!

Sim   funus interim
procedit. sequimur, ad sepulcrum uenimus.
in ignem impositast, fletur. interea haec soror
quam dixi ad flammam accessit imprudentius,   130
satis cum periclo. ibi tum exanimatus Pamphilus
bene dissimulatum amorem et celatum indicat.
accurrit, mediam mulierem complectitur.
"mea Glycerium," inquit "quid agis? quor te is perditum?"
tum illa, ut consuetum facile amorem cerneres,   135
reiecit se in eum flens quam familiariter!

Sos   quid ais?

Sim   redeo inde iratus atque aegre ferens.
nec satis ad obiurgandum causae. diceret:
"quid feci? quid commerui aut peccaui, pater?
quae sese in ignem inicere uoluit, prohibui.   140
seruaui." honesta oratiost.

Sos   recte putas.
nam si illum obiurges uitae qui auxilium tulit,
quid facias illi qui dederit damnum aut malum?

Sɪᴍ uenit Chremes postridie ad me clamitans
     indignum facinus: comperisse Pamphilum   145
     pro uxore habere hanc peregrinam. ego īllud sedulo
     negare factum, ille instat factum. denique
     ita tum discedo ab illo ut qui se filiam
     neget daturum.
Sᴏs   non tu ibi gnatum—?
Sɪᴍ   ne haec quidem
     satis uehemens causa ad obiurgandum.
Sᴏs   qui? cedo.   150
Sɪᴍ "tute ipse his rebus finem praescripsti, pater.
     prope adest quom alieno more uiuendumst mihi.
     sine nunc meo me uiuere interea modo."
Sᴏs qui igitur relictus est obiurgandi locus?
Sɪᴍ si propter amorem uxorem nolet ducere,   155
     ea primum ab illo animum aduortenda iniuriast.
     et nunc id operam do, ut per falsas nuptias
     uera obiurgandi causa sit, si deneget.
     simul sceleratus Dauos si quid consili
     habet, ut consumat nunc quom nil obsint doli,   160
     quem ego credo manibus pedibusque obnixe omnia
     facturum, magis id adeo mihi ut incommodet
     quam ut obsequatur gnato.
Sᴏs   quapropter?
Sɪᴍ   rogas?
     mala mens, malus animus. quem quidem ego, si sensero—
     sed quid opust uerbis? sin eueniat quod uolo,   165
     in Pamphilo ut nil sit morae, restat Chremes
     qui mi exorandus est, et spero confore.
     nunc tuŏmst officium has bene ut assimules nuptias,
     perterrefacias Dauom, obserues filium
     quid agat, quid cūm īllo consili captet.
Sᴏs   sat est,   170
     curabo.
Sɪᴍ   eamus nunciam intro. i prae, sequar.

                           Sɪᴍᴏ

     non dubiumst quin uxorem nolit filius.
     ita Dauom modo timere sensi, ubi nuptias
     futuras esse audiuit. sed īpse exit foras.

Davos Simo

ia⁸	DAV	mirabar hoc si sic abiret et eri semper lenitas

ia⁸　DAV　mirabar hoc si sic abiret et eri semper lenitas　　175
ia²　　　　　　　　　　uerebar quorsum euaderet,
ia⁸　　　　　　　qui postquam audierat non datum iri filio uxorem suo,
tr⁷　　　　　　　numquam quoiquam nostrum uerbum fecit neque id aegre tulit.
　　SIM　at nunc faciet neque, ut opinor, sine tuo magno malo.
ia⁸　DAV　id uoluit nos sic necopinantis duci falso gaudio　　180
　　　　　sperantis iam amoto metu, interoscitantis opprimi,
　　　　　nĕ esset spatium cogitandi ad disturbandas nuptias:
　　　　　astute!
　　SIM　　　　carnufex quae loquitur?
　　DAV　　　　　　　　erus est neque prouideram.
　　SIM　Daue!
　　DAV　　　hem! quid est?
　　SIM　　　　　ehodum, ad me!
　　DAV　　　　　　　　quid hĭc uolt?
　　SIM　　　　　　　　　　quid ais?
　　DAV　　　　　　　　　　　qua de re?
　　SIM　　　　　　　　　　　　rogas?
　　　　mĕum gnatum rumor est amare.
　　DAV　　　　　　　　　id populus curat scilicet.　　185
　　SIM　hocine agis an non?
　　DAV　　　　　ego uero istuc.
　　SIM　　　　　　　　sed nunc ea me exquirere
　　　　iniqui patris est. nam quod antehac fecit nil ad me attinet.
　　　　dum tempus ad eam rem tulit, siui animum ut expleret suom.
　　　　nunc hic dĩes aliam uitam adfert, alios mores postulat.
　　　　dehinc postulo, siue aequomst te oro, Daue, ut redeat iam in uiam.　　190
　　　　hoc quid sit? omnes quĭ amant grauiter sibi dari uxorem ferunt.
　　DAV　ita aiunt.
　　SIM　　　　tum si quis magistrum cepit ad eam rem improbum,
　　　　ipsum animum aegrotum ad deteriorem partem plerumque applicat.
　　DAV　non hercle intellego.
　　SIM　　　　　　non? hem!
　　DAV　　　　　　　　　non. Dauos sum, non Oedipus.
　　SIM　nempe ergo aperte uis quae restant me loqui?
　　DAV　　　　　　　　　　　sane quidem.　　195
ia⁶　SIM　si sensero hodie quicquam in his te nuptiis
　　　　fallaciae conari quo fiant minus,
　　　　aut uelle in ẽa re ostendi quam sis callidus,

ꞁ⁸ uerberibus caesum te in pistrinum, Daue, dedam usque ad necem,
  eă lege atque omine ut, si te inde exemerim, ego pro te molam.   200
  quid? hoc intellexti? an nondum etiam ne hoc quidem?

Dav   immo callide.
  ita aperte ipsam rem modo locutu's, nil circumitione usus es.

Sim ubiuis facilius passus sim quam in hac re me deludier.

Dav bona uerba, quaeso!

Sim   irrides? nil me fallis. sed dico tibi,
  ne temere facias, neque tu haud dicas tibi non praedictum. caue!   205

ꞁ iii]   DAVOS

ꞁ⁸ enĭmuero, Daue, nil locist segnitiae neque socordiae,
  quantum intellexi modo senis sententiam de nuptiis.
  quae si non astu prouidentur, me aut erum pessum dabunt.
  nec quid agam certumst, Pamphilumne adiutem an auscultem seni.
  si illum relinquo, eĩus uitae timeo; sin opitulor, hũius minas,   210
  quoi uerba dare difficilest. primum iam de amore hoc comperit;
  me infensus seruat ne quam faciam in nuptiis fallaciam.
  si senserit, perii; aut si lubitum fuerit, causam ceperit
  quo iure quaque iniuria praecipitem in pistrinum dabit.

ꞁ⁶ ad haec mala hoc mi accedit etiam: haec Andria,   215
  si ista uxor siue amicast, grauida e Pamphilost,
  audireque ēorumst operae pretium audaciam.
  nam inceptiost amentium, haud amantium.
  quidquid peperisset decreuerunt tollere.
  et fingunt quandam inter se nunc fallaciam   220
  ciuem Atticam esse hanc. "fuit olim quidam senex
  mercator. nauem is fregit apud Andrum insulam.
  is obiit mortem." ibi tum hanc eiectam Chrysidis
  patrem recepisse orbam paruam. fabulae!

ꞁ⁸ miquidem hercle non fit ueri simile; atque ipsis commentum placet. 225
ꞁ⁶ sed Mysis ab ea egreditur. at ego hinc me ad forum ut
ꞁ⁸ conueniam Pamphilum ne de hac re pater imprudentem opprimat.

ꞁ iv]   MYSIS

ꞁ⁷ audiui, Archylis, iamdudum: Lesbiam adduci iubes.
  sane pol ĩlla temulentast mulier et temeraria
  nec satis digna quoi committas primo partu mulierem.   230

ia⁸

tamen eam adducam. importunitatem spectate aniculae
quia compotrix eius est. di, date facultatem, obsecro,
huic pariundi atque illi in aliis potius peccandi locum.
sed quidnam Pamphilum exanimatum uideo? uereor quid siet.
opperiar, ut sciam numquidnam haec turba tristitiae afferat.   235

[I v]   PAMPHILVS MYSIS

ia⁸	PAM	hocinĕst humanum factu aut inceptu? hocin officium patris?
tr⁷	MYS	quid īllud est?
	PAM	pro dēum fidem, quid ĕst, si haec non contumeliast?
ia⁸		uxorem decrerat dare sese mi hodie. nonne oportuit
		praescisse me ante? nonne prius communicatum oportuit?
ia²	MYS	miseram me! quod uerbum audio! 240
tr⁷	PAM	quid? Chremes, qui denegarat se commissurum mihi
		gnatam sūam uxorem, id mutauit quia me immutatum uidet?
ia⁸		itane obstinate operam dat ut me a Glycerio miserum abstrahat?
ia²		quod si fit pereo funditus.
tr⁸		adeon hominem esse inuenustum aut infelicem quemquam ut ego sum! 245
tr²^		pro deum atque hominum fidem,
tr⁸		nullon ego Chremetis pacto affinitatem effugere potero?
tr⁷		quot modis contemptus, spretus! facta transacta omnia. em!
		repudiatus repetor. quăm ŏb rem? nisi si id est quod suspicor:
		aliquid monstri alunt. ea quoniam nemini obtrudi potest, 250
		itur ad me.
	MYS	oratio haec me miseram exanimauit metu.
ia²	PAM	nam quid ego dicam de patre? ah!
ia⁸		tantamne rem tam neglegenter agere! praeteriens modo
tr⁷		mi apŭd forum: "uxor tibi ducendast, Pamphile, hodie" inquit. "para,
		abī domum." id mihi uisust dicere: "abī cito ac suspende te." 255
		obstipui. censen me uerbum potuisse ullum proloqui? aut
		ullam causam, ineptam saltem, falsam, iniquam? obmutui.
		quod si ego rescissem id prius, quid facerem si quis nunc me roget:
		aliquid facerem ut hoc ne facerem. sed nunc quid primum exsequar?
		tot me impediunt curae, quae meum animum diuorsae trahunt: 260
ia⁸		amŏr, misericordia huius, nuptiarum sollicitatio,
		tum patris pudor, qui me tam leni passus est animo usque adhuc
		quae mēo quomque animo lubitumst facere. ēine ego ut ăduorser? ei mihi!
		incertumst quid agam.
	MYS	misera timeo "incertum" hoc quorsus accidat.
		sed nunc peropust aut hunc cum ipsa aut de illa aliquid me aduorsum hunc
		loqui. 265

dum in dubiost animus, paullo momento huc uel illuc impellitur.

PAM   quis hīc loquitur? Mysis, salue.

MYS   o salue, Pamphilē.

PAM   quid agit?

MYS   rogas?

laborat e dolore atque ex hoc misera sollicitast, diem
quia olim in hunc sunt constitutae nuptiae. tum autem hoc timet,
ne deseras se.

PAM   hem! egone istuc conari queam?   270

egŏn propter me illam decipi miseram sinam,
quae mihi suom animum atque omnem uitam credidit,
quam ego animo egregie caram pro uxore habuerim?
bene et pudice eīus doctum atque eductum sinam
coactum egestate ingenium immutarier?   275
non faciam.

MYS   haud uerear si in te solo sit situm,
sed uĭm ŭt queas ferre.

PAM   adeon me ignauom putas,
adeon porro ingratum aut inhumanum aut ferum,
ut neque me consuetudo neque amor neque pudor
commoueat neque commoneat ut seruem fidem?   280

MYS   unum hoc scio, hanc meritam esse ut memor esses sui.

PAM   memor essem? o Mysis, Mysis, etiam nunc mihi
scripta illa dicta sunt in animo Chrysidis
de Glycerio. iam ferme moriens me uocat.
accessi, uos semotae, nos soli. incipit: 285
"mi Pamphile, huius formam atque aetatem uides,
nec clam te est quăm īlli nunc utraeque inutiles
et ad pudĭcitiam et ad rem tutandam sient.
quod ego per hanc te dexteram et genium tuom,
per tuăm fidem perque huius solitudinem   290
te obtestor ne abs te hanc segreges neu deseras.
si te in germani fratris dilexi loco
siue haec te solum semper fecit maxumi
seu tibi morigera fuit in rebus omnibus,
te isti uirum do, amicum, tutorem, patrem;   295
bona nostra haec tibi permitto et tuăe mando fide."
hanc mi in manum dat. mors continuo ipsam occupat.
accepi, acceptam seruabo.

MYS   ita spero quidem.

PAM   sed quor tu abis ab īlla?

MYS   obstetricem accerso.

	P A M	propera. atque audin?

uerbum unum cauĕ de nuptiis, ne ad morbum hoc etiam—

| | M Y S | teneo. | 300 |

[II i]   C H A R I N V S B Y R R I A P A M P H I L V S

tr⁸   C H A quid ais, Byrria? datŭrne illa Pamphilo hodie nuptum?

       B Y R   sic est.

tr⁷   C H A qui scis?

       B Y R   apud forum modo e Dauo audiui.

       C H A   uae misero mihi!

ia⁸   ut animus in spe atque in timore usque antehac attentus fuit,

             ita, postquam adempta spes est, lassus cura confectus stupet.

tr⁸   B Y R quaeso edepol, Charine, quoniam non potest id fieri quod uis,   305

tr⁷   id uelis quod possit.

       C H A   nil uolo aliud nisi Philumenam.

       B Y R   ah!

tr⁸   quanto satiust te id dare operam qui istum amorem ex animo amoueas,

tr⁷   quam id loqui quo magis lubido frustra incendatur tua!

ia⁸   C H A facile omnes quom ualemus recta consilia aegrotis damus.

             tu si hic sis aliter sentias.

       B Y R   age age, ut lubet.

       C H A   sed Pamphilum   310

             uideo. omnia experiri certumst priusquam pereo.

       B Y R   quid hic agit?

       C H A ipsum hunc orabo, huic supplicabo, amorem huic narrabo meum.

             credo, impetrabo ut aliquot saltem nuptiis prodat dies.

             interea fiet aliquid, spero.

       B Y R   id "aliquid" nil est.

       C H A   Byrria,

             quid tibi uidetur? adeon ad eum?

       B Y R   quidni? si nil impetres,   315

             ut te arbitretur sibi paratum moechum, si illam duxerit.

tr⁷   C H A abin hinc in malam rem cum suspicione istac, scelus?

ia⁶   P A M Charinum uideo. salue.

       C H A   o salue, Pamphile.

tr⁷   ad te aduenio spem, salutem, auxilium, consilium expetens.

       P A M neque pol consili locum habeo neque ad auxilium copiam.   320

             sed istuc quidnamst?

       C H A   hodie uxorem ducis?

       P A M   aiunt.

CHA	Pamphile,
	si id facis, hodie postremum me uides.
PAM	quid ita?
CHA	ei mihi!
	uereor dicere. huic dic, quaeso, Byrria.
BYR	ego dicam.
PAM	quid est?
BYR	sponsam hic tuam amat.
PAM	nĕ ĭste haud mecum sentit. ehodum, dic mihi:
	num quidnam amplius tibi cŭm illa fũit, Charine?
CHA	ah, Pamphile! 325
	nil.
PAM	quam uellem!
CHA	nunc te per amicitiam et per amorem obsecro,
	principio ut ne ducas.
PAM	dabo equidem operam.
CHA	sed si id non potest
	aut tibi nuptiae hae sunt cordi—
PAM	cordi?
CHA	—saltem aliquot dies
	profer, dum proficiscor aliquo ne uideam.
PAM	audi nunciam.
	ego, Charine, ne utiquam officium liberi esse hominis puto, 330
	quom is nil mereat, postulare id gratiae apponi sibi.
	nuptias effugere ego istas malo quam tu adipiscier.
CHA	reddidisti animum.
PAM	nunc si quid potes aut tu aut hic Byrria,
	facite, fingite, inuenite, efficite qui detur tibi.
	ego id agam mihi qui ne detur.
CHA	sat habeo.
PAM	Dauom optume 335
	uideo, quoius consilio fretus sum.
CHA	at tu hercle haud quicquam mihi,
	nisi ea quae nil opus sunt scire. fugin hinc?
BYR	ego uero ac lubens.

[II ii]

DAVOS CHARINVS PAMPHILVS

r⁷	DAV	di boni, boni quid porto! sed ubi inueniam Pamphilum,
		ut metum in quo nunc est adimam atque expleam animum gaudio?
	CHA	laetus est nescioquid.

Pam	nil est. nondum haec resciuit mala.	340
Dav	quem ego nunc credo, si iam audierit sibi paratas nuptias—
Cha	audin tu illum?
Dav	—toto me oppido exanimatum quaerere.
	sed ubi quaeram? quo nunc primum intendam?
Cha	cessas alloqui?
Dav	abeo.
Pam	Daue, ades, resiste.
Dav	quis homost qui me—? o Pamphile,
	te ipsum quaero. euge, Charine! ambo opportune. uos uolo.	345
Pam	Daue, perii!
Dav	quin tu hoc audi.
Pam	interii!
Dav	quid timeas scio.
Cha	mea quidem hercle certe in dubio uitast.
Dav	et quid tu, scio.
Pam	nuptiae mi—
Dav	etsi scio?
Pam	—hodie—
Dav	obtundis, tam etsi intellego?
	id paues ne ducas tu illam, tu autem ut ducas.
Cha	rem tenes.
Pam	istuc ipsum.
Dav	atque istuc ipsum nil periclist. me uide.	350
Pam	obsecro te, quam primum hoc me libera miserum metu.
Dav	em
	libero. uxorem tibi non dat iam Chremes.
Pam	qui scis?
Dav	scio.
	tuos pater modo me prehendit. ait tibi uxorem dare
	hodie, item alia multa quae nunc non est narrandi locus.
	continuo ad te properans percurro ad forum ut dicam haec tibi.	355
	ubi te non inuenio, ibi escendo in quendam excelsum locum.
	circumspicio: nusquam. forte ibi huius uideo Byrriam.
	rogŏ: negat uidisse. mihi molestum. quid agam cogito.
	redeunti interea ex ipsa re mi incidit suspicio: "hem!
	paullulum opsoni, ipsus tristis, de improuiso nuptiae.	360
	non cohaerent."
Pam	quorsumnam istuc?
Dav	ego me continuo ad Chremem.
	quom illo aduenio, solitudo ante ostium. iam id gaudeo.
Cha	recte dicis.

Pam	perge.
Dav	maneo. interea introire neminem
	uideo, exire neminem, matronam nullam in aedibus.
	nil ornati, nil tumulti. accessi, intro aspexi.
Pam	scio: 365
	magnum signum.
Dav	num uidentur conuenire haec nuptiis?
Pam	non opinor, Daue.
Dav	"opinor" narras? non recte accipis.
	certa res est. etiam puerum inde abiens conueni Chremi:
	holera et pisciculos minutos ferre obolo in cenam seni.
Cha	liberatus sum hodie, Daue, tua opera.
Dav	ac nullus quidem! 370
Cha	quid ita? nempe huic prorsus illam non dat.
Dav	ridiculum caput!
	quasi necesse sit, si huic non dat, te illam uxorem ducere,
	nisi uides, nisi senis amicos oras, ambis.
Cha	bene mones.
	ibo, etsi hercle saepe iam me spes haec frustratast. uale.

[II iii]

Pamphilvs Davos

r⁷

Pam	quid igitur sibi uolt pater? quor simulat?
Dav	ego dicam tibi. 375
	si id suscenseat nunc quia non det tibi uxorem Chremes,
	ipsus sibi esse iniurius uideatur, neque id iniuria,
	prius quam tŭom ut sese habeat animum ad nuptias perspexerit.
	sed si tu negaris ducere, ibi culpam in te transferet.
	tŭm ĭllae turbae fient.
Pam	quiduis patiar.
Dav	pater est, Pamphile: 380
	difficilest. tum haec solast mulier. dictum factum inuenerit
	aliquam causam quam ob rem eiciat oppido.
Pam	eiciat?
Dav	cito.
Pam	cedo igitur quid faciam, Daue?
Dav	dic te ducturum.
Pam	hem!
Dav	quid est?
Pam	egŏn dicam?
Dav	quor non?

a⁶

PAM   numquam faciam.
DAV   ne nega.
PAM   suadere noli.
DAV   ex ēā re quid fiat uide.   385
PAM   ut ab illa excludar, hoc concludar.
DAV   non itast.
          nempe hoc sic esse opinor: dicturum patrem
          "ducas uolo hodie uxorem." tu "ducam" inquies.
          cedo quid iurgabit tecum? hic reddes omnia
          quae nunc sunt certa ei consilia incerta ut sient   390
          sine ŏmni periclo. nam hoc haud dubiumst quin
          Chremes tibi non det gnatam, nec tu ēā causa minueris
          haec quae facis, ne is mutet sūam sententiam.
ia⁸   patri dic uelle, ut, quom uelit, tibi iure irasci non queat.
          nam quod tu speres "propulsabo facile uxorem his moribus;   395
          dabĭt nemo," inueniet inopem potius quam te corrumpi sinat.
          sed si te aequo animo ferre accipiet, neglegentem feceris.
          aliam otiosus quaeret. interea aliquid acciderit boni.
PAM   ităn credis?
DAV   haud dubium id quidemst.
PAM   uidĕ quo me inducas.
DAV   quin taces?
PAM   dicam. puerum autem ne resciscat mi esse ex illa cautiost.   400
          nam pollicitus sum suscepturum.
DAV   o facinus audax!
PAM   hanc fidem
          sibi me obsecrauit, qui se sciret non deserturum, ut darem.
DAV   curabitur. sed pater adest. cauĕ te esse tristem sentiat.

[II iv]   SIMO DAVOS PAMPHILVS

ia⁶   SIM   reuiso quid agant aut quid captent consili.
          DAV   hic nunc non dubitat quin te ducturum neges.   405
                    uenit meditatus alicunde ex solo loco.
                    orationem sperat inuenisse se
                    qui differat te. proin tu fac apud te ut sies.
          PAM   modo ŭt possim, Daue!
          DAV   crede, inquam, hoc mihi, Pamphile,
                    numquam hodie tecum commutaturum patrem   410
                    unum esse uerbum, si te dices ducere.

Byrria Simo Davos Pamphilvs

Byr	erus me relictis rebus iussit Pamphilum
	hodie obseruare ut quid ageret de nuptiis
	scirem. id propterea nunc hunc uenientem sequor.
	ipsum adeo praesto uideo cum Dauo. hoc agam.

     415

Sim utrumque adesse uideo.

Dav   em serua.

Sim   Pamphile!

Dav quasi de improuiso respice ad eum.

Pam   ehem, pater!

Dav probe.

Sim   hodie uxorem ducas, ut dixi, uolo.

Byr nunc nostrae timeo parti quid hīc respondeat.

Pam neque istic neque alibi tibi erit usquam in me mora.

Byr   hem!   420

Dav obmutuit.

Byr   quid dixit?

Sim   facis ut te decet,

quom istuc quod postulo impetro cum gratia.

Dav sum uerus?

Byr   erus, quantum audio, uxore excidit.

Sim i nunciam intro, ne in mora, quom opus sit, sies.

Pam eo.

Byr   nullane in re esse quoiquam homini fidem!   425

uerum illud uerbumst, uolgo quod dici solet,

omnis sibi malle melius esse quam alteri.

ego illam uidi; uirginem forma bona

memini uideri. quo aequior sum Pamphilo,

si se illam in somnis quam illum amplecti maluit.   430

renuntiabo, ut pro hoc malo mihi det malum.

Davos Simo

Dav hic nunc me credit aliquam sibi fallaciam

portare et ea me hic restitisse gratia.

Sim quid Dauos narrat?

Dav   aegre quicquam nunc quidem.

Sim nilne? hem!

Dav   nil prorsus.

Sim   atqui exspectabam quidem.   435

Dav praeter spem euenit, sentio. hoc male habet uirum.

SIM   potin es mihi uerum dicerē?

DAV   nil facilius.

SIM   nŭm īlli molestae quippiam hae sunt nuptiae
        huiusce propter consuetudinem hospitae?

DAV   nil hercle, aut, si adeo, biduist aut tridui   440
        haec sollicitudo (nosti?), deinde desinet.
        etenim ipsus secum id recta reputauit uia.

SIM   laudo.

DAV   dum licitumst ei dumque aetas tulit,
        amauit; tum id clam. cauit ne umquam infamiae
        ea res sibi esset, ut uirum fortem decet.   445
        nunc uxore opus est: animum ad uxorem appulit.

SIM   subtristis uisus est esse aliquantum mihi.

DAV   nil propter hanc rem, sed ĕst quod suscenset tibi.

SIM   quidnamst?

DAV   puerilest.

SIM   quid id est?

DAV   nil.

SIM   quin dic, quid est?

DAV   ait nimium parce facere sumptum.

SIM   mene?

DAV   te.   450
        "uix" inquit "drachumis est opsonatum decem.
        non filio uidetur uxorem dare.
        quem" inquit "uocabo ad cenam mēōrum aequalium
        potissumum nunc?" et, quod dicendum hic siet,
        tu quoque perparce nimium. non laudo.

SIM   tace!   455

DAV   commoui.

SIM   ego istaec recte ut fiant uidero.
        quidnam hoc est rei? quid hĭc uolt ueterator sibi?
        nam si hic malist quicquam, ĕm īllic est huic rēī caput.

[III i]   MYSIS SIMO DAVOS LESBIA (GLYCERIUM)

MYS   ita pol quidem res est ut dixti, Lesbia:
        fidelem haud ferme mulieri inuenias uirum.   460

SIM   ab Andriast ancilla haec? quid narras?

DAV   itast.

MYS   sed hĭc Pamphilus—

SIM   quid dicit?

Mys	—firmauit fidem.
Sim	hem!
Dav	utinam aut hic surdus aut haec muta facta sit!
Mys	nam quod peperisset iussit tolli.
Sim	o Iuppiter,

Sim o Iuppiter,
quid ego audio? actumst, sīquidem haec uera praedicat.   465
Les bonum ingenium narras adulescentis.
Mys   optumum.
sed sequere me intro, ne in mora illi sis.
Les   sequor.
Dav quod remedium nunc huic malo inueniam?
Sim   quid hoc?
adeon est demens? ex peregrina? iam scio. ah!
uix tandem sensi stolidus.
Dav   quid hic sensisse ait?   470
Sim haec primum affertur iam mi ab hoc fallacia:
hanc simulant parere, quo Chremetem absterreant.
Gly Iuno Lucina, fer opem, serua me, obsecro.
Sim hui! tam cito? ridiculum. postquam ante ostium
me audiuit stare, approperat. non sat commode   475
diuisa sunt temporibus tibi, Daue, haec.
Dav   mihin?
Sim num immemores discipuli?
Dav   ego quid narres nescio.
Sim hicin me si imparatum in ueris nuptiis
adortus esset, quos mihi ludos redderet!
nunc huius periclo fit, ego īn portu nauigo.   480

[III ii]

LESBIA SIMO DAVOS

a⁴ Les adhuc, Archylis, quae adsolent quaeque oportent
signa esse ad salutem, omnia huic esse uideo.
nunc primum fac ista ut lauet, poste deinde
quod iussi dari bibere et quantum imperaui
a⁴ᐱ   date; mox ego huc reuortor.   485
a⁶   per ecastor scitus puer est natus Pamphilo.
a⁸   deos quaeso ut sit superstes, quandōquidem ipsest ingenio bono,
quomque huic est ueritus optumae adulescenti facere iniuriam.
Sim uel hoc quis non credat qui te norit abs te esse ortum?
Dav   quidnam id est?
Sim non imperabat coram quid opus facto esset puerperae,   490

sed postquam egressast illis quae sunt intus clamat de uia.
o Daue, itane contemnor abs te? aut itane tandem idoneus
tibi uideor esse quem tam aperte fallere incipias dolis?
saltem accurate ut metui uidear certe si resciuerim.

DAV   certe hercle nunc hic se ipsus fallit, haud ego.

SIM   edixin tibi,   495
interminatus sum ne faceres? num ueritu's? quid re tulit?

ia⁶   credon tibi hoc nunc, peperisse hanc e Pamphilo?

DAV   teneo quid erret et quid agam habeo.

SIM   quid taces?

ia⁸   DAV   quid credas? quasi non tibi renuntiata sint haec sic fore.

SIM   min quisquam?

DAV   eho! ăn tute intellexti hoc assimulari?

SIM   irrideor.   500

DAV   renuntiatumst. nam quĭ ĭstaec tibi incidit suspicio?

SIM   qui? quia te noram.

DAV   quasi tu dicas factum id consilio meo.

SIM   certe enĭm scio.

DAV   non satis me pernosti etiam qualis sim, Simo.

SIM   egŏn te?

DAV   sed si quid tibi narrare occepi, continuo dari
tibi uerba censes.

SIM   falso?

DAV   itaque hercle nil iam muttire audeo. 505

ia⁷   SIM   hoc ego scio unum, neminem peperisse hic.

DAV   intellexti.

ia⁸   sed nilo setius referetur mox huc puer ante ostium.
id ego iam nunc tibi, ere, renuntio futurum, ut sis sciens,
ne tu hoc posterius dicas Daui factum consilio aut dolis.

tr⁷   prorsus a me opinionem hanc tŭam esse ego amotam uolo. 510

SIM   unde id scis?

DAV   audiui et credo. multa concurrunt simul
qui coniecturam hanc nunc facio. iam prius haec se e Pamphilo
grauidam dixit esse. inuentumst falsum. nunc, postquam uidet
nuptias domi apparari, missast ancilla ilico
obstetricem accersitum ad eam et puerum ut afferret simul. 515
hoc nisi fit, puerum ut tu uideas, nil mouentur nuptiae.

tr⁴^   SIM   quid ais? quom intellexeras

tr⁷   id consilium capere, quor non dixti extemplo Pamphilo?

DAV   quis igitur eum ab illa abstraxit nisi ego? nam omnes nos quidem
scimus quam misere hanc amarit. nunc sibi uxorem expetit. 520
postremo id mi da negoti. tu tamen idem has nuptias

perge facere ita ut facis, et īd spero adiuturos deos.

SIM immo abi intro. ibi me opperire et quod parato opus est para.

ₐ⁶ non impulit me haec nunc omnino ut crederem.

atque haud scio an quae dixit sint uera omnia. 525

sed parui pendo. illud mi multo maxumumst

quod mi pollicitust ipsus gnatus. nunc Chremem

conueniam, orabo gnato uxorem. si impetro,

quid alias malim quam hodie has fieri nuptias?

nam gnatus quod pollicitust, haud dubiumst mihi, id 530

si nolit, quin ēum merito possim cogere.

atque adeo in ipso tempore eccum ipsum obuiam.

[III iii]

SIMO CHREMES

ₐ⁸ SIM iubeo Chremetem—

CHR   o te ipsum quaerebam.

SIM   et ego te. optato aduenis.

CHR aliquot me adierunt, ex te auditum qui aibant hodie filiam

meăm nubere tuō gnato. id uiso tune an illi insaniant. 535

SIM ausculta pauca, et quid ego te uelim et tu quod quaeris scies.

ₐ² CHR ausculto. loquere quid uelis.

ₐ⁶ SIM per te dēos oro et nostram amicitiam, Chreme,

quae incepta a paruis cum aetate accreuit simul,

perque unicam gnatam tuam et gnatum meum, 540

quoius tibi potestas summa seruandi datur,

ut me adiuues in hac re atque ita uti nuptiae

fuerant futurae, fiant.

CHR   ah! ne me obsecra.

quasi hoc te orando a me impetrare oporteat!

alium esse censes nunc me atque olim quom dabam? 545

si in remst utrique ut fiant, accersi iube.

    sed si ex ea re plus malist quam commodi

utrique, id oro te in commune ut consulas,

quasi si illa tua sit Pamphilique ego sim pater.

SIM immo ita uolo itaque postulo ut fiat, Chreme, 550

neque postulem abs te ni ipsa res moneat.

CHR   quid est?

SIM irae sunt inter Glycerium et gnatum.

CHR   audio.

SIM ita magnae ut sperem posse auelli.

CHR   fabulae!

SIM   profecto sic est.
CHR   sic hercle ut dicam tibi,
       amantium irae amoris integratiost.   555
SIM   ĕm, ĭd te oro ut ante eamus. dum tempus datur
       dumque eius lubido occlusast contumeliis,
       prius quam harum scelera et lacrumae confictae dolis
       redducunt animum aegrotum ad misericordiam,
       uxorem demus. spero consuetudine et   560
       coniugio liberali deuinctum, Chreme,
       dein facile ex illis sese emersurum malis.
CHR   tibi ita hoc uidetur. at ego non posse arbitror
       neque illum hanc perpetuo habere neque me perpeti.
SIM   qui scis ergo istuc, nisi periclum feceris?   565
CHR   at ĭstuc periclum in filia fieri grauest.
SIM   nempe incommoditas denique huc omnis redit
       si eueniat, quod di prohibeant, discessio.
       at si corrigitur, quot commoditates uide.
       principio amico filium restitueris,   570
       tibi generum firmum et filiae inuenies uirum.
CHR   quid ĭstic? si ita istuc animum induxti esse utile,
       nolo tibi ullum commodum in me claudier.
SIM   merito te semper maxumi feci, Chreme.
ia⁷   CHR   sed quid ais?
SIM   quid?
CHR   qui scis eos nunc discordare inter se?   575
SIM   ipsus mihi Dauos, qui intumust ēorum consiliis, dixit.
       et ĭs mihi suadet nuptias quantum queam ut maturem.
       num censes faceret, filium nisi sciret eadem haec uelle?
       tute adeo iăm ĕius uerba audies. heus! euocate huc Dauom.
       atque eccum uideo ipsum foras exire.

[III iv]   DAVOS SIMO CHREMES

ia⁷   DAV   ad te ibam.
SIM   quidnamst?   580
DAV   quor uxor non accersitur? iam aduesperascit.
SIM   audin?
ia⁸   ego dudum non nil ueritus sum, Daue, abs te ne faceres idem
       quod uolgus seruorum solet, dolis ut me deluderes
       propterea quod amat filiūs.
DAV   egon istuc facerem?
SIM   credidi,

idque adeo metuens uos celaui quod nunc dicam.

DAV   quid?

SIM   scies.   585

nam propemodum habeo iam fidem.

DAV   tandem cognosti qui siem?

SIM   non fuerant nuptiae futurae.

DAV   quid? non?

SIM   sed ea gratia

simulaui uos ut pertemptarem.

DAV   quid ais?

SIM   sic res est.

DAV   uide!

numquam istuc quiui ego intellegere. uah! consilium callidum!

SIM   hoc audi: ut hinc te introire iussi, opportune hic fit mi obuiam.

DAV   hem!   590

numnam perimus?

SIM   narro huic quae tu dudum narrasti mihi.

DAV   quidnam audio?

SIM   gnatam ut det oro uixque id exoro.

DAV   occidi!

SIM   hem!

quid dixtī?

DAV   optume inquam factum.

SIM   nunc per hunc nullast mora.

CHR   domum modo ibo, ut apparetur dicam, atque huc renuntio.

SIM   nunc te oro, Daue, quoniam solus mi effecisti has nuptias—   595

DAV   ego uero solus.

SIM   —mihi corrigere gnatum porro enitere.

DAV   faciam hercle sedulo.

SIM   potes nunc, dum animus irritatus est.

DAV   quiescas.

SIM   age igitur, ubi nunc est ipsus?

DAV   mirumni domist.

SIM   ibo ad eum atque ēadem haec quae tibi dixi dicam itidem illi.

DAV   nullus sum!

quid causaest quin hinc in pistrinum recta proficiscar uia?   600

nil est preci loci relictum. iam perturbaui omnia:

erum fefelli, in nuptias conieci erilem filium,

feci hodie ut fierent insperante hoc atque inuito Pamphilo.

ēm ăstutias! quod si quiessem, nil euenisset mali.

sed ēccum ipsum uideo. occidi!   605

utinam mi esset aliquid hic quo nunc me praecipitem darem!

[III v]   PAMPHILVS DAVOS

tr⁸   PAM   ubi ílle est scelŭs qui perdidit me?
       DAV   perii!
       PAM   atque hoc confiteor iure
             mi obtigisse, quandoquidem tăm iners tam nulli consili sum.
tr⁷   seruon fortunas meas me commisisse futtili!
ia⁸   ego pretium ob stultitiam fero. sed inultum numquam id auferet.   610
       DAV   posthac incolumem sat scio fore me, nunc si deuito hoc malum.
       PAM   nam quid ego nunc dicam patri? negabon uelle me, modo
             qui sum pollicitus ducerē? quă ăudacia id facere audeam?
             nec quid nunc me faciam scio.
       DAV   nec mequidem, atque id ago sedulo.
             dicam aliquid me inuenturum, ut huic malo aliquam producam moram.   615
       PAM   oh!
       DAV   uisus sum.
       PAM   ehodum, bone uir, quid ais? uidĕn me consiliis tuis
             miserum impeditum esse?
       DAV   at iam expediam.
       PAM   expedies?
       DAV   certe, Pamphile.
       PAM   nempe ut modo.
       DAV   immo melius spero.
       PAM   oh! tibi ego ut credam, furcifer?
             tu rem impeditam et perditam restituas? em quo fretus sim,
             qui me hodie ex tranquillissuma re coniecisti in nuptias!   620
tr⁷   an non dixi esse hoc futurum?
       DAV   dixti.
       PAM   quid meritu's?
       DAV   crucem.
             sed sine paullulum ad me redeam. iam aliquid dispiciam.
       PAM   ei mihi,
             quom non habeo spatium ut de te sumam supplicium ut uolo!
             namque hoc tempus praecauere mihi me, haud tĕ ŭlcisci sinit.

[IV i]   CHARINVS PAMPHILVS DAVOS

da⁴   CHA   hoccinĕst credibile aut memorabile,   625
cr⁴   tanta uecordia innata quoiquam ut siet
             ut malis gaudeant atque ex incommodis
             alterius sua ut comparent commoda? ah!
             idnest uerum? immo id est genus hominum pessumum, in

denegando modo quis pudor paullum adest.   630
post ubi tempus promissa iam perfici,
tum coacti necessario se aperiunt,
et timent et tamen res premit denegare.
ibi tum eorum impudentissuma oratiost:
"quis tŭ es? quis mihi's? quor meam tibi? heus!   635
       proxumus sum egomet mihi."
at tamen "ubi fides?" si roges,
nil pudet hic, ubi opus; illi ubi
       nil opust, ibi uerentur.   638a
sed quid agam? adeamne ad eum et cūm eo iniuriam hanc expostulem?
ingeram mala multa? atque aliquis dicat "nil promoueris."   640
multum. molestus certe eī fuero atque animo morem gessero.

PAM   Charine, et mĕ ĕt tĕ īmprudens, nisi quid di respiciunt, perdidi.
CHA   itane "imprudens"? tandem inuentast causa: soluisti fidem.
PAM   quid "tandem"?
CHA   etiamnunc me ducere istis dictis postulas?
PAM   quid īstuc est?
CHA   postquam me amare dixi, complacitast tibi.   645
heu me miserum, qui tuom animum ex animo spectaui meo!
PAM   falsus es.
CHA   non tibi sat esse hoc solidum uisumst gaudium,
nisi me lactasses amantem et falsa spe produceres?
habeas.
PAM   habeam? ah! nescis quantis in malis uorser miser,
quantasque hic suīs consiliis mihi conflauit sollicitudines   650
meus carnufex.
CHA   quid īstuc tam mirumst de te si exemplum capit?
PAM   haud istuc dicas, si cognoris uel me uel amorem meum.
CHA   sciŏ. cum patre altercasti dudum et is nunc propterea tibi
suscenset nec te quiuit hodie cogere illam ut duceres.
PAM   immo etiam, quo tu minus scis aerumnas meas,   655
hae nuptiae non apparabantur mihi
nec postulabat nunc quisquam uxorem dare.
CHA   sciŏ. tu coactus tuă uoluntate es.
PAM   mane.
nondum scis.
CHA   scio equidem illam ducturum esse te.
PAM   quor me enicas? hoc audi. numquam destitit   660
instare ut dicerem me ducturum patri,
suadere, orare usque adeo donec perpulit.

ia⁸	CHA	quis homo istuc?	

ia⁸ CHA quis homo istuc?
PAM Dauos.
CHA Dauos?
PAM interturbat.
CHA quăm ŏb rem?
PAM nescio,
nisi mihi dēōs satis scio fuisse iratos qui auscultauerim.
ia⁶ CHA factum hoc est, Daue?
DAV factŭm.
CHA em! quid ais, scelus? 665
at tibi di dignum factis exitium duint!
eho, dic mi, si omnes hunc coniectum in nuptias
inimici uellent, quod nisi hŏc consilium darent?
DAV deceptus sum, at non defetigatus.
CHA scio.
DAV hac non successit, alia aggrediemur uia; 670
nisi si id putas, quia primo processit parum,
non posse iam ad salutem conuorti hoc malum.
PAM immo etiam. nam satis credo, si aduigilaueris,
ex unis geminas mihi conficies nuptias.
DAV ego, Pamphile, hoc tibi pro seruitio debeo, 675
conari manibus pedibus noctesque et dies,
capitis periclum adire, dum prosim tibi.
tŭōmst, si quid praeter spem euenit, mi ignoscere.
parum succedit quod ago; at facio sedulo.
uel melius tute reperi, me missum face. 680
PAM cupio. restitue in quem me accepisti locum.
ia⁸ DAV faciam.
PAM at iăm hŏc opŭst.
DAV em. sed manĕ. concrepuit a Glycerio ostium.
PAM nil ad te.
DAV quaero—
PAM hem! nuncin demum?
DAV at iăm hŏc tibi inuentum dabo.

[IV ii]   MYSIS PAMPHILVS CHARINVS DAVOS

ia⁷ MYS iam ubiubi erit inuentum tibi curabo et mecum adductum
tŭōm Pamphilum. modo tu, anime mi, noli te macerare. 685
PAM Mysis!
MYS quis est? ehĕm, Pamphile! optume mihi te offers.

PAM   quid id est?

MYS orare iussit, si se ames, era iăm ut ăd sese uenias.
uidere ait te cupere.

PAM   uah! perii! hoc malum integrascit.
sicin mĕ ătque illam opera tua nunc miseros sollicitari!
nam idcirco accersor nuptias quod mi apparari sensit.   690

CHA quibus quidĕm quam facile potuerat quiesci, si hic quiesset!

DAV age, si hic non insanit satis suă sponte, instiga.

MYS   atque edepol
ea res est, proptereaque nunc misera in maerorest.

PAM   Mysis,
per ŏmnis tibi adiuro deos numquam ēam me deserturum,
non si capiundos mihi sciam esse inimicos omnis homines.   695
hanc mi expetiui, contigit, conueniunt mores. ualeant
qui inter nos discidium uolunt. hanc nisi mors mi adimet nemo.

MYS resipisco.

PAM   non Apollinis magis uerum atque hoc responsumst.
si poterit fieri ut ne pater per me stetisse credat
quo minus hae fierent nuptiae, uolo. sed si id non poterit,   700
id faciam, in procliui quod est, per me stetisse ut credat.
quis uideor?

CHA   miser, aeque atque ego.

DAV   consilium quaero.

PAM   forti's.
sciŏ quid conere.

DAV   hoc ego tibi profecto effectum reddam.

PAM iăm hŏc opus est.

DAV   quin iam habeo.

CHA   quid est?

DAV   huic, non tibĭ habeo, ne erres.

CHA sat habeo.

PAM   quid facies? cedo.

DAV   dies hic mi ut satis sit uereor   705
ad agendum, ne uacuom esse me nunc ad narrandum credas.
proinde hinc uos amolimini; nam mi impedimento estis.

PAM ego hănc uisam.

DAV   quid tu? quŏ hĭnc te agis?

CHA   uerum uis dicam?

DAV   immo etiam.
narrationis incipit mi initium.

CHA   quid me fiet?

DAV	eho tu, impudens, non satis habes quod tibi dieculam addo,	710
	quantum huic promoueo nuptias?	
CHA	Daue, at tamen—	
DAV	quid ergo?	

DAV eho tu, impudens, non satis habes quod tibi dieculam addo, 710
    quantum huic promoueo nuptias?
CHA   Daue, at tamen—
DAV   quid ergo?
CHA ut ducam.
DAV   ridiculum!
CHA   huc face ad me ut uenias, si quid poteris.
DAV quid ueniam? nil habeo.
CHA   at tamen si quid.
DAV   age, ueniam.
CHA   si quid,
    domi ero.
DAV   tu, Mysis, dum exeo, parumper me opperire hic.
MYS quapropter?
DAV   ita factost opus.
MYS   matura.
DAV   iăm, ĭnquam, hic adero. 715

[IV iii]

MYSIS DAVOS

ia⁶ MYS nilne esse proprium quoiquam! di uostram fidem!
    summum bonum esse erae putabam hunc Pamphilum,
    amicum, amatorem, uirum in quouis loco
    paratum. uerum ex ēo nunc misera quem capit
    laborem! facile hic plus malĭst quam illic boni. 720
    sed Dauos exit. mĭ homo, quid ĭstuc, obsecro, est?
    quo portas puerum?
DAV   Mysis, nunc opus est tua
    mihi ad hanc rem exprompta memoria atque astutia.
MYS quidnam incepturu's?
DAV   accipe a me hunc ocius
    atque ante nostram ianuam appone.
MYS   obsecro, 725
    humine?
DAV   ex ara hinc sume uerbenas tibi
    atque ēas substerne.
MYS   quăm ŏb rem id tute non facis?
DAV quia, si forte opus sit ad erum iurato mihi
    non apposisse, ut liquido possim.
MYS   intellego.
    noua nunc religio in te istaec incessit. cedo. 730
DAV moue ocius te, ut quid agam porro intellegas.

pro Iuppiter!

MYS   quid ĕst?

DAV   sponsae pater interuenit.
repudio quod consilium primum intenderam.

MYS nesciŏ quid narres.

DAV   ego quoque hinc ab dextera
uenire me assimulabo. tŭ ŭt subseruias   735
orationi, ut quomque opus sit, uerbis uide.

MYS ego quid agas nil intellego. sed si quid est
quod mea opera opus sit uobis, ut tu plus uides,
manebo, ne quod uostrum remorer commodum.

[IV iv]   CHREMES MYSIS DAVOS

a⁶   CHR reuortor, postquam quae opus fuere ad nuptias   740
gnatae paraui, ut iubeam accersi. sed quid hoc?
puer herclest. mulier, tun posisti hunc?

MYS   ubi ĭllic est?

CHR non mihi respondes?

MYS   nusquamst. uae miserae mihi!
reliquit mĕ homo atque abiit.

DAV   di uostram fidem!
quid turbaest apŭd forum! quid ĭlli hominum litigant!   745
tum annona carast. quid dicam aliud nescio.

MYS quor tu, obsecro, hic me solam—?

DAV   hem! quaĕ haĕc est fabula?
eho, Mysis, puer hic undest? quisue huc attulit?

MYS satĭn sanu's qui me id rogites?

DAV   quĕm ego igitur rogem
qui hic neminem alium uideam?

CHR   miror unde sit.   750

DAV dictura's quod rogo?

MYS   au!

DAV   concede ad dexteram.

MYS deliras. non tute ipse—?

DAV   uerbum si mihi
unum praeterquam quod te rogŏ faxis, caue!
male dicis? undest? dic clare.

MYS   a nobis.

DAV   hahae!
mirum uero impudenter mulier si facit   755
meretrix.

CHR	ab Andriast haec, quantum intellego.
DAV	adeon uidemur uobis esse idonei
	in quibus sic illudatis?
CHR	ueni in tempore.
DAV	propera adeo puerum tollere hinc ab ianua.
	mane. cauĕ quoquam ex istoc excessis loco. 760
MYS	di te eradicent! ita me miseram territas.
DAV	tibi ego dico an non?
MYS	quid uis?
DAV	at etiam rogas?
	cedo, quoium puerum hic apposisti? dic mihi.
MYS	tu nescis?
DAV	mitte id quod scio. dic quod rogo.
MYS	uostri.
DAV	quoius nostri?
MYS	Pamphili.
DAV	hem! quid? Pamphili? 765
MYS	eho, ăn non est?
CHR	recte ego hăs semper fugi nuptias.
DAV	o facinus animaduortendum!
MYS	quid clamitas?
DAV	quemne ego heri uidi ad uos afferri uesperi?
MYS	ŏ hominem audacem!
DAV	uerum. uidi Cantharam
	suffarcinatam.
MYS	dis pol habeo gratiam 770
	quom in pariundo aliquot adfuerunt liberae.
DAV	nĕ ĭlla illum haud nouit quoius causa haec incipit:
	"Chremes si positum puerum ante aedis uiderit,
	sūam gnatam non dabit." tanto hercle magis dabit.
CHR	non hercle faciet.
DAV	nunc adeo, ut tu sis sciens, 775
	nisi puerum tollis, iăm ego hunc in mediam uiam
	prouoluam teque ibidem peruoluam in luto.
MYS	tu pol homo non es sobrius.
DAV	fallacia
	alia aliam trudit. iam susurrari audio
	ciuem Atticam esse hanc.
CHR	hem!
DAV	coactus legibus 780
	eam ŭxorem ducet.
MYS	aŭ ŏbsecro, an non ciuis est?

CHR	iocularium in malum insciens paene incidi.
DAV	quis hīc loquitur? o Chreme, per tempus aduenis.
	ausculta.
CHR	audiui iam omnia.
DAV	anne haec tu omnia?
CHR	audiui, inquam, a principio.
DAV	audistin, obsecro? em
	scelera! hanc iam oportet in cruciatum hinc abripi.
	hic ĕst ille. non te credas Dauom ludere.
MYS	me miseram! nil pol falsi dixi, mi senex.
CHR	noui omnem rem. est Simo intus?
DAV	est.
MYS	ne me attigas,
	sceleste. si pol Glycerio non omnia haec—
DAV	eho, inepta, nescis quid sit actum?
MYS	qui sciam?
DAV	hic socer est. alio pacto haud poterat fieri
	ut sciret haec quae uoluimus.
MYS	praediceres.
DAV	paullum interesse censes, ex animo omnia,
	ut fert natura, facias an de industria?

785

790

795

IV v]

CRITO MYSIS DAVOS

a⁶

CRI	in hac habitasse platea dictumst Chrysidem,
	quae sese inhoneste optauit parere hic ditias
	potius quam in patria honeste pauper uiueret.
	eīus morte ea ad me lege redierunt bona.
	sed quos perconter uideo. saluete.
MYS	obsecro,
	quem uideo? estne hic Crito, sobrinus Chrysidis?
	is est.
CRI	o Mysis, salue.
MYS	saluos sis, Crito.
CRI	itan Chrysis—? hem!
MYS	nos quidĕm pol miseras perdidit.
CRI	quid uos? quo pacto hic? satine recte?
MYS	nosne? sic
	ut quimus, aiunt, quando ut uolumus non licet.
CRI	quid Glycerium? iăm hīc suōs parentis repperit?
MYS	utinam!
CRI	an nondum etiam? haud auspicato huc me appuli.

800

805

nam pol si id scissem numquam huc tetulissem pedem.
semper eius dictast esse haec atque habitast soror.
quae illīūs fuere possidet. nunc me hospitem   810
litis sequi quăm hīc mihi sit facile atque utile
aliorum exempla commonent. simul arbitror
iam aliquem esse amicum et defensorem ēī. nam fere
grandicula iam profectast illinc. clamitent
me sycophantam, hereditatem persequi   815
mendicum. tum ipsam despoliare non lubet.

DAV ŏ optume hospes!
MYS   pol, Crito, antiquom obtines.
CRI duc me ad eam quando huc ueni ut uideam.
MYS   maxume.
DAV sequăr hos. nolo me in tempore hoc uideat senex.

[V i]   CHREMES SIMO

tr⁷ CHR satis iam satis, Simo, spectata erga te amicitiast mea.   820
          satis pericli incepi adire. orandi iam finem face.
          dum studeo obsequi tibi, paene illusi uitam filiae.
     SIM immo enīm nunc quom maxume abs te postulo atque oro, Chreme,
          ut beneficium uerbis initum dudum nunc re comprobes.
     CHR uidĕ quam iniquos sis prae studio. dūm id efficias quod cupis,   825
          neque modum benignitatis neque quid me ores cogitas.
          nam si cogites remittas iam me onerare iniuriis.
     SIM quibus?
     CHR   at rogitas? perpulisti me ut homini adulescentulo
          in alio occupato amore, abhorrenti ab re uxoria,
          filiam ut darem in seditionem atque in īncertas nuptias,   830
          eius labore atque eius dolore gnato ut medicarer tuo.
          impetrasti. incepi, dum res tetulit. nunc non fert: feras.
          illam hinc ciuem esse aiunt, puer est natus: nos missos face.
     SIM per ego te dēŏs oro, ut nĕ īllis animum inducas credere,
          quibus id maxume utilest illum esse quam deterrumum.   835
          nuptiarum gratia haec sunt ficta atque incepta omnia.
          ubi ea causa quam ob rem haec faciunt erit adempta his, desinent.
     CHR erras. cum Dauo egomet uidi iurgantem ancillam.
     SIM   scio.
     CHR   at
          uero uoltu, quom ibi me adesse neuter tum praesenserat.
     SIM credo, et id facturas Dauos dudum praedixit mihi. et   840
          nescio quī īd tibi sum oblitus hodie ac uolui dicere.

DAVOS CHREMES SIMO DROMO

r7   DAV   animo nunciam otioso esse impero—
     CHR   em Dauom tibi!
     SIM   unde egreditur?
     DAV   —meŏ praesidio atque hospitis.
     SIM   quid ĭllud malist?
     DAV   ego commodiorem hominem aduentum tempus non uidi.
     SIM   scelus,
           quemnam hic laudat?
     DAV   omnis res iam est in uado.
     SIM   cesso alloqui?   845
     DAV   erus est. quid agam?
     SIM   o salue, bone uir.
     DAV   ehĕm, Simo! o noster Chremes!
           omnia apparata iam sunt intus.
     SIM   curasti probe.
     DAV   ubi uoles accerse.
     SIM   bene sane. id enĭmuero hinc nunc abest.
           etiam tu hoc respondes: quid ĭstic tibi negotist?
     DAV   mihin?
     SIM   ita.
     DAV   mihin?
     SIM   tibi ergo.
     DAV   modŏ introii—
     SIM   quasi ego quam dudum rogem.   850
     DAV   —cum tŭō gnato una.
     SIM   anne est intus Pamphilus? crucior miser.
           eho, non tu dixti esse inter eos inimicitias, carnufex?
     DAV   sunt.
     SIM   quor igitur hic est?
     CHR   quid ĭllum censes? cŭm ĭlla litigat.
     DAV   ĭmmŏ uero indignum, Chreme, iam facinus faxo ex me audies.
           nescioquis senex modo uenit—ellum—confidens catus.   855
           quom faciem uideas uidetur esse quantiuis preti.
           tristis seueritas inest in uoltu atque in uerbis fides.
     SIM   quidnam apportas?
     DAV   nil equidem nisi quod ĭllum audiui dicere.
     SIM   quid ait tandem?
     DAV   Glycerium se scire ciuem esse Atticam.
     SIM   hem!
           Dromŏ, Dromo!

	DAV	quid est?	
	SIM	Dromo!	
	DAV	audi.	
	SIM	uerbum si addideris—Dromo!	860
ia⁸	DAV	audi, obsecro.	
	DRO	quid uis?	
	SIM	sublimem intro rape hunc quantum potest.	
	DRO	quem?	
	SIM	Dauum.	
	DAV	quãm õb rem?	
	SIM	quia lubet. rape, inquam.	
	DAV	quid feci?	
	SIM	rape.	
	DAV	si quicquam inuenies me mentitum occidito.	
	SIM	nil audio.	
tr⁷		ego iam te commotum reddam.	
	DAV	tamen etsi hoc uerumst?	
	SIM	tamen.	
ia⁸		cura asseruandum uinctum atque (audin?) quadrupedem constringito.	865
ia⁶		age nunciam. ego pol hodie, si uiuo, tibi	
		ostendam erum quid sit pericli fallere,	
		et īlli patrem.	
	CHR	ah! ne saeui tanto opere.	
	SIM	o Chreme,	
		pietatem gnati! nonne te miseret mei?	
		tantum laborem capere ob talem filium!	870
		age, Pamphile. exi, Pamphile. ecquid te pudet?	

[V iii]   PAMPHILVS SIMO CHREMES

	PAM	quis me uolt? perii! pater est.	
ia⁶	SIM	quid ais, omnium—?	
	CHR	ah!	
		rem potius ipsam dic ac mitte male loqui.	
	SIM	quasi quicquam in hunc iam grauius dici possiet.	
		ain tandem, ciuis Glyceriumst?	
	PAM	ita praedicant.	875
	SIM	"ita praedicant"? õ īngentem confidentiam!	
		num cogitat quid dicat? num facti piget?	
		uidĕ num eius color pudoris signum usquam indicat.	
		adeo impotenti esse animo ut praeter ciuium	
		morem atque legem et suī uoluntatem patris	880

	tamen hanc habere studeat cum summo probro!
PAM	me miserum!
SIM	hem! modŏne id demum sensti, Pamphile?
	olim istuc, olim quom ita animum induxti tuom
	quod cuperes aliquo pacto efficiundum tibi,
	ēōdem die istuc uerbum uere in te accidit.
	sed quid ego? quor me excrucio? quor me macero?
	quor meăm senĕctutem huius sollicito amentia?
	an ŭt pro huius peccatis ego supplicium sufferam?
	immo habeat, ualeat, uiuat cŭm ĭlla.
PAM	mi pater!
SIM	quid "mi pater"? quasi tŭ hŭius indigeas patris.
	domus, uxor, liberi inuenti inuito patre.
	adducti qui illam hinc ciuem dicant. uiceris.
PAM	pater, licetne pauca?
SIM	quid dices mihi?
CHR	at
	tamen, Simo, audi.
SIM	ego audiam? quid audiam,
	Chremē?
CHR	at tandem dicat.
SIM	age, dicat. sino.
PAM	ego me amare hanc fateor. si id peccarest, fateor id quoque.
	tibi, pater, me dedo. quiduis oneris impone. impera.
	uis me uxorem ducere? hanc uis mittere? ut potero feram.
	hoc modo te obsecro ut ne credas a me allegatum hunc senem.
	sine me expurgem atque illum huc coram adducam.
SIM	adducas?
PAM	sine, pater.
CHR	aequom postulat. da ueniam.
PAM	sine te hoc exorem.
SIM	sino.
	quiduis cupio dum ne ab hoc me falli comperiar, Chreme.
CHR	pro peccato magno paullum supplici satis est patri.

Line numbers: 885, 890, 895, 900

CRITO CHREMES SIMO PAMPHILVS

CRI	mitte orare. una harum quaeuis causa me ut faciam monet,
	uel tu uel quod uerumst uel quod ipsi cupio Glycerio.
CHR	Andrium ego Critonem uideo? certe is ĕst.
CRI	saluos sis, Chreme.
CHR	quid tu Athenas insolens?

Line number: 905

[V iv]

CRI   euenit. sed hicinest Simo?

CHR   hic.

CRI   Simo, men quaeris?

SIM   eho tu, Glycerium hinc ciuem esse ais?

CRI   tu negas?

SIM   itane huc paratus aduenis?

CRI   qua re?

SIM   rogas?

tune impune haec facias? tune hic homines adulescentulos   910
imperitos rerum, eductos libere, in fraudem illicis?
sollicitando et pollicitando eōrum animos lactas?

CRI   sanun es?

SIM   ac meretricios amores nuptiis conglutinas?

PAM   perii! metuo ut substet hospes.

CHR   si, Simo, hunc noris satis,
non ita arbitrere. bonus est hic uir.

SIM   hic uir sit bonus?   915
itane attemperate euenit, hodie in ipsis nuptiis
ut ueniret, antehac numquam? est uero huic credundum, Chreme.

PAM   ni metuam patrem, habeo prŏ īlla rĕ īllum quod moneam probe.

SIM   sycophanta!

CRI   hem!

CHR   sic, Crito, est hic. mitte.

CRI   uideat qui siet.
si mihi perget quae uolt dicere, ea quae non uolt audiet.   920
ego īstaec moueo aut curo? non tu tūŏm malum aequo animo feras?
nam ego quae dico uera an falsa audierim iam sciri potest.
Atticus quidam olim naui fracta ad Andrum eiectus est
et īstaec una parua uirgo. tŭm īlle egens forte applicat
primum ad Chrysidis patrem se.

SIM   fabulam inceptat.

CHR   sine.   925

CRI   itane uero obturbat?

CHR   perge.

CRI   tum is mihi cognatus fuit
qui ēum recepit. ibi ego audiui ex illo sese esse Atticum.
is ibi mortuost.

CHR   eius nomen?

CRI   nomen tam cito? Phania? hem!
perii! uerum hercle opinor fuisse Phaniam. hoc certo scio,
Rhamnusium se aiebat esse.

CHR   o Iuppiter!

ia⁸

CRI	eadem haec, Chreme, 930
	multi alii in Andro audiuere.
CHR	utinam id sit quod spero! eho, dic mihi,
	quid eam tum? suămne esse aibat?
CRI	non.
CHR	quoiam igitur?
CRI	fratris filiam.
CHR	certe meast.
CRI	quid ais?
SIM	quid tŭ ais?
PAM	arrige auris, Pamphile.
SIM	qui credis?
CHR	Phania illic frater meus fuit.
SIM	noram et scio.
CHR	is bellum hinc fugiens meque in Asiam persequens proficiscitur. 935
	tum illam relinquere hic est ueritus. postilla hoc primum audio
	quid īllo sit factum.
PAM	uix sum apud me. ita animus commotust metu,
	spe, gaudio, mirando tanto hoc tam repentino bono.
SIM	nĕ īstam multimodis tūam inueniri gaudeo.
PAM	credo, pater.
CHR	at mi unus scrupulus etiam restat qui me male habet.
PAM	dignus es 940
	cum tūa religione, odium. nodum in scirpo quaeris.
CRI	quid istud est?
CHR	nomen non conuenit.
CRI	fuit hercle huic aliud paruae.
CHR	quod, Crito?
	numquid meministi?
CRI	id quaero.
PAM	egon huius memoriam patiar meae
	uolŭptati obstare, quŏm ego possim in hac re medicari mihi?
	non patiar. heus, Chreme, quod quaeris Pasibulast.
CHR	ipsast.
CRI	east. 945
PAM	ex ipsa miliens audiui.
SIM	omnis nos gaudere hoc, Chreme,
	te credo credere.
CHR	ita me dī ament, credo.
PAM	quod restat, pater,—
SIM	iamdudum res redduxit me ipsa in gratiam.
PAM	o lepidum patrem!

de uxore, ita ut possedi, nil mutat Chremes?
CHR   causa optumast,
nisi quid pater ait aliud.
PAM   nempe id.
SIM   scilicet.
CHR   dos, Pamphile, est   950
decem talenta.
PAM   accipio.
CHR   propero ad filiam. eho, mecum, Crito!
nam illam me credo haud nosse.
SIM   quor non illam huc transferri iubes?
PAM   recte admones. Dauo ego īstuc dedam iam negoti.
SIM   non potest.
PAM   qui?
SIM   quia habet aliud magis ex sese et maius.
PAM   quidnam?
SIM   uinctus est.
PAM   pater, non recte uinctust.
SIM   haud ita iussi.
PAM   iubĕ solui, obsecro.   955
SIM   age, fiat.
PAM   at matura.
SIM   eo intro.
PAM   o faustum et felicem diem!

[V v]   CHARINVS PAMPHILVS

ia⁸   CHA   prouiso quid agat Pamphilūs. atque eccum.
PAM   aliquis me forsitan
putet non putare hoc uerum. at mihi nunc sic esse hoc uerum lubet.
tr⁷   ego dēorum uitam propterea sempiternam esse arbitror
quod uolŭptates ēorum propriae sunt. nam mi immortalitas   960
partast, si nulla aegritudo huic gaudio intercesserit.
sed quĕm ego mihi potissumum exoptem quoī nunc haec narrem dari?
CHA   quid īllud gaudist?
PAM   Dauom uideo. nemost quem mallem omnium.
nam hunc scio mea solide solum gauisurum gaudia.

[V vi]   CHARINVS PAMPHILVS DAVOS

tr⁷   DAV   Pamphilus ubinam hic est?
PAM   Daue!

Dav	quis homost?
Pam	ego sum.
Dav	o Pamphile! 965
Pam	nescis quid mi obtigerit.
Dav	certe. sed quid mi ŏbtigerit scio.
Pam	et quidem ego.
Dav	more hominum euenit ut quod sim nanctus mali
	prius rescisceres tu quam ego illud quod tibi euenit boni.
Pam	Glycerium mea suŏs parentis repperit.
Dav	factum bene!
Cha	hem!
Pam	pater amicus summus nobis.
Dav	quis?
Pam	Chremes.
Dav	narras probe. 970
Pam	nec mora ullast quin eam uxorem ducam.
Cha	num ille somniat
	ea quae uigilans uoluit?
Pam	tum de puero, Daue—
Dav	ah! desine.
	solus est quem diligant di.
Cha	saluos sum si haec uera sunt.
	colloquar.
Pam	quis homost? Charine, in tempore ipso mi aduenis.
Cha	bene factum!
Pam	audisti?
Cha	omnia. age, me in tūīs secundis respice. 975
	tuos est nunc Chremes. facturum quae uoles scio ĕsse omnia.
Pam	memini. atque adeo longumst illum me exspectare dum exeat.
	sequere hac me. intus apŭd Glycerium nunc est. tu, Daue, abī domum,
	propera, accerse hinc qui auferant eam. quid stas? quid cessas?
Dav	eo.
	ne exspectetis dum exeant huc. intus despondebitur. 980
	intus transigetur si quid est quod restet.
Ω	plaudite!

ANDRIA: COMMENTARY

THE DIDASCALIA

The ancient MSS of T. prefaced each play with a brief, formulaic set of production notes we call *didascaliae*. The name recalls Aristotle's Διδασκαλίαι,
from διδάσκαλοι ("directors"), a work of theater-history based on the
archons' official archive at Athens. The Roman didascaliae, however, are
neither official nor authoritative. Rome of the mid-Republic lacked a state
archive, and what records magistrates kept would have remained their
personal property after holding office. (The *commentarii aedilium* sometimes evoked in this context are a scholarly fiction.) The information in
the Terentian didascaliae, which includes a recognizable factual record
along with stray bits of information that are as tantalizingly suggestive as
they are maddeningly corrupt, probably derives, ultimately, from the acting company's own annotated scripts, which came to be amalgamated,
regularized (and possibly supplemented) by subsequent antiquarian
research of the kind first associated with Varro and his teacher, Aelius
Stilo, in the first century BCE.

(For the didascaliae, see Klose 1966, Deufert 2002: 94–6, Goldberg
2005: 69–75, and for the work of the early Roman philologists who helped
create them, Zetzel 2018: 27–34).

The didascalia for *An.* is missing from the MSS, but Don.'s introductory
essay preserves information that must ultimately derive from that source.
Though the text is corrupt, its difficulties probably reflecting Don.'s own
occasional confusion over a garbled source before being further cor-
rupted in the course of his own transmission, it preserves both sound
information about the play's original production and intriguing hints of
revival performances. The version offered here is that of Cioffi 2017: 2.
The most problematic bits, the results of either early interpolation or later
corruption, are enclosed in square brackets.

prima facta est: the didascaliae regularly report the order of composition
of the play in question, though not always accurately. The claim that *An.*
was T.'s first play is congruent with the testimony of the ancient *vita* (3)
and with its position as first in all the MSS.

ludis Megalensibus: the Megalenses, held on the Palatine hill, honored
Cybele, the Asian Magna Mater, whose arrival at Rome in 204 marked
a turning point in the Second Punic War (Gruen 1990: 5–33). Pl.'s
Pseudolus was staged at the dedication of her temple in 191. The official
dates of the festival were 4–10 April, but since the Roman calendar in the

160s ran some two months ahead of the sun, the Megalenses in T.'s day actually took place in late January. The Palatine provided a comparatively intimate venue for staging plays, so it may be significant that four of T.'s six comedies were produced at this festival. See Introduction 2.

M. Fuluio M.' Glabrione aedil. curul.: the aediles were the junior magistrates who supervised the Megalensia. The aedileship conferred membership in the Senate but was not required for holding higher office. The responsibility for staging games, however, gave ambitious politicians an immediate opportunity to gain public recognition by the lavishness of their display, and it may be significant that these aediles, Marcus Fulvius Nobilior (the son of Ennius' patron) and Manius Acilius Glabrio, who held office in 166, both went on to win the consulship, Glabrio in 159 and Nobilior in 154. For the utility of games in launching political careers, see Shatzman 1975: 159–64, Gruen 1992: 188–97.

Q. Minucio Thermo L. Valerio: these are thought to be the names of two additional aediles, though who exactly they are and when they held office is uncertain. A Lucius Valerius Flaccus, perhaps son of the aedile in 163 (and consul of 152) who sponsored the production of T.'s *Hau.*, was consul in 131. No Quintus Minucius Thermus is attested for his period. If Flaccus is correctly identified and Thermus served with him as aedile, the year could not have been earlier than 136 (Linderski 1987). The implication of a revival performance of *An.* in the later second century is congruent with testimony in the didascalia to *Ph.*, which hints at a revival of that play possibly as late as 106 (Tansey 2001).

egerunt: the technical term for producing a play (*OLD* 25).

L. Atilius Praenestinus et L. Ambiuius Turpio: L. Ambivius Turpio is firmly fixed in the tradition as T.'s producer (Brown 2002: 229–35). Lucius Atilius of Praeneste is also mentioned in the didascaliae of *Hau.*, *Eun.*, *Ph.*, and *Ad.* Whether he was Turpio's business partner, an actor in Turpio's troupe, or the later producer of revival performances is unknown.

Flaccus Claudi: Flaccus, the slave of Claudius, composed the music (*modos fecit*) for all of T.'s plays. (*filius* was probably added to Don.'s text by someone who did not recognize the idiom identifying a slave by his owner's name in the genitive.) The mention of Flaccus in all the didascaliae acknowledges his importance to the production and recalls more generally the prominent role of tibicines in the social, civic, and religious life of Rome. In addition to the dramatic festivals, they performed at banquets, processions, and rituals of many kinds; their temporary withdrawal to Tibur over a perceived slight to their collegium, an event Livy dates to

311 BCE, became the stuff of legend (Liv.9.30–5–10, Val. Max. 2.5.4, Ov. *Fast.* 6.651–92).

tibiis paribus "on pipes of equal length." The tibia (Gk. *aulos*) consisted of two double-reed pipes played simultaneously, though they could vary in length, i.e. *pares* or *impares*. The sound was probably closer to the modern oboe than the medieval shawm. Right- and left-handed tibiae were of different pitches, perhaps better suited either to lighter or to more serious plays or to recitative or song, but the testimony is confused and contradictory. The lack of clarity in Don.'s phrase *dextris uel sinistris* leads it to be bracketed. For the tibia, see Moore 2012: 35–63, and for the role of music in performance, Marshall 2006: 234–44.

tota "throughout" (*OLD* 3a), i.e. with no change, an odd thing to say since T. is explicit about having made changes to his model. Corruption is likely. The didascaliae to *Ph.*, *Hec.*, and *Ad.* use *tota* to describe the accompaniment, e.g. *Ph.*'s *tibiis inparibus tota* ("with unequal pipes throughout"), while all surviving didascaliae specify the Greek source, either *Graeca Menandru* or, in the case of *Ph.*, *Graeca Apollodoru*. Don.'s original text probably said something similar.

edita "performed" (*OLD* s.v. *edo*² 12).

M. Marcello C. Sulpicio consulibus: Marcus Claudius Marcellus and Gaius Sulpicius Galus were consuls in 166, thus confirming the date of this first production.

PERSONAE

The Bodmer codex of Menander (iii/iv CE) introduces each play in the collection with a list in order of appearance of the characters and their roles, τὰ τοῦ δράματ(ος) πρόσωπα. The MSS of T. have no such feature, though the illustrated MSS preface all plays but *Eun.* with a somewhat fanciful display of masks. The lists of characters customarily found in modern editions are instead derived from the scene headings in the Codex Bembinus, which identifies the figures in each scene by name and character type, the list for *An.* (the one play largely missing from the Bembinus) then reconstructed on that model. The characters' names are unexceptional. Fourth-century Greek comedy, rooted as it was in the daily life of its time, drew its names from the world it knew. Thus, "Pamphilus" (lit. "Loved by all"), so appropriate as a name for a comic lover and the title of a play by Eubulus, recurs in fragments of Philemon, Menander, and Apollodorus and is also an extremely common citizen name at Athens

(*PA* 11524–60). So too with most other names. New Comedy's tendency to favor the familiar in this way was later obscured by Pl., whose adaptations for the Roman stage took special delight in significant names like Pseudolus and Sceledrus, absurd names like Therapontigonus Platagidorus, or simply names with a sound distinctly foreign to Roman ears like Mnesilochus and Acroteleutium. T. gives us the parasite Gnatho ("Jaw"), but largely reverts to the Greek practice: even his one soldier, Thraso ("Audacious") in *Eun.*, sports a name well attested in Attica (*PA* 7375–95).

Naming conventions for both Greek and Roman traditions distinguished slave names from citizen names, *meretrices* from *matronae*, secondary cooks and pimps and parasites from major players. Names thus worked in conjunction with masks and costumes to make characters readily identifiable by their dramatic roles, at least in a general way (Brown 1987). For the different treatment of names by Pl. and T., see Duckworth 1952: 346–50.

Simo (Σίμων, *PA* 12684–12709): a *senex* also in Pl. *Mos.* and *Ps.*, the father in Men. *Eun. Rhet. Her.* 1.9.14 appropriates the name for a comic scenario; "Simo" is a generic comic dupe at Hor. *Ars* 237–8.

Sosia (Σωσίας, *PA* 13175–82): a slave name in *Hec.* and Pl. *Am.*; also in Men. *Kolax, Perik.* and *Perinthia*, though not necessarily a slave in those roles.

Dauos: a very frequent slave-name in Men., also in *Ph.* and the title figure of a play by Caecilius. "Davos" becomes in later tradition the very embodiment of trickery, so that the reference at Hor. *S.* 1.10.40–1, *arguta meretrice potes Dauoque Chremeta | eludente senem comis garrire libellos* is probably not specifically to *An.* 740–89. Cf. Hor. *Ars* 237.

Mysis: the name is found only here.

Pamphilus (Πάμφιλος, *PA* 11524–60): also the young husband of *Hec.*

Charinus (Χαρῖνος, *PA* 15434–58): also an *adulescens* in Pl. *Mer.* and *Ps.*, and in Men. *Messenia*.

Byrria: the Gk. form Pyrrhias is a slave name in Men. *Dysk., Sik.*, and (by restoration) *Perinthia*.

Lesbia: not otherwise found in comedy.

Glycerium: not otherwise found in comedy, though Glykera is the young woman of Men. *Perik.* The name returns in that form at Hor. *C.* 1.19.5, 1.30.3, 1.33.2 and 3.19.28.

Chremes (Χρέμης, *PA* 15566–70): also a *senex* in *Hau.* and *Ph.*, but an *adulescens* in *Eun.* Antiphanes *PCG* 189.22 treats it as a generic name in comedy.

Crito (Κρίτων, *PA* 8817–28): a *senex* in *Ph.*, addressed in a fragment of Diodorus, *PCG* 1.

Dromo: a slave name in *Hau.* and *Ad.*, Pl. *Aul.*, Men. *Sik.*, Euangelos, *PCG* fr. 1, P. Oxy. 2329.

ARGUMENTUM

Each play of T. is preceded by a twelve-line *argumentum* in iambic senarii that the Bembine codex identifies as the work of C. Sulpicius Apollinaris, the second-century grammarian whose students included Aulus Gellius and the future emperor Pertinax (Holford-Strevens 2003: 83–6, Zetzel 2018: 88–92). Compressing a Terentian plot into twelve senarii was not easy, as oddities of emphasis and omission in these *periochae* show all too clearly, but Sulpicius' learning, which Gellius greatly admired, is readily apparent. He must have been a keen student of the comic idiom, and, like the author of *An.*'s post-Terentian alternative ending (Appendix I), he drew heavily on genuine features of Terentian diction. Noteworthy examples of that debt include:

1 meretriculae: comedy makes full use of diminutives, which can suggest affection, derision, and sometimes simply small size. *An.* includes *seruolos* (83), *aniculae* (231), *pisculos* (369), *dieculam* (710), *grandicula* (814), and *adulescentulos* (910).

3 dat fidem: for the idiom, cf. *hanc fidem | sibi me obsecrauit . . . ut darem* (401–2).

4 nam: introducing a new stage in the narrative, as at 51.   **desponderat**: *despondi* (102).

5 gnatam: *gnati* (49)   **Chremetis**: the Gk. gen. also at 247.   **ut +** indic. "as soon as." Cf. *ut hinc te introire iussi* (590).

7 quid animi: part. gen. is esp. common with neut. prns., e.g. *id negoti* (2).

8 suasu: an extremely rare noun, but found at *Ph.* 730 and as a variant reading at Pl. *Per.* 597.

9 ut uidit: as *ut comperit* (5).   **puerulum**: cf. *meretriculae* (1).

11 insperato: *insperante hoc* (603).

PROLOGUE

Plays of Pl. commonly introduce themselves either at the outset or early in the action with a monologue announcing the author and title, acknowledging a purported Greek model, and providing some orientation to the setting, characters, and action to come. The practice, derived with appropriate modifications from an expository device of Greek New Comedy, became so regular a feature that plays lacking such a prologue, e.g. *Curculio* and *Epidicus,* are often thought to have lost one in transmission. T. introduces each of his plays in a somewhat different way. Title and source are still identified, but he foregoes the explicitly expository function of the prologue, offering instead a speech defending his artistic program against what he represents as the carping of older rivals, who appear to resent his fresh approach to playwriting. Energetic Youth thus stands up to the objections of Old Age as the generational conflict at the heart of so many New Comedy plots is recast as an exercise in poetics.

The innovation is not entirely without precedent: argumentative speeches are hardly new to drama. The *parabaseis* of Aristophanic comedy most readily come to mind, but prologue-speakers, too, have often been given a case to plead. Mercury, for example, represents himself as Jupiter's *orator* when introducing *Amphitruo* (19–20, 34) because he believes the spectators, whom he calls the play's *arbitri,* might otherwise have difficulty understanding its unusual premise and accepting the gods' unusual roles (16, cf. *Capt.* 67 *iudices iustissimi, Poen.* 58 *uos iuratores estis*). Mercury, however, is an *orator* only in the general sense of ambassador or legate. While T.'s prologue-speaker is also an *orator* (and, like Mercury, uses the term at *Hau.* 11 and *Hec.* 9), this *orator* is quite specifically a legal advocate. His language, long recognized as rhetorical in style and tone, is explicitly and overtly forensic as he presents charges and counter-charges that make the fact of T.'s Greek models, not simply what they are but what he did in adapting them, the focus of attention, and his speech adopts the four-part structure of *exordium* (1–8), *narratio* (9–16), *argumentatio* (17–23), and *conclusio* (24–27) familiar from rhetorical handbooks. Whether the quarrel represented so artfully here is true (or in what sense it is true) hardly matters, and that is just as well since understanding these charges and the aesthetic objections behind them has long been frustrated by the elusive language and deliberate instability of T.'s evolving defense. Scholars today therefore read skeptically the arguments that earlier generations (e.g. Duckworth 1952: 61–5, Mattingly 1959) were more inclined to accept at face value. Exactly how T. ruined plays by his method of adaptation or stole from his fellow dramatists or lost the vigor of the traditional *palliata* style or unfairly advanced his career through the influence of well-connected patrons – all questions raised in the course of one or another of these prologues and debated over centuries of subsequent Terentian scholarship – are, and are likely to remain, largely unresolved.

Building literary judgments into a prologue is another gambit that is not entirely new. Pl. jokes about the different expectations aroused by comedy and tragedy (*Am.* 51–63, *Capt.* 61–2, *Poen.* 1–4) and even feigns distaste for comedy's dependence on dirty jokes and scurrilous characters (*Capt.* 56–58). When *Casina* was reproduced at some point after his death, its revival was justified by likening the new plays of the time to a debased coinage (9–10). What sets the *An.* prologue apart is its narrow focus on the creative process and the extensive critical vocabulary it employs to identify elements of composition (*argumentum, oratio, stilus*), to acknowledge a debt to predecessors (*auctores*), to contrast different approaches to adaptation (*neglegentia, diligentia*), and – if it is indeed a critical term and not simply a rhetorical feint – to describe T.'s own technique of composition (*contaminari*).

Whose voice do we hear advancing this argument? Two later plays appear to cast the manager of T.'s acting troupe, the aged Ambivius Turpio, as his spokesman (*Hau.* 41–5, *Hec.* 9–27), while other prologues feature an advocate less explicitly identified but still clearly speaking on behalf of the company, i.e. *Eun.* 19 / *Ad.* 3 *quam [fabulam] acturi sumus, Ph.* 33 *noster grex.* Ambivius' first words in *Hau.* imply that young men are normally assigned to deliver prologues (*Hau.* 1–2 *partis seni | poeta dederit quae sunt adulescentium*), but even that degree of characterization is uncertain in the case of *An.* This first speaker is almost completely anonymous and self-effacing: save for a parenthetic *quaeso* (8) and a reference to "our" poet (*hic noster*, 19), his speech is phrased entirely in the third person. The advocate thus remains subordinate in every possible way to the poet whose case he is presenting.

T.'s prologues are much discussed, important both for the light they are thought to shed on his working methods and more generally for their place in the long history of ancient literary criticism. Papaioannou 2014 provides a helpful overview. Their rhetorical quality was first explored by Leo 1960a (1898) 135–49, with their specific echoes of contemporary legal advocacy developed in detail by Gelhaus 1972 and Goldberg 1983. Gowers 2004 first drew attention to the possibility of significant thematic links between each ostensibly extra-dramatic prologue and the play that follows. For their recollection of the Old Comedy *parabasis*, see Ehrmann 1985 and Arnott 1985. A more recent line of inquiry, well represented by Sharrock 2009: 78–83, looks to a possible echo of the *Aetia* prologue, with Luscius standing in for Callimachus' Telchines. Attention has also been directed toward the role of these prologues in shaping later literary discourse, initially through the satires of Lucilius. For this approach, see Caston 2016, Keane 2018.

The meter is, as for all spoken verse in Roman drama, the iambic senarius.

1 poeta: by T.'s day this Gk. loan word was well established in Latin, applied to Naevius in the famous barb *malum dabunt Metelli Naevio poetae* (Ps.-Ascon., p. 215 Stangl) and the epigram quoted by Gell. 1.24.2 *flerent diuae Camenae Naeuium poetam*, used by Pl. of dramatists generally at *Curc.* 591, *Men.* 7, *Mil.* 211 (of Naevius?), *Ps.* 401, and regularly by T. of himself in these prologues, which consistently speak of him in the third person. Thus, *hic noster*, 19. He is never identified by name.   **quom**: T.'s text regularly distinguishes the conj. *quom* from the prep. *cum*. So too *quor* for *cur* (Introduction 4.1).   **animum . . . appulit**: a nautical metaphor, says Don., derived from the beaching of ships. Used again at 446. Not every reader understood it: Don. records the more obvious *attulit* as a variant, clearly a *lectio facilior*.

2 id . . . negoti: the part. gen. is common with neut. prns. (*SEL* II 25–34). The gen. sg. in the second declension is regularly -ī in Republican Latin (Weiss 2020: 239–40).

3 populo ut placerent: word order puts some emphasis on *populo*. In speaking of his patrons at *Ad.* 19 *qui uobis uniuorsis et populo placent*, T. appears to distinguish his immediate audience from the Roman people as a whole. Here, however, the appeal is clearly to that larger group, an appeal for favor difficult to reconcile with the hypothesis that "T.'s target audience was really only the fathers and more particularly the sons of Rome's elite" (Fantham 2004: 29).   **quas fecisset fabulas**, i.e. *fabulae quas fecisset*. Attraction of the antecedent to the case of the rel. prn. is common in T., a manifestation of what linguists call "left dislocation" (Halla-Aho 2018: 62–145). ποιέω (and thus ποιητής), not γράφω, is the Gk. verb for composing a play: thus Menander, in a famous anecdote, tells a friend, ἔγωγε πεποίηκα τὴν κωμωιδίαν (ap. Plut. *Moral.* 347f = T 11 K–T). T. (as also Pl.) uses *scribere* (1, 5) and *facere* interchangeably, and so too *fabula* and *comoedia* (26), though a distinction between *fabula* as a generic term for a play and *comoedia* as an artistically marked form has been suspected for Pl. (Hunter 2014: 16–23).

4 multo: abl. of degree of difference with *aliter*.

5 prologis: a rhetorical pl., since this is almost certainly T.'s first prologue. In the fifth century, πρόλογος was a common term for the first part of a play, i.e. action before entry of the chorus (e.g. Ar. *Ran.* 119–21); by

the later third century it referred to introductory speeches, as the hetaira Gnathaena's joke about the frigidity (ψυχρότής) of Diphilus' prologues shows (Athen. 580a). This is the first appearance of the term in
extant Latin, scanned *prōlogos* on analogy with *prōloqui*. At *Ph.* 14 it also
means an introductory speech; at *Hau.* 11 and *Hec.* 9 it means the prologue-speaker.   **scribundus**: *scribendum* at 1. Variation between old-
and new-style spelling is common in T.'s text. Whether the MSS preserve
his own practice is unknown, but similar variation is found in Cic., e.g.
Mur. 41 showing *dicundi* beside *decernendi* and *audiendi*, with comparable
inconsistency found in the Gallus papyrus (P. Qaṣr Ibrîm inv. 78–3–11),
a deluxe book roll probably written between 50 and 25 BCE.   **operam
abutitur**: *abutor* is consistently constructed with the acc. in T. (*Ph.* 413)
and Pl. (*Bac.* 360, *Per.* 262, *Poen.* 1199, *Trin.* 686), *utor* more commonly
with the expected abl. (*SEL* II 208, 216–17, 352–3).

6 qui = *ut* (*OLD* s.v. *qui²* 4), introducing a cl. of purpose. In origin an
abl. or instrumental form of prn. *quis* or *qui*, it can also mean "how" or
"why."   **argumentum narret**: despite T.'s implication here, exposition
was only one function of a dramatic prologue, and not always the primary
one. Thus Pl. *Trin.* 16–17 *sed de argumento ne exspectetis fabulae:* | *senes qui
huc uenient, i rem uobis aperient.* Cf. Pl. *As.* 1–15, *Truc.* 1–21.

7 ueteris poetae: Don. identifies T.'s critic as Luscius Lanuvinus, ranked
ninth of the ten poets in the notorious canon of Volcacius Sedigitus (ap.
Gell. 15.24). Posterity seems to have agreed with T.'s claim at *Eun.* 8, *ex
Graecis bonis Latinas fecit non bonas.* Far less is known about him, however,
than is hypothesized. See Garton 1972: 41–139, Wright 1974: 78–9,
Manuwald 2011: 242–3. *uetus*, also at *Hau.* 22 and *Ph.* 1, may allude not
just to Luscius' age, but to his outdated style of playwriting. T., in contrast,
takes pride in his newness, e.g. *Hau.* 28–30.   **maledictis** "slanders," an
idea readily paired with *maleuolus*. Cf. *Rhet. Her.* 2.12 *homines natura mali-
uolos et maledicos.*

8 uitio dent "reckon as a fault" (*OLD* s.v. *uitium* 1b), a pred. dat. (*NLS* §68).
uitium of faulty dramaturgy also at *Hau.* 30, *Ad.* 5; *malefacta* at 23; *peccata*
at *Hau.* 33. The single *poeta* of 7 is now a rhetorical plural.   **quaeso**
"please" (*OLD* 3), in origin a desiderative of *quaero* (Ernout and Meillet
1994: 550). It is one of Latin's more formal ways to soften a request, often
used in appeals to gods (Barrios-Lech 2016: 117–18).   **animum aduortite**: the standard phrase in Pl. for "pay attention," e.g. *Am.* 38, 393, *Capt.*
388, *Cas.* 393, 413, and the reading of all MSS here. Elsewhere, however,
T. writes *animum attendite* (*Eun.* 44, *Ph.* 24) and *aequo animo attendite* (*Hec.*
28), and so *attendite*, a variant known to Don. and in the version of the

line quoted by the fourth-century encyclopedist Nonius (p. 57L), is preferred by some editors (e.g. OCT, Brown). Cf. a fragment of Cic. quoted
by Quint. 4.1.74 *hoc, quaeso, iudices, diligenter attendite*. This is in either case
the language of advocacy.

9 Andriam et Perinthiam: for what is known of these plays, see Appendix
II.

10 norit . . . nouerit: both fut. pf. The contracted, more colloquial pf.
forms of *nosco* are the normative forms in comedy, with the longer forms
retained, most often at line-end, for metrical convenience. Cic. *Or.* 157,
citing *Ph.* 384 (*noras*, mid-line) and 390 (*noueras*, line-end), distinguishes
the longer, "proper" form (*recte dici*) from the "familiar" one (*usitate*). The
idea of knowing (and not knowing) will assume thematic significance in
the course of the play.

11 et tamen: this is the great eighteenth-century critic Richard Bentley's
emendation of the MSS reading *sed tamen*. For the neg. statement followed
by *et tamen* introducing an alternative, cf. 59. So too *Eun.* 23–4.   **ita**,
pro ualde (Don.). The basic distinction here between plot and words is a
commonplace, attributed to Men. (ἡ ὑπόθεσις v. τὰ στιχίδια, T 11 K–T),
resurfacing at Pl. *Trin.* 707 *hic agit magis ex argumento et uorsus meliores facit*
("This one sticks closer to the plot and makes better lines"), and is not so
far from the dictum attributed to the elder Cato, *rem tene, uerba sequentur*
(*Ad M. filium* fr. 15J, cf. Cic. *De or.* 3.125).

12 dissimili oratione . . . ac stilo: after famously calling plot (μῦθος = *argumentum*) the soul of a play, Arist. *Poet.* 1450b1–15 went on to distinguish
the substance of what was said (διάνοια) from the words used to say it
(λέξις). T.'s distinction between *oratio* and *stilus* carries this idea into Latin.
As Don. says, *oratio ad res refertur, stilus ad uerba*. So at *Hau.* 27 *oratio* refers
to the substance of his rivals' slanders, not simply their words, and *Hau.*
46 *in hac est pura oratio* describes a play dependent on talk (what he calls a
stataria, 36) rather than broad action (37–40).

13 quae conuenere: the 3 pl. perf. in *-ēre* was by the second century already
an archaism with a solemn ring, used regularly by Cato in history and oratory and as the marked form in Ennius, who used both it and *-erunt*. The
longer forms are over twice as frequent in Pl., but T. shows a slight preference for *-ēre* (26x) over *-ērunt* (22x) and *-ĕrunt* (1x). Caesar and Cicero
would generally avoid *-ēre*, but it returned as a stylistic accent for Livy (56
percent in the first decade, 10 percent in the fifth) and predominates
in Virgil. (The data is from Bauer 1933. Good summaries by Clackson
and Horrocks 2011: 100–1, Weiss 2020: 416–18.) T. is deliberately vague

about what he actually took from *Perinthia*. Someone, perhaps as late as the grammarian Aemilius Asper in the second century CE, eventually compared his plays in some detail with their Greek models, but only scattered (and meager) remains of the results eventually found their way into Don.'s commentary. See Appendix II.3.

14 transtulisse, sc. *se*. The acc. subj. is often omitted when easily supplied by the context.   **usum**, sc. *esse*.

15 isti: pejorative here and at 21, probably with an overtone of trial language (*OLD* 5b).   **factum**: the construction elides the distinction between verb and noun. So at *Hec.* 647 *non tibi illud factum minus placet quam mihi*, we can understand *illud factum* as "that thing done" or simply "that deed."   **in eo** "in this matter."

16 contaminari non decere fabulas: the regularity of the line, with neither elisions nor resolutions, gives it an epigrammatic feel. T. clearly refers to the importation of material from Men.'s *Perinthia* to his new *Andria*, a practice he would continue in *Eun.*, which incorporates characters taken from Men.'s *Kolax* (*Eun.* 30–4), and in *Ad.*, which features a scene imported from Diphilus (*Ad.* 6–11). Don. thus quotes this line ad 959.3, noting a putative borrowing from Men.'s *Eunouchos*. Here he glosses *ex multis unam non decere facere*. This is, however, the only thing clear about the line, which by leaving so much unsaid has become the single greatest crux in Terentian studies. Are these the actual words of T.'s critics, or his own distortion of their complaint recast to his advantage? How does what he did "contaminate," and is the play somehow spoiled by his "contamination" of the primary play (in this case, the Latin *Andria*) or the play he pillaged in the process of creating it (the Gk. *Perinthia*)? And spoiled for whom, the audience being offered an unfaithful version of its model or fellow dramatists, whose stock of new plays for adaptation has been further reduced by making two plays into one? T.'s further references to the practice at *Hau.* 16–19 and *Eun.* 19–34, where plagiarism is added to the charge, only add to the confusion. The problem, together with its history, is discussed in detail by Papaioannou 2014: 30–43, Germany 2016: 157–67.

17 intellegendo ut nil intellegant: T. plays on multiple senses of *intellego*, notably "understand" (*OLD* 1) and "appreciate" (*OLD* 4).

18 Naeuium Plautum Ennium: three predecessors listed in roughly chronological order. The first two were highly successful writers of *palliata* comedies, Naevius (d. ca. 200 BCE) ranked third in Volcacius' canon and Plautus (d. ca. 184 BCE) ranked second. Ennius (d. 169 BCE) is then something of a surprise in this company. He was famous for tragedy, not comedy, and appears last on Volcacius' list, and there only *antiquitatis causa*. Perhaps even more surprising is the absence of T.'s immediate predecessor Caecilius (d. 168 BCE), who heads Volcacius' list (so too Cic. *De opt. gen. or.* 2) and features in the biographical tradition as something of a patron for the younger dramatist (*Hec.* 14–15, *Vit. Ter.* 3; see Wright 1974: 87–126, Manuwald 2011: 234–42). Varro *Sat. Men.* 399B thought he excelled in plot construction (*in argumentis Caecilius poscit palmam*), and since dramatic structure is the main point at issue here, a reference to Caecilius would surely have been appropriate.

19 auctores "models" (*OLD* 8). The noun is predicative. *Eun.* 25 will look again to Naevius and Plautus. There is no further mention of Ennius, though *Eun.* 590 parodies a line of Ennian tragedy. T.'s claim might be thought at best disingenuous, since his significant departures from the traditional *palliata* style are readily apparent. Some examples of that difference are discussed by Wright 1974: 131–51.

20–21 The claims here are nearly as problematic as the charge of *contaminari*, which is probably (given the rhetorical context) by design, since vague claims are more difficult to refute than specific ones. How does carelessness (*neglegentia*) become a virtue and diligence (*diligentia*) a fault? (At 71, *neglegentia* is hardly a positive trait.) Reproducing the structural integrity of his model was never a priority for Pl. – *Casina* gleefully suppresses the climax engineered by Diphilus (*Cas.* 64–6), while the underlying plot of *Stichus*, ostensibly based on a second *Adelphoe* of Men., is impossible to recognize – but scholars have looked in vain in his work for signs of "contamination" in anything like T.'s sense (Schaaf 1977: 11–14, Fraenkel 2007(1960): 417–19). How, then, did T. "emulate" his predecessors' *neglegentia*? He seems in fact to have remained so faithful to the basic outline of his primary model that spotting his occasional alterations was at one time central to Terentian scholarship, their identification being the perceived key to discovering his originality. What separates that level of care from a pedantry that makes *diligentia* into something *obscura*?

22 dehinc "therefore" (*OLD* 1a). Scanned as a monosyllable, an ex. of synizesis.   **porro** "hereafter" (*OLD* 2).

23 malefacta . . . sua: T. will make good on this threat at *Hau.* 31–4, *Eun.* 10–13, *Ph.* 6–8 describing scenes in his rival's plays that he finds illogical or conceptually absurd.

24 fauete: *uos ergo fauorem facite* (Don.). This is again the language of advocacy. Thus Quint. 4.1.73 *nam iudices et in narratione nonnumquam et in argumentis ut attendant et ut faueant rogamus*.   **adeste** "pay attention"

(*OLD* 19). So too *Hau.* 35, *Ph.* 30, and frequently in Pl., e.g. *Am.* 151, *Poen.* 126, *Trin.* 22.   **cognoscite** "investigate," again with a legal connotation (*OLD* 4).

25 pernoscatis: T. is fond of this intensifying prefix, esp. (though not exclusively) with verbs, e.g. *persolui* (39), *perduxere* (81), *perterrefacias* (169), *percurro* (355), etc. The verb introduces two successive ind. questions, *ecquid spei sit relicuom* and [*utrum comoediae*] *quas posthac faciet . . . spectandae an exigendae sint.*   **spei**: part. gen. (2n.).   **relicuom**: scanned as four syllables.

26 de integro "afresh" (*OLD* 3a). T. calls a play *integra* (rather than *noua*) when emphasizing that it is new to the Roman stage, e.g. *Hau.* 4–5 *ex integra Graeca integram comoediam | hodie sum acturus* ("Today I will be performing a fresh comedy from a fresh Greek play").   **comoedias**: 3n. for the case.

27 exigendae, sc. *e scaena. exigo* is almost a technical term for failure here and at *Hec.* 12, 15. So Don. ad *Hec.* 15.4 *fabulae aut stare dicuntur aut exigi.*   **prius** = *priusquam (spectatae sint).*

[I.i] Simo, Sosia, [porters] (28–171)

The text we read begins with words, but the play we see begins with action as a line of porters enters carrying provisions for a feast. How many porters there are and how lavish the provisions is uncertain. Davos will grow suspicious because these preparations seem meager (360, 450–6), and the illustrated MSS of T. show only two porters carrying (among other things) a rack of fish and what looks like a pheasant. The procession that tramps across the stage could nevertheless be significantly longer: the maids we see carrying the *meretrix* Bacchis' clothing and jewelry in *Heauton timorumenos* (381) are later described as *plus decem* (451). Whether Simo and Sosia, his freedman, lead or follow this procession is also uncertain, though a delayed entrance, at least by Simo, would provide time for the necessary change of costume if, as is at least possible, the prologue-speaker was to reappear in this role. There would in either case be significant stage business – heavy loads inevitably invite broad gestures and sight gags – before Simo engages Sosia in the dialogue that begins the exposition proper.

The scene is, in an important sense, T.'s creation. Men.'s *Andria* opened with an expository monologue by the young man's father, but T. substituted for that speech a dialogue modeled on what he found in *Perinthia.* That play, we are told, began instead with the father in conversation with

his wife. (See Appendix II.3.2.) What part she then took in the ensuing action is unknown. What *is* known is that T. replaced her with the
freedman Sosia, a significant change because it eliminated at the outset
the opportunity to provide a female perspective in a play that will be
conspicuously lacking in them. This Sosia is what ancient critics called a
"protatic" character (προτατικὸν πρόσωπον, lit. "a character to advance
a point"), a figure introduced solely to turn an expository scene into a
conversation, like Davos of *Phormio*, Philotis and Syra of *Hecyra* (Don.
ad *An*. Prf. 1.8, 28, *Ph*. 35; Duckworth 1952: 108–9). In the course of
his career, T. would perfect the technique of expository dialogue (only
Adelphoe opens with an expository monologue), but even here in his first
such effort, the subtlety with which he presents the expository material is
noteworthy. It is not just a matter of slipping in details like the names and
situations of all the principal figures – Sosia (28), Simo (41), Pamphilus
(61), Chrysis (85), Chremes (99), Glycerium (134), Davos (159) – but
of how, in the course of explaining action, he also reveals character. The
key to it all is Sosia, whose deadpan obsequiousness brings to the fore
Simo's more overbearing qualities and whose own singular virtues, *fides
et taciturnitas* (34), will emerge as the central themes of the play.

Like all initial scenes of exposition in Terence, the dialogue is spoken
in iambic senarii.

28 uos: Simo addresses the porters.   **istaec:** *ista* + *c(e)* neut. acc. pl.
Reinforced demonstratives of this type are frequent in comedy and well
attested in colloquial Latin, e.g. at Pompeii (*CIL* I² 2451), Vindolanda
(343.14 at http://vindolanda.csad.ox.ac.uk). Simo accompanies the
words with a sweeping gesture from the porters' burdens to the house
door (thus *intro*).   **auferte:** not just to carry, but to carry away. The
porters, eager to hear what Simo will say to Sosia, nevertheless linger,
which necessitates Simo's impatient second command. Though scansion mandates the elision of *aufert(e) abite*, a significant pause between
the two words is required to accompany the stage business, followed by
another pause as the porters finally exit. Only then does Simo turn to his
freedman.

29 ades dum: imper., softened by the enclitic adverb *dum* (*OLD* 2a), i.e.
"stay a minute." Simo will be less peremptory with Sosia than he was with
the porters.   **paucis,** sc. *uerbis* (abl.). A verb of speaking is understood.
Maltby 1979: 144 notes that five of the six occurrences of this phrase in T.
come in the speech of old men, which tends *not* to be brief. (The sixth is
in the pretentiously elevated speech of the parasite Gnatho, *Eun*. 1067).

Long-windedness may be thought a trait of the old.   **dictum puta**: lit. "consider it said." Sosia immediately seeks to oblige.

30 nempe: Sosia anticipates a further instruction. The adv. introduces the following question in terms of its expected answer (*OLD* 2).   **ut . . . haec**: the ind. command depends on an implied *uis*, readily supplied from *uolo* above (cf. 165–6). *haec* then echoes *istaec*: "So you want these things [i.e. what the porters have now carried inside] to be properly seen to?" Don., glossing *curentur recte* as *diligenter coquantur* ("carefully prepared"), refers the phrase specifically to preparation of the meal. For the casting of Sosia as a cook, see Introduction 3.1.1.

31 mea ars: if Sosia is a cook, the expertise in question would be the art of cookery.   **hoc**: abl. with *amplius*.   **possit**: subjunc. in a characterizing clause (*SEL* I 289).

32–33 arte . . . eis [*sc.* **artibus**]: Simo plays on *ars* "technical skill" (*OLD* 1) and *artes* "personal qualities" (*OLD* 4).

34 fide et taciturnitate: loyalty and discretion will emerge as dominant themes of the play as Pamphilus is torn between obligations to his father and to Glycerium. Desirable traits in a freedman, e.g. Cic. *Fam.* 13.22.2 commending the *libertus* Hammonius *quod est in patronum suum officio et fide singulari*, they are emphatically *not* the qualities of the traditional comic cook.   **exspecto quid uelis**: a polite invitation, repeated at 45, to come to the point, which Simo will do only at 51. T. here further delays exposition of the plot, concentrating first on the revelation of character.

35 ego postquam: T. regularly thrusts words to the front of a clause for emphasis; *ego* always figures prominently in Simo's thinking, and he certainly enjoys the memory of his own benevolence.   **a paruolo** "from very small." So Micio, of his adopted nephew Aeschinus: *eduxi a paruolo* (*Ad.* 48). Though not a home-born slave (*uerna*), Sosia's upbringing has been entirely within Simo's household. Early manumission seems not to have been uncommon at Rome; T. was himself said to have been freed *mature* (*Vita T.* 1, and on the various motives for manumission, Treggiari 1969: 11–20, Hunt 2018: 117–22).   **ut** "how;" cf. *Eun.* 127–28 *tute scis . . . mea consilia ut tibi credam omnia.*

36 iusta et clemens "fair and lenient," not adjs. commonly associated with the slave condition. (Micio, the easy-going brother of *Ad.*, claims for himself a *clemens uita*, 42.) This is, of course, only Simo's view, but Sosia does not (or is not in a position to) contradict him. Dacier cites

[Longinus] *Subl.* 44.3 here for the concept of "justified slavery" (δουλεία δικαία), but the treatise itself goes on to quote, perhaps more appropriate to Sosia's situation, Hom. *Od.* 17.322–3: "the day of slavery takes away half a man's manhood." Pl. *Am.* 166–75 reflects that more common view as the Plautine Sosia comments on how hard life is for the slave of a rich man.

37 libertus: the *aduocati* of Pl. *Poen.* 504 ff. are the only other characters identified as freedmen on the Roman stage. See Rawson 1993.

38 propterea quod: a causal clause stating a fact (*NLS* §241), with the correlative adv. used to provide emphasis, e.g. Pl. *Am.* 297–8 *nunc propterea quod me meus erus | fecit ut uigilarem…* ("now, particularly because my master kept me up all night…").   **seruibas**: fourth conj. verbs can form a metrically convenient imperf. in *-ibam* as well as the more familiar *-iebam*. Thus *seruiebat* at *Ph.* 83 (Palmer 1961: 270–1, Weiss 2020: 440, 566–7). Don. remarks on the choice of imperf. over perf. here to stress the duration of Sosia's service.   **liberaliter**: lit. "like a free person," high praise in a society built upon the labor of slaves. So later of Glycerium, *honesta ac liberali* (123), and *Eun.* 473 of a supposed eunuch, *quam liberali facie.* T. seems to use the term with no discernible irony. A maxim ascribed to Men., ἐλευθέρως δούλευε· δοῦλος οὐκ ἔσῃ ("Serve freely; you will not be a slave," p. 108 Jäkel), plays on the oxymoron, but whether ironically or with the complacency of the rich when advising the poor is unknown.

39 quod: acc. rel. prn. anticipating *pretium.*   **summum pretium**, i.e. freedom.   **persolui**: the verb suggests not simply giving, but fulfilling an obligation.

40 in memoria habeo: Sosia sounds noncommittal, as if recalling the condition of servitude rather than the manumission. Don. nevertheless takes it to mean *non sum ingratus.*   **haud muto factum**: lit. "I'm not changing what I've done [i.e. the manumission]." The implication that Simo *could* do so troubled Don., who thought it out of character and understood the expression to mean simply *non me paenitet facti.* He may be right. A mechanism to revoke the freedom of a *libertus ingratus* became an issue in the first century CE (Suet. *Cl.* 25.1, Tac. *Ann.* 13.26–7), but is unattested in the Republic. Cic. seems only to have wished he could revoke the manumission of the disloyal Chrysippus (*Att.* 7.2.8). The situation was different at Athens, where revocation was possible if the terms of manumission were not met (Zelnick-Abramowitz 2005: 308–15).

41 tibi . . . quod placeat: an example of prolepsis. By setting *tibi* in the *si*-clause, Sosia literally puts his patron before himself. He knows how to speak to Simo's priorities.

42 gratum . . . gratiam: deliberate word-play.　　**aduorsum te** = *tibi*.　　**habeo gratiam**: lit. "I have gratitude." The related idioms are *gratias agere* "to thank" and *gratiam referre* "to return a favor." Sosia says what a former master would certainly like to hear, though his words might carry an ironic undertone to any *liberti* in the audience.

43 istaec commemoratio: the account of his manumission by Simo.

44 immemori: since the verbal noun *exprobratio*, like its cognate verb *exprobro*, is commonly constructed with the dat. of the person being reproached, edd. emend the MSS, which (along with Don. and OCT) read gen. *immemoris*. The difference, if there is one, would be between a reproach to someone who is unmindful and a reproach to someone for being unmindful. Sosia has already, of course, declared himself *memor* (40).　　**benefici**: gen in -*i* is regular in Republican Latin (Weiss 2020: 239–40). Most easily understood with *immemori*. A slave's obligations to his master did not end with manumission: deference (*obsequium*) and also specific duties (*operae*) were still expected of the *libertus*. The precarious position of a freedman lacking a patron's support may at least in part lie behind Sosia's markedly deferential tone. See Treggiari 1969: 68–78, Mouritsen 2011: 152–4, Hunt 2018: 128–30, and for depictions of manumission in comedy, Richlin 2017: 418–34. Given the recurrence of *An.* in rhetorical studies, Cic. may well have had this situation in mind at *De or.* 2.206, when Antonius notes that affection is better secured by holding out *spes utilitatis futurae quam praeteriti benefici commemoratio*.

45 quin . . . tu dic: formed from the old instrumental case of the prn. stem *qui-* + neg. part. -*ne, quin* in colloquial Latin frequently retains its original sense "why not?" and readily combines with an imper., e.g. *Hau.* 890 *quin tu ausculta*, *Ph.* 350 *quin tu hoc age* (Barrios-Lech 2016: 86–9).　　**uno uerbo**: another invitation for Simo to come to the point, which he will not do until 51.　　**quid est**: use of the indic. in questions of fact that might be thought indirect looks back to an earlier paratactic structure, the difference between "tell me what you want" and "tell me, what do you want?" (*NLS* §179, Stephens 1985, Clackson and Horrocks 2007: 171–2). **uelis**: commonly constructed with acc. of the thing and acc. of the person (*SEL* II 251); Simo's statement at 50 might suggest supplying *facere* to complete the thought. The subjunc. (more correctly an optative) of *uolo* is often used to reinforce the idea of desire.

46 praedico, i.e. *prae* + *dico* (3), not to be confused with *praedico, praedicare* "to declare," as at 875 *ain tandem ciuis Glyceriumst? :: ita praedicant.*

47 has . . . nuptiae: the first indication in the text that what we saw carried into Simo's house were materials intended for a feast. *has* is attracted to the case of the rel. clause, where *ueras* is understood, i.e. *hae nuptiae, quas credis esse ueras, non sunt uerae*.

48 quor: the spelling *cur* did not take hold until the late Republic. Always a monosyllable with a long vowel.   **igitur**: normally in second position in T. (21x, e.g. *An.* 154), but can be found even in fourth (*Hau.* 857) and as late as sixth position (*Ph.* 572–3).

49–50 Cic. *Inv.* 1.33 quotes these lines to illustrate the concept of *partitio*, a methodical statement of the individual topics to be covered in a speech, and Simo will, in good rhetorical fashion, follow his own outline: *gnati uitam* (51–154), *consilium meum* (155–67), *quid facere te uelim* (168–70). Don. ad 49, ever alert to T.'s rhetorical qualities, further subdivides these categories.

49 gnati: a synonym for *filius/a* in comedy (131 v. 318 occurrences), which distinguished between the noun *gnatus/a* (cf. *gigno*, Gk. γίγνομαι) and the participle of *nascor, natus/a*. That distinction faded in the course of the Republic. Thus, in epitaphs, *gnatos duos creauit* in the mid-Republic (*CIL* 1.1211 = 17.5 Courtney) but *[amor] quem dedit natae suae* by the first century (*CIL* 1.1214 = 20.3 Courtney).

51–142 Cic. *de Or.* 2.326–7 praises this entire section for the way T. mixes detail and dialogue, using stylistic variety to make a long narrative lively and engaging.

51 nam "well then," settling into the promised narrative (*OLD* 6).   **ex ephebis**: at Athens, young male citizens between the ages of eighteen and twenty (ἔφηβοι) spent those two years undergoing military training and serving on garrison duty along the frontiers of Attica as a kind of citizen education. Though T. will sometimes remove an explicitly Athenian reference (the deme-name Halai becomes *in his regionibus* at *Hau.* 63) or explain it (e.g. the Athenian law of the *epikleros* at *Ph.* 125–6), forms of *ephebeia* came to be widespread in the Hellenistic world and apparently required no such circumlocution (Kennell 2015). Cf. *Eun.* 290, 824; Pl. *Mer.* 40, 61. Caecilius even entitled a play *Synephebi* (*The Ephebes Together*). Besides adding a touch of local color, the term identifies Pamphilus as an *adulescens* of at least twenty.

52 The line has long been suspect. As transmitted, it has an extra syllable, and *antea* is not otherwise found in Roman comedy, which elsewhere uses the colloquial *ante*. Barsby's choice of *erat* for MSS *fuit* at least saves a syllable by an easy elision. OCT obelizes *liberius . . . potestas*, while other editors solve the problem by deleting from *Sosia* to *potestas,* which they explain as a gloss intended to explain the change of status *ex ephebis* that found its way into the text.   **potestas**: the context continues to be specifically Greek, since a Roman *adulescens* would remain *in patria potestate* and thus, at least in theory, enjoy little such freedom (Watson 1971: 28–33, Krause 2011: 629–33); cf. the reference to Chremes' *potestas* below, 541.

53 quī: in origin an Old Latin instrumental, this interrog. adv. often means "why?" or, as here, "how?"   **posses**: deliberative subjunc. suggesting an impossibility in the past, as *Eun.* 831 *quid facerem?* "What was I to do?"   **ingenium** "character," as at 275.

54 dum "as long as." The time of this clause is co-extensive with that of the main clause.   **magister**, i.e. *paidagogos*, the slave assigned to escort a young master to his lessons, who often becomes in the process both chaperone and mentor, like Lydus of Pl. *Bac.* (420–34) and Syrus of *Ad.* (962–3). Simo must be speaking generically: Davos, he of *mala mens, malus animus* (137), seems hardly suited to have curbed anyone's wilder impulses. For the social practice, see Bonner 1977: 38–45; in comedy, Fantham 1972: 35–8.   **itast** "so it is!" A common expression of agreement in a language lacking a single word for "yes" (*OLD* 11a). Sosia needs to make his presence felt.

55 Simo continues, taking no notice of Sosia's interjection.   **plerique omnes** "just about all." The more logical order *omnes plerique,* where the second word limits the first, yields to this common form of the expression, e.g. *Ph.* 172, *Hau.* 830; Pl. *Trin.* 29. The metrical convenience of *plērī(que) ōmnēs* is often thought to be a factor, though Naevius begins a Saturnian with the phrase (*BP* fr. 49 Str. / 54 M *plerique omnes subiguntur . . .*). Don. thought it an archaism.   **adulescentuli**: diminutives are more common in colloquial than in formal Latin. Pl. clearly liked the sheer sound as well as the nuance of them, e.g. *Cas.* 40 *primulo crepusculo, Ps.* 68 *papillarum horridularum oppressiunculae* (Duckworth 1952: 334–5, Palmer 1961: 77–8). T.'s use of diminutives is more restrained and more likely to be semantically significant (Minarini 1987: 87–91, and more generally Müller 1997: 239, Karakasis 2005: 31–2), e.g. the hint of condescension at *Hec.* 619 *odiosa haec est aetas adulescentulis,* though at line end metrical convenience may well be the determining factor.

56–60 Simo's catalogue sets out the activities and values appropriate for the aristocratic youth of Athens as described by Isocrates (7.45) and Menander, e.g. *Sa.* 14–17.

56 ut animum . . . adiungant: this explanation of the preceding *quod* comes as a consecutive noun clause (*NLS* §168).   **studium** "pastime" (*OLD* 4). Not a serious occupation, as the preceding indef. adj. indicates.

57 alere: the verb has both *equos* and *canes* as obj. Both animals were used in hunting.   **ad philosophos:** a verb needs to be supplied. Don. suggests *audire* or *sectari*. The young men who followed Socrates around Athens may come to mind, but philosophical discourse had appeal at Rome, too. In ca. 167, around the very time of *Andria*, the Pergamese scholar Crates of Mallos lectured at Rome (in Greek), probably on the interpretation of Homer (Suet. *Gram.* 2.1). The lingering appeal was such that a *senatus consultum* of 161 sought to ban philosophers (and rhetoricians) from the city, evidently to no avail: in 155, crowds flocked to hear the Academic philosopher Carneades, then on a diplomatic mission to Rome, set out through arguments *in utramque partem* alternative definitions of justice. Cato professed outrage at what he took to be his insincerity (Cic. *Rep.* 3.6, Plut. *Cato* 22.4–5; for the SC of 161, Suet. *Gram.* 25.1, Gell. 15.11.1, Gruen 1990: 171–7). Trimalchio's boast, *nec umquam philosophum audiui,* suggests the other side of an enduring cultural divide (Petron. *Sat.* 71.12).

58 horum . . . nil: the obj. of *studebat*. The normally intrans. verb may take an acc. of the person or thing affected, e.g. Pl. *Mil.* 1437 *minus has res studeant, Truc.* 337 *illum student iam.*

59 mediocriter: picking up *nil egregie praeter cetera.* "In moderation" or "with moderate success" (*OLD* s.v. *mediocritas* 4)? Simo has escaped the torments of Strepsiades, who at the beginning of Aristophanes' *Clouds* frets over his son's ruinous preoccupation with horses, but the following account makes "not to excel" sound like an aristocratic virtue. Cato would encourage his son to explore Greek learning but not take it too seriously (*inspicere, non perdiscere, Ad Marcum filium,* fr. 1 = Plin. *Nat.* 29.14).

60 non iniuriā "not unreasonably," adverbial abl. Thus *Eu.* 433 (another ingratiating response to an overbearing patron) *metuebant omnes iam me. :: haud iniuria.*

61 apprime: *admirabiliter* (Don.), not a word in the classical vocabulary. It appears first in Liv. Andron. *Od.* fr. 10 M *adprimus Patroclus.*   **ut:** introduces a consecutive noun clause in apposition to *id* (*NLS* §168).   **ne quid nimis:** a verb like *agas* is understood. Sosia recasts Simo's description as the proverbial μηδὲν ἄγαν. Lower status characters in comedy are among those most prone to such clichés, *sententia non incongrua seruo, quia est peruolgata* (Don.).

62 Simo continues his speech, echoing but not taking explicit notice of Sosia's interjection. As throughout the scene, the establishment of character precedes an account of action.   **sic**: colloquial for *talis* (*OLD* 5a), e.g. *sic, Crito, est hic* (919).   **omnis**: acc. pl., obj. of the following hist. infin.

63 quibus . . . quomque: the tmesis (lit. "splitting") gives added weight to each component, as if "anyone at all."   **dēdĕre**: significantly stronger than *dare*, as *Hau.* 681 *dedo patri me nunciam* ("I forthwith give myself over to my father"); contrast 688 *da te mihi uicissim*, meaning little more than "Grant me a favor in return."

64–65 Pamphilus is described as the ideal companion, always the follower, never the leader. That the strong-willed Simo praises such a character is striking: whether what he says of his son is true is another matter.

65 ita ut "that's the way to . . ." The phrase, with variations of meaning, becomes something of a mannerism for Simo in this scene: 77 and 80, then 542, with Davos perhaps mocking him at 522.   **facillume** "very easily." *quam* would be required to suggest "as easily as possible."

66 laudem: not just praise, but with the moral connotation of being praiseworthy; cf. the contrast between *laus* and *uitium* at *Ad.* 5, 418. Later in the century, Scipio Hispanus (pr. 139 BCE) would proudly claim in his epitaph, *maiorum optenui laudem* ("I maintained the high reputation of my ancestors," *CIL* 1.5 = 13 Courtney).   **inuenias . . . pares**: 2 per. pres. sg. generalizing subjunc. (*NLS* §119).

67 hoc tempore: moralizers like Sosia tend to think of themselves as living in an Iron Age.

68 obsequium: Sosia gives Simo's *obsequi* (64) a decidedly negative spin. Cic. quotes the line at *Am.* 89 as a general, though regrettable truth. By the time of Jerome, *Ep.* 116.31 it was a *uulgare prouerbium* (Otto 1890: 368). His teacher Don. ad 67 comments, "This sentiment is condemned by intelligent people, since a flatterer (*adsentator*) owes compliance (*obsequium*), a friend truth." That is indeed the tenor of Roman moralizing texts, e.g. Lucil. 694W/611M and 695W/953M, Cic. *Am.* 91–2, Sen. *Ep.* 3, but a freedman's experience may well have encouraged a different view. Cf. the claim at Tac. *Ann.* 13.26.5 that freedmen should expect *per idem obsequium retinendi libertatem per quod adsecuti sint*. By Tacitus' day, *obsequium* defined the freedman's duty to his former master, but it does not appear to have that technical sense here (Watson 1971: 53–4, Rawson 1993: 223). Sosia is probably speaking aside (thus Barsby): otherwise, his sardonic comment would, quite uncharacteristically, contradict his patron. Simo, in any case, again takes no notice.

69 mulier quaedam: Simo knows her name (85) but withholds it to let the narrative build momentum.   **triennium**: acc. of duration modifying *abhinc* (constructed with an abl. only at Pl. *Most.* 494).

70 ex Andro: the northernmost island of the Cyclades, a reluctant ally of Athens in the fifth century and an object of contention between Macedonia and Egypt in the fourth. In Terence's day, it was ruled by Pergamon.   **huc uiciniae**: part. gen. as in the common expression *ubi gentium.* So too *Ph.* 95 *hic uiciniae* "here in this neighborhood." Thus Don., who also preserves the alternative reading *uiciniam* (acc. of the goal of motion) and found this phrase redundant. The MSS read *huic uiciniae,* as if dat. with *commigrauit.* Comic convention, of course, puts Chrysis' house literally next door. So too in *Sa.,* where the poor Nikeratos is the next-door neighbor of the rich Demeas.

71 inopia: not simply poverty (*paupertas, Ph.* 94, 903, *Ad.* 496), but lack of resources (*Hau.* 929, *Ad.* 105). At 798, her cousin Crito will claim a virtue in living *pauper.*   **cognatorum neglegentia**: Athenian law obliged her closest male relative to arrange a suitable marriage for an orphaned daughter, less out of sympathy for her situation than to protect the assets of the household. That necessity motivates the plots of, e.g., Men.'s *Aspis* and Apollodorus' *Epidikazomenos* / T.'s *Phormio* (MacDowell 1978: 95–9, Todd 1993: 228–31). The requirement in other *poleis* may have been less stringent (her kinsman Crito of Andros certainly proves less than sympathetic to her situation, 796–9), but the description here seems designed to arouse the sympathy of audiences at Athens or, presumably, at Rome.

72 aetate integra "unblemished youth," as at *Eun.* 473.

73 ei! a (monosyllabic) exclamation, usually by males, of pain and foreboding (Müller 1997: 138).   **quid . . . mali**: the part. gen. is much preferred to an adj. in agreement (*NLS* §77 ii).   **Andria**: T. seems to make clear here and at 85 which of the two women from Andros is the play's title figure. Don. thought this a metatheatrical moment: *nomen ostendit et mulieris et fabulae.* At 215, however, Davos will refer to Glycerium as *haec Andria.*   **apportet**: another metatheatrical hint, since the verb can mean not just importing things or, as here, trouble, but bringing a play onto the stage (Pl. *Men.* 3; *Ph.* 24).

74–79 Simo recounts the Andrian woman's progress at Athens from impoverished respectability to the more lucrative life of a *meretrix.* Since no sources of information are provided, how much of this is fact and how much is based on supposition remains unclear. That a single, foreign woman could support herself at Athens (or Rome) by spinning and weaving is hardly credible: Simo is dealing in stereotypes.

74 parce ac duriter: at *Ad.* 45 the urbane Micio describes his country brother Demea as living *semper parce ac duriter*, which he does *not* think desirable.

75 lana et tela: the traditional mark of female respectability in the Greco-Roman world. Thus the virtue of Antiphila is confirmed by her dedication to the loom at *Hau.* 276–95, and so too of Lucretia at Liv. 1.57.9. Cf. the summarizing epitaph of the good wife Claudia, *domum seruauit, lanam fecit* (Courtney 17 = *CIL* I² 1211, ca. 135–120 BCE).   **quaeritans**: frequentative (contrast *quaerens*) indicating habitual action (Weiss 2020: 425). Dacier detected a note of pathos in the word, suggesting earnest action for meager reward.

76 amans: the substantive part. (e.g. Ov. *Am.* 1.9 *militat omnis amans*) introduces a new subject as the narrative moves from one stage (*primo*) to the next (*sed postquam*).

77 item "similarly," i.e. *pretium pollicens*. The implication is not just of a second lover, but the beginning of a sequence of lovers.   **ingeniumst omnium | hominum**: Simo attributes the change of occupation not to an individual weakness of character but to human nature generally (Don.). Crito of Andros will take a less generous view (796–8). At *Hau.* 446–7, the moralizing Chremes acknowledges the role of economic necessity in such a choice.

78 procliue "inclined," with the connotation of a downward slope.   **ad lubidinem**: the noun often carries connotations of sexual desire (e.g. 308, 557; *OLD* 3), unlike the more general idea of happiness or pleasure represented by *uoluptas* (e.g. 944, 960). Simo offers the outsider's view of sex work as a life of pleasure; comedy is, however, capable of presenting a quite different view when seen from the inside, e.g. *Hau.* 388–91. See Marshall 2013, Richlin 2017: 105–26.

79 condicionem "the proposition" (*OLD* 3). The word may also be used of a marriage proposal (e.g. *Hec.* 241, *Ph.* 579).   **dehinc**: indicating future time. Contrast *adhinc*, referring to the past (69).   **quaestum**: an occupation for pay, esp. (though not necessarily) a disreputable one like, in comedy, that of a slave dealer (Pl. *Capt.* 98) or a *leno* (*Ad.* 206). Cic. *Off.* 1.150–1 addresses the connotations of the term.   **occipit**: hist.

pres. after the aorist perf. *accepit*. Such a combination is common in narrative (*SEL* I 14–15). The sequence is logical, since the second action only began after completion of the first, though (as becomes clear at 105), both actions are now entirely in the past.

80–98 From this point on, Simo's narrative is based on his own observations and inquiries, and yet – as becomes increasingly apparent in the course of the play – the picture he paints is at best incomplete. Nothing he says can be taken at face value.

80 forte: Simo speaks as if his son had no active role in what follows.

81 perduxere: the prefix *per-* may imply reluctance on Pamphilus' part (*OLD* 1d). Thus Don. comments *inuitum isse Pamphilum*. His acquiescence is of a piece with the description above, 64. The perf. in *-ēre*, which Pl. largely confined to solemn and mock-solemn passages, e.g. *Am.* 216 *haec ubi legati pertulere…*, is common in T., though by the later first century, it had come to sound distinctly archaic and poetic. See 13n.   **esset**: from *sum, esse* or *edo, ēsse*? Not even Don. was sure. *Eun.* 574 *essem una quacum cupiebam* clearly means "I would be together with the girl I wanted," but 88–9 below suggests that Pamphilus was being dragged off specifically to dinner parties.   **meum**: a striking hyperbaton, esp. with the strong stop at line end. The loose order may hint at colloquial speech.

82 egomet: the metrically convenient enclitic particle, often added to a prn., may here be genuinely emphatic as Simo shifts the focus of his narrative from his son to himself.   **mecum**: a verb of saying or thinking is easily supplied from the context. Diaeresis here, the metrical equivalent of the printed colon, marks the beginning of the direct quotation.

83 habet: *proprie de gladiatoribus* says Don., recalling the crowd's cry *hoc habet* after the striking of a decisive blow (cf. Pl. *Most.* 715, *Rud.* 1143). If, as Don. also says, *captus est* just above means "ensnared" (*OLD* 5), we might think of the retiarius' net, with Chrysis as the retiarius.   **obseruabam**: context suggests an inceptive imperf., i.e. "I began to watch…"   **mane**: Simo will learn what he can from behavior observed the morning after the night before.   **illorum seruolos**: young slaves (hence the dimin.) regularly escorted their masters around town, a particularly desirable custom in a city lacking street lights and police. Cf. *Ad.* 26–7 acknowledging Aeschinus' retinue.

84 rogitabam: the frequentative suggests a certain urgency.   **heus**: the interjection is commonly used to get attention or to call someone back, like Eng. "Hey!" It is not limited by class or gender: thus *Hau.* 743 (slave to slave), *Hec.* 339 (slave to mistress), 522 (husband to wife), *Ad.* 882

(slave to master), though women seem to use it only when addressing social inferiors, as *Eun.* 594 (Hofmann 1951: 15–16, Müller 1997: 102–5, Barrios-Lech 2016: 162–6).   **puer**: like Gk. παῖ, the usual address to a slave, e.g. *Ph.* 152, *Hec.* 719, *Eun.* 624.

85 sodes: contraction of *si* + *audes* = "please," softening the imper., as *Ad.* 517, 643. A word of masculine diction in T. and primarily addressed to social inferiors (Müller 1997: 94–5; Carney 1964 considers the exceptions to be dramatically significant). Women in T. say *amabo* (Müller 1997: 96–7, Barrios-Lech 2016: 116–17).   **heri . . . habuit**: adv. and tense stress the transitory nature of relations with Chrysis. Like Eng. "have," *habuit* can carry a sexual connotation, directly as Pl. *Bac.* 1080 *duxi, habui scortum* ("I did hire, I did have a prostitute") and in the sense "keep," as *Ad.* 389 of Ctesipho's *psaltria* (*an domi est habiturus*), where Don. glosses *quia haberi uxor dicitur et haberi mulier, cum coit.* See Adams 1982: 187, Bagordo 2001: 66–7. Chrysis, however, is neither *scortum* nor *psaltria*; a *meretrix* of her class could choose her clients, an important distinction (Adams 1983: 321–7, Davidson 1997: 112–27). Simo may be deliberately disparaging in his word choice.   **Chrysidem** "Goldie" (χρυσός), also the name of a *hetaira* in Menander's *Kolax* (fr. 4 K–T) and the common-law wife (παλλακή) of Demeas in *Samia.* She is the title character in a play by Antiphanes, appears in a fragment of Timocles (fr. 27), and possibly in Menander's *Misoumenos* (P. Oxy. 4408, 5198), though in those cases her characterization is unclear.

86 teneo "I understand" (*OLD* 23).

87 The line presents a metrical challenge. The Athenian name Νικήρατος implies the scansion Nicēratum, which gives the senarius an extra *longum.* Some editors solve the problem by deleting *nam*, others by deleting *tum.* (OCT obelizes from *nam* to *simul.*) Since the prosody of Greek names in Latin varies, a third possibility is to scan Nicēratum on the analogue of Sīmo for Σίμον, with the following two syllables lightened by prosodic hiatus followed by iambic shortening. Brown solves the problem by reading *eam* for *simul*, which also provides an obj. for *amabant.*   **simul**: a *meretrix* might well entertain multiple clients as, perhaps most notoriously, Thais does at the end of *Eun.*

88 eho: an interjection to attract attention, often followed by a voc., and then (as here) a question or, as at 184, an imper. (Müller 1997: 105–6, Barrios-Lech 2016: 166–8).   **quid . . . quid**: the first is the obj. of a verb understood (e.g. *agit*); the second introduces the coming answer.   **symbolam**: the contribution, usually financial, to a dinner party, an aristocratic Greek practice (δεῖπνον ἀπὸ συμβολῶν) frequently mentioned in

Greek comedy, e.g. Ar. *Ach.* 1211, Alexis fr. 15, Eubulus fr. 72, Timocles fr. 8. Allusions to the custom in Roman comedy (*Ph.* 339, *Eun.* 540; Pl. *Cur.* 474, *Epid.* 125, *St.* 432) retain the Greek term, but when Cic. refers to a similar practice in a Roman context, he says *collecta a conuiua* (*De or.* 2.233). These lines on Chrysis' domestic arrangements became the inspiration for Thornton Wilder's description of her household in *The Woman of Andros* (Introduction 3.4.2).

90 The imperfects in this passage reflect Simo's continued anxiety: one good report would not satisfy him.   **nil . . . quicquam** "nothing whatever." The pleonasm is emphatic and colloquial, as at *Hec.* 400, *Eun.* 884, *Ph.* 80, 250, *Ad.* 366. The personal equivalent *nemo quisquam* is found at *Hec.* 67, *Eun.* 226, 1032.

91 enimuero: the particle introduces a further confirmation of the preceding statement (*OLD* 2).   **spectatum** "tested" (*OLD* 6c), with *eum* understood.

92 continentiae: defined by Cic. *Inv.* 2.164 as the quality *per quam cupiditas consili gubernatione regitur*. Simo, it will turn out, could hardly be more mistaken.

93–95 The general statement introduced by *nam* explains and justifies the preceding conclusion about Pamphilus.

93 qui: understanding *is qui* requires us to supply *cuius* with *animus* in the following clause. Don. seems to prefer (*scilicet*) to understand *animus qui*, which avoids the grammatical change of subj.   **ingeniis**: *pro hominibus* (Don.), like Eng. "characters."   **conflictatur** "engages" (depon., *OLD* 3), usually suggesting some kind of struggle, e.g. *Ph.* 505 *cum huius modi . . . ut conflictares malo* ("to grapple with this sort of trouble").   **eiusmodi**, i.e. the sort of people who gather around Chrysis.

94 tamen: Don. felt the lack of a preceding *licet* or *quamquam*, but *tamen* often stands at the end of a sentence (and a verse) in T. to mark a concession, i.e. "nonetheless" or "after all" as at *Hau.* 678, 712, 1012, etc.

95 scias: generalizing subjunc., as 66.   **posse**, sc. *eum*.   **ipsum** "of his own accord" (*OLD* 7).   **habere modum** "to take control" (*OLD* 5b).

96 quom . . . tum: emphasis rests on the second, less expected action, e.g. *Ph.* 187 *quom mihi paueo, tum Antipho me excruciat animi* ("Not only am I frightened for myself, but Antipho torments me to the core."). The indic. is normal for a variety of *quom*-clauses in early Latin (*SEL* I 79–85, *NLS* §231).   **uno ore** "with one voice." T. then creates a noteworthy alliterative string by following with the common collocation *omnes omnia* (e.g. *Hec.* 867, *Ad.* 299).

97 dicere et laudare: hist. inf., almost always two or more standing for imperf. rather than perf. conjugated verbs. Quint. 9.3.58 postulated an ellipsis of *coepi* in this construction, but its origin is in fact uncertain (*NLS* §20–1, Weiss 2020: 486–7).   **fortunas**: Don. thought the pl. here ἐμφατικώτερον.

98 qui: the antecedent is supplied by *meas*.   **haberem**: mood and tense likely determined by *dicere et laudare*. Simo seems to be reporting, with evident pleasure, what he was told. A causal rel. cl. in early Latin would more likely have an indic. verb (*SEL* I 137–8, *NLS* §159), though T. may use either or, as at 272–3 below, both moods in succession.

100 ultro "of his own accord" (*OLD* 5). Cf. *Ad.* 471–2 (Aeschinus seeking to make amends for the offense to Sostrata's daughter) *ad matrem uirginis | uenit ipsus ultro . . .* Chremes' proposal would, at least in the world of comedy, normally come from the prospective bridegroom's side, e.g. Pl. *Aul.* 256–7, *Poen.* 1155–7, *Tri.* 571.   **unicam**: so the fathers suppose, perhaps with a hint here that a surprise is in store.

101 cum dote summa: a dowry of ten talents is offered at 951 (with n.). Mention of the dowry is a traditional part of the betrothal formula, but Simo's prominent reference to it here is striking, *summa* perhaps taken as a measure of Chremes' appreciation of the young man's presumed virtues.   **daret**: the expected verb in phrases of formal betrothal like *uxorem dare* and *in matrimonium dare* (*OLD* 4a), but since Chremes is only proposing a marriage, "offer" comes closer to the sense here, as similarly in his review of the situation at 545.

102 despondi: like *dare*, a verb normally referring to actions by the prospective bride's parent, e.g. *Ad.* 670 (of Sostrata's daughter) *quis despondit? quis dedit?* ("Who betrothed her? Who gave her away?") The technicality troubled Don., who presumed some older usage behind it: *ex uetere more, quo spondebat etiam petitoris pater.* It is easier simply to understand a more general sense, "I promised" (*OLD* 2). Consultation with the young people themselves would be neither expected nor required. Cf. the agreement between the two fathers at Men. *Sa.* 113–18. At 238–9, Pamphilus' complaint is not that he was not consulted but only that he was not informed before the marriage was announced. There was, however, no doubt some variation between what the law allowed and actual family practice. For Athens, see MacDowell 1978: 86, and for Rome, Treggiari 1991: 176–80.   **hic . . . dies**, i.e. *hodie*. This is, presumably, why Sosia and Simo

have been shopping for provisions.　　　**dictust**: for the contraction, see
Pezzini 2015: 52–3.

103 quor non = *quominus*, as found at Cic. *Nat. D.* 1.95 *quid obstat quominus
sit beatus?*　　　**uerae**: echoing 47. Sosia virtually repeats the question
posed at 48.　　　**audies**: the stock reply to such a question, as at *Hec.* 177,
Pl. *Epid.* 499. At *Eun.* 571, T. seems to play on the artificiality of the expository convention when Chaerea replies, *tacitus citius audies.*

104 fere: the adv. qualifies *paucis*, i.e. "just a few."　　　**quibus**: the rel.
prn. does the work of *postquam*, as Caes. *BGall.* 3.23.2 *paucis diebus quibus
eo uentum erat.* For the prep. in such expressions of time, cf. Cic. *de Or.*
1.168 *in his paucis diebus* "within the last few days."

105 uicina haec: said with a gesture toward the neighboring house, thus
providing another expository detail.　　　**factum bene**: Sosia inverts the
conventional response to such news, *male factum* (e.g. *Ph.* 751; Cic. *Att.*
15.1.1; Catull. 3.16). His apparent callousness could be excused, at least
in part, by recollection of how grasping the *meretrix mala* of comic stereotype could be, e.g. Bacchis of *Hau.*, Acroteleutium of Pl. *Mil.* Chrysis' true
character has yet to emerge.

106 beasti, sc. *me.* Syncopated perf.　　　**ei**: *metui* can be constructed with
dat. of the per. for whom the fear is felt and *a* + abl. for its source, but
Sosia's *ei! uereor* above (73) suggests this may instead be again the exclamation. Thus Martin 1964: 3.　　　**ibi tum**: a colloquial redundancy, also
in narrative at 131, 223, 634. Simo continues his account, again taking no
notice of Sosia's interjection.

107 frequens = *frequenter* (*OLD* 5).

109 collacrumabat: the compound suggests both that he joined the lam-
entation and that it was intense. Cf. the epitaph for Plautus preserved by
Gell. 1.24.3 *et Numeri innumeri simul omnes conlacrimarunt.*

110 sic, not *hoc.* The effect, says Don., is to take us back to the moment of
the thought, not simply to report it in hindsight. The distinction matters
since this initial impression turns out to be erroneous, as Simo will soon
discover.　　　**consuetudinis**: often used to describe relationships with a
sexual component (Glycerium at 279, 439 and Phanium at *Ph.* 161; with
a wife at 560 and *Hec.* 404). Thus *consuetum amorem* at 135.

111 familiariter: a *familiaris* is a member of the extended household that
Romans called a *familia.* Thus the play on *familia, familiaris,* and *familiariter* at Pl. *Am.* 352–9 as that Sosia insists with increasing desperation that
he is *huius familiai familiaris.* Here *familiariter* = "like a member of the family," despite what Simo takes to have been a *parua consuetudo.*

112 mihi . . . patri: emphatic order, "for me, his father." Simo naturally thinks of himself.

113–14 haec . . . omnia . . . officia: a notable hyperbaton, the order reflecting the sequence of Simo's thought.

114 mansueti "gentle" (*OLD* 3). Don. distinguishes the *animus* shown toward his friends from the *ingenium* shown to the departed Chrysis. He finds *mansuetus* an odd word to describe Pamphilus' treatment of the older woman.   **officia**: here, as at 236 and 330, the sense is closer to "behavior" (*OLD* 1) than to "duty" or "obligation" (*OLD* 4), as at 168, 236.   **multis**, sc. *uerbis*. Cf. *paucis*, 29.

115 eius, i.e. *Pamphili*.   **prodeo**: something of a set expression for attendance at a funeral, as Varro *R.* 1.69.2 *rogat ut ... in funus postridie prodeamus*.

116 nil . . . mali "no trouble." *malum* and its cognates often hints at the particular kind of trouble or trickery that generates comic plots.   **etiam** "as yet."   **hem:** a common exclamation in T., a versatile particle with a range of meanings from incredulity or surprise (as here) to sarcasm (435) to annoyance (683) or outright anger (919) depending on context (Luck 1964: 15–16, Müller 1997: 121–3). Sosia is responding to the implications of *etiam mali*.

117 ecfertur: the *vox propria* in the funeral context (*OLD* 3) as at Pl. *Most.* 1001 *unum uidi mortuom ecferri foras*. Don. nevertheless thought it a Grecism (ἐκφέρω), citing by way of counter-example Virgil's substitution at *G.* 4.255–6, *corpora . . . exportant tectis*. For the funeral scene as it would have been envisioned by a Roman audience, see the source material collected by Hope 2007: 113–56.

118 unam "one in particular" (*OLD* 8). Word order creates the emphasis. The following diminutive might suggest a certain daintiness as Simo lingers over each of its syllables.

119 forma: descriptive abl. The assertive Simo is nevertheless at a loss for words. (He is more articulate at 123.) Sosia then volunteers the most mundane of the possibilities (so, too, Byrria at 428). Dacier admired the propriety (*bienséance*) of Simo's unwitting, glowing description of his future daughter-in-law. Glycerium ought at this point to be visibly pregnant, but T. leaves unclear how much time has elapsed between this funeral and the dramatic present, when Glycerium is about to give birth. See 216n.

120 adeo = *tam* (*OLD* 4).   **ut nil supra**: similar expressions at *Eun.* 427, *Ad.* 264. Cic. adds a form of *posse* to the phrase at *Att.* 13.19.2, *Fam.* 14.1.4.

121–2 praeter ceteras: a deliberately striking repetition.

123 honesta ac liberali: *honesta* carries connotations of respectability (*OLD* 4a); *liberali* connotes nobility of bearing (*OLD* 3). Cf. Cic. *Cael.* 6 *forma et species fuit liberalis*. Simo, in a subtle bit of foreshadowing, is taken aback by the qualities of the young woman who will become (and be proved worthy of becoming) his daughter-in-law. The concepts, however natural-sounding in Latin, are no less Greek: Plangon, who, like Glycerium here, will need to have her status restored in Men.'s *Heros*, is identified at the outset as ἐλευθέριος καὶ κοσμία (40).   **pedisequas**: female attendants, part of Chrysis' retinue; cf. the crowd of *ancillae* (739, 744) that accompanies Bacchis on her entrance at *Hau.* 723. Chrysis has evidently done well for herself at Athens.

124 sororem: not quite the case, as it turns out. There is a similar relationship between Thais and Pamphila in *Eun.*   **aiunt**: no more authoritative an affirmation than Eng. "they say," e.g. 321, 833.

125 ilico: "on the spot," temporal.   **animum** = *me* (*OLD* 2a).   **attāt**: an expression of pain in Attic tragic diction (ἀτταταῖ, Soph. *Phil.* 743, 790) becomes in Latin an indication of surprise (e.g. *Eun.* 228–9, *Hec.* 449–50), often, as here, with an added touch of alarm or dismay (Müller 1997: 133). It seems to have been genuinely colloquial, since even Cato uses it: *attat!, noli, noli scribere, inquam, istud* (*ORF*[3] 173.7). Disyllabic interjections sometimes lengthen the final vowel: cf. *eugē*, 345 and Eng. "hurrāh!"

126 hinc illae lacrimae: the phrase became proverbial for any sudden revelation quite independent of tears shed, e.g. Cic. *Cael.* 61; Hor. *Epist.* 1.19.41. The tears here are, of course, those shed by Pamphilus (109).

127 quorsum euadas: obj. of *timeo.* cf. 176 *uerebar quorsum euaderet.* The verb has a similar, negative connotation at *Ad.* 509.

128 ad sepulcrum: as context suggests, the place where the final rites are to be performed, not necessarily a tomb.   **vēnimus**: perf. verbs often occur together with hist. pres. in narrative passages, e.g. Pl. *Aul.* 371–87, *Cur.* 329–63; *Hau.* 121–41, *Ph.* 862–7, and below, 353–65. Whether the (aorist) perf. is being used to distinguish single, completed actions in the account from continuous actions is not certain. See the exx. at *SEL* I 14–17.

129: fletur: Don. finds in the impers. verb a suggestion that the weeping is universal. It certainly emphasizes the action over the agents of that action (Weiss 2020: 405–6).

131 satis "enough," adv. (*OLD* 8)   **periclo**: the regular form in T. Pl. also uses the longer, metrically convenient forms of *periculum,* esp. at line end, e.g. *Capt.* 740 *periclum uitae meae tuo stat periculo.* The syncopation of unstressed vowels was a feature of the spoken language. For its effect on poetic diction, see Coleman 1999: 38–40. **exanimatus** "breathless," but with the added connotation of agitation, as at 234, 342.

132 dissimulatum . . . celatum: the predicative use of the perf. pass. part. extends the action of the subject, the equivalent of a subordinate clause, i.e. "love that was . . ." (*NLS* §91). The device is well established in comedy, less common in what remains of second-century prose. A good, if rare example occurs in a speech of Scipio Aemilianus, fr. 33M: *vi atque ingratis coactus cum illo sponsionem feci, facta sponsione ad iudicem adduxi, adductum primo coetu damnavi, damnatum ex voluntate dimisi.* ("Compelled by force and ungrateful men, I entered into a contract with him. Once the contract was made, I brought him before the judge. Having brought him before the judge, I secured a conviction at the first hearing, and once he was convicted, I voluntarily let him go.") It seems to be a mark of literary rather than colloquial style. (So Laughton 1964: 147–56 analyzing the part. in Cic.'s correspondence.)

133 mediam, i.e. "around the waist" (*OLD* 2). So, too, *Ad.* 316 (describing something like a wrestler's move), *sublimen medium primum arriperem et capite in terra statuerem.*

134 mea Glycerium: the adj. agrees with the gender of the person, not the name, which is in form a neut. diminutive of Glykera. Plautine *meretrices* frequently sport names of this type (e.g. Acroteleutium, Philocomasium, Phoenicium), but this is the only example in T. "Sweetie" suits a member of Chrysis' household; her proper name, as we eventually learn, is the more respectable sounding Pasibula (945). **inquit**: vocal mimicry was an established feature of Greek comic acting (Csapo 2002: 135–8, Davis 2003: 55–65), and the subtle demarcation of quoted speech was among Menander's technical refinements (Nünlist 2002: 243–7). It could be overdone, as Quint. 11.3.91 observes, but orators, too, might need to speak in the voice of another, which was among the skills to be developed from the study of drama (Quint. 11.1.39–41, cf. 10.1.69–71 on the virtues of Menander). **perditum**: supine. The construction with a verb of motion is common in comedy, including examples where the supine has an expressed obj., e.g. Pl. *Truc.* 559 *perditum se it*; *Hau.* 315 *laudem is quaesitum?* (*SEL* I 453–6).

135 consuetum, i.e. "longstanding." Word order emphasizes the pred. adj. **cerneres**: consecutive subjunc., the tense stressing the logical connection between the action (*reiecit*) and this result (*NLS* §164). Her action leaves no room for doubt, *non "suspicarere" dixit sed "cerneres"* (Don.).

136 quam familiariter: contrast 111n. Here the adv. suggests not just an acquaintance, but something much closer to the Eng. cognate. So Ampelisca, in fending off the wolfish Sceparnio as he tries to get his hands on her at Pl. *Rud.* 419–20 *aha! nimium familiariter / me attrectas.* For an analogous exclamation at line end, cf. *Eun.* 178, *labascit uictus uno uerbo quam cito!*

137 quid ais? an expression in T. commonly of surprise, as here, or, as at 184, to direct the course of the conversation, e.g. "What have you got to say?" (*OLD* s.v. *aio* 6, Müller 1997: 45–6, Barrios-Lech 2016: 172–6). Simo, as usual, ignores the interruption.

138 nec "and yet" + neg. (*OLD* s.v. *neque* 5). Simo is not just annoyed by what he has seen but frustrated by his inability to hold his son accountable. **satis** (sb.) + gen. (*OLD* 1b). For the construction, using *ad* + gerund to avoid a second gen. with *causae*, cf. Cic. *Att.* 12.27.3, *habemus satis temporis ad cogitandum.* T. often omits forms of *sum* in such short sentences, e.g. 138, *Ad.* 121, 264, 792. (Don. cites V. *Aen.* 2.314 *nec sat rationis in armis.*) **diceret**: past contrary-to-fact condition with the protasis (*si obiurgarem*) suppressed. The imperf. subjunc. in such conditions is common in Republican Latin (*NLS* §199).

139–41 Simo imagines the inevitable reply. For a similar use of quotation in an imagined rejoinder, compare Sannio's musings at *Ad.* 233–5. Cf. the effectiveness of directly reported speech at 134, 221.

139 commerui: used in a bad sense. The corresponding positive verb is *promereo.* Simple *mereo* can be used in either sense, negative (281, 621) or positive (351).

140 prohibui: the obj. is readily supplied from the preceding rel. clause.

141 honesta oratio "a reasonable response." Cic. *Off.* 2.69 uses the phrase to grant the attraction of a claim his argument aims to supersede, but the echo is probably coincidental. For *oratio* referring to the content of speech, see 12n.

142 uitae. dat. as at *Ad.* 155 *ferte misero ac innocenti auxilium.* The prolepsis is typical for T.

143 illi: in the sense "to do . . . with regard to" (*OLD* 22b), *facio* commonly takes either a dat., e.g. Cic. *Att.* 7.3.2 *quid enim tibi faciam, qui illos libros deuorasti?* ("What should I do with you, who has devoured those books?"), or an abl., e.g. Cic. *Sest.* 29 *quid hoc homine facias . . .?* ("What can you do with such a man . . .?"). T. uses the abl. at 614, 709. **damnum aut malum**: harm to property or person respectively. Simo again takes no particular notice of Sosia's words.

144 uĕnit: hist. pres. as the narrative resumes; cf. *ecfertur*, 117.   **postridie**: news travels fast, and, as at 99, Chremes responds to what he had heard on the street.   **clamitans**: the frequentative is emphatic rather than literal, as at *Ad.* 60, where *saepe* is required to complete the sense, *uenit ad me saepe clamitans: quid agis, Micio?*

145 indignum facinus "a scandalous thing." A stock phrase, used nine times by T., only four times by Pl. *facinus* in early Latin means simply "a thing done" (thus *pulcherrimum facinus, Ph.* 870) and does not acquire the sense of "crime" until the early first century, e.g. *Rhet. Her.* 2.69 *dicimus uoluntario facinori nullam esse excusationem* ("We say there is no excuse for an intentional crime"). The phrase appears as an exclamation in direct speech at *Eun.* 70, *Hec.* 376, *Ad.* 173, 447, 669. Here the punctuation treats it as an opening exclamation in the speech of Chremes reported after *clamitans*. Don., however, seems to have understood *indignum facinus [se] comperisse*, with the following clause *Pamphilum . . . peregrinam* offered to specify the deed.

146 pro uxore: Clinia's love for the "Corinthian" Antiphila *ut pro uxore haberet* describes a similar problem at *Hau.* 96–8. It was a serious crime at Athens to disguise a liaison with a foreign woman as a legal marriage: that was the basis for the action against Stephanus and Neaera in [Dem.] 59. To treat such a woman as a common-law wife (παλλακή) – the relationship we find in Menander's *Samia* between Demeas and Chrysis, and in real life between Pericles and Aspasia – was perfectly acceptable, at least for older men. The outrage here is not legal but moral. Chremes, understandably enough, is angered by the discovery that his prospective son-in-law may have his affections seriously engaged elsewhere. See also 297n.   **hanc peregrinam**: the prn. adds to the pejorative overtones of the word. Cf. Don. ad 469 *mulieres enim peregrinae inhonestae ac meretrices habebantur.*

147 negare: 97n.   **factum**: what is the deed being denied? Simo has himself seen evidence of a *consuetus amor* (135). How serious it is and whether it constitutes an obstacle to a legitimate marriage are the issues for him. Chremes naturally has a somewhat different view, as he will make explicit at 828–32.   **instat**: an unusual construction. Don., who calls it an archaism, cites Pl. *Mer.* 242 *instare factum simia* ("The monkey insisted that it happened").   **denique**: the argument evidently continued for some time.

148 ita . . . ut qui "in the eventual understanding that..." *qui* is the indef. adv. = Gk. πως (*OLD* 6b), not easily rendered in Eng. Edd. sometimes print *utqui.*

149–50 One of the few moments of genuine dialogue in the scene. Sosia naturally wonders why even now, at this moment of apparent crisis, Simo has not confronted his son. Note the two changes of speaker in a single line.

150 qui: adv.   **cĕdŏ**: this imper. particle (pl. *cette*, in comedy only at Pl. fr. 160 *cette patri meo*), in origin an aorist <*kedō with iambic shortening (Meiser 1998: 185, Weiss 2020: 449, 462), can mean either "hand over" (*OLD* 1) or, as here, "tell me" (*OLD* 2). Simo then again imagines Pamphilus' supposed rejoinder.

151 tute ipse: doubly emphatic. Pamphilus will in fact demonstrate the ability to evade moral responsibility that Simo imagines here.   **his rebus**: deliberately vague. Simo is as eager as Pamphilus to avoid defining the full nature of the relationship with Glycerium.   **praescripsti** = *praescripsisti*. Syncopated forms are esp. common in the 2 pers. perf. act. indic. (as here) and the plupf. subjunc.

152 adest quom: the *quom*-clause provides the subj. of *adest*.   **alieno more**: another evasive euphemism. Simo will say something similar in his own voice at 189.

153 sine "allow." The imper. of *sino*, here constructed with acc. and inf. (*OLD* 2b), has a variety of colloquial meanings centering on requests and permission, e.g. 622, 900, 902. For the full range of constructions, see *SEL* I 234–5.   **meo . . . modo**: in deliberate contrast with *alieno more*. The implication is that Pamphilus' relationship with Glycerium would be acceptable so long as it ended by the time of his marriage. The lenient Micio expresses a similar view at *Ad.* 147–53.

155 nolet: edd. prefer to read this fut. indic. here (with Don.) over the subjunc. *nolit* of the MSS since Simo considers this situation a real possibility. Contrast *eueniat* at 165. A pres. with fut. sense is common in the apodosis, e.g. Pl. *Bac.* 911, *Capt.* 209; *Eun.* 382, *Ad.* 347.

156 ea, i.e. Pamphilus' refusal.   **primum**: adv. The refusal would be Pamphilus' first actionable offense. Simo is proposing a test or, given his suspicions, a trap. (Scafuro 1997: 354–77 claims entrapment as the central issue of the play.)   **animum aduortenda iniuriast**: the idiom that often means simply to pay attention (8n.) here takes on a hostile sense, i.e. not just an *iniuria* to be noticed, but one that deserves to be punished. Cf. 767 *o facinus animaduortendum!*

157 operam do = *curo*, with *id* as its obj. A similar construction at 307. What follows is the *consilium* promised at 49–50.   **falsas**: a sham since Chremes has at this point withdrawn his consent to the marriage.

158 uera: The play on *falsas* is striking, with the future less vivid construction that follows standing in contrast to the certainty of *si nolet . . . est* just above.

159–64 The following portrait of Davos builds on the traditional hallmarks of the comic *seruus callidus*: *sceleratus* and *malus*, a hatcher of *consilia* and *doli* to trick his master. Moore 1998: 36–41 surveys the type. In what hints at a major reversal of comic roles, Simo instead schemes to thwart the schemer by hatching his own plan to forestall and misdirect the slave's efforts. In this play, as McCarthy 2004: 103 notes, trickery "operates more as a characterising device than as a plot device." For Simo's description of Davos as an implicit recognition of comic convention, see Introduction 3.2.

159 simul: Simo's plan is in two parts. The first was directed at his son; the second now aims at his slave.

160 ut consumat: dependent, like *ut . . . causa sit* above, on *operam do* (157).   **quom** "when."   **nil doli**: whatever scheme Davos plans should prove harmless because it will be directed against a false target.

161 manibus pedibusque: recalling Homeric χερσίν τε ποσίν τε (*Il.* 20.360), the phrase (repeated at 676) is proverbial, like "tooth and nail" or "might and main."

162 id: anticipates the *ut*-clause.   **adeo** "moreover" (*OLD* 6b).   **mihi . . . gnato**: word order puts some stress on the prn. and then makes possible an artfully balanced chiasmus. On the purported motive for Davos' mischief, cf. the enthusiasm with which Pl.'s Pseudolus, in the process of helping young Calidorus, contracts for the tricking of his old master.

163 quapropter: a question posed purely for the audience's benefit. A man raised *a paruolo* in Simo's household would surely know Davos' character perfectly well. Simo's reply – *rogas?* – may be a tacit acknowledgment of the convention, as at *Eu.* 571.

164 mens . . . animus: the distinction is between the seat of thought (*OLD* 1) and the seat of intention (*OLD* 7). Cf. Ar. *Pax* 1086 δόλιαι ψυχαί, δόλιαι φρένες.   **quidem**: the emphatic particle often follows a rel. prn. (Solodow 1978: 96–9). Alliteration enhances the effect, though not as strikingly as 691.   **sensero**: use of the indic. strengthens the threat, which hardly needs to be completed. For that completion, cf. 196.

165 opust: for the contraction (also at 265, 638a), see Pezzini 2015: 170–5.   **eueniat**: the subjunc. suggests that Simo thinks this outcome less likely than the unwillingness he envisioned at 155 (and represents as fact at 172), in which case his reported denial to Chremes at 147 would have been at best disingenuous.

166 nil . . . morae "no delay," i.e. in accepting the marriage. A similar construction at 420, but with the sense "obstacle" (*OLD* 8), not "delay."   **restat:** indic. because Simo is more confident of his putative course of action than of the need for it. Cf. 920, *si perget . . . audiet.*

167 exorandus: *ex* + *oro*, not just to beseech, but to persuade. This is the reading of the MSS. Don. reports as an alternative *cui . . . expurgandus* [sc. *Pamphilus*], which OCT prints. Since the way to win over Chremes would be to have him excuse Pamphilus' past conduct, the difference in sense is slight.   **confore:** a very rare verb, here supplying a fut. pass. inf. of *conficio*. For the sense, cf. *Ad.* 946 *hoc quom confit quod uolo* ("since this thing is coming about, which I want").

168 nunc: Simo at last comes to the instructions promised at 50.   **tuomst officium:** introduces a series of indirect commands.   **bene . . . assimules:** the instruction to further the preparations for the (sham) wedding is consistent with the casting of Sosia as a cook.

169 perterrefacias: an impressive verb found only here in classical Latin. The usual verb is *perterreo*.

171 curabo: echoing 30 (*ut coquus,* Don.)   **nunciam:** in this emphatic compound, *-i-* is not the palatal glide (Eng. *y* /j/) of *iam*, but vocalic. The word is therefore always trisyllabic in comedy (Weiss 2020: 67–8).   **i prae:** this and *abi prae* (e.g. *Eun.* 499, *Ad.* 167) are something of an exit formula like προάγετε and πρόαγε at Men. *Dys.* 866, 906.   **sequar:** there is equally good support in the MSS for *sequor*, as at *Eun.* 908. The issue is as much dramaturgic as textual: Does Simo immediately follow Sosia inside, in which case *i prae* suggests an uncharacteristic courtesy on Simo's part, or is it an order to exit, with a promise to follow after some interval, as at Pl. *Am.* 544, *Cist.* 773, *Mil.* 1353? If the former, Simo must exit and return almost immediately to deliver the brief monologue of 172–4; if the latter, he stays behind to address the audience and does not leave the stage until 205. This second interpretation seems to be how Don. envisioned the action (*substitit senex,* ad 172; *non recessit de loco senex,* ad 173). Both interpretations, however, raise significant problems of dramaturgy. See Introduction 3.1.2.

[I.ii] Simo (172–4)

Simo remains on stage to deliver a brief "link" monologue (Prescott 1939) making the transition from the expository scene that ends with

Sosia's exit to the next move in the plot, which will center around Davos. It is a moment for Simo to take the audience into his confidence, as monologues performed in the intimate performance venues of second-century Rome so often do.

172 non dubiumst: what was expressed to Sosia as a possibility at 155–8 is now stated as fact.

173 ita: introduces the reason for the previous statement (*OLD* 14), where later Latin would use a causal particle like *nam* or *enim*.   **modo** "recently" (*OLD* 5). When? Those who posit an exit and immediate return for Simo after 171 assume he refers here to a chance encounter inside, where he has just observed Davos' response to the preparations for what the slave does not realize is a sham wedding. The alternative explanation, encouraged by Davos' coming statement that Simo has neither said anything to anyone nor appeared vexed (175–8), is to understand *nuptias* as referring back to the original agreement with Chremes. It would have been Davos' alarm on that earlier occasion that fed the suspicion mentioned at 161–3.

Simo, Davos (175–205)

The mood changes as the *tibicen* is heard for the first time, and he will continue to play almost without pause until 269. The rhythms are still largely iambic, but the long octonarius line makes possible a variety of musical effects. For T.'s use of octonarii, see Moore 2012: 182–4.

A scene like this, where one character enters and at first either ignores or fails to observe another already on stage, was often expanded for comic effect by Pl. T., as might be expected, is usually more restrained in such situations (Bain 1977: 156–61, Fraenkel 2007: 151–4). Here Simo stands to one side as Davos enters from the house, either muttering to himself or, like Simo before him, speaking directly to the audience. However *callidus* we may expect him to be, though, he opens with a confession of perplexity. The emphasis throughout the scene will be on character development as master and slave jockey for advantage.

175 mirabar . . . si: the following potential subjunc. indicates that the thing eliciting surprise was not to be expected, e.g. *Ph.* 490 *mirabar si tu mihi quicquam afferres noui* ("I thought it would be strange if you were offering me anything new"). An indic. verb would create instead a neg. statement of a fact, e.g. *Hau.* 525 *minimeque miror Clinia hanc si deperit* ("I'm hardly surprised if Clinia is mad about her").   **hoc**: i.e. Pamphilus' conduct, subj. of *abiret*.   **sic abiret** "get off this way" (*OLD*

7c). A colloquial phrase. Thus Catull. 14.16 *non non hoc tibi, salse, sic abibit* ("No, wise guy, you won't get away with it like this"). Don. thought a gesture should accompany *sic*, as Eng. "just like that," with a snap of the fingers.   **eri**: the standard term used by a slave for a master, e.g. 183, 208, 412, etc. Direct address is then either *ere* or (often) by name. Forms of *dominus/a* are rare except in generic reference to the master–slave relationship. See Dickey 2002: 77–81, Richlin 2017: 22–4.   **semper**: Don. was unsure whether the adv. should be understood with *lenitas* or *uerebar* (Scafuro 1997: 374–5); most modern translators understand it with *uerebar*.   **quorsum euaderet**: 127n.

178–9 The shift to trochaic rhythm in these two lines is noteworthy, and even more noteworthy is the variation between them. The fact that the first (– –), fourth (– –), and final (– ◡|–) feet of the two lines are metrically identical heightens the contrast with the opposing patterns of substitution in the remaining feet. Simo seems to contradict Davos metrically as well as substantively.

178 quoiquam nostrum, i.e. any member of the household. This would seem to exclude Sosia, consistent with the idea that the *libertus* was brought in as an outside contractor.

179 An aside addressed to the audience, further suggesting that the initiative will, contrary to comic expectation, continue to lie with the *senex*, not the *seruus*.   **nunc faciet**: answers Davos' *numquam fecit*.   **tuo magno malo** "big trouble for you." For the poss. adj. in agreement in an objective sense, cf. *Ph.* 1016 *nam neque neglegentia tua neque odio id fecit tuo* ("He didn't do it out of disregard or dislike for you"). Similarly, *Hau.* 307 *desiderio tuo* ("longing for you"). *malum*, as so often in comedy (e.g. 431, 611), stands as a virtual euphemism for punishment.

180 id: anticipates the sequence that runs from *nos* to *opprimi*, a striking ex. of T.'s ability to weave a set of ideas into a tight syntactic structure.   **falso gaudio**, i.e. the belief that Chremes' intervention has relieved Pamphilus of the obligation to marry. So far, Davos has been taken in by Simo's ruse.

181 interoscitantis (*inter* = "at intervals," *OLD* 12 + *oscito*), lit. "between yawns." Eng. might say "caught napping." The word appears only here in Latin literature.

183 astute! Don. imagines an emphatic gesture and shake of the head to accompany this exclamation.   **carnufex**, lit. "meat-maker." The Latin word for executioner, a loathed profession (cf. Cic. *Rab. Post.* 15), becomes a frequent term of abuse in comedy (also of Davos at 651, 852).

Simo continues to speak aside, but Davos now at least becomes aware of his presence.   **erus**: the slave's customary term for the master, *dominus* being reserved for more general references to the master–slave relationship, e.g. *Ad.* 555 (Syrus speaking) *scire equidem uolo quot mihi sint domini* ("I'd really like to know how many masters I have").   **prouideram**: both the literal and figurative senses are appropriate here.

184 The six changes of speaker as the two play off each other in this one line are remarkable. For the role of meter in establishing the timing for such rapid exchanges, see Marshall 2006: 243–4.   **Daue!** slaves, like free people, are regularly addressed by name in Roman comedy, unlike in Men., where even named slaves are often addressed simply as παῖ ("boy"). *puer* is not used in this general way (Dickey 2002: 235).   **hem**: 116n. Davos, still speaking aside, ignores Simo's summons.   **ehodum**: the interjection (88n.) + *dum*. An imperative is implied, which Davos again ignores.   **quid ais?** 137n. Davos will at last acknowledge his master but pretend to take this colloquial attention-getter literally as a genuine request for information. In treading at the border of insolence, Davos would be acting out the fantasies of any slaves in the audience. The contrast with the obsequious Sosia could not be more pronounced.

185 rumor: Simo withholds the fact that he believes he has seen evidence of Pamphilus' infatuation with his own eyes (129–36).   **id**, i.e. *gnatum amare*. Davos' sarcasm has an edge to it: given his social position, Simo might well think his son's conduct would be a subject of gossip, as in happier days it apparently was (*hac fama impulsus Chremes…*, 99).

186 hocine = *hoc* + -*ce* + *ne*.   **agis** "pay attention" (*id est audis*, Don.), as at Pl. *As.* 1 *hoc agite sultis, spectatores* ("Pay attention to this, spectators, if you please"). Simo does not like to be ignored or to have his concern disregarded.   **istuc**: answering *hocine*, with *ago* understood.   **ea . . . exquirere**: not an ind. statement but an acc. + inf. noun-phrase, the equivalent of "my inquiring into these things," which provides the subj. for the following *est* (*NLS* §25); cf. *Eun.* 1071 *uos non facere inscitast* ("[the fact] that you're not doing it is foolish"). Simo has of course already made such inquiries (83–98) but is now (*nunc*) prepared to let bygones be bygones.

187 quod antehac fecit, i.e. whatever Pamphilus was up to at Chrysis' house. Young men in comedy are permitted, often even expected to sow plenty of wild oats without consequences (to themselves) so long as they turn respectable when eventually called upon. So Micio, in brushing aside the reports of Aeschinus' conduct, *non est flagitium . . . adulescentulum | scortari* *neque potari* (*Ad.* 101–2). Those less accommodating, e.g. Menedemus of *Hau.* and Demea of *Ad.*, would in Simo's terms be *iniqui patres,* and they suffer the consequences of their strictness.

188 tulit "permitted" (*OLD* 21). The verb with this sense is normally unqualified, e.g. 443 *dumque aetas tulit, Hec.* 594 *dum aetatis tempus tulit.*   **siui**: the verb in T. is normally followed by an inf., e.g. 153, 271, or a subjunc. alone, e.g. 165, 622, but *ut* + subjunc. is also found at *Hec.* 590 and *ne* + subjunc. at *Hau.* 90. Pamphilus will acknowledge the truth of this claim at 262–3.

189 hic dies: the day announced for the wedding.   **uitam,** i.e. the circumstances of living (*OLD* 7) and thus readily paired with *mores,* as *Ad.* 758 *hancin uitam! hoscin mores!* Simo expects his son to adjust his behavior to his new condition.   **adfert**: this is the expected verb and found in all MSS of T., but the MSS of Cic., who quotes the line at *Fam.* 12.25.5, read *defert.* OCT prints *defert* in deference to Cic.; the most recent editor of the letters (Shackleton Bailey), in deference to the Terentian MSS, prints *adfert.* T. probably wrote *adfert,* and Cic., quoting from memory, got it wrong.

190 te oro, Daue: a stronger verb than *postulo.* It is a measure of Simo's earnestness that he makes such a request, softened by *siue aequomst,* of his slave.   **in uiam,** sc. *rectam.* Don. calls the expression proverbial.

191 hoc quid sit? sc. *quaeris.* In anticipating Davos' question, Simo substitutes *sit* for what would have been *est* in the notional "original" utterance; cf. *Ad.* 84 *quid fecit?* :: *quid ille fecerit?* Prolepsis is common in such questions (*SEL* I 335).   **omnes . . . grauiter . . . ferunt**: Simo's generalization shows little regard for the bride's perspective on a marriage contracted under such circumstances, but T. is quite capable of representing the other side. Thus Chremes' (admittedly belated) objection to the union at 828–32. The line is metrically striking. Making *quī* in the third foot the first element of a resolved *longum* results in hiatus and a lightening of the syllable: thus the scansion *quĭ ămant.* In addition, though the iambic octonarius commonly features either a caesura in the middle of the fifth foot or diaeresis after the fourth foot (Introduction 5.3.I.B), syntax here suggests a pause in the middle of the *fourth* foot, since *grauiter* must be understood with *ferunt* (cf. 650). As often, a metrical norm yields to the demands of sense (Questa 2007: 350–1).

192 ita aiunt: studiously non-committal. So too Pamphilus at 321 *hodie uxorem ducis?* :: *aiunt.*   **tum**: in introducing a further consideration (*OLD*

9), Simo takes an indirect approach to Davos' feigned ignorance.   **magistrum**: 54n.   **ad eam rem**, i.e. affairs of the heart.   **improbum**: delayed for effect, as if Simo is choosing his words with care. It is a much gentler term than *sceleratus* (154), not to mention *mala mens, malus animus* (164).

193 ipsum "on its own" (*OLD* 7), i.e. without an honest guide.   **aegrotum** "lovesick," as at 559, *Hau.* 100. Don. nevertheless claims that *aegrotum* is, properly speaking, said of the body, *aeger* of the mind. Love as a sickness (νόσος / *morbus*) is something of a comic cliché (Flury 1968: 88–9, Fantham 1972: 14–18).   **ad deteriorem partem** "for the worse."   **applicat**: subj. is the *magister improbus*.

194 hercle: the oath, functionally an emphatic particle, is among the most common in T. Like *mehercle*, it is used only by men: *in ueteribus scriptis neque mulieres Romanae per Herculem deiurant neque uiri per Castorem* (Gell. 11.6.1). See Maltby 1985: 115–17, Müller 1997: 139–42.   **hem!** here probably a snort of annoyance or incredulity (*interiectio est irascentis*, Don.), but Davos continues to feign ignorance.   **non Oedipus**: the story of Oedipus and the Sphinx was familiar to Roman audiences (e.g. Pl. *Poen.* 443–4). Being likened to a riddling monster would only add to Simo's exasperation.

195 nempe . . . uis "so you want . . ." (*OLD* 2b).   **aperte . . . loqui**, i.e. not in "riddles." The mild hyperbaton puts some emphasis on *aperte*.   **quidem**: emphatic, much like so-called μέν solitarium (Solodow 1978: 94–6).

196–8 The music abruptly stops to introduce Simo's threat. This is the first of five short reversions to iambic speech (the others come at 226, 318, 486, 497–8) marking significant turns of direction, a kind of metrical punctuation (Moore 2013: 92–3). The deliberate pace, as Don. notes, makes the threat seem almost to blaze out (*sic pronuntiatur ut <in> singulis uerbis ardeant minae*).

196 si sensero: though the protasis of a factual condition referring to the future will naturally be in the fut. perf., the apodosis may be either fut., as here (*dedam*, 199), or pres. with future force, as at 565 (*qui scis . . . nisi periclum feceris?*). Simo's emphasis creates a tightly interlocked word order: understand *si sensero te hodie quicquam fallaciae in his nuptiis conari . . .*   **hodie**: here, as at 866, Simo probably means lit. "today," but *hodie* in threats is often little more than an emphatic particle (*OLD* 3). Thus Don. ad *Ad.* 215 *hodie non tempus significat, sed iracundam eloquentiam ac stomachum.*

197 quo . . . minus: instrumental *quo* with the comparative creates the equivalent of *ne* to introduce neg. purpose (*NLS* §150). Cf. 700. It is not yet quite the conjunction *quominus* that later Latin used to introduce clauses of prevention. The expression must have puzzled Don.'s students, for he glosses *quominus <fiant>impediturum.*

198 callidus: the *vox propria* for the comic slave, *qui exercet dolos* (Don. ad *Ad.* 417). Thus Simo at 583 *quod uolgus seruorum solet, dolis ut me deluderes.* The term, along with its attendant values, is common in Pl. (*Am.* 268, *As.* 257, *Bac.* 643, *Epid.* 428, *Per.* 455, *Ps.* 385, 725), but appears elsewhere in T. with this sense only at *Eun.* 1011 (of Parmeno, ironically) and *Ph.* 591 (of the parasite Phormio, *callidiorem neminem*). Ironic, even metatheatrical overtones are likely here as Simo seeks to deny Davos his traditional role (Sharrock 2009: 143–5).

199 The music resumes with Simo's specific threat made here in the apodosis.   **in pistrinum**: lit. donkey's work (as depicted on the tomb of the baker Eurysaces in Rome), to be chained to a mill and made to rotate the millstone was one of the most savage of slave punishments and for a household slave like Davos would amount to a death sentence. Cf. the horrific scene described by Apul. *Met.* 9.11–13. The frequent references to the mill in Pl., e.g. *Mos.* 17, *Poen.* 827, *Ps.* 494, 499, probably lie behind the story that having lost his fortune, he was himself consigned to work at a mill (Gell. 3.3.14).   **dedam**: 63n. Don., at pains to distinguish *dare* (*quod repetas*) and *dedere* (*ad perpetuum*), says *damus etiam amicis, dedimus tantum hostibus.* There is certainly an air of finality to Simo's threat.   **usque ad necem**: added almost as an afterthought, to be taken with *uerberibus caesum.* Having warmed to his task, Simo piles on the details.

200 ea lege atque omine: *lege*, says Don., *ad homines, omine ad rem diuinam.* Barsby treats the phrase as a hendiadys ("on the solemn condition"), but Simo clearly adds words to add weight to the threat. Thus Ashmore, "on these terms and with this assurance."   **ut . . . molam**: a stipulative clause with subjunc. after *lege*. Cf. Pl. *Mos.* 360 *sed ea lege ut offigantur bis pedes, bis bracchia* ("but on the condition that both feet and both hands be bound"). *molo* is the *vox propria* for working at a mill, e.g. *Ph.* 249 (heading a list of slave punishments) *molendum esse in pistrino.*   **pro te** "in your place."

201 quid? "well?" A common start to an impatient question or set of short questions (*OLD* s.v. *quis*[1] 10, Müller 1997: 48). Cf. American "What, me worry?" representing "an incredulous comment on a previously mentioned proposition" (Lambrecht 2001: 1061).   **intellexti**: 151n.   **nondum**

. . . ne . . . quidem: an emphatic double negative.   **callide**: a wry, borderline insolent echo of *callidus* above (198), as is *aperte* just below (202).

202 ita: 173n.   **ipsam rem**: no longer just Pamphilus' marriage, as at 198, but now the risk of being sent to the mill.   **locutu' s**: an example of prodelision, with apocope of the final *-s* of *locutus*. For second person contraction, see Pezzini 2015: 90–4.   **usus es**: Don. preserves a variant reading *usor*, an otherwise unattested agent noun of *utor*, i.e. "you're not one for beating around the bush."

203 ubiuis "in any [other] matter" (*OLD* c).   **passus sim**: there is no discernible difference between a potential subjunc. in the perf. and one in the pres., e.g. Pl. *Truc.* 349 *ego istos qui nunc me culpant confutauerim* but *Ba.* 149 *ut te usurpem lubens!* The perf. in this construction, most familiar from *faxim* and *ausim*, is usually described as aoristic (*SEL* I 202–3, *NLS* §119).   **deludier**: the pres. pass. inf. in *-ier* was already an archaism by the later third century (Karakasis 2005: 51–2, Clackson and Horrocks 2007: 100, Weiss 2020: 474). In Pl. and T. it is generally confined to line-ends, the only exceptions in T. being *Hec.* 827 and *Ad.* 535.

204 bona uerba should be words of good omen (*OLD* s.v. *bonus* 17b), as if to counter the ill-omened *me deludier.* Eng. in that case might say something like "Heaven forbid!" The expression is, however, ambiguous: Davos could be understood to be wishing that Simo's words come true.   **quaeso**: here a word of exaggerated politeness, certainly spoken ironically, as Simo's *irrides?* shows (Müller 1997: 97–8).   **nil me fallis**: a lit. translation of what Don. preserves of Men.'s original line, νῦν δ' οὐ λεληθάς με (fr. 33 K–T). See Appendix II. In his eagerness to avoid being fooled by Davos, Simo will instead fool himself, as Davos later observes (*hic se ipsus fallit, haud ego*, 495).

205 ne . . . facias: both the pres. and the perf. subjunc. are used in prohibitions; cf. Pl. *Epid.* 148 *ne feceris.*   **neque . . . haud**: the negatives, commonly separated by a word, strengthen each other, e.g. Pl. *Bac.* 1037 *neque ego haud committam*, *Men.* 371 *neque id haud inmerito tuo.* See Lindsay 1907: 131. Editors therefore print *haud* here, adopted from Don., over MSS *hoc*, though this is the only example of a double neg. in T.

    With one last threat (*caue!*), Simo exits . . . but in which direction? His command to Sosia at 171 (*i prae, sequar*) seems to mandate an entry into his house, but his return at 404 appears to be from the forum, where he encountered Pamphilus (253–4) and attracted the notice of Charinus' slave, Byrria (414). That would require an exit here in that direction, since an exit into the house and subsequent reappearance from the forum would be a serious violation of dramatic practice, which almost without exception shows consistency in the staging of exits and returns to the stage (Duckworth 1952: 119–20).

[I.iii] Davos (206–27)

Now alone, Davos urges himself to greater effort – but accomplishes very little. He neither develops the theme of urgency as his Plautine counterparts Libanus (*Asinaria*) and Acanthio (*Mercator*) do, nor does he seize the opportunity to announce some great counterstroke in the manner of a Chrysalus (*Bac.* 925–78) or Pseudolus (*Ps.* 574–93). At 209 his self-address turns almost imperceptibly into an appeal to the audience for sympathy, and at 215 he slips from deliberation to direct exposition for their benefit. Spectators may well begin to wonder what kind of *callidus* this Davos will turn out to be.

206 enimuero: 91n. Don. hears a note of anxiety in the adv.   **Daue:** self-address with encouragement to greater action is something of a comic convention, e.g. Pl. *As.* 249, *Mer.* 112; *Hau.* 668–78. (The self-address of Syrus at *Ad.* 763, introduced in similar terms, is self-congratulatory.)   **segnitiae atque socordiae:** probably heard as dat., as at 601 (*nil preci loci*) and *Ph.* 547 (*nullus locus preci*), though T. also writes *obiurgandi locus* (154). *segnitia* implies lack of energy, *socordia* lack of will. Cf. Pl. *As.* 253 *quin tu aps te socordiam omnem reice et segnitiem amoue* ("why not shake off all sluggishness and rid yourself of sloth").

207 quantum adv. "so far as" (*OLD* s.v.) Davos from the outset reveals some limit to his understanding of Simo's plans.

208 quae = *nuptiae*, though in effect, "the situation."   **astu:** abl. of *astus* ("cunning") functions as an adv. Cf. *astute* (183).   **erum,** i.e. *Pamphilum*, as the context makes clear. (Simo is called Davos' *erus* at 183, 846). When required, the distinction between "master" and "young master" is made by saying *erilis filius* (= τρόφιμος), as at 602, or *erilis filius minor* (*Eun.* 289).   **pessum dabunt** "it will sink," lit. "send to the bottom" (*OLD* s.v. *pessum* c).

209 certumst "settled" (*OLD* 2b), always an impersonal construction. The dependent question (*quid agam*) is then specified by a second such question. (*-ne . . . an*).   **auscultem** "obey" (*OLD* 2).

210 illum, i.e. *Pamphilum.*   **uitae:** dat., the construction distinguishing fear *for* something from a thing feared (*minas*). Whether Pamphilus in

his despair might actually be thought capable of taking his own life could
be doubted, but the unsuccessful lover's threat of suicide is a comic convention, e.g. Pl. *Cist.* 639–41, *Mer.* 469–73, *Ps.* 89–90 (Flury 1968: 78–81,
Dutsch 2012).

211 uerba dare "to hoodwink" (*OLD uerbum* 6), a colloquial expression,
words being thought inherently unreliable: *decipere est eum, qui cum rem
exspectet, nihil inueniet praeter uerba* (Don. ad *Eun.* 24). Davos presumably
speaks from experience; cf. Simo's allusion to past encounters, 159–
63.   **primum**: to be followed by *hoc etiam* (215).   **comperit**: normally
constructed with an acc. obj. (90) or a clause (145–6). The reference is to
Simo's discovery at the funeral of Chrysis (135–6).

212 infensus "relentless" (*OLD* 2), here used adverbially, as adj. representing states of mind often are (*NLS* §88n.), e.g. *Ph.* 236 *inuitus feci* ("I acted
unwillingly"), *Ad.* 711 . . . *ne forte inprudens faciam quod nolit: sciens cauebo*
("... so I don't by chance do something he doesn't like. I'll be deliberately
careful.").   **seruat** "keep watch on" (*OLD* 2).   **quam** = *aliquam.*

213 senserit, sc. *fallaciam.*   **perii** "I'm done for." The perf. describing
a state that carries into the pres. easily extends to the future, especially
in the apodosis of a condition, e.g. Pl. *Am.* 320 *perii, si me aspexerit*; T.
Eu. 1064–5 *si te in platea offendero . . . periisti.* Given the severity of Simo's
threat, the stock comic expression of despair gains a certain edge.   **aut
si lubitum fuerit** "or if he [just] feels like it." The owner's power over a
slave was, for most practical purposes, unlimited. This alternative possibility (some editors prefer to bracket *aut*) offers wry acknowledgment that
Simo could take this action even without evidence of *fallacia*.   **causam**
"pretext" (*OLD* 5).   **ceperit**: the fut. perf. in a main clause is rare and
often difficult to explain. The logic here seems to be that Simo must first
have settled on the pretext before he can take the action. For the linguistic problem of the tense choice, see de Melo 2007: 21–50.

214 quo iure quaque iniuria "whether rightly or wrongly." Don. calls the
expression proverbial.   **praecipitem**, sc. *me.* Davos appears to be rattled
by Simo's threat.

215–24 The music stops. Exposition is conventionally presented in spoken verse, and so it is here as Davos provides information that Simo does
not (yet) know. He is at this point clearly addressing the audience, not
simply reviewing the situation in his own mind.

215 mi accedit: Davos, mindful of his role as *callidus*, readily makes
Pamphilus' troubles his own.   **etiam** "in addition" (*OLD* 3).

216 ista: the word may include an element of disapproval or distaste, e.g. of Ctesipho's *psaltria* at *Ad.* 388, 558, but there is clearly no such connotation at 483, *fac ista ut lauet.*   **uxor**: Pamphilus wants to think of her this way (273), though *amica* is closer to the truth of the situation at this point. See 295n. Both nouns are predicative.   **grauida**: the chronology of Glycerium's pregnancy is unclear. At Chrysis' funeral some weeks before – it would require at least a few weeks for the news of her death to reach Andros and bring her kinsman Crito to Athens to settle her estate (795–816) – Pamphilus was able to grab her around the waist to pull her from the pyre (133), behavior hardly suggesting a woman in an advanced state of pregnancy, yet she will soon give birth (473). Nor does Simo, who was watching her closely then, have any reason to believe she can be in childbirth now (474–5). T. seems untroubled by the oddity (close reading of *Hec.* reveals an analogous problem), but it has not gone unnoticed by critics (Scafuro 1997: 366–9; for *Hec.*, Goldberg 2013: 203–4).

217 eorum audaciam: Davos implies that the couple working together has concocted this tale. *audacia* frequently has a negative connotation in T., e.g. *Eu.* 958 *qua audacia / tantum facinus audet?*   **operae pretium** "worth the trouble" (*OLD pretium* 2b). The expression has a very long history, solemnized by Ennius (*audire est operae pretium procedere recte, / qui rem Romanam . . . augescere uoltis, Ann.* 494–5 Sk.), parodied by Hor. (*audire est operae pretium procedere recte / qui moechis non uultis, S.* 1.2.37–8), and everything in between. It is especially common as an introductory formula (Fraenkel 1957: 81–2).

218 inceptio: the verbal noun, which normally means "a beginning," here must mean "an undertaking" (thus *OLD* 2). Cf. 925 *fabulam inceptat!*   **amentium, haud amantium**: an easy pun in Latin, e.g. Pl. *Mer.* 82 *amens amansque.* Verbal play of this sort, common in Pl., is comparatively rare in T. Examples in Duckworth 1952: 350–6. Throughout this passage, Davos implies a relationship both longstanding and consensual.

219 quidquid peperisset, i.e. regardless of whether male or female, a decision that surprised Don. The exposure of unwanted children, especially girls, is a common theme in comedy, e.g. Posidippus fr. 12 *PCG* υἱὸν τρέφει πᾶς κἂν πένης τις ὢν τύχη / θυγατέρα δ' ἐκτίθησι κἂν ᾖ πλούσιος ("a son everyone raises, even if he happens to be poor, but a daughter he exposes, even if he is rich"); *Hau.* 625–6 (Sostrata to her husband, Chremes) *meministi me grauidam et mihi te maxumo opere edicere, / si puellam parerem, nolle tolli?* (Allusions to the practice also at *Hec.* 400, *Ph.* 647.) The frequency of exposure in real life, and thus the relationship of dramatic convention to actual practice, remains controversial. See Patterson 1985: 115–16

(Greece), Harris 1994: 3–11 and Carroll 2018: 174–7 (Rome), Scafuro 1997: 272–8 (comedy and myth).   **decreuerunt**: a verb of strong resolution and most often a manifestation of power. Thus the despairing Pamphilus, *uxorem decrerat [pater] dare sese mi hodie* (238).   **tollere**: the technical term for acknowledging a legitimate child, a reference to the father's literal act of picking up the new-born infant (*OLD* 2).

220 fingunt: a colorful verb of invention; cf. 334 *facite, fingite, inuenite, efficite*.   **quandam . . . fallaciam**: Davos inevitably thinks in terms of schemes and dismisses out of hand a story that Glycerium, who never forgot her true identity (945–6), knows to be the truth.

221 ciuem Atticam esse: this would solve Pamphilus' problem at a stroke. In Menander's Athens, a legal marriage required both parties to be citizens, and marriage was the easiest way to resolve the awkwardness of an ill-timed pregnancy (Todd 1993: 177–9, Scafuro 1997: 211–16).   **fuit olim**: like Eng. "once upon a time." The caesura after *hanc* creates in delivery an effect much like the editor's quotation marks as Davos affects, without benefit of *aiunt* or other preamble, the voice and manner of his young charge. Slipping into direct speech in the course of a narrative (*ad mimeticum transit*, Don.) was a favorite comic technique (e.g. *Hec.* 131, 148, *Ad.* 60–3 and above, 134n.). The simplicity of the narrative that follows reflects Davos' disdain for the invention, while the alternation of end-stopped and run-on lines seems calculated to bring the senarii as close as possible to the language of prose. (For the sentence structure, see Goldberg 1986: 44–6.)

222 nauem . . . fregit "was shipwrecked" (*OLD* 1c), an idea more logically expressed either by a passive construction, e.g. Pl. *Rud.* 505 *pol minime miror nauis si fractast tibi* or by the cognate noun, e.g. Vitr. 6 Prf. 1 *Aristippus . . . naufragio cum eiectus ad Rhodiensium litus . . .*

223 obiit mortem: a common expression (e.g. Pl. *Aul.* 15; *Hau.* 271, *Ph.* 1019; Cic. *Brut.* 78), though *obiit* can carry the meaning alone, e.g. Lucr. 3.1042 *ipse Epicurus obit*. The quotation ends here, as it began, with a metrical pause as Davos returns to his own voice and completes the narrative as an indirect statement.   **ibi tum**: 106n.   **hanc eiectam**: the necessary inference in this highly compressed narrative is that the merchant was traveling with a young child, who survived the shipwreck. A fuller version will be provided by the Andrian Crito at 923–36.

224 paruam: she would thus be too young to recognize any of her Attic relatives, as Don. notes in a fit of rationality.   **fabulae!** "stories!" with the further idea of nonsense (*OLD* 3). Cf. Simo's response to Crito's account at 925, *fabulam inceptat*. It is purely a term of dismissal at *Hau.* 336 (*uera causast.* :: *fabulae!*), but here the literal and colloquial senses combine to create a moment laced with ironies. Davos will prove to be an unreliable as well as over-confident narrator: the story is actually true, not a *fallacia* invented by the young couple but an account Pamphilus heard directly from Glycerium (923–46). Neither Davos nor Simo recognizes the truth of this when he hears it, and each of them is ultimately stymied not by the other, but by the eventual revelation of that truth. Further, since the implications of Davos' narrative would be immediately obvious to an audience steeped in comic conventions, the spectators enjoy from early on a knowledge superior to that of the ostensible *seruus callidus*. And finally, since *fabula* is also T.'s word for a play (3, 16: then *Hec.* 1, *Eu.* 23, 25, 33, *Ph.* 4, *Ad.* 7), it is hard to avoid hearing an unwitting, metatheatrical reference to the artificialities of the genre. Sharrock 2009: 145–50 explores the resulting interplay of fact and fiction, understanding and misunderstanding, confidence and overconfidence.

225 Davos rounds off his monologue with a return to accompanied octonarii.   **mĭquidem**: enclitic *quidem* causes the preceding long vowel to be shortened, a process called enclisis (Questa 2007: 153–7).   **atque** "and yet" (*OLD* 9).   **ipsis**, i.e. Pamphilus and Glycerium. It is striking how Davos thinks of them throughout as a couple.   **commentum** "fiction" (*OLD* 2), in Davos' vocabulary, a synonym for *fabula* and *fallacia*.

226 Stage doors were notoriously noisy, their creaking and banging as they open to admit a new character often, though not invariably, noticed in the script either by *(con)crepuit*, e.g. Pl. *Am.* 496, *Bac.* 234; *Hec.* 521, *Eu.* 1029, or simply by acknowledging the sound, e.g. Pl. *Mil.* 1377 *hinc sonitum fecerunt fores* (so too in tragedy, e.g. Accius 29R/244W *sed ualuae resonunt regiae*). T. provides the expected cue for Mysis' entrance at 682. In the present case, an (unscripted) commotion at the door of Glycerium's house is sufficient to stop the music and attract the attention of Davos, who must turn to see the emerging figure before delivering this line as Mysis' entrance cue. For the convention, see Duckworth 1952: 116–17 and for its Greek precedent, Bader 1971.

sed: the conj. used to interrupt a previous line of thought (*OLD* 2a) is common in introducing an entrance formula (e.g. 174, 682, *Hec.* 521, *Ph.* 840). Menander used ἀλλὰ γάρ and καὶ γάρ in a similar way (Frost 1988: 5–6).   **Mysis**: an ethnic slave name, like Syrus/Syra (i.e. "the Syrian"). Mysia was a region of Asia Minor abutting the south shore of the Sea of Marmara.   **ab ea**, sc. *Glycerio*. The maid attends Glycerium so closely that, while the expression may stand loosely for *ab aedibus Glycerii* (cf. *Hau.* 510 *a me nescioquis exit* "somebody is coming out of my house"), a more direct, personal reference well suits the situation.   **me**, sc. *conferam*.   **ut**: Davos' resolution comes as something of an anticlimax. To do nothing more than warn Pamphilus of his father's suspicions is hardly an advance on the *segnitia* and *socordia* he began by renouncing, and as it turns out, Simo encounters him first. This decision, clearly articulated here for the audience's benefit, is emphasized by the return of the music.

[I.iv] Mysis (228–35)

The pregnant Glycerium is in fact going into labor as her maid Mysis emerges from the house to fetch a midwife. Mysis' first words are spoken back inside, a common device in both Greek and Roman comedy to hint at life beyond the narrow confines of the stage (Duckworth 1952: 125–6; Frost 1988: 7–8). Archylis, the addressee, need not be visible to the audience, and by 229 Mysis must have turned to speak directly to them, since her private opinion of Lesbia is clearly not intended for Archylis' ears.

Mysis' entrance is set apart from the preceding scene by a shift from iambic to trochaic rhythm, but the music will shift back again to iambics at 234 to signal the long-awaited appearance of Pamphilus, prefiguring the metrical variations that will come to characterize the following scene.

228 Archylis: the name, derived from ἄρχω ("to lead"), suggests a woman of some authority in the household. Thus *iubes*.   **iamdudum**: Don. was unsure whether to understand the adv. with *audiui* or with *iubes*; with a perf. verb it means "some time ago" (*OLD dudum* 1b), with a pres. it means "for a long time now" (*OLD dudum* 2b). The characteristic diaeresis after the fourth foot of this septenarius encourages the reading *audiui iamdudum* reflected in the punctuation here.   **Lesbiam**: the midwife. The drunkenness and unsteadiness attributed to her are stereotypical of old women in comedy, e.g. the *uinosissuma* Leana of Pl. *Curc.* 77 *multibiba atque merobiba* and the *anus* similarly bribed with a vat of wine at *Cist.* 541–2. Her very name, says Don. ad 226, suggests these traits, since Lesbos was known for the quality of its wine. A fragment of Menander's *Perinthia* describes comparable behavior at a drinking party: οὐδεμίαν ἡ γραῦς ὅλως | κύλικα παρῆκεν, ἀλλ᾿ ἔπιε τὴν ἐν κύκλῳ ("the old woman not once passed up a single cup but drank from it at every round," fr. 5 Körte/4 Sandbach). Whether this old woman is the midwife of *Perinthia*, however, remains uncertain. Midwives were generally well trained and well compensated professionals (French 1986: 71–3), and at 459 and again at 481, T.'s Lesbia shows no sign of either drunkenness or incompetence.

229 pol: colloquial *pol* (as also *edepol*), in origin an oath by Pollux, functions here as an emphatic particle after *sane*. It is an expression favored by Mysis (also at 459, 770, 778, 790, 803, 817) and comes to characterize female speech in T. (Adams 1984: 50–3; Müller 1997: 142–3), though in *An.* Pamphilus uses it at 320, Crito at 808, and Simo at 866.   **temulenta**: of a woman also at *Eun.* 655, *uinolentus* of a man at *Ph.* 1017, though any gender distinction does not continue into later Latin; so Cic. *Sest.* 20 *temulentus* of the consul A. Gabinius.   **temeraria** "thoughtless" (*OLD* 3) and thus unreliable, a significant deficiency in a midwife.

230 primo partu: a first pregnancy might be especially difficult. Mysis indicates both her genuine concern for Glycerium and the fact that her young charge was a *uirgo* before meeting Pamphilus.

231 spectate: the verb is a clear indication that Mysis is addressing the audience directly.   **aniculae**: the dimin. of *anus*, here used in a disparaging way.

232 compotrix: not otherwise found in classical Latin, though Cic. twice uses the masc. equivalent *compotor* contemptuously of Antony's entourage (*Phil.* 2.42, 5.22).   **eius**, i.e. of Archylis.   **obsecro**: like Eng. "please," often simply an expression of politeness (Adams 1984: 55–8, Müller 1997: 100–1, Barrios-Lech 2016: 117–18), here comes closer to its ritual sense of entreaty (*OLD* 1b). It is frequently used by Mysis to soften a request (721, 725, 747, 781, 800) and in T. is largely a female expression, the male equivalent being *quaeso*.

233 huic, i.e. Glycerium, recipient of the *facultatem*.   **illi**, i.e. Lesbia, recipient of the *locum*.   **in aliis** "when dealing with other [women]" (*OLD* s.v. *in* 42).   **locum** "opportunity" (*OLD* 14).

234 The shift in rhythm, accompanied as at 226 by *sed*, ends the monologue proper with the cue for another entrance.

quidnam: the particle strengthens the interrogative, e.g. "why, then . . ." (*OLD* 7b; Müller 1997: 76–7). Cf. *numquidnam* just below, *quidnamst* at 321.   **exanimatum**: 131n.   **siet**: archaic forms of the pres. subjunc. (*siem, sies, siet*) generally occur at line end, probably for metrical convenience. They appear within the line only twice in T. (*Hec.* 637, *Ad.* 83).

235 turba "commotion," referring to Pamphilus' upset state. Cf. *Eun.* 947 (responding to an impassioned outburst) *quae illaec turbast?*   **tristitiae** "unhappiness," (*OLD* 1), part. gen. with *numquidnam*.   **afferat**: since early Latin did not invariably employ the subjunc. in an ind. quest., it here may have some potential force, i.e. "may bring" (*SEL* I 326–7). Elision of gen. *-ae* is unusual, leading Leo 1912: 353 to suggest reading *ferat*.

[I.v] Pamphilus, Mysis (236–300)

Mysis retreats to one side as Pamphilus enters from the forum, where he encountered his father and was informed (peremptorily, to judge from his account at 254) that the marriage to Chremes' daughter is once again in prospect. Mysis will voice her dismay at this news in a series of asides (237, 240, 251, 264–5) before being recognized by Pamphilus, who assures her of his unfailing loyalty to Glycerium.

Unlike Pl., who regularly built songs around runs of anapaests, bacchiacs, and cretics as well as iambo-trochaic rhythms, T. creates an impressive musical entrance for Pamphilus entirely of iambs and trochees. The scene is no less effective for that, its emotional charge created by rhetorical flourishes like anaphora (236) and chiasmus (239–40) and enhanced by rapid shifts between long iambic and trochaic lines punctuated at intervals by dimeters (240, 244, 252) to mark changes in the direction of his thought. Pamphilus' extended declaration of loyalty then gains added point by the sudden end to the music as he explains himself in *senarii* (270–98).

The dramaturgy of the scene is much discussed, especially the role of Mysis, whose continued presence is sometimes thought to be a Terentian innovation. Though her speaking part is certainly small, Don. believed she made a major contribution by firming Pamphilus' resolve to resist his father's plans for a marriage (ad 236), an ability he ascribed to her characteristically female *calliditas* (ad 265, 268, 281). See Brown 2012, and for T.'s musical innovation in the scene, Denzler 1968: 119–21, Moore 2013: 93–7.

236 humanum: the *humanum* (Menander's ἀνθρώπινος) distinguishes people from beasts or insensate things (e.g. *Hec.* 214 *me omnino lapidem, non hominem putas*). What then constitutes conduct befitting a human being becomes a recurring theme in T., e.g. *Hec.* 86, 214, 499, 553; *Hau.* 99, 1046; *Eu.* 880; *Ad.* 145, 471, 687, as it was in Men. before him, e.g. *Asp.* 164, *Mis.* 302, *Perik.* 137, *Sa.* 17–22, fr. 650 K–T, *Asp.* 395, *Dys.* 105, *Sa.* 35. Since it is a sensibility hard to parallel in Pl. (*Mer.* 319 and *Most.* 814 come the closest), T. is often credited with introducing this concern to the Romans (Haffter 1953: 96–100, Bianco 1962: 226–33, Ludwig 1968: 180), but there is often something slightly off kilter about his moralizers. Thus the most famous declaration of Terentian *humanitas*, *Hau.* 77 *homo sum: humanum nil a me alienum puto*, excuses a busybody who will later be justly faulted as *iniquos* (1011) and for acting *nimis inhumane* (1045). Here in *An.*, the moral sensibility may be undercut by what, seen from a different perspective, appears to be largely a reflection of Pamphilus' self-centeredness. **factu aut inceptu** "to do or [even] to conceive." The inverted order reflects Pamphilus' agitated indignation. The supine in -*u* appears in a wider variety of expressions than in later Latin, where it is largely restricted to a more limited number of adjectives (*SEL* I 457, *NLS* §153). The form is in origin probably a fourth declension dative like *neglectu* (*Hau.* 357) and *uestitu* (*Ad.* 63). See Weiss 2020: 472–3. The text follows Don. The MSS read *factum aut inceptum.*   **officium**: 114n.

237 illud: Mysis, commenting aside, responds as much to the alarming tone as to the substance of Pamphilus' words. The momentary change of rhythm emphasizes her dismay and prefigures the metrical alternations to come. (Note, however, that without iambic shortening the line becomes another octonarius, which would continue the iambic sequence until 241.)   **pro deum fidem**: as an interjection in this (and similar) expressions, *pro* does not govern the case of what follows, e.g. with voc. *pro Iuppiter* (732). The acc. in this set phrase was probably heard as exclamatory, but a verb might be supplied, as in the noteworthy comic expansion of Caecilius, *Synephebi* 211–12R (201–2W) *pro deum popularium omnium omnium adulescentium | clamo postulo obsecro oro ploro atque inploro fidem.* The archaic gen. *deum* becomes fixed in this formulaic phrase: Cic. *de Or.* 155–6 complains of modernizers, who prefer to say *pro deorum fidem* and the like.   **contumeliast**: this is, as structured, the noun that explains *hoc* in 236, though Pamphilus seems more intent on venting his indignation and despair than identifying its cause. Ill treatment of a wife (*Ph.* 972, *Hec.* 165), of a friend (*Hau.* 566), or even a *meretrix* (*Eu.* 48, 865, 877) may be called *contumelia*, but the word is not commonly used to describe a father's treatment of his son.

238 decrerat: 219n., and for the betrothal formula *uxorem dare*, 101n.

238–9 nonne oportuit | . . . ante? "Shouldn't I have known about it beforehand?" *oportuit* is normally constructed with a pres. inf. (*NLS* §123 n. i), e.g. *Ph.* 70 *regem me esse oportuit* ("I should have been a nabob!"). The perf. inf., together with the redundant *ante*, simply emphasizes that the action mentioned did not happen, e.g. *Eu.* 981–2 *oportuit | rem praenarasse me* ("I should have told you about it earlier."). So too with the impers. *communicatum [esse].* See *SEL* I 427–8.

240 uerbum: here a connected utterance, not simply a single word (*OLD* 10); cf. *Ad.* 952 *nunc meum illud uerbum facio . . .* ("Now I make my own that saying . . ."); *Ph.* 342 *quid istuc uerbist?* ("What kind of expression is that?"). Contrast 256, *uerbum ullum* "a single word." Mysis fears that Pamphilus may be compelled to accept a different wife. Her iambic dimeter rounds off the first part of Pamphilus' impassioned song. A shift to predominantly trochaic rhythms will mark the change of subject in the second part.

241 quid? 201n. Pamphilus now turns his thought to his prospective father-in-law.   **denegarat**: Simo reported this decision in similar terms at 144–9.

242 mutauit . . . immutatum: this type of word-play, a kind of *figura ety-mologica*, is found as early as Liv. Andron., e.g. *ornamento incedunt gnobilid ignobiles* (3 R), and becomes a frequent ornament of dramatic diction, especially in accompanied verse. See Haffter 1934: 10–43 (17–23 for Terentian examples), Wills 1996: 248–53. *mutauit* is a true perf. indicating past action continuing into the pres., while pluperf. *denegarat* represents an action completed at a prior time, e.g. *Eun.* 654 *uirginem quam erae dono dederat miles uitiauit* (*SEL* I 48–9). To his credit, Pamphilus' loyalty to Glycerium remains *immutatum* throughout, however pusillanimous his conduct may on occasion be.

243 miserum: predicative. Pamphilus implies, somewhat egotistically, that Chremes' purpose in dragging him from Glycerium is to make him *miser*. Such self-centeredness is a trait he shares with his father (e.g. 112).

244 pereo: like *miser*, part of the comic lover's traditional vocabulary, e.g. Pl. *Ps.* 300 *ita miser et amore pereo*. The pres. referring to future time is common in such conditions, e.g. *Ph.* 201–2 *quod si eo meae fortunae redeunt, Phanium, abs te ut destrahar,* | *nullast mihi uita expetenda*. See *SEL* I 65.

245 adeon hominum esse inuenustum: the exclamatory inf., more frequent in T. than in Pl., appears to be colloquial, largely restricted to expressions of annoyance or regret (*SEL* I 423–5, Palmer 1961: 318).   **inuenus-tum**: the adj. commonly means "unattractive" or "ungainly," but here must mean something like "unlucky in love." T. may have derived that sense from Menander, e.g. ἀναφρόδιτης εἰμί τις ("I'm someone unsuccessful in love," *Phasma* 84).

247 ego: the enclitic prn. serves to emphasize *nullo*. For the phenomenon, see Adams 1994: 141–51.   **Chremetis**: Gk. gen. (Χρέμητος), but Lat. *Chremi* at 368. Similarly, Lat. acc. *Chremem* at 361, *Chremetem* at 472, 533. Lack of standardization in the treatment of Greek proper names provides convenient metrical options.   **affinitatem**: a connection by marriage, constructed here (as often) with a gen. of the person with whom the alliance is made. Latin regularly distinguishes *affines* (in-laws) from *cognati* (blood relatives). Pamphilus will in the end seek precisely this connection.

248 contemptus, spretus! Pamphilus, characteristically, thinks of the arranged marriage first off as an insult to himself.   **facta trans-acta omnia** "signed, sealed, and delivered." Don. says the phrase was

proverbial.   **em**: in origin the truncated imper. of *emere* ("to take"), this
demonstrative adv. often accompanies an emphatic pronoun, e.g. *em tibi!*
("Get that!" *Ph.* 847) or an imper., e.g. *em serua!* ("Hey, watch out!" *Ad.*
172), but may by itself indicate indignation and surprise, e.g. *Hec.* 63 *em
duxit!* ("Well, guess what! He married!"). That seems to be the sense here.
See Luck 1964: 62, Müller 1997: 115-17.

249 nisi si: a colloquial pleonasm equivalent to *nisi* alone (*OLD* 7).
nescio may be understood, the sense being, "I don't know why, unless
perhaps . . ." Cf. 671 *nisi si id putas* . . . ("unless you think that . . .").

250 aliquid monstri: why did Chremes change his mind? Pamphilus, who
has never seen Chremes' daughter, imagines she is so ugly he must accept
whatever son-in-law is offered him. While *aliquod monstrum* would itself be
insulting, Don. hears a *duplex contumelia* in the partitive construction, as at
Hec. 643-4 *sed quid mulieris | uxorem habes?* ("What sort of a woman do you
have for a wife?")   **obtrudi**: the Pamphilus of *Hec.*, having yielded to
a similar demand, explains himself in similar terms, *numquam ausus sum
recusare eam quam mi obtrudit pater* (295).

251 itur: perhaps with hostile intent (*OLD* 7), i.e. "They come for me."
Don. cites as parallels Pl. *Ps.* 453 *itur ad te, Pseudole* and Verg. *A.* 9.423-4
ense recluso | ibat in Euryalum.

252 nam: when introducing a question, the particle simply indicates
impatience rather than any logical connection to what precedes (*OLD* 7,
Müller 1997: 76).

253 agere: 245n. *eum* is understood.   **praeteriens**: Pamphilus treats
this as a chance encounter. Thus *neglegenter* ("casually").

254-5 Direct quotation, doubtless marked in delivery by a change in posture and tone as the speaker assumes the voice of another, again enlivens
the narrative. See 221n.

256 censen = *censesne*, with an indefinite second pers. sing. The verb
with this sense often suggests a mistaken belief, e.g. Pl. *Am.* 134-5 (of
Alcumena, tricked by Jupiter) *illa illum censet uirum | suom esse.*

257 causam "excuse" (*OLD* 5).   **obmutui**: like *obstipui* just above, a confession of helplessness.

258 quod: conj. Contrast 244, where *quod* provides the subj. of *fit*.   **si
ego rescissem**: the apodosis *aliquid facerem* only comes in the next line; in
his agitation, Pamphilus jumbles the order of his thoughts. For the tense
sequence, see de Melo 2007: 75-6.

259 ut . . . ne: a common collocation to introduce negative purpose in Republican Latin, where *ut* is the subordinating conjunc. and *ne* the negating adv. (*OLD* s.v. *ne*¹ 5). So too at 327, 699, 834, 899. Further exx. in *SEL* I 258.

260 diuorsae: *pro in diuersa*, Don. For an adj. used adverbially, qualifying the action of the verb rather than the noun in agreement, cf. Pl. *Merc.* 470 *diuorsus distrahor* and 107 above, *aderat frequens*.

261 huius, i.e. *de Glycerio*. Objective gen., as are the following *nuptiarum* and *patris*.   **sollicitatio** "worry," here the equivalent of *sollicitudo*. Never a common word, *sollicitatio* more often means "incitement." Cf. the distinction between Eng. solicitude and solicitation.

262 pudor: not just a sense of shame, but displeasure with oneself for being found morally deficient. Thus the indulgent father Micio believes *pudor* and *liberalitas* to be more effective tools for child-rearing than *metus* (*Ad.* 57–8). See Kaster 1997: 4–9. The concern does Pamphilus credit: he tempers his annoyance with the acknowledgment that his father has some legitimate moral as well as legal claim on him. These four *curae*, serious and incompatible, quite understandably weigh him down.   **leni . . . animo** = *leniter*. The abl. of *animus* readily combines with an adj. to produce the equivalent of an adv. in phrases like *aequo animo* "fairly" (34) and *animo praesenti* "resolutely" (*Eun.* 769).

263 quae . . . quomque: tmesis (63n.).   **ut aduorser**: the "repudiating question" introduced by *ut* (*OLD* 44) is often found in comedy with or without an introductory *-ne*, e.g. *Eun.* 771, *Ph.* 304, 874; Pl. *Aul.* 690, *Bac.* 375. For the subjunc. in this construction, see Palmer 1961: 311–12, *NLS* §175.   **ei**: 73n.

264 incertumst quid agam: Pamphilus' impassioned outburst ends with a bathetic thud. The *adulescentes* of Roman comedy frequently find themselves similarly *incertus*, e.g. Chaerea (*Eun.* 295), Pamphilus (*Hec.* 121, 450), Antipho (*Hau.* 660).   **quorsus**: a variant of *quorsum*, which is the MSS reading here. Since this leaves the line a syllable short, Bentley solved the problem by emending to *quorsus*. A less elegant solution retains *quorsum* and reads *incertumst* for *incertum*.   **accidat** "may lead" (*OLD* s.v. *accido*¹ 5c). Cf. 127 *quorsum euadas*.

265 peropust: T. readily adds the intensive prefix *per-* to adjs., advs., and verbs, e.g. *pergrauis* (*Hec.* 292), *perbenigne* (*Ad.* 702), *perdoceo* (*Hau.* 361). Its attachment to a noun is unparalleled.   **ipsa**, i.e. Glycerium. For *ipsus/a* as a synonym for *erus/a* (*OLD* s.v. *ipse* 12), cf. 360 *ipsus tristis* ("the master's annoyed"). **aduorsum hunc**: though a slave, Mysis will not hesitate to address Pamphilus directly.

266 paullo momento: *paullum* is more commonly an adv. or substantive, but an adj. also at *Ad.* 876, *paullo sumptu*. Don. understands *momentum* to be the weight that tips the scale (*OLD* 7b). **huc uel illuc**: modern readers may well think of Lesbia's sparrow *circumsiliens modo huc modo illuc* (3.9), but the extant Don. cites Catullus only once, at 718 below.

267 quis hic loquitur? Pamphilus catches something of Mysis' aside and then turns in the direction of her voice. This stock expression, used as a scene moves from overheard monologue to genuine dialogue, is also found in T. at *Eun.* 86, *Hau.* 517, *Ph.* 739, as well as 783 below. The formula has significant Greek precedent, e.g. *CGF* 282.16 τίς ἐστιν ὁ λαλῶν; (Bain 1977: 158–61). Marshall 1999 relates the convention to the requirements of masked performance, where the actor, lacking peripheral vision, can only see what is directly before him and must turn in the direction of the sound to recognize another character. **o salue**: what is the force of the optional interjection, which introduces some 6 percent of T.'s vocatives? Pleasure or surprise are both possible, as Don. notes, though either would of course be feigned. See Müller 1997: 125, Dickey 2002: 225–9. **Pamphilē**: the inevitable pause at the change of speaker lengthens the naturally short vowel (*breuis in longo*), a reminder that scansion generally reflects the dramatic needs of delivery and not the other way around. The chiasmus of the exchanged greeting is a characteristically Terentian elegance. **quid agit?** "How is she?" Glycerium so occupies his thoughts that the subj. need not be expressed.

268 laborat . . . sollicitast: the former verb represents physical distress (*OLD* 6), the latter emotional distress (*OLD* 3). **dolore**: the pain of childbirth, as *Ad.* 289 (of the very pregnant Pamphila) *modo dolores . . . occipiunt*. **ex hoc** anticipates the following *quia*-clause. **diem . . . in hunc**: for *in* + acc. indicating an appointed time (*OLD* 23a), cf. Pl. *Most.* 700 *res parata est mala in uesperum huic seni* ("A bad time has been readied for this old man this evening"). This is the day originally set by Simo and Chremes for the wedding of their children (102).

270–98 Pamphilus' earnestness is emphasized by the turn from song to speech as the *tibicen* ceases to play. His sincerity in these lines is beyond question, his words surely intended to reflect well on him, but here Roman dramatic conventions and modern sensibilities diverge markedly. Even a conservative Roman, mindful that the *adulescens* Pamphilus was in no position to treat any woman *pro uxore*, might nevertheless excuse his youthful exuberance as Davos will purport to do (443–5) and, for example, the strait-laced Hegio of *Adelphoe* does for Aeschinus (470–1). We today may not so readily forget that Pamphilus has gotten an innocent girl pregnant and that her one public response to this condition was an attempt at self-immolation (129–36).

270 hem! 116n. The unelided particle here suggests denial, a stronger response than, e.g., repudiating *quid?* (201n.).   **conari**: Pamphilus would not even attempt to abandon her.

271 propter: causal (*OLD* 5). Cf. *Hec.* 833 *haec tot propter me gaudia illi contigisse laetor* ("I'm glad all these joys came to him through me").   **decipi**: the verbs of deceiving in T. are *fallo* (204, 493, 602, 902) and *deludo* (203, 583). *decipio* is to deprive of an expectation, e.g. *Ph.* 927 *non est aequom me propter uos decipi* ("it's not right that I lose out for your sake").

273 egregie "especially" (*OLD* 2b).   **pro uxore**: so Chremes had heard, though Simo tries hard to believe otherwise (145–53). Pamphilus' confirmation of his serious intent prefigures the clash to come between father and son.   **habuerim**: the subjunc. is likely generic, providing the reason for the declaration made in the main clause (*NLS* §155–6, *SEL* I 292–3), while indic. *credidit* just above and structurally parallel simply makes a statement of fact. The rules governing the use of subjunc. and indic. were in any case fluid in T.'s day (98n.).

274 bene et pudice: at *Hau.* 225–6 it is important to know that Antiphila is, though linked to the hard bitten professional Bacchis, *bene et pudice eductam, ignaram artis meretriciae*. The statement is, in effect, a promise that she will in the end prove to be a suitable wife for Clinia. So here with Glycerium, despite having been raised in Chrysis' household.   **eius . . . ingenium**: a remarkable hyperbaton, the modifiers *doctum, eductum,* and *coactum* being more important than their noun.

275 coactum egestate: as happened to Chrysis in her migration from Andros to Athens, 69–79. Where *paupertas* is essentially a financial condition (*Ph.* 903, *Ad.* 496), *egestas* suggests a broader lack of resources (*Ph.* 733, *Ad.* 303, paired with *inopia* at *Ad.* 104–5).   **immutarier**: 203n.

276 uerear: the tense of the subjunc. was not used in early Latin to distinguish a hypothetical condition in the future from an unrealized one in the present. The pres. subjunc. thus regularly appears in both protasis and apodosis of both types: only later did the pres. subjunc. come to indicate a future condition and the imperf. a condition unrealized in the present (*NLS* §197, *SEL* I 273–4; extended discussion in de Melo 2007: 70–7).

277 uim: i.e. the pressure that Simo may bring to bear, which, given Pamphilus' self-confessed *patris pudor*, seems a real possibility. The scansion *uĭm ŭt* is the result of prosodic hiatus combined with iambic shortening. **ut queas**, sc. *uereor*. Thus *ut* to introduce a negative clause of fearing.

277–80 Pamphilus again waxes rhetorical with parallelism (*adeon . . . adeon*), symmetrical strings of adjs. (*ingratum . . . ferum*) and nouns (*consuetudo . . . pudor*), word-play (*commoueat / commoneat*) and the two chiastically positioned result clauses.

277 ignauom: the adj. means either faint-hearted (*OLD* 3) or ignoble (*OLD* 4). Don. thinks the former: *qui non est perseuerans*.

278 aut inhumanum aut ferum: notably redundant, since the *humanum* in T. is what separates people from beasts (236n.). Pamphilus in his passion does not lack a *copia uerborum*.

279 consuetudo: 110n.   **pudor**: presumably something different from the *patris pudor* of 262. Mysis' intervention appears to have shifted his thoughts entirely towards Glycerium. As Don. observes, *non enim dixit "adeon me obsequentem patri . . ."*

280 commoueat neque commoneat "move or motivate" (Brown). **fidem**: Pamphilus continues to phrase his obligation in terms of Glycerium. *non dixit "ut contemnam patrem"* (Don.).

281 memor sui: the reflexive prn. looks back to *hanc*.

282 essem: another repudiating subjunc. (263n.).   **o Mysis, Mysis**: an emphatic repetition, as at *Eun.* 91, *Hec.* 856, *Ad.* 253. Altering the tone would raise the emotional pitch, *primum uocandi, alterum increpandi est* (Don.).

283 scripta . . . in animo: as we might say, "engraved on my heart."

284–97 Critics have long been impressed by the poignancy of Chrysis' dying request and the nobility with which Pamphilus accepts the responsibility thrust upon him. Anne Dacier found this scene particularly moving ("I know nothing better written or more touching than these twelve verses," 1688: 64–5), as did Benedetto Croce nearly three centuries later: "The vow made to the dying Chrysis was sacred, and he will not loosen his grip upon that hand which she placed in his, and which he gripped as he swore the oath" (1966 [1936]: 796). Yet Pamphilus' reliability as a narrator is not beyond question. Is he reporting Chrysis' actual words, simply his memory of those words, or is this speech largely the invention of his own uneasy conscience? A definitive view is hardly possible. Much depends on whether we emphasize the earnestness with which he aspires to do right by Glycerium or the self-centeredness and self-indulgence that caused the problem in the first place. The one sure thing is that T. creates a character with a psychological complexity not easily paralleled in his Roman predecessors.

284 ferme moriens, i.e. "near death." T. can use *ferme* simply as an intensifier, e.g. 460 *haud ferme* "scarcely at all."

285 Pamphilus sets the scene in four short bursts chiastically arranged with single verbs at beginning and end. Whether *nos* includes Glycerium or means that only Pamphilus and Chrysis were present at this interview is not entirely clear from what follows.

286 mi Pamphile: the endearing vocative *mi*, suggesting an earnestness that is here as much cajoling as affectionate, is often associated with female speech patterns (Adams 1984: 68–73, Dickey 2002: 220–2, Dutsch 2008: 53–5), but it is not limited to women. Pamphilus is said to have exclaimed *mea Glycerium* (134); Cic. uses it in correspondence both intimate (e.g. *Att.* 14.12.1 *o mi Attice*) and professional (*Fam.* 7.5.3 *mi Caesar*). Don. detects a note of *blandimentum* in Chrysis' manner, for which see Barrios-Lech 2016: 118–20.   **huius formam**: the demonstr. prn. might be taken as a sign of Glycerium's presence. So too at 290, 293. Her *forma* had at once caught Simo's attention (119–20); at *Ph.* 93–108 the *forma* of the young girl in mourning is what first attracts Antipho and his friends.

287 te: acc., as regularly after *clam* in early Latin.   **quăm ĭlli**: 277n.   **utraeque**: the pl. commonly refers to sets or groups but can also refer to a natural pair (*OLD* 3b), e.g. *Hau.* 394 (of a monogamous couple) *utrique ad utrisque uero deuincimini*.

288 rem "property" (*OLD* 1). Cf. *Ph.* 393 *si talentum rem reliquisset decem* ("if he'd left an estate worth ten talents").   **tutandam**: to be understood with each noun in turn, *pudicitiam* looking back to *formam*, *rem* to *aetatem*.   **sient**: 234n.

289 The MSS here transmit an unmetrical line: *quod ego te per hanc dexteram oro et ingenium tuum*. Don. supplies the variant *genium*, which must be correct: cf. Pl. *Capt.* 977 *per tuum te genium obsecro*. The other easy correction to produce an acceptable senarius is to move *te* and delete *oro* (thus both OCT and Barsby); Brown prefers to read *dextram* and retain *oro*. *dexteram* is otherwise found in T. only at line end (734, 751, *Eun.* 775), though the longer (and older) form could be thought appropriate in this prayer formula.

quod "wherefore" (*OLD* 1b). The adv. links the request to the preceding statement. **per hanc te dexteram**: slipping the personal prn. between the prep. and its obj. is idiomatic in this prayer formula, as at 538 and 834 below. For the effect of such positioning, see 247n. Chrysis would presumably have grasped Pamphilus' hand at this point in her plea. **genium**: the *genius* is the spiritual part of the individual, not unlike Gk. δαίμων. Cf. Men. fr. 714.1–3 K–T ἅπαντι δαίμων ἀνδρὶ συμπαρίσταται | εὐθὺς γενομένῳ μυσταγωγὸς βίου | ἀγαθός ("a spirit stands beside each man from the moment of birth, an initiator for good in life"). Thus "by the god who watches over you" (Brown), or more colloquially, "by your own better self" (Barsby).

290 fidem "loyalty" (*OLD* 8). Cf. Pl. *Capt.* 405 (on the relationship of slave to master) *neque med umquam deseruisse te neque factis neque fide*. **huius solitudinem**: at Athens, even a citizen woman without an obvious male guardian (κύριος) would be in an extremely vulnerable position and a non-citizen woman even more so. Thus Sostrata of *Ad.* anxiously looks to the support of her late husband's kinsman Hegio (455–8) and Thais of *Eun.*, whose situation more closely parallels that of Chrysis, actively seeks a male protector (147–9). Davos thus has reason to fear Simo's ability to have Glycerium driven from the city (381–2). Don. records the variant reading *sollicitudinem* here, i.e. "concern for her," but that is widely treated as a *lectio facilior*.

291 abs te: the standard forms of the prep. are *a* before consonants and *ab* before vowels, but T. consistently writes *abs te* (489, *Hec.* 223, *Hau.* 399). **segreges . . . deseras**: Don. is hard pressed to distinguish between these two verbs, ultimately taking the former closely with *fidem* and the latter with *solitudinem*, but the duplication probably owes more to the solemnity of the entreaty than to any semantic difference.

292–4 si . . . siue . . . seu: the sequence is additive, not disjunctive. Each reason adduced is thought true (*OLD* s.v. *siue, seu* 1).

292 in germani fratris . . . loco "like my own brother" (Barsby). A *germanus* is a brother with the same father and mother; as an adj. the word extends its meaning to "true" or "genuine" (*OLD* 3). For its connotations, see Bannon 1997: 69–72.

293 maxumi: gen. of value. Cf. *Ad.* 891–2 *hominem maxumi* | *preti te esse*.

294 morigera "obliging." This and its near synonym *morigeratus* (*Ad.* 218) appear only once each in T., who prefers the expression *morem gerere*, e.g. *Ad.* 214 *adulescenti morem gestum* [sc. *esse*] *oportuit*. Don. finds the expression there particularly suited to a *leno* or *meretrix*.

295 uirum . . . patrem: Chrysis entrusts Glycerium to his care in terms not to be taken literally. Though she will require protection (290n), Pamphilus is not positioned to act as either husband or guardian (*tutor* = προστάτης, at Athens the sponsor and legal representative of a resident foreigner). For *patrem*, cf. Catull. 72.3–4 *dilexi tum te . . . | pater ut gnatos diligit et generos.* When Mysis at 718 applies a similar string of nouns to Pamphilus, Don. cites the famous scene at *Il.* 6.429–30, where Andromache calls Hector father, mother, and brother as well as husband.

296 bona "property." This may not be hers to bequeath: at 795, her kinsman Crito arrives from Andros to lay claim to it as her legal heir. Chrysis – or is it Pamphilus? – may be deliberately denying her Andrian connection. **fide**: Gell. 9.14.21 calls this fifth declension dat. sg. the choice of those *qui purissime locuti sunt*. The form has some MS support here, and *diē, rē,* and *fidē* are all attested in Pl., e.g. *Cist.* 245 *meae fide concredita.* See Ernout 1953: 70–1, Weiss 2020: 274.

297 in manum dat: a temptation since the time of Don. (*confirmatae sunt legitimae nuptiae per manum conuentionem*) has been to understand this and the *accepi* that follows as the formal language of betrothal, and it is certainly true that Pamphilus regards Glycerium *pro uxore* (146, 273). The phrase, however, seems to mean little more than "to entrust to one's care" – so Cic. *Fam.* 7.5.3 (in recommending Trebatius to Caesar) *hominem tibi ita trado, de manu, ut aiunt, in manum tuam* – and commentators have increasingly moved away from assigning it a technical meaning. See Williams 1968: 400–2, Brown 2012: 42–4. **occupat** "seizes hold" (*OLD* 4b). A melodramatic expression to end a melodramatic scene.

298 accepi, acceptam: participial resumption, a kind of *figura etymologica* (242n.), is a stylistic device with a long history in various registers of Latin. See Laughton 1964: 17–19, Wills 1996: 311–15. **quidem** "certainly" (*OLD* 1). The post-positive adv. puts emphasis on the verb. Contrast 399 *itan credis?* :: *haud dubium id quidemst.* ("You think so?" :: "No doubt that for sure is it.")

299 quor tu abis ab illa? Having heard that Glycerium is in labor (268), Pamphilus at last wonders why Mysis is not with her. If, as Don. thinks, his question is a veiled reproach, Pamphilus blithely ignores the fact that he is himself the cause of the delay. **audin** = *audisne*, in effect a command rather than a question (Barrios-Lech 2016: 168–71). Having just ordered her to hurry away, Pamphilus now calls her back.

300 caue: *deest "dicas"* (Don.), *ne* being optional in this neg. command (*NLS* §130 ii). **de nuptiis**, i.e. the proposed marriage with Chremes' daughter. The missing verb would be, e.g., *accedat*.   **teneo**: 86n. An exit line. Mysis does not need Pamphilus to complete the thought; she has already said something similar to him (268–9).

[II.i] Charinus, Byrria, Pamphilus (301–37)

Charinus and his slave Byrria enter. They are so deep in conversation that they do not at first notice Pamphilus, who has (presumably) retreated to the opposite end of the stage. Since they had no place in the initial exposition, T. is careful here to identify them and hint at their role in the developing action. Thus the almost immediate introduction of their names (301, 305) and the fact that Charinus is, like Pamphilus, a young man in love (306). For T.'s addition of this pair and its structural consequences, see Introduction 3.1.3.

301 quid ais, Byrria? 137n. The stock question, here combining surprise with indignation, immediately reveals the topic of their conversation. Menander's *Dyskolos* opens in similar fashion as Chaireas phrases as a question the subject of what is evidently an ongoing conversation: τί φῂς; ἰδὼν ἐνθένδε παῖδ' ἐλευθέραν . . . ἐρῶν ἀπῆλθες εὐθύς; ("What's that you say? You saw a free-born girl from here . . . and came away immediately love-stricken?" 50–2).   **Byrria**: Greek names in comedy generally follow the closest Latin declensional pattern. Thus, the first declension Πυρρίας becomes Latin Byrria, with -ă in nom. and voc. (Questa 2007: 84) and *b* replacing π (as also φ) in the loan word (Leumann 1977: 158; thus Cic. *de Or.* 160 *Burrum semper Ennium, numquam Pyrrhum*).   **illa**, i.e. Chremes' daughter.   **nuptum**: supine after *datur* (*OLD* s.v. *nubo* 1b).

302 qui: 53n. Charinus is at first understandably reluctant to believe this news.   **e Dauo**: the prep. indicates the source of the knowledge (*OLD* 14c). The claim is consistent with Davos' exit *ad forum* at 227 to find Pamphilus. Though unable to locate his young master there, he did apparently encounter Byrria and passed on this news (cf. 357–8). The detail helps integrate Charinus and Byrria into the dramatic structure provided by the original *Andria*, though where Byrria afterward met his master and what motivates their appearance here are unspecified.   **uae misero mihi!** a formulaic expression of distress, also found at 743, *Hec.* 605, *Hau.* 250, 917, *Ad.* 301, 327, 383. The particle is stronger than *ei* and not restricted to male speech (Adams 1984: 54–5, Müller 1997: 136–7).

303 ut: answered by *ita* in the following line. Charinus is not so distraught that he cannot construct an extended, well-balanced sentence.   **usque antehac** "up until now."   **attentus** "intent" (*OLD* 2).

304 cura confectus "thoroughly worn out with care" (*OLD* s.v. *conficio* 13b). The alliteration and fifth-foot caesura make clear that *cura* belongs with *confectus*.

305 edepol: 229n. The prefix is often explained as the intensive particle *e-* (cf. *ecastor*) combined with *-de-*, perhaps derived from *deiue*, archaic voc. of *deus* (for which see Weiss 2020: 242–3).   **quoniam . . . possit**: Don. calls this sentiment proverbial, which is also how it appears at Aug. *C. D.* 14.25. The wisdom of the lower classes in comedy often takes proverbial form: cf. 61 (Sosia), 805 (Mysis).

306 uelis: the jussive subjunc. stands in for the missing imper. of *uolo*.   **possit**: the subjunc. is generic (*NLS* §155–6). Contrast factual *potest* just above.   **nil . . . aliud**: more emphatic, as Don. notes, than if he had said *nullam aliam*.   **Philumenam**, i.e. Φιλουμένην ("Beloved"). This is the one occasion, save for the spurious ending (998), where Chremes' daughter is given a name. It is, unlike Glycerium (134n.), a name appropriate to a respectable woman, e.g. Pamphilus' wife in *Hec.* and the ingenue in Menander's *Sikyonios*.

307 satiust = *satius est*. The comparative is followed, as often, by an inf. clause (*OLD* A.7) with *id* anticipating the *qui*-clause. Cf. 157n.   **qui** = *ut* (*OLD qui²* 4). Cf. 6, also 334, 402.

308 quo magis: answers the preceding *qui*.   **lubido**: 78n. This is T.'s most common word for desire, often with erotic overtones. *cupiditas* (*Hau.* 208; *Ph.* 821) is more generic, *desiderium* (*Hau.* 307, 753; *Hec.* 88) more specifically a longing for something lost.   **incendatur**: fire is a common metaphor in the language of love (Fantham 1972: 7–11). Cf. Pl. *Curc.* 54 (another slave advising his master) *fumo comburi nil potest, flamma potest.*

309 The honest, if somewhat stolid Charinus matches platitude with platitude. Dacier traced the general sentiment here back to [A.] *Pr.* 263–5 ἐλαφρόν ὅστις πημάτων ἔξω πόδα | ἔχει, παραινεῖν νουθετεῖν τε τοὺς κακῶς | πράσσοντας ("It is easy for one who has his foot out of trouble to give advice and to admonish those faring badly"). A version is also found in a later tragic fragment (*TrGF* Adesp. 342), suggesting a cliché that might easily have found its way eventually into Men. and from there to T.'s Charinus. Illness is another metaphor common in erotic discourse (Fantham 1972: 18).

310 hic: the adv., i.e. "here (in my place)," though Don. takes it as the demonstr. prn.   **sentias**: 276n.   **age age**: an expression of acquiescence, perhaps with a hint of impatience in the repetition (Müller 1997: 114).

310–11 sed Pamphilum | uideo: after rejecting his slave's advice, Charinus turns away and having done so, catches sight of Pamphilus. The direct question he addresses to Byrria at 314 suggests that the intervening lines 312–14 are spoken to himself and that at 311 and 314 Byrria is commenting aside on his master's declaration.   **certumst**, sc. *mihi*. A common expression of resolution, e.g. *Hau.* 466–7 *si certumst tibi | sic facere* ("If that's what you've decided to do . . ."). **hĭc**: said with a gesture toward Charinus.

312 Diaeresis at the end of the fourth foot divides this line into equal parts, the first containing two clauses of supplication and the second explaining the basis for the appeal. Don., keen to make fine distinctions, associates *oro* with requests for *bona, supplico* with the escape from *mala*. The three verbs in *-abo* and the absence of resolutions are also noteworthy.

313 prodat "postpone" (*OLD* 4). *aliquot dies* is the direct obj., the construction being analogous to 615 *huic malo aliquam producam moram*. Such a delay would not of course be in Pamphilus' power to grant.

314 nil est: Byrria recognizes the pipe-dream for what it is.

315 quid: Lat. says "What?" where Eng. more naturally says "How?"   **adeon** = *adeone*. Not a deliberative quest. but a request for advice, so the indic. comes naturally (*NLS* §169, *SEL* I 22–4).   **quidni?** *NLS* §173.   **impetres**: the verb has two objects, the simple acc. *nil* followed, as often, by an *ut*-clause (*OLD* 1b), which here represents an alternative. *nil* thus becomes the equivalent of "nothing else," as more fully at 306 *nil uolo aliud nisi Philumenam*.

316 moechum: the Greek loan-word (μοιχός) was always the colloquial Latin term for this type of sexual transgressor. *adulter*, which by the late Republic was preferred in educated and legalistic discourse, appears only once in Pl. (*Am.* 1049, but *moechus* at 135) and never in T. (At *Cas.* 976, Pl. seems to gloss *in adulterio* with *dum moechissat*.) See Adams 1983: 351–3, and for the Greek background, Todd 1993: 276–9, Scafuro 1997: 474–9.

317 abin hinc in malam rem: one of many variants on a stock, relatively mild imprecation, e.g. Pl. *Capt.* 877, *Epid.* 78; *Eun.* 536, *Ph.* 930. *abin* = *abisne*.   **istāc** = *ista* + *-ce* "that of yours." These deictic forms of the personal adj. and prn. (cf. 28n.) are listed in *OLD* s.v. *istic*[1].   **scelus**: a mild term of abuse (*OLD* 3; Dickey 2002: 168–70).

318 Charinum uideo: at the sound of Charinus' voice, raised in annoyance at his slave's cheekiness, Pamphilus breaks off his reverie, or whatever was occupying him, and turns toward Charinus. The resulting exchange of greetings as the two catch sight of each other across the stage is a fixture in comedy, though usually played more broadly in Pl. than in T. For its variants, see Marshall 1999: 120–4. The momentary halt to the music marks the scene's turn in a new direction.

319 Diaeresis after the second foot sets off the following participial phrase, where the nouns are arranged in alliterative pairs. The jingle *auxilium consilium* is well within Roman norms. Cf. Enn. *TrRF* F 23.8 *fana flamma deflagrata*, Cic. *De con.* 8 (Courtney) *o fortunatam natam*, and in prose, Cato *ORF*³ 58 *quid illos . . . opinamini animi habuisse.*

320 ad auxilium: as at 138, the construction with *ad* avoids a second gen. Pamphilus replies in reverse order to the request for help and advice.

321 quidnamst: 234n.   **aiunt**: an evasive reply. "*aiunt*," says Don., *de ea re dicimus, quam uolumus esse falsum.*

322 facis . . . uides: for the tense, 244n.   **postremum** (adv.) "for the last time" (*OLD* 2). The dark allusion could be to suicide, a common threat of frustrated lovers in comedy (210n.), or to service abroad as a mercenary, as Men.'s Moschion contemplates (*Sa.* 623–38) and T.'s Clinia apparently did (*Hau.* 115–17).   **quid ita?** "Why is that?" (*OLD* s.v. *quis*¹ 16). Charinus' allusion to self-destruction motivates this expository question. It is necessary since to this point Pamphilus is apparently unaware of – and some in the audience may yet be unsure of – Charinus' feelings for Chremes' daughter.

323 uereor: the verb can suggest not fear but hesitation, e.g. *Ad.* 269 *uereor coram in os te laudare* ("I'm reluctant to praise you openly to your face").   **quid est?** passing the explanation on to Byrria requires Pamphilus to ask again. The repetition and consequent delay in getting an answer to an expository quest. is itself a comic device, muted here in T. but richly exploited by Pl., e.g. *Cur.* 1–19, *Ps.* 1–22.

324 ne: the asseverative particle (Gk. νή) commonly precedes the word, usually a personal prn., that it emphasizes, e.g. 772 (*ne illa*), 939 (*ne istam*). Prosodic hiatus is the preferred scansion here since elision would obscure the emphatic syllable.   **mecum sentit** "agrees with me" (*OLD* 6b).   **ehodum**: the same collocation at 184. Pamphilus now turns to address Charinus directly.

325 quidnam amplius: under normal circumstances, a young, unrelated Athenian male would have had limited opportunities even to see, let alone become acquainted with the daughter of a respectable citizen like

Chremes. In the world of comedy, though, almost anything is possible, from an innocent chance encounter (e.g. *Ph.* 91–118) to an opportunistic rape (e.g. *Hec.* 822–9). And at the back of Pamphilus' mind in asking the question is probably the history of his own relationship with Glycerium. Phaedria asks a similar question at *Eun.* 143–4 *ad uirginem animum adiecit.* :: *etiamne amplius?* | :: *nil.* There, however, the girl in question was believed to be a *citharistria*, and so expectations were conceivably different. For the visibility of women in Athenian everyday life, a much-debated subject, see Todd 1993: 201–12, Fantham et al. 1994: 101–13, Trümper 2012: 288–96; for the representation of love in comedy, Brown 1993; and for the difficulties in evaluating comedy's representation of legal realities, Scafuro 1997: 1–19.   **ah**: the MSS read *aha*, a particle of strong denial in Pl., e.g. *Rud.* 419–20 (Ampelisca fending off Sceparnio) *aha! nimium familiariter* | *me attrectas.* It is not otherwise found in T., who instead uses *ah* in a wide variety of situations (Müller 1997: 126–30). In delivery, it could be the difference between a sigh (*āh*) and an emphatic shake of the head (*ăhă*). For Charinus' denial, cf. Men. *Aspis* 290–1 (Chaireas on his love for Kleostratos' sister) οὐθὲν ποήσας προπετὲς οὐδ' ἀνάξιον | οὐδ' ἄδικον ("I've done nothing hasty or unworthy | or improper").

326 quam uellem! an unfulfilled wish (*OLD* 11). Pamphilus is thinking not of Charinus' unhappiness but of his own: a liaison with Charinus might have preempted his own planned marriage to Chremes' daughter.   **per amicitiam et per amorem**: why Pamphilus, his *amicus*, would not already know of his *amor* is left unexplained.

327 principio: introducing a first proposal (*OLD* 2). The alternative comes with *sed si.*   **ut ne**: 259n.   **dabo . . . operam**: 157n.

328 tibi . . . cordi: a set expression (*OLD* 5b). The dat. is probably locative rather than predicative (*NLS* § 8 i).   **aliquot dies**: Charinus makes the request prefigured at 313, but here *dies* is an acc. of duration. Cf. Pl. *Curc.* 240 *quin tu aliquot dies perdura* ("Why don't you put up with it for a few days . . ."). *nuptias* is easily supplied as the obj. of *profer.*

329 proficiscor: Charinus mitigates the threat implied at 322.

330 ne utiquam "by no means." Generally written as two words in comedy.   **officium liberi . . . hominis**: 114n. *liber* means not simply "free," i.e. not a slave, but conducting oneself with the dignity and grace of the ideal citizen, what the Anglophone world used to call "a gentleman." Thus in *Ad.*, Aeschinus' compromising of Sostrata's (citizen) daughter is an *inliberale facinus* (449), and the worst accusation leveled at the urbane Micio is that he has acted *inliberaliter* (664).

331 gratiae apponi "to be reckoned a favor" (*OLD* s.v. *appono* 8). For the dat., most often an abstract noun, cf. 444–5 *ne umquam infamiae | ea res sibi esset* (*SEL* II 171–7). Pamphilus wants no special credit (*gratia*) for doing what is in his own interest.

332 adipiscier: 203n. *uis* is understood.

334 facite . . . efficite: the four verbs, as Don. notes, all describe actions to be conceived or effected, an example of what Cic. *de Or.* 37 would call the *uerborum copia et eorum constructio* that made T. a favored text for rhetorical study. The order is chiastic, the two verbs of action framing the two verbs of invention, but the two simple verbs also form an alliterative pair followed by the two compound verbs, with all united by homoioteleuton. This is the *lectus sermo* for which Cicero praises T. in a famous epigram preserved by Suet. in his *Vita Terenti*. **qui**: 307n. **detur**, sc. *uxor*. The subj. is Chremes' daughter. It is a futile exhortation. Charinus and Byrria will prove unable to do much of anything to further their own interests, a fault of character that the author of the alternative ending to *An.* may have set out to remedy (Appendix I).

335 qui ne: since the clause, like 334, expresses purpose, its negation is *ne*. **sat habeo**: a phrase of agreement or contentment (*OLD* s.v. *satis* 4). Three centuries and more after T., Tac. (*Ann.* 15.25.7) and then Gell. (13.17.2) were still writing *satis habere*, but the expression had become distinctly archaic by the time of Don. in the fourth century (*sic antiqui . . . dicebant*). **Dauom**: we last saw Davos leaving for the forum in search of Pamphilus (227).

336 quoius: like dat. *quoi*, the normal spelling in T.'s day and still used into the second century CE. It is almost always scanned as a monosyllable in T. (Questa 2007: 77–8). Quint. knew these pronominal forms as a boy and called the change to *cui* an improvement (1.7.27). See Weiss 2020: 372–4, and for the forms, *OLD* s.v. *qui*[1]. **consilio fretus**: the dependence of a young master on his slave is of course the comic norm. How worthy Davos is of this trust and how well he fulfills that role remain to be seen. **at tu**: Charinus turns to Byrria, making a pointed contrast with Davos. **haud quicquam**, sc. *mones*.

337 quae nil opus sunt scire: this quasi-personal construction with *opus* (*OLD* 13) appears again at 740 *quae opus fuere ad nuptias*. Byrria has in fact brought news (301) and offered advice (305–8); Charinus has simply not liked what he was told. **fugin** = *fugisne*, a *de facto* command. Cf. *audin*, 299n. **lubens** = *lubenter*. Cf. *frequens*, 107. Byrria is sent away, destination and purpose unspecified, though probably toward the forum (357).

When he reappears at 412, he will claim to be acting under instructions, presumably having met his master offstage sometime after Charinus' exit at 374, but the dramaturgy is less than tight.

[II.ii] Davos, Charinus, Pamphilus (338–74)

Though characters in comedy normally return from the direction of their last exit, Davos is not now returning directly from the forum, where he had failed to find Pamphilus but did encounter Byrria (302). He will thus explain in some detail how he took a detour, in the course of which he made an important discovery (356–69).

Davos' eagerness here to bring Pamphilus his news and his initial inability to find him, though Pamphilus remains in plain sight to the audience, are hallmarks of a stock routine in Roman comedy, the so-called running slave (*seruus currens*). In its full form (e.g. Pl. *Merc.* 111–33), the messenger enters in haste, tunic pulled high and cloak thrown over his shoulder, looks in increasing agitation everywhere but in the right direction as he declares his intentions, and when at last he is brought to a standstill by his now impatient master, he is at first too breathless to deliver the urgent message. T. would ridicule his rival, Luscius Lanuvinus, for incorporating such a hackneyed scene in one of his plays (*Hau.* 31–2), but this is nevertheless the first of four such scenes played more or less straight in T.'s own comedies (*Ph.* 179–99, 841–60; *Ad.* 299–329), and two more with noteworthy inversions of its conventions (*Hec.* 430–43, 799–815). It is therefore reasonable to infer that in this scene Davos enters at a run (338), fails to see his master, and is preparing to hurry off again when Pamphilus calls out to him (344). Whether the two of them stood at opposite ends of the stage, thus lending the comic business an element of logic, or Pamphilus stands closer to stage center with Davos running farcically around him, is impossible to determine. For the scene and its possible Greek origins, see Duckworth 1936 and 1952: 106–7, Csapo 1989 and 1993, and for T.'s use of the convention, Lowe 2009.

The scene continues the trochaic rhythm of the preceding action, though the tempo may accelerate to match Davos' livelier antics.

338 boni quid "what good [news]." *quid* constructed with a gen. of the whole (*NLS* §77 ii) is most commonly paired in comedy with *boni*, e.g. Pl. *Cist.* 539, *Most.* 370, *Ps.* 1067; *Hec.* 851, and *mali*, e.g. Pl. *Aul.* 370, *Am.* 570; *Hec.* 418. Here the play on *boni*, first adj. and then substantive in different cases, a form of polyptoton, also creates an effective chiasm.

340 nescioquid: acc. of the internal obj., defining the nature or the cause of the verbal idea inherent in *laetus* (*NLS* §13(ii)). Cf. 362 *id gaudeo* ("I was happy about it"), *Hec.* 321 *pauitare nescioquid* ("trembling with some kind of fever"). Don. thought the construction required explanation, *deest "propter," ut sit propter nescioquid.*   **haec . . . mala**, i.e. the marriage to Chremes' daughter. Davos in fact learned of this before Pamphilus (173–4).

341 quem: the acc. subj. of *quaerere* (342). Its antecedent is *Pamphilum* (338). Davos' syntax takes no account of the intervening exchange between Charinus and Pamphilus, since he does not hear it.

342 toto . . . oppido "all over town." *oppidum*, also at 382 (again Davos speaking) and *Ad.* 715. *urbs* becomes more common in T., with no apparent difference in connotation: *Hau.* 191, *Ph.* 517, *Hec.* 175, 589, *Eun.* 973, *Ad.* 949.   **exanimatum**: Pamphilus' usual state (131, 234).

343 intendam, sc. *gradum*.   **cessas alloqui?** "Why don't you speak to him?" *cesso* + inf. suggests hesitation or tardiness in taking an action (*OLD* 1b). Cf. 845 *cesso alloqui?*, *Ph.* 252 *sed quid cessas hominem adire?*

344 abeo: Davos starts to leave, presumably in the direction from which he came since Pamphilus must call him back. This is the MSS reading. Don. knew *habeo* as an alternative: cf. 498 *quid agam habeo*. On that reading, Davos would be announcing some unspecified resolution, but not his intention to leave.   **quis homo**: Davos responds to the voice before identifying the speaker. The tunnel vision imposed by the mask encourages such slow recognition.   **ades**: 29n.

345 euge: one of a group of Greek exclamations – *attat* and *papae* are the other common ones – that come into colloquial Latin from Gk. (Müller 1997: 133–4). Where εὖγε expresses approval or confirmation, e.g. Plato *Grg.* 494c εὖγε, ὦ βέλτιστε ("Good man! Well said!"), its Latin cousin indicates pleasure, often tinged with surprise. Thus *Ad.* 911 (stern Demea, suddenly addressed as *pater lepidissume*) *euge! iam lepidus vocor*. The second vowel, short in Gk., is lengthened here: OCT prints *eugae*, found in some MSS. of Pl.   **ambo opportune**, sc. *adestis* (Don.).

346 perii! the usual expression of a despairing lover (Müller 1997: 134–5).   **quin**: 45n.   **timeas**: subjunc. in the ind. quest., the expected mood in classical Latin but still optional in the time of T. (*NLS* §178–9, Clackson and Horrocks 2007: 171–2).

347 in dubio "at risk" (*OLD* 9).   **quid**, sc. *timeas.* Davos presumably learned of Charinus' situation from Byrria when the two met in the forum (302).

348 etsi "even if" (*OLD* 1). Davos does not simply know a fact, viz. that the marriage was proposed; he has grasped the full situation, viz. that the proposed wedding is a sham. That difference in knowledge is reflected in the difference between *scio* and *intellego.* Cf. 506.   **obtundis**: also used absolutely at *Ph.* 515, though *auris*, as Pl. *Cist.* 116, or *me*, as *Ad.* 113, might be understood. The metaphor, says Don., comes from metal-working. Thus Brown, "You're banging on about it . . ."

349 id: anticipates the following cl. of fear. The first *tu* is Pamphilus, the second Charinus. It is easiest to imagine Davos standing between them and gesturing to each in turn.   **ut** = *ne non*, as often in early Latin (*SEL* I 252–5, *NLS* §188).

350 istuc ipsum "that very thing." Possibly an exclamatory acc. as commonly in expressions of despair (*miseram me!* 240), outrage (*indignum facinus!* 144), dismissal (*ridiculum caput!* 371), and in oaths, e.g. *pro Iuppiter hominis stultitiam!* (*Ad.* 366). Here, however, where a verbal idea is easily supplied, the acc. might more readily be explained as the obj. of *tenes* understood, though whether a Latin-speaker would register this distinction between obj. and exclamation could be doubted.   **atque**: 225n.   **periclist**: part. gen. For the form, 131n.   **uide me**: the colloquial Latin equivalent of Eng. "Trust me!" (*OLD* 4a).

351 obsecro: 232n.   **em**: 248n. This versatile particle is sometimes the verbal accompaniment to an action, e.g. *Ph.* 52 (handing over a sack of coins) *accipe, em!*, *Ad.* 172 (preparing for a blow) *em, serua!* The stage business here may therefore parody the touch of the lictor's staff (*festuca*) in a formal *manumissio uindicta*, though extant Roman comedy never adopts the legal formulae for manumission directly. Cf. the manumission of Syrus (*liber esto*) and then his wife at *Ad.* 959–81, and for comparable scenes in Pl., Richlin 2017: 419–24. Watson 1971: 48–9 reviews the legal language of manumission. There is in any case a calculated irony in the young master representing freedom as the gift of his slave.

352 qui: 150n.   **scio**: at 116, Simo introduces a similar explanatory narrative with *scies*, which is also found here in one tenth-century MS (Par. lat. 10304) and was preferred by Bentley. It may well be the better reading.

353 modo me prehendit: Davos refers to the encounter at 184. *prehendit* could be pres. or perf. A perf. would set the time for the following narrative in the past, which then continues in hist. pres.; a pres. would instead mark the beginning of that narrative sequence.   **dare**: the acc. subj. (*se*), readily supplied from *ait*, is readily omitted. So, too, at 450, 470, 688.

354 alia multa: that would be Simo's declared willingness to forgive Pamphilus' earlier habits (187–90) and the threats he directs at Davos (196–205). T. avoids repeating what the audience has already heard, but by calling attention to the omission, he also encourages us to note Davos' eagerness to pass over information unflattering to himself and possibly unsettling to the two *adulescentes*.

355 continuo: not strictly true. Davos omits his protracted moment of indecision (206–27).

356 ibi: correlated with *ubi* to indicate a chronological sequence (*OLD* 2b).   **in quendam excelsum locum**: during the day, the Roman forum, rather like modern Rome's Campo dei Fiori, would have been crowded with stalls, shoppers, and passers-by of all kinds. Retreat to a high point, such as the podium of a temple or the base of a monument like the Maenian column, would have been a sensible strategy under the circumstances. For the everyday pandemonium of the forum, see Russell 2016: 47–9. Conditions in the agora at Athens would not have been much different.

357–65 The short, incomplete sentences as the narrative unfolds reflect the urgency of Davos' efforts and the inexorable progress of his deductions. Whether his expectations of the wedding preparations he does *not* see at the homes of Simo and Chremes reflect Athenian or Roman practice is unclear. Comedy often blurs such differences. Thus the burlesque ceremony staged at Pl. *Cas.* 798–854 is based largely on Greek ritual but comes embroidered with Plautine elements (Williams 1958: 17–20). Considerable activity by the two households would in either case be expected, and keeping the details vague allows audience members to imagine what they wish. For Athenian wedding arrangements generally, see Oakley and Sinos 1993: 11–21; for Roman rites, Dixon 1992: 64–5; for the difficulty of deducing actual practice from literary evidence, Hersch 2013/2014.

357 huius . . . Byrriam "his slave Byrria," with a gesture toward Charinus. A slave's master is commonly identified by the gen., e.g. Flaccus Claudi in Don.'s didascalic note.

359 redeunti, i.e. to Simo's house. For the pres. part. doing the work of a clause, see Laughton 1964: 20–3 and above, 132n.   **hem!** 116n.

360 paullulum opsoni "a teensy bit of food." The idea reappears at 450, along with the cognate verb *opsono*. *opsonium*, a Greek loan word (ὀψώνιον) that became naturalized in Latin, is used in either sing. or pl. to denote the provisions for a meal. Davos must be referring to the supplies we saw carried into Simo's house at the outset. Were they really *paullulum*? and if so, why were Sosia's services required to supervise their procurement and preparation? It is a question of T.'s own making, since Sosia and the porters are his creation.   **ipsus** "the master" (*OLD* 12). This metrical equivalent of nom. *ipse* is common in drama. See Ernout 1953: 96.   **tristis:** not sad, but in a bad mood. Thus *Ad.* 79 (of the ever-sour Demea) *tristem uideo*.   **de improviso** "unexpectedly" (*OLD* 2).

361 quorsumnam istuc? "Where is this heading?" For -*nam* as a strengthening particle, cf. *quidnam*, 234n.   **Chremem:** Lat. acc., but Gk. acc. *Chremetem* at 472. See 247n.

362 illo = *illuc*.   **ostium:** the only distinction between *ostium* and *fores* is metrical shape, e.g. *Ad.* 637 *sed quis ostium hic pulsauit?* followed by *tune has pepulisti fores?* (*Ad.* 638). Since wedding rituals normally began at the bride's house, with a very public procession to the house of the groom being an important part of the ceremony, significant bustle before Chremes' house door would have been expected. For the customary Roman procession (*domum deductio*), see Hersch 2010: 140–4, and for its Greek equivalent, Vérilhac and Vial 1998: 312–23.

363 recte dicis: Charinus agrees with Davos' deduction. He does not himself have direct knowledge of what is happening at Chremes' house.

364 matronam nullam: to be significant, the detail must be suggesting something more than the absence of a living wife for Chremes. A married woman, *nympheutria* at Athens and *pronuba* at Rome, had a significant role in both forms of marriage ritual, so the presence of such a woman here might be expected. See Vérilhac and Vial 1998: 297, 368–9; Hersch 2010: 191–9.

365 nil ornati . . . tumulti: gen. of definition (*NLS* §72 (5)). A few fourth declension nouns in early Latin receive a gen. in -ī on the model of *dominus, dominī* (Ernout 1953: 66–7, Clackson and Horrocks 2007: 103–4, Weiss 2020: 270). In early usage, *ornatus* ordinarily refers to dress, e.g. *Eun.* 546 (on seeing Chaerea in the eunuch's costume) *qui hic ornatus?* ("What's this get-up?"), *Hec.* 11 *orator ad uos uenio ornatu prologi* ("I come to you as an advocate in the dress of a prologue-speaker") or personal accouterment, e.g. Pl. *Rud.* 428 (Ampelisca come to fill a water jar) *sapienti ornatus quid uelim indicium facit* ("For anyone smart, my equipment makes clear what I want"). Here it must mean decoration, as Cic. *Ver.* 2.1.58 *uidi . . . forum comitiumque adornatum ad speciem magnifico ornatu* ("I saw the forum and *comitium* decked out to all appearances with magnificent decoration"). **accessi**: the narrative now slips from hist. pres. to perf. tenses.

366 magnum signum: Pamphilus seems reluctant to move from this clue to its logical conclusion. His hesitation, in contrast to Charinus' ready agreement (*recte dicis*), leads to Davos' next impatient question.

367 non opinor: another hedge. Given his emotional state, Pamphilus' reluctance to believe is understandable.   **narras** = *dicis*, as 434, 461, etc.   **accipis** "interpret" (*OLD* 20).

368 etiam: introduces an additional point by way of confirmation (*OLD* 3). Don. thus glosses *pro praeterea*.   **puerum**: a male slave (*OLD* 5).   **Chremi**: the Lat. second declension gen. ending is confirmed by Don. Most MSS read the equally possible Gk. Chremis.

369 holera et pisciculos minutos "greens and a few teeny fish." The dimin. + *minutos* stresses the modesty of the provisions. Cf. Men. *Per.* fr. 6 τὸ παιδίον | εἰσῆλθεν ἑψητοὺς φέρον ("the slave | went in bringing some tiny fish").   **ferre**: hist. inf.   **obolo** "an obol's worth." Abl. of price (*NLS* §87 (i)) and a very small sum. In fourth-century Athens, jury pay was a modest three obols (i.e. half a drachma) a day, while a workman's daily wage ranged, depending on the level of skill, from nine to fifteen obols.

370 opera: an effort made (*OLD* 1c), as distinct from *opus*, a work done (*OLD* 1). Cf. the fatuous boast of M. Livius ap. Cic. *Sen.* 11 *mea opera, Quinte Fabi, Tarentum recepisti* ("By my effort, Quintus Fabius, you regained Tarentum").   **ac**: mildly adversative (*OLD* s.v. atque 9).   **nullus**: as an adv., a colloquial, emphatic negative (*OLD* 6), e.g. *Eun.* 216 *tam etsi nullus moneas* ("even without your reminder"), Cat. 8.14 *cum rogaberis nulla* ("when you're not asked for at all"), Cic. *Att.* 11.24.4 *Philotimus non modo nullus uenit . . .* ("Not only did Philotimus not appear . . .").

371 quid ita? 322n.   **nempe**: the particle introduces a question seeking further information (*OLD* 3b).   **prorsus**: the adv. strengthens the following negative (*OLD* 2b).   **caput**: by synecdoche standing for the whole person (*OLD* 7), in comedy as likely to express affection as abuse, e.g. *Ad.* 966 and Pl. *Mil.* 725 *o lepidum caput!*

372 quasi necesse sit: Don., ever the rhetorician, notes that Davos' correction identifies the relief Charinus feels as based on a faulty syllogism (*uitiosum* ἐνθύμημα).

373 uides = *prouides* (Don.).   **senis amicos oras, ambis**: friends
of Chremes are meant. Cf. Pl. *Mil.* 69 (of the women said to flock to
Pyrgopolynices) *orant, ambiunt, exopsecrant.* Davos' advice is essentially a
more explicit version of what Pamphilus had urged at 333–4.

374 etsi . . . saepe iam "even if often before now." Charinus suggests either
that previous approaches to Chremes were unsuccessful or that he has
lacked the courage to make such approaches. Either might explain the
suggestion that he solicit the support of Chremes' friends. At 975, however, there will be no indication that Charinus' suit would be unwelcome
or unsuccessful.

Charinus exits, presumably to find Chremes' friends, though there is
no subsequent indication that he actually makes an appeal to them or
that it meets with any success. Whether he leaves to stage right or left is
unclear, though by Roman stage convention his return at 625 should be
from the same direction.

[II.iii] Davos, Pamphilus (375–403)

OCT's scene division here is quite artificial: after Charinus' exit, the
action continues without noticeable pause and in the same meter. (Thus
the ninth-century Vat. lat. 3868, which marks the beginning of each scene
with an illustration of its characters, has a continuous text with no picture
at this point.) The ensuing dialogue between Davos and Pamphilus, however, does have its own distinct metrical shape. It falls into three almost
equal parts, nine lines of trochaic septenarii (375–83), followed by ten of
iambic senarii (384–93) and then ten of iambic octonarii (394–403). For
this structure and its effects, see Moore 2013: 99–100.

375 sibi uolt "aims at" (*OLD* 16).

376 id suscenseat: the neut. prn., which anticipates the following *quia*-
clause, specifies the cause of Simo's anger. Cf. the anticipatory *id* at 180,
349.

377 iniurius: a very rare word outside comedy, and then applied only to
actions (Cic. *de Off.* 3.89, Liv. 43.5.5).

378 perspexerit "investigated," constructed here with an ind. quest.
tuom ut sese habeat animum "how *your* mind is disposed" (*OLD* s.v. *habeo*
21b). The eagerness to contrast Pamphilus' attitude with Simo's leads to
the prolepsis of *tuom.* Davos' logic would be easier to follow if lines 378
and 377 were transposed, as some editors, e.g. Brown, do. Barsby prints
the traditional MSS order but translates with the lines reversed.

379 negaris = *negaueris*.   **ibi** "in that case" (*OLD* 3c). Davos has in fact divined Simo's thinking as set out in the conversation with Sosia, 155–8.

380 illae turbae: probably "the usual sort of trouble" (*OLD* s.v. *ille* 4), although the prn. could be essentially demonstrative, pointing to a source in Simo's anger. The pl. of *turba* is common in this colloquial sense (*OLD* 1d).   **pater est**: a timely reminder of Simo's power over the situation.

381 solast mulier: as (presumably) a non-citizen woman, Glycerium would be particularly vulnerable to bullying and victimization of all sorts. As the *meretrix* Thais, in a similar legal situation, explains to her lover at *Eun.* 147–9 *sola sum: habeo hic neminem | neque amicum neque cognatum. quam ob rem, Phaedria, | cupio aliquos parere amicos beneficio meo.*   **dictum factum**: *prouerbium celeritatis* (Don.), or as we would say, "no sooner said than done." So too at *Hau.* 760, 904, and Enn. *Ann.* 314 Sk. *dictum factumque facit frux* ("the honest man makes the word the deed").   **inuenerit**: for the fut. perf. in a main clause, cf. *ceperit*, 213n.

382 oppido: *ex oppido, ex ciuitate* (Don.). Understanding the adv. *oppido* "altogether," common in Pl. and T., is not impossible here: cf. Pl. *Am.* 299 *oppido interii* ("I'm completely done for"). This may be why Don. felt the need for a gloss. The noun and adv. may in fact be etymologically related (de Vaan 2008: 431).

383 cedo: 150n.   **quid faciam?** the archetypal quest. of comic *adulescens* to *seruus*. The version at *Eun.* 46 *quid igitur faciam?* became famous, quoted by Cic. *N.D.* 3.72, four times by Quint., and echoed by Pers. 5.171–3. *faciam* is deliberative subjunc. (*NLS* §172).   **hem!** 116n. The suggestion, so opposite to his intention, takes Pamphilus completely by surprise.

384 The music ceases as Davos explains the reasoning behind his plan.   **ne nega**: *ne* + pres. imper., where the later language regularly uses *ne* + perf. subjunc. or the imper. *noli/nolite* (cf. *suadere noli* just below), is common in early and colloquial Latin, generally in short phrases. Thus *ne obsecra* (543), *ne saeui* (868). Exx. in *SEL* I 362, *NLS* § 128 (ii).

386 excludar . . . concludar: a deliberate jingle. Cf. *auxilium consilium*, 319n. *concludar* may suggest confinement like an animal (Fantham 1972: 47). To be shut out of a house is a recurrent motif in comedy (Pl. *Men.* 668–71, 698, *Truc.* 758; T. *Ad.* 119, *Eun.* 49, 88; Afran. 377–8R), as might be expected with housedoors so conspicuous a feature of the *scaenae frons*. There may also be talk of cajoling (Pl. *Mer.* 408–9, *Per.* 569–73) or attacking them (T. *Ad.* 102–3; Turp. 199–200R). Thraso actually launches such an assault at *Eun.* 771–87. It can, however, be the wife rather than the mistress who does the excluding (for Menaechmus I it is both in succession), and only the opening scenes of *Curc.* combine elements familiar from the *exclusus amator* topos of later elegy (Tib. 1.2; Prop. 1.16; Ov. *Am.* 1.6).   **hoc** = *huc.*

387 dicturum patrem: ind. statement after *opinor.* For Davos' use of direct speech in what follows, see 221n.

388 ducas uolo: *ut* is optional in the construction *uolo* + jussive subjunc. meaning "I want you to" (*SEL* I 215–16, Barrios-Lech 2016: 106–9). Davos anticipates almost exactly Simo's words at 418.

389 hic "in this case" (*OLD* s.v. *hic*² 5).

389–90 omnia . . . certa ei consilia, i.e. the sham wedding. Davos will use Simo's self-confidence against him.

391 sine omni periclo: comedy regularly uses *omnis* with *sine* rather than *ullus*, e.g. Pl. *Trin.* 338 *quia sine omni malitiast.* Also *Aul.* 215, *Truc.* 565, Cic. *de Or.* 2.5 *sine omni quidem sapientia.*   **hoc**: anticipates the following *quin*-clause.

392 minueris "modify [a course of action]" (*OLD* 4b). Perf. subjunc. in a prohibition (*SEL* I 171–2, *NLS* §128).

393 haec quae facis, i.e. what Davos is now telling him to do, but does this mean not objecting to the marriage or not continuing to see Glycerium? Don. understands the former. On that reading, *ea causa* anticipates *ne is mutet.*

394 The iambic rhythm continues, but once again set to music. Moving to the longer, accompanied octonarius line helps vary the pace of Davos' extended explanation.   **uelle**, sc. *te.*   **quom uelit** "when(ever) he wants." Davos hopes to deprive Simo of the initiative.   **non queat** = *nequeat*, which is why the conj. in this neg. clause of purpose is *ut* rather than *ne.*

395 quod speres "suppose you were hoping." *quod* + subjunc. suggesting a contingency (*OLD* 6c) is found several times in T.: *Hau.* 671–2, *Eun.* 785 and 1064, *Ad.* 162–3. The effect is concessive, though the subjunc. is in origin potential. The construction may derive from legal language: cf. the mock contract at Pl. *As.* 757 *quod illa aut amicum aut patronum nominet . . .* ("should she identify him as a friend or patron . . ."). **his moribus**: the *mores* in question would be his continued liaison with Glycerium. Cf. Chremes' reaction upon learning of it as described by Simo, 144–9.

396 inueniet, sc. Simo.   **inopem**, i.e. a bride without a dowry. Strictly speaking, neither Athenian nor Roman marriage required a dowry (προίξ, *dos*), but it was desirable both as a social statement and as protection for the bride's interests, since it remained her property and would have to be returned in the event of divorce. So in Pl. *Trin.*, Lysiteles' father objects to a marriage *sine dote* (*egone indotatam te uxorem ut patiar?* 378), and the girl's brother will be similarly outraged by the proposal: *me germanum meam sororem in concubinatum tibi,* | *si sine dote <dem>, dedisse magis quam in matrimonium* (690–1). The inability to provide a dowry could require a family to accept an otherwise unattractive match, as an unreformed Pamphilus might appear to be. For the dowry and what it represents, see Todd 1993: 215–16 (Athens), Watson 1971: 24–7 (Rome).   **corrumpi**: the customary fear of comic moralizers, e.g. *Ad.* 97 (Demea's complaint to Micio about Aeschinus) *tu illum corrumpi sinis.*

397 aequo animo "with resignation" (*OLD* s.v. *aequus* 8). Contrast 24, where the phrase means "fair-minded" (*OLD* 6c).   **accipiet**: 367n.   **feceris**: the fut. perf. may here represent the immediate result of the action described in the subordinate clause. So de Melo 2007: 40.

398 otiosus "acting in a leisurely manner" (*OLD* 1b).   **interea**: so, too, Charinus at 314, *interea fiet aliquid, spero.* Davos' "plan" amounts to no more than delay in hope that something will turn up, as of course it will, though from an entirely unexpected direction. Those who caught the hint at 224 might detect a metatheatrical allusion here.

399 uide "consider" (*OLD* 16b).   **quin**: 45n.

400 dicam, sc. *me uxorem ducturum esse.* Repeating the verb of a command or suggestion, as *dicam* here answers Davos' *dic* at 394, is a common way for colloquial Latin to express agreement or affirmation (Thesleff 1960: 12–17, Müller 1997: 191–2).   **puerum**: a child, without reference to its sex. Cf. Davos' noncommittal *quidquid peperisset,* 219.   **ne resciscat**: the standard verb for discovery in Roman comedy, often (as here) expressing a wish to avoid it. The connotation, says Gell. 2.19, is of revealing something hidden. Thus the Pamphilus of *Hec.*, eager to avoid the revelation of his priggishness: *placet non fieri hoc itidem ut in comoediis* | *omnia omnes ubi resciscunt* (866–7). Simo will in fact make this discovery at 459–64.   **cautiost** = *cauendum est* (*SEL* I 233).

401 suscepturum, sc. *me.* In this sense, *suscipio* (*OLD* 4) becomes the equivalent of *tollo* (219n.).   **facinus**: 145n. Not really a surprise for Davos (219).   **fidem**: a promise (*OLD* 2). Logically the obj. of *darem* but brought into the main clause for emphasis.

402 qui = *ut* (307n.). *se* is obj. of *deserturum.* The sense is *me obsecrauit ut sibi fidem darem qui sciret se [me] non deserturum.*

403 curabitur: the vague impersonal allows Davos to avoid committing himself to a course of action. Contrast Sosia's *curabo* at 171.   **caue:** *caue* + subjunc. creates a more polite command than *noli*. Since it is inherently neg., the conj. *ne* is optional (*SEL* I 232–4, *NLS* §130, Zetzel 1974).

[*II.iv*] *Simo, Davos, Pamphilus (404–11)*

The music stops with Simo's entrance, which is evidently from the forum, where Pamphilus encountered him (253–4). He will not see his son and Davos until 416. The action is soon complicated further by Byrria's entrance at 412, which must be from the same direction since he is following Simo (414). Byrria will see Davos and Pamphilus almost immediately (415) but remains unobserved by all the others as he overhears their conversation and comments on it in asides to the audience. The result is what Marshall 2006: 166–7 calls a split-focus scene, where attention is shifted back and forth between and among characters. The easiest way to imagine this particularly complex interplay is for Davos and Pamphilus to move across the stage at 403, momentarily out of Simo's line of sight as they continue their conversation, while Simo moves toward the center. Byrria will then establish himself unseen opposite them. The scene heading of Vat. lat. 3868 (9v) shows an arrangement much like this, with Byrria to the left, Simo in the center, Pamphilus and Davos to the right, though actual stage practice may not be the direct inspiration for the miniature.

404 reuiso: *redeo ut uideam* (Don.). As often in comedy, a character explains the reason for his entrance. So, too, Byrria (412–14), Chremes (740–1), Charinus (957). Simo appears to assume for himself the purpose he had previously assigned, in almost precisely the same terms, to Sosia (170).

405 hic: Don. hears a note of disdain in the use of the demonstr. prn. instead of a noun, e.g. *senex* or *pater*.   **quin . . . neges:** colloquial Latin avoided the periphrastic fut. subjunc. that strict tense sequence might expect (*NLS* § 187 (b), de Melo 2007: 57–60, 87–9). Thus Pl. *Poen.* 183–4 *quid tu dubitas quin extemplo . . . fur leno siet?* ("Do you doubt that the pimp will immediately be a thief?"), where the idea of futurity is established by *extemplo*, not by *siet*.

406 meditatus "having rehearsed a speech" (*OLD* 4). So Moschion in Men. *Sa.* 94–5, as well as Pl. *Amph.* 197, *Aul.* 550, *Mil.* 944. *Pers.* 45–6 applies the term to actors rehearsing their lines: *tragici et comici | numquam aeque sunt meditati.* Don. quotes Men. fr. 37 K–T εὑρετικὸν εἶναί φασι τὴν ἐρημίαν | οἱ τὰς ὀφρῦς αἴροντες ("eye-brow raisers [i.e. philosophers] say a deserted spot is the place for solving problems"), a gloss perhaps more relevant to *ex solo loco* than to *meditatus*.

408 qui: either the adv. (307n.) or the rel. prn. as a true abl., with *orationem* as antecedent.   **differat te** "to confound you" (*OLD* 2), although the lit. meaning "to pull apart" echoes in the background. Cf. Pl. *Ps.* 359 *iam ego te differam dictis meis*.   **apud te** "in your senses" (*OLD* 11), i.e. "keep your wits about you." At 937 *vix sum apud me* means "I'm scarcely in my right mind." Cf. *Hau.* 920–1 *prae iracundia, | Menedeme, non sum apud me*.   **sies**: 234n.

409 ut: like *utinam*, used to express a wish (*OLD* 42), strengthened here by *modo*.   **inquam**: more an emphasizer than a verb of saying, e.g. *Hec.* 214 *egon? :: tu, inquam, mulier* (Müller 1997: 180).   **hodie**: 196n.

410–11 numquam . . . commutaturum patrem | unum esse uerbum "that your father will exchange not a single word" (*OLD* s.v. *commuto* 5a). The clause explains the preceding *hoc*.

[II.v] Byrria, Simo, Davos, Pamphilus (412–31)

Byrria was sent away at 337 for an unspecified reason and in an unspecified direction. Now he returns, in obedience, he says, to an instruction to keep his eye on Pamphilus. When and where he received this instruction and why Charinus should suddenly have become suspicious of Pamphilus after having left him on seemingly good terms (374) are not explained. As written, the scene is T.'s invention. Roman productions were not limited, as Athenian productions were, to three speaking actors, and here he exploits the dramatic possibilities of that expanded cast. This is the first scene in the play that requires four speaking parts (the others are 459–67, 684–708, 861–6, and 904–52), and T. uses it for maximum effect as the response to Davos' improvised strategy by Simo and by the uncomprehending Byrria produces a richly comic combination of misdirection and misunderstanding. For the three-actor convention in New Comedy, see Frost 1988: 2–3, for the use of four speakers in T., Lowe 1997, and for the size of T.'s company, Marshall 2006: 120–5.

The developing action continues uninterrupted despite the notional scene division and is particularly noteworthy for the comments that go unheard by other characters present onstage. How should we understand the delivery of what are broadly termed asides? The mechanics of masked performance, where lack of peripheral vision means that even characters in close proximity may not see each other and that speech will be clearest when directed "out front" makes such comments easiest to deliver effectively as addresses to the audience. For examples of the device, see Bain 1977: 105–20 (Greek) and Duckworth 1952: 109–14 (Roman), and for staging asides under the conditions of ancient performance, Marshall 1999: 115–24.

412 relictis rebus "having dropped everything" (*OLD* s.v. *relinquo* 3). Similar expressions at *Hau.* 840, *Eun.* 166.

414 id "for this reason" (*OLD* 13). An internal acc. looking back to *ut scirem. propterea* "accordingly" then gives the reason for this action, viz. *erus iussit.*   **hunc** = Simo. Byrria, who must have caught sight of Simo in the forum, now follows him onstage in the hope of being led to Pamphilus.

415 ipsum, i.e. Pamphilus.   **adeo**: 162n.   **praesto**: adv.   **agam**: 186n. Byrria announces his intention to eavesdrop on their conversation.

416 em serua "Watch out now!" Davos realizes that Simo has at last spotted them and is approaching.

417 quasi de improuiso: Davos' stage direction for the role he wants Pamphilus to play. An unambiguous instruction like this helps identify *ehem* as an expression of surprise (Müller 1997: 106–8).

418 probe: as again at 421 and 423, Davos is either encouraging Pamphilus with marks of approval unheard by Simo (and Byrria) or is commenting to the audience on Pamphilus' performance. The practicalities of performance may suggest the latter. (His coaching of Mysis at 751 will raise a similar question of interpretation.)   **ut dixi**: Simo here says almost exactly what Davos had imagined at 388 and what Pamphilus reported at 254. Use of *uolo* makes for a more peremptory instruction than a pres. imper. *uelim* would have been a kinder alternative (Barrios-Lech 2016: 106–8).

420 neque istic neque alibi "neither in this nor in anything else." The advs. are locative in origin, but both *istic* (*OLD* 2) and *alibi* (*OLD* 3) acquire this extended meaning.   **mora** "obstacle" (*OLD* 8c). Cf. Pl. *St.* 710 *non mora erit apud me.*   **hem!** Byrria is thoroughly taken aback and rendered almost speechless by Pamphilus' apparent reversal.

421 obmutuit: said of Simo, no doubt with a hint of satisfaction at having read the old man correctly.   **quid dixit?** said of Pamphilus. Byrria can still not believe his ears. (Asides can be overheard – at 592 Simo catches something of Davos' aside; at Pl. *Mil.* 1348–50 Palaestrio must make a quick recovery when overheard by the soldier – but there is no dramatic gain in imagining Byrria's question as referring to Davos' *obmutuit*.)   **ut te decet**: Pamphilus' acquiescence sits well with his somewhat imperious father. If, as Davos thought, Simo was taken aback by this apparent turn of events, he recovers quickly and begins working to regain the initiative.

422 postulo: *iuste uolo*, says Don., who distinguishes this from the other verbs of requesting, *petimus enim precario, poscimus imperiose*. Thus *Hau.* 1025–7 (Clitipho entreating his mother) *obsecro . . . quod peto aut uolo, parentes meos ut commonstres mihi*, *Hau.* 606 (Bacchis naming her price) *mille nummum poscit*.

423 sum uerus? "Wasn't I right?" In the absence of an interrogative marker, intonation must make the difference between a statement and a question, e.g. *rogas?* (163, 184, 267, 762, 909). So too with longer utterances. Thus Cic. *Mil.* 60 *Clodius insidias fecit Miloni?* is confirmed as a question by Cic.'s introduction, *age uero, quae erat aut qualis quaestio?* Cf. Quint. 11.3.176 on the contribution of voice to meaning. Here, however, Davos' words could be equally well understood as a triumphant exclamation (*sum uerus!*), especially if addressed, in counterpoint with Byrria, to the audience.   **excidit**: with abl., a verb of deprivation (*OLD* s.v. *excido*[1] 6).

424 nunciam: 171n.   **in mora** "delay." Pamphilus will now exit into the house.

425 fidem: Eng. usage invites distinctions that T., with the single word at his disposal, did not have to make. Chrysis' reported appeal to Pamphilus' *fides* at 290 suggests loyalty (*OLD* 8). At 401, *fides* is a promise (*OLD* 2), at 586, confidence (*OLD* 12). Here the connotation is trustworthiness (*OLD* 9b), or perhaps good faith (*OLD* 7). Having no reason to doubt the sincerity of the scene played out before him, Byrria naturally concludes that Pamphilus has abandoned his pledge to avoid the marriage (326–32). For the exclamation, cf. 245, *Ad.* 38.

426 uerbum "saying" (*OLD* 10), primarily an early usage (e.g. *Eun.* 732, *Ad.* 803–4, 952–4), where, as Don. notes, later Latin would say *sententia*. Cf. 61n. on Sosia's recourse to proverbial wisdom.   **uolgo**: adv. abl. Cf. *Hau.* 421 *aut illud falsumst quod uolgo audio | dici* ("or it's untrue what I hear commonly said").

427 melius "[something] better."

428 illam, i.e. Chremes' daughter. She is evidently not the *monstrum* of Pamphilus' imagination (250). How and under what circumstances Byrria saw her remains unexplained. Glycerium, too, is described as *forma bona* (119).

429 memini uideri: the pres. inf. is regular with *memini* when recalling a personal experience, e.g. Pl. *Cist.* 552–3 *mihi ab hippodromo memini adferri* *paruolam | puellam* ("I remember a very young girl was brought to me from the racecourse"). An omitted acc. subject (here it is *eam*) can be easily supplied, e.g. *Hec.* 822–3 *memini abhinc menses decem fere ad me . . . | confugere anhelantem . . .* ("I remember that around ten months ago he came rushing to me all out of breath . . ."). For Byrria to say, "She seemed, as I recall, to be a nice-looking girl," makes good sense, but all MSS actually read *uidere* here, which Don. glosses *memor sum me uidisse*. Because that is not nearly as satisfactory a meaning, edd. universally emend to *uideri*, for which Don.'s otherwise garbled note offers indirect support.   **quo** "for which reason" (*OLD* s.v. *quo*² 1)   **aequior** "rather sympathetic to" (*OLD* 7).

430 illum, sc. *Charinum.*

431 malo . . . malum: a play on *malum* as "misfortune" (*OLD* s.v. *malum*¹ 2) and *malum* as punishment. Cf. the famous barb directed at Naevius, *dabunt malum Metelli Naeuio poetae* (Ps.-Ascon., p. 215 Stangl). Byrria is fatalistic about the slave condition. He now exits in search of Charinus and will not return.

[II.vi] Davos, Simo (432–58)

With Pamphilus and then Byrria off the stage, the action continues without pause, still in iambic senarii. Though taken aback by Pamphilus' unexpected agreement to the marriage, Simo remains suspicious and searches for ways to regain control even as Davos presses his advantage and teases him for the audience's benefit.

432 hic . . . credit: a comment to the audience. Simo, of course, has good reason to suspect trickery and has been on his guard from the beginning. Thus his warning to Davos at 196–200. The two appear continuously aware of their roles as *iratus senex* and *seruus callidus* and of what a comedy therefore expects of them.

433 ea . . . gratia "for this purpose" (*OLD* 7c). *causa* would be more common in later Latin.

434 narrat: 367n. Davos' immediate reply confirms that this question is addressed directly to him and is not an aside to the audience.   **aegre . . . quidem**: the MSS read *aeque*, which Don. took to mean "no more now than before" with reference to their previous encounter, when Davos repeatedly dodged Simo's questions (185–205), but it is difficult to derive that sense from the Latin since while *aeque* suggests a comparison, *quicquam* looks to a negative that is not present. Of the proposed emendations, *aegre*, first suggested in a dissertation by Ludwig Schopen in 1821 (and adopted by Brown) offers the easiest fix, viz. "hardly anything just now."

435 hem! 116n.   **prorsus**: 371n.   **atqui**: the adv. introduces a strong denial of the previous statement (*OLD* 1a). Simo was expecting some excuse and is not sure what to make of Davos' refusal to rise to his challenge.

436 A comment aside to the audience.   **hoc male habet uirum**: "This has the man off balance" (*OLD* s.v. *habeo* 21a).

437 potin es = *potisne es*. Both *potis* (and *pote*) + the appropriate form of *sum* and *possum* are found in Pl. and T. (cf. *siquid potes*, 333). The older expression, from which *possum* is derived (Weiss 2020: 455), remained in colloquial use through the late Republic, e.g. Cat. 72.7. Virgil revived *potis (est)* as an archaism (*Aen.* 3.671, 9.796, 11.148), and it continued in later poetry as a metrically convenient variant (Ernout 1953 §256, Fordyce 1961: 203–4).   **dicerē**: the pause before a change of speaker can have the effect of lengthening a naturally short vowel, thus making a light syllable heavy, an ex. of what metricians call *breuis in longo*.

438 num: in comedy, the interrogative adv. may reflect anxiety, doubt, irony, or surprise on the part of the questioner, e.g. Pl. *Men.* 620–1 *num ancillae aut serui tibi responsant? :: nugas agis.* ("Are the maids or slaves answering you back?" :: "You're blathering."), T. *Ph.* 846 *num tu intellegis quid hic narret? :: num tu?* ("Do you understand what he's saying?" :: "Do you?"). Here, since Davos' ability to tell the truth could be doubted, Simo's skepticism probably lies just under the surface: cf. 578 *num censes faceret . . . ?* ("Do you suppose he would do that . . . ?"). See *SEL* I 473–4, Bailey 1953: 121–2.   **quippiam** "at all" (*OLD* s.v. *quispiam²* 1c), the neut. sing. used adverbially.

439 hospitae: a gentler alternative to Simo's earlier *peregrinam* (146). He may be deliberately affecting a neutral, conciliatory tone: *consuetudo* was Pamphilus' own word for his relationship with Glycerium (279). The striking hyperbaton *huiusce . . . hospitae*, though hardly unprecedented in T. (e.g. 471 *haec . . . fallaciam*), is the result of emendation: the MSS read *propter huiusce hospitae consuetudinem*, which does not scan. A less radical solution preserves the word order by restoring the archaic genitive *hospitāī*, found with some frequency in Pl. but elsewhere in T. only at *Hau.* 515 *Cliniāī* (also by emendation). See Questa 2007: 58, Weiss 2020: 251.

440 hercle: 194n.   **adeo** "indeed" (*OLD* 8), the particle simply adding emphasis to *si. sunt molestiae* is understood. Davos immediately follows his firm declaration with a hedge.

442 recta . . . uia "in the right way." The text is uncertain. All MSS read *eam rem* (not *id*) and some include *recta*, but the combination produces an unmetrical line. Since *viā* can itself convey the required meaning (*OLD* 6d), *rectā* may be an intrusive gloss, but *eam rem* might just as readily have replaced *id*. The sense, at least, is clear.

443 laudo: a colloquial expression of approval (*OLD* 2). Cf. *Ph.* 139–40 *in me omnis spes mihist.* :: *laudo.* ("All my hope is within myself." :: "Good for you!"). Davos will play on the expression below, 455.   **licitumst**: T. uses both the deponent and active perf. of *licet*, e.g. *Hau.* 819 *quam non licitumst tangere*, but *Hau.* 965 *tibi non licuit.*   **ēī**: for the scansion, see Questa 2007: 73.   **dumque aetas tulit**: Davos, knowing what his master would most like to hear, echoes Simo's own words at 188. Cf. *Ad.* 151–2 (Micio's hope for Aeschinus) *dixit uelle uxorem ducere.* | *sperabam iam deferuisse adulescentiam.* That youth is the appropriate time for love affairs is a common sentiment, e.g. Cic. *Cael.* 43–5, Hor. *Carm.* 1.19.15–16, Sen. *Phaed.* 446–8.

444 clam: not strictly true, especially not after the events at Chrysis' funeral (133–6), but Davos' effort to cast Pamphilus' behavior in the best possible light has truth to it. It was certainly able to generate the *fama* that initially led Chremes to propose a marriage (99–101).   **infamiae**: dat. 331n.

445 fortem "honorable" (*OLD* 4b), like Gk. καλός. For this moral sense, cf. Pl. *Trin.* 1133 *eum sororem despondisse suam in tam fortem familiam.* The connotations of *humanum* are significantly broader (236n.).

446 animum ad uxorem appulit: Davos speaks the truth (273), though not the truth that Simo is meant to hear. For the expression, cf. 1 *poeta . . . animum ad scribendum appulit.* The echo, if deliberate, may support the kind of thematic link suggested by Gowers 2004: 163, "It is as though T. presents us with a contrived personal or professional predicament that the plays then take up . . .".

447 subtristis: the prefix, a mark of "reduced intensity" (*OLD*), also generates *submoneo* "drop a hint" (*Eun.* 570) but is significantly more productive in Pl., e.g. *submerus* "nearly pure" (*St.* 273), *subrufus* "reddish" (*Cap.* 648), *subausculto* "eavesdrop" (*As.* 586, *Mil.* 993), etc. Pamphilus' moral dilemma is taking a toll on him.   **aliquantum** "a bit." Simo is reluctant to abandon his skepticism.

448 quod: neut. acc. prn. for the cause of displeasure + dat. of the person (*OLD* s.v. *suscenseo* b). Cf. *Ph.* 361 *adulescenti nil est quod suscenseam* ("There's nothing for me to be angry about with the young man"). Here, the *quod*-cl. is the subj. of *est* and, since Davos wants his statement to be heard as a fact rather than a possibility, he uses the indicative.

449 Davos' feigned reluctance forces Simo to coax the lie out of him. It is a masterful bit of improvisation working from Simo's *subtristis*. For the rapid change of speaker, cf. 184n.   **quin dic**: 45n.

451 drachumis . . . decem: abl. of price. Latin speakers might facilitate the pronunciation of a Greek consonant cluster by adding a vowel (anaptyxis). Thus μνᾶ becomes *mina*, τέχνη *techina*, Ἀλκμήνη Alcumena. Ten drachmas for a wedding feast would certainly be a small sum: at Pl. *Men.* 219, Erotium allocates *tris nummi*, at the time probably understood as six drachmas, to provision a dinner for three. At *Ad.* 370 the generous Micio is said to have approved half a mina, i.e. fifty drachmas, to provision a party of four. For the price of things in Roman comedy, where values were not always aligned with reality, see Duckworth 1952: 275–6.   **est opsonatum**: impers. pass. of the deponent *opsonor*, but there is also MS support for personal *opsonatus*, which is no less appropriate.

453 quem . . . meorum aequalium: the sg. prn. reflects the severe limitation imposed on Pamphilus' notional choice.

454 potissimum "in preference to the others" (*OLD* 2a). Cf. 962 *quem ego mihi potissimum optem . . . dari?* ("Whom would I more want to appear . . . ?"). **quod** = *si*, introducing a contingency (*OLD* 6b). Cf. Pl. *Cas.* 275 *quod nunc liceat dicere* ("If I may now say so"). Davos takes some care in faulting his master.

455 quoque "indeed" (*OLD* 4). Davos stresses the extent of Simo's miserliness.   **perparce**, sc. *sumptum facis*. T. is fond of this intensifying prefix, which is most frequently attached to verbs (25n.)   **non laudo**: a cheeky echo of Simo's *laudo* (443).

456–8 The duel between master and slave plays out not only through their dialogue but through parallel addresses to the audience.

456 commoui: addressed to the audience and unheard by Simo.   **uidero**: Simo responds to this unexpected twist as best he can. The fut. perf. carries the specific sense "I'll see to it," where the simple fut. means "I'll see [something]." Thus *Ad.* 845 *ego istuc uidero* ("I'll see to that"), but *Eun.* 1009 *numquam pol hominem stultiorem uidi nec uidebo* ("I've never seen nor will I see a more foolish man"). For the idiom, see de Melo 2007: 47–8. It carries over into Classical Latin as well, e.g. Cic. *Cael.* 35 *sed uidero hoc posterius . . .* ("but I will see to this matter later . . .").

457 rei: part. gen., here scanned *rēī*.   **uolt . . . sibi**: 375n.   **ueterator** "the old rogue." So too of the slave Syrus at *Hau.* 889, of Hannibal at Lucil. 826M/953W, *uetus* implying long-standing habit rather than chronological age.

458 illic: prn., said with a gesture toward Davos.   **rei**: dat., always scanned as a monosyllable (Questa 2007: 61).   **caput** "ring-leader" (*OLD* 13). Cf. *Ad.* 568 (to the clever Syrus) *sentit te esse huic rei caput.*

[III.i] Mysis, Simo, Davos, Lesbia (Glycerium) (459–80)

As Mysis returns with the midwife Lesbia (cf. 299–300), Simo and Davos retreat to one side and overhear them. This second four-speaker scene again splits the focus, shifting between Mysis and Lesbia in one conversation and Simo and Davos either speaking together or in independent comments aside. The offstage cry of Glycerium in childbirth (473) will add a further complication.

459–60 A similar idea similarly expressed opens the scene at *Hec.* 58–9 *per pol quam paucos reperias meretricibus | fidelis euenire amatores, Syra.*

458 Lesbia: first named at 228. Use of the name here immediately identifies the new character as the midwife Mysis was sent to fetch.

460 haud ferme "hardly ever" (*OLD* 3b).   **inuenias**: as at 66, the potential subjunc. with an indef. 2nd pers. sing. introduces a general statement (*NLS* §119).

461 Simo has long had his eye on the neighboring house (83–4) and witnessed Chrysis' funeral (115–36), so he could easily have some idea of Mysis' identity. The first words printed here as a question could thus well be assigned to him, but the rest of the line is more problematic. Barsby follows the MSS allocation of speakers. OCT, which punctuates the opening words as a statement, assigns *quid narras?* to Davos, while Victor 1996b: 372–3 has *ab Andriast ancilla haec* spoken aside by Davos and assigns the remainder of the line to Lesbia, responding to Mysis. As printed here, *quid narras?*, usually an expression of surprise or incredulity, e.g. *Ph.* 135 *duxit.* :: *quid narras?* :: *hoc quod audis*, would have to be the equivalent of *quid ais?* seeking confirmation of a preceding question, as at *Eun.* 334 *eho nonne hoc monstri similest? quid ais?* :: *maxume.* ("Well, isn't this something monstrous? What do you think?" :: "Absolutely!").

462 hem! Simo is understandably shocked by this apparent contradiction of Davos' earlier assurance, *animum ad uxorem appulit* (446). Yet it will soon be Davos' turn to be momentarily taken aback by developments.

464 iussit, sc. Pamphilus (219).

465 actumst "we're done in" (*OLD* 21c). Simo might expect to overcome Pamphilus' wandering affections by force of will, but the birth of a child would certainly end all hope of Chremes' assent to marriage with his daughter.   **sīquidem**: 225n.

467 illi, i.e. *Glycerio*. With Lesbia's *sequor*, the pair exit into Glycerium's house.

468 remedium . . . huic malo: the faint medical connotation (also at *Ph.* 185, *Ad.* 294) is all but lost elsewhere, where *remedium* means little more than "solution," e.g. *Ph.* 200, 617, 824. See Fantham 1972: 14–18. Mysis' loose tongue threatens to give the game away.   **quid hoc?** the reference is to Mysis' revelation, which the ever-suspicious Simo finds difficult to believe.

470 sensi: the verb suggests a fullness of understanding. Don. invokes Cic., slightly misquoting *Cat.* 1.8 *non solum uideam, sed etiam audiam planeque sentiam.*   **sensisse**: *se* is understood. Davos has registered the fact, if not the substance, of Simo's aside. (Cf. Pl. *Mil.* 381 *etiam muttis? Mos.* 512 *quid tute tecum loquere?*) Though Don. imagines Simo thinking aloud to himself here, Republican stage practice as determined by the focusing power of the masks, the relatively small stage space, and the close proximity of the spectators rather suggests direct address to the front. Simo and Davos each seeks to take the audience into his confidence, adding another dimension to their rivalry.

471 primum: adv. Simo has long suspected some *fallacia* by Davos (159–60, 196–200) and now mistakes the truth for the beginning of some such scheme.   **ab hoc**, i.e. *a Dauo*.

472 hanc simulant parere: the suspicion is not beyond the realm of comic possibility, as Pl. *Truc.* 384–411 and 448–81 show, though Glycerium is a world away from Pl.'s calculating Phronesium. Both Pl. (*Capt.* 1031) and T. (*Eun.* 39) identify the *pueri suppositio* as something of a comic cliché.

473 Iuno Lucina: Glycerium calls upon the Roman goddess of childbirth, *ab eo, quod in lucem producat* (Don.); *Cat.* 34.13–14 treats *Lucina Iuno* as a cult title of Diana. In Menander, says Don., the appeal was to Artemis, as apparently also at *Georg.* 112. There are similar cries at Pl. *Aul.* 691–2 and T. *Ad.* 486–7. In addition to these scenes, Gell. 3.16.1–4 (and 2.23.18 quoting Caecilius' *Plocium*) recalls other such moments, as does Schol. Theoc. 2.66b (ap. *Andria* fr. 35 K–T). So too, perhaps, Plat. *Rep.* 395e, Turp. 179R, Afran. 346–8R. Comic convention thus relegates to an off-stage cry what in reality would have been a scene of elaborate preparation and then considerable activity (French 1986: 73–7, McWilliam 2013: 265–7).

474 hui! A favorite exclamation of surprise, wonder, or disgust in T. (fifteen examples to only four in Pl.), often suggesting something close to a whistle (Müller 1997: 130–1). Transliteration of this sound as it was heard in colloquial speech carries over into the informal prose of the late Republic, used both by Cic. (*Att.* 5.19.1, 13.21.5, 13.35.2) and his correspondents Caelius (*Fam.* 8.15.2) and Cassius (*Fam.* 15.19.4).

475 audiuit, sc. Glycerium. She would, thinks Simo, have taken her cue from Mysis and Lesbia.

476 temporibus, *id est per tempora* (Don.). Dacier understood this as language drawn from the theater, where the proper sequencing of an action can be integral to its dramatic effect. Cf. *Eun.* 10–13, where T. faults his rival for an illogical ordering of speeches.   **tibi**: dat. of agent. Cf. *Ph.* 321 *iam instructa sunt mi in corde consilia omnia.*

477 discipuli: at 192 Simo likened Davos to a *magister improbus*. He must mean Glycerium and Mysis, who he believes are carrying out a charade, but why does he use the masc. pl.? Don. records several explanations, none very satisfactory, and himself includes Pamphilus in the reference, which suits the grammar better than the context. Some modern commentators (e.g. Ashmore, Brown) call this a generalizing pl., though the reference is in fact specific.

478–80 Simo turns to address the audience, eager to claim credit for having recognized Davos' "trick." His three lines employ three discrete metaphors: military (*imparatum . . . adortus esset*), sport (*ludos redderet*), and commerce (*in portu nauigo*).

478 hicin = *hic* + *ne*, said with a gesture toward Davos. Cf. *hocine* (186).

479 mihi ludos redderet: a variant on the common expression *ludos facere* + dat. (Pl. *Mos.* 427, *Truc.* 759) or acc. (Pl. *Am.* 571, *Bac.* 1090, *Per.* 803).

480 periclo: abl. Simo believes that his escape from difficulty comes at Davos' expense.   **in portu nauigo**: the safe harbor metaphor is (or becomes) proverbial, e.g. Cic. *Fam.* 9.6.4 (to Varro) *quod his tempestatibus es prope solus in portu* ("because in this stormy weather you almost alone are safe in port").

[III.ii] Lesbia, Simo, Davos (481–532)

Lesbia emerges from Glycerium's house, largely repeating back through the door the instructions she has just given inside. Her words show no sign of the *temulenta mulier et temeraria* that Mysis had led us to expect

(229–30). There may be tension here between the old woman of comic stereotype and the expected competence of the midwife (228n.), much as T. put Sosia in the position of cook but without the cook's expected mannerisms. Lesbia does, however, sing in bacchiacs, the only bacchiacs in all of T., and their slow, halting rhythm could perhaps suggest unsteadiness. (For these characteristics of dramatic bacchiacs, see Moore 2012: 197–9; for their scansion here, Questa 2007: 438–9.) The timing of her appearance further inflames Simo's suspicions, and he proceeds to entangle himself in a snare of his own making. Davos is only too happy to encourage his error.

481 Archylis: Lesbia's reappearance here mirrors Mysis' entrance at 228.   **oportent**: verbs normally used impersonally can take a subj. in Pl. and T., though usually a neut. prn., e.g. *Ad.* 754 *non te haec pudent?* (*NLS* §209n.).

482 ad: purpose (*OLD* 41). Don. quotes *Hau.* 207 *haec sunt tamen ad uirtutem omnia* ("All this is to preserve their morals").   **huic**, sc. Glycerio.

483 lauet: intrans. Don. quotes Menander λούσατ' αὐτὴν αὐτίκα ("bathe her at once," fr. 36 K–T), which also shows that T. has turned iambic-trochaic speech into song.   **poste**: adv. This archaic forerunner of *post* is restored by edd. for metrical reasons, since the alternative, the trisyllabic scansion of *deinde*, is not found until the poetry of late antiquity. *poste* is also metrically necessary at *Eun.* 493, Pl. *As.* 915, *Most.* 290, and Enn. *Ann.* 218 Sk.

484 quod iussi dari bibere: the Byzantine scholar Photius quotes what appears to be the original prescription from Menander's Ἀνδρία: καὶ τεττάρων | ὠιῶν μετὰ τοῦτο, φιλτάτε, τὸ νεόττιον ("and afterwards, dear, the yolk of four eggs," fr. 37 K–T). T.'s generalizing of the original detail has encouraged much, albeit inconclusive discussion of his tendency to universalize (good summary by Ludwig 1968: 178 n. 29). Elimination of Menander's chatty φιλτάτε may give the midwife a more business-like tone, a tone Don. ad 485 heard as the *auctoritas et iactantia medicorum*.   **bibere**: the inf. to express purpose is the regular construction in early Latin, e.g. Pl. *Pers.* 821 *bibere da* (*NLS* §28, further examples with a variety of verbs in *SEL* I 418–19).

485 The promise goes unfulfilled. Lesbia exits and will not return.

486 The one line sure to have the greatest effect on Simo is spoken, not sung.   **per . . . scitus**: the intensifier is easily detached, e.g. *Hec.* 58 *per pol quam*, Cic. *De or.* 1.205 *pergrata perque iucunda*. *scitus*, lit. "possessing knowledge" (perf. part. *scisco*) quickly becomes a general term of praise (*OLD* 4).

ecastor: the oath by Castor is a woman's oath, while swearing by Pollux (*pol, edepol*) is common to women and men. So Gell. 11.6, on Varro's authority (Adams 1984: 50–4, Müller 1997: 142–4).

487 superstes: the wish stands as a matter-of-fact reminder of antiquity's high rate of infant mortality, often estimated at 20–30 percent in the Roman world. That was why, says Aristotle, children were not named until the seventh day after birth (*HA* 7.588a8–10); the Roman naming custom was after the eighth or ninth day (Macr. 1.16.36). See Parkin 2013: 45–50, Carroll 2018: 147–51. **quandōquid+em**: 225n. **ipse**, i.e. Pamphilus. So, too, the description at 98, *gnatum tali ingenio praeditum*, which at that time Simo found so pleasing.

488 est ueritus: 323n., and for the indic. after *quom*, 96n. **adulescenti**: also used of a woman at *Ph.* 794, *Hec.* 661. At 118, Glycerium is introduced as *adulescentula*.

489 uel "for example" (*OLD* 4b). Simo offers a reason for thinking the midwife's appearance is contrived. **qui te norit**: 10n. Much will turn on what Simo knows – or thinks he knows (502, 503, 914, 934).

490–1 Simo, like Davos before him (220–4), mistakes the truth for a fiction, though with the further twist that this "truth" emerges through one of comedy's distinctly striking fictions, viz. the inside conversation carried out to the street (Duckworth 1952: 125–6). The effect is among T.'s most overt metatheatrical gestures. See Sharrock 2009: 147–50.

490 coram: Don. distinguishes this adv. directed *ad certas personas* from *palam*, directed *ad omnes*. **quid opus facto esset**: the necessity is expressed by a neut. prn. subj. and abl. perf. part. used impersonally of the action required (*OLD* 12c). Cf. 523 *quod parato opus est*. A supine is sometimes used instead, e.g. *Hau.* 941 *ita dictu opus est*. **puerperae**: dat.

491 clamat: not literal shouting. Simo exaggerates for effect. Cf. 144n.

493 quem . . . incipias: a rel. cl. following *idoneus* (as also following *aptus* and *dignus*) is invariably subjunc., but whether to be categorized as final or consecutive is unclear (*NLS* §158).

494 accurate: the adv. responds to *tam aperte* above, with a verbal idea, e.g. *me fallere debebas*, understood from *fallere dolis*. **metui**: pass. inf. **certe** "at least" (*OLD* 2), taken closely with *metui*.

495 Spoken aside, with a mocking echo of Simo's *certe* and *fallere*. **edixin**: Simo refers to the warning at 196–200.

496 interminatus sum "forbid with threats" (*inter* + *minatus*). Cf. Pl. *Capt.* 791 *eminor interminorque ne quis mi opstiterit obuiam* ("I warn and I threaten that nobody stand in my way"). **ueritu's**: 323n. **quid re tulit?** "what was the use?" The perf. of *refert*, regularly written as two words.

497 credon: 315n. **hoc**: anticipates the following inf. cl.

498 teneo: 86n. **quid ... quid**: the first means "in what respect?" (*OLD* s.v. *quis*[1]15); the second means "what?" (*OLD* 2b). The line is spoken aside, as Simo's *quid taces?* makes clear. The momentary shift to speech in lines 497–8 signals the importance of the moment as Davos conceives a new stratagem.

499 credas: answering Simo's *credo* (497). For the subjunc., 191n. **haec**, i.e. the apparent *fallacia*. The neut. pl. here becomes sing. at 501.

500 min = *mihi* + *ne*. **tute**: the emphatic prn. is vaguely insolent, as if Davos finds it difficult to credit Simo with recognizing the "plot." Thus Simo's reply, *irrideor*.

501 qui? "how?" (*OLD* s.v. *quid*[2]1).

502 te noram: cf. 159–60. Simo will be misled by his own suspicions.

503 enim: often simply an emphatic particle in early Latin, e.g. *Ad.* 656 *quid illas [dicere] censes? nil enim.* ("What do you think they say? Nothing at all.").

504 egon te? sc. *non pernouerim.* **si ... occepi**: the protasis of a factual condition. Davos knows his man.

504–5 dari | tibi uerba: 211n. **falso?** adv. Simo is being ironic. **muttire**: also at *Hec.* 865–6 *neque opus est | adeo muttito* ("there is no need for even whispering"). It is, like *musso* and its frequentative variant *mussito*, derived from the idea of being able to say no more than "mu" (Varro *L.* 7.101: cf. μύζω). Colloquial Eng. might say "not a whisper."

506 hoc ... unum: 497n. Simo emphasizes his certainty in the matter where he is in fact most completely in error. **intellexti**: 348n.

507 nilo setius "nevertheless" (*OLD* s.v. *setius* 2c). **referetur ... puer**: even a sham birth would, presumably, require a baby to display. Cf. Pl. *Truc.* 401–9. The details of Davos' improvised story will continue to develop with further telling: 513–15, 768–70. His passive construction neatly avoids acknowledging an agent for the imagined charade. (Most MSS read *deferent*, which spoils the effect.)

508 ere: 183n.   **ut sis sciens**: the same expression at 775, Pl. *Poen.*
1038. Its appearance in the SC de Bacanalibus of 186 BCE (*CIL* 1.581.23)
senatuosque sententiam utei scientes esetis ("and that you be aware of the
Senate's decree") suggests an echo of legal usage, where *sciens* means
"knowingly," e.g. in the oath quoted by Cic. *Fam.* 7.1.2 and Fest. 102.11 *si
sciens fallo* ("if I knowingly swear falsely . . .") and the law ascribed to Numa
(*Leges Regiae* 12) *siqui hominem liberum dolo sciens morti duit* ("If anyone
knowingly puts to death a free man . . ."). Davos thus purports not just to
inform, but to forewarn Simo.

510 prorsus: with *amotam* "utterly removed" (371n.).

511 unde: the adv. can mean either "from whom" (*OLD* 2) or "from what
source" (*OLD* 3). Simo, in his eagerness to determine responsibility, may
well mean the former, but Davos answers as if having heard the latter.

512 quī "by which means" (*OLD* s.v. *qui²* 3).   **haec** = Glycerium. Davos
begins his series of lies with a fragment of truth (216).

514 ilico: 125n.

515 accersitum: supine of purpose with direct obj. (134n.), immediately
followed by an adverbial cl. of purpose.

516 hoc: anticipates *ut uideas*.   **nil**: adv. (*OLD* s.v. *nihil* 11).   **mouentur** "interfere with" (*OLD* 9b). The use of pres. for fut. is a colloquial
touch, occurring most often with neg. expressions, e.g. *Ph.* 486 *audi obsecro
. . . :: non audio* (*SEL* I 18–21).

517 quid ais? 137n. Simo's half-line breaks the run of septenarii and turns
the conversation in a new direction.

518 capere, sc. *eam.*

519 Davos evades Simo's probing quest. by responding with a purely rhetorical quest. of his own.   **abstraxit**: said (more truthfully) of Chremes
at 243.   **omnes nos**: who are these *nos*? The response of Pamphilus'
friends to Simo's initial queries may have been disingenuous (86–9), but
at 444 Davos said the affair was kept secret.

520 amarit = *amauerit.* Davos echoes his words at 446.

521 id . . . negoti: Don. understands the business in question to be the
baby about to be left on the doorstep, presuming a contrast with Simo's
responsibility for *has nuptias.*   **tu tamen idem** "meanwhile, *you*"
(Barsby), understanding *idem* as reinforcing *tu.* This was Don.'s reading,
though he considered *tandem* a possible alternative. OCT prefers *tamen-
dem*, i.e. *tamen + -dem*, which Lindsay also read at Pl. *Merc.* 595 and *Mil.*

585. Some addition is necessary, since the MSS reading *tamen* leaves the line one syllable short.

523 immo: Simo will not take instruction from Davos, contradicting him with three imperatives in this single line.   **parato opus est**: 490n.

The music ceases with Davos' exit into the house. Simo then turns to address the audience. It is important for us to know that he remains skeptical of Davos' story.

525 haud scio an: in T. an expression of hesitation or doubt, e.g. *Hau.* 999 *etiam haud scio anne uxorem ducat* ("Perhaps he'll even marry"), *Ph.* 774 *etiamne id dubiumst?* :: *haud scio hercle . . . an mutet animum.* ("Is there still any doubt?" :: "For all I know . . . he could change his mind.").

526 parui: gen. of value. There is latent irony in Simo's refusal to count as important the baby who will turn out to be his own grandchild. So too in the title scene of Men. *Epitr.* 218–375, when Smikrines adjudicates the fate of a foundling and its birth tokens.   **maxumum** "most important."

527 quod, i.e. Pamphilus' professed willingness to marry.   **ipsus** = *ipse.* It matters most that Simo has heard this from Pamphilus directly and not simply through an intermediary.   **Chremem**: 247n. on the declension of Greek proper names.

529 quid = *quor* (*OLD* s.v. *quis*[1] 16).   **alias** "at another time" (*OLD* 1).   **malim**: delib. subjunc. after a pres. indic. in the protasis referring to fut. time, e.g. *Ad.* 531 *si hic pernocto, causae quid dicam?* ("If I stay here all night, what excuse shall I give?").

530 quod "in view of the fact that" (*OLD* s.v. *quod* 10).

531 si nolit, i.e. if he changes his mind.

532 adeo "in fact" (*OLD* s.v. *adeo*[2] 8).   **eccum**: an interj. formed from *ecce* + the appropriate acc. prn. ending. Thus also *eccos, eccam, eccas,* etc.

[III.iii] Simo, Chremes (533–80)

Having convinced himself that the marriage is again a real possibility, Simo must now overcome Chremes' not unreasonable objection to Pamphilus as a son-in-law. His neighbor, a deeply concerned but not equally domineering parent, remains skeptical but at last gives his reluctant consent. The power of such fathers to settle the affairs of their children, the very power that had so offended Pamphilus (236–9), is well within the norms of ancient family life. In extant comedy, the only time a prospective bride is consulted about a proposed marriage occurs at Men.

Mis. 968–9, where we are told Krateia was asked whether she wished to marry Thrasonides: "ναί," φησί, "πάππα, βούλ[ομαι." ("Yes, Papa," she said, "I do wish it.") The emphasis of these two Terentian fathers on the *commodum* and *utile* may yet seem particularly cold, even callous, to modern ears.

As often in T., the meter changes here with the introduction of a new character. The rhythm remains iambic throughout, with unaccompanied speech to ensure the clarity of its central argument, but the scene begins and ends with music, a passage of octonarii rounded off by an iambic dimeter to set apart Chremes' entrance (533–7) and then returning to song with septenarii once an agreement is reached (575).

533 iubeo Chremetem: a polite greeting that would have continued with *saluere*, but Chremes is in no mood for such niceties. Cf. *Ad.* 460–1 (the meeting of two old and old-fashioned acquaintances) *saluere Hegionem plurumum | iubeo. :: oh te quaerebam ipsum: salue Demea.* For the greeting, see Barrios-Lech 2016: 186, and for the Gk. acc., 247n. **optato** "in accordance with one's wishes" (*OLD*), an adv. formed from *optatus* + the adverbial suffix -*o*, as *continuo, dolo, merito*, etc. (Weiss 2020: 385).

534 ex te: the position is emphatic. Chremes is particularly angered that even after his explicit refusal (147–8), Simo should persist in speaking of the marriage. **auditum**, sc. *esse*. Chremes could have said *se audisse*. The impers. construction suits the vagueness of his sources. **aibant**: for the metrically convenient form (*aiebat* at 930), cf. *seruibas*, 38n.

535 uiso, *ad uidendum uenio* (Don.). **id**: anticipates the following ind. quest.

536 quid . . . quod: ind. quest. followed by rel. cl., both being obj. of *scies*. **te uelim**: 45n.

538–43 Simo's opening appeal is modest in tone and carefully constructed: two invocations (538, 540), each modified by a rel. cl. (539, 541), followed by the actual request, which ends with a finely wrought alliteration (542–3).

538 per te deos oro: for the word order in this formula of supplication, see 289n. **Chreme**: this is, after the initial greeting, the first of four line-ending voc. in the scene (550, 561, 574). They are marks of Simo's earnestness as well as his regard for his neighbor (Barrios-Lech 2016: 203–4).

539 simul "together with" (*OLD* 6b), i.e. their *amicitia* strengthened as they grew up. Simo stresses their common bond before making his request.

540 unicam: as at 100, a misleading detail, since the plot will come to turn on the discovery of a second daughter (923–37).

541 quoius: 336n.   **potestas** "opportunity" (*OLD* 5b). At 52, in an explicitly Greek context (*ex ephebis*), Simo spoke of Pamphilus' own *liberius uiuendi potestas*. That now, in a conversation between fathers, he should thrust a *potestas seruandi* upon Chremes could be heard by Romans as a delegation of parental authority. Simo is taking a much softer line with Chremes than he had with Pamphilus or Davos.

542 uti = *ut*.

543 fuerant: the plupf. often functions as a simple past tense with no suggestion of priority, e.g. *Ph.* 399–400 *id si falsum fuerat, filius | quor non fefellit?* ("If it was untrue, why didn't your son refute it?"), *Hau.* 661 *uiuitne illa quoi tu dederas?* ("Is the woman to whom you gave her still living?"). For the alliteration and word play, cf. 832 (also spoken by a senex).   **ne me obsecra**: 384n.

545 atque "than" (*OLD* 13a), as regularly after words of implied comparison like *alius, magis, talis*, e.g. *Ad.* 597 *numquam te aliter atque es in animum induxi meum* ("I've never regarded you as other than as you are").

546 in remst utrique "if it's advantageous to each of them" (*OLD* s.v. *res* 13b).   **fiant**, sc. *nuptiae*.   **accersi**: the standard verb in comedy for bringing the bride to the groom's house, as at 581, 741, 848. For the accompanying procession, see 362n.

548 utrique: the repeated emphasis on a common good for both their children is a noteworthy feature of Chremes' character, though Don. ad 547, reading these lines as an argument from utility, takes *utrique* as referring instead to the two fathers (*mihi et tibi, non alteri utile, alteri inutile*). Modern commentators do not take that view.   **id**: the anticipatory prn., here looking to the coming *ut*-clause, seems to be a mannerism of Chremes (cf. 535).   **oro te**: Chremes responds to Simo's *te oro* (538) with a parallel appeal.

549 quasi si: for the pleonasm, cf. *nisi si*, 249n.

550 immo: the particle introduces a correction (*OLD*f), e.g. *Eun.* 562 *narra istuc quaeso quid sit.* :: *immo ego te obsecro hercle ut audias.* ("Explain, please, what is going on." :: "I'd like you, please, to listen.").   **postulo**: 422n.

552 irae "bad feelings," often in this sense constructed with *inter* (*OLD* 2), e.g. *Hec.* 310 *pueri inter sese quam pro leuibus noxiis iras gerunt!* ("What grudges children bear each other over trivial complaints!"). At 576

Simo will identify Davos as the source of this information, but when Davos could have told him this is unclear. Only the announcement of Pamphilus' new-found willingness to marry has been dramatized (440–6, 519–20). **audio** "I'm listening" (*OLD* 10), said with a note of skepticism. So Don., *ironia, mox "fabulae!"*

553 magnae, sc. *irae.* **fabulae!** 224n.

555 integratio "renewal." The word appears only here among classical authors. The verb agrees with the complement, not the subj. *irae.* The sentiment, which has a proverbial ring, finds a parallel in Men. 567 K–T ὀργὴ φιλούντων ὀλίγον ἰσχύει χρόνον ("the anger of lovers lasts a short time"), a line quoted without context by the late anthologizer Stobaeus. Attribution to the Greek *Andria* is thus uncertain.

556 em: the particle adds urgency to the request, e.g. *Hau.* 866 *em istuc uolueram, Ad.* 169 *em sic uolo.* **id**, i.e. the reconciliation implied by 555. It is the obj. of *ante eamus* "forestall" (*OLD* 4a).

557 lubido: 308n. **occlusast** "restrained" (*OLD* 2c), an unusual metaphoric use. Fantham 1972: 62 compares Pl. *Mil.* 605, *Trin.* 188 *linguam occludere.* Cf. the metaphoric sense of *claudier* at 573.

558 harum: *inuidiosius*, says Don., recalling the *meretricum contumelias* of *Eun.* 48. Simo imagines Glycerium's entire household conspiring to ensnare his son.

559 aegrotum: 193n. Simo seems to acknowledge Pamphilus' lingering attraction to Glycerium, which at 562 he will refer to vaguely as *illa mala.* His position is much like that attributed to Laches in *Hec.*, who forced marriage on a son still infatuated with a *meretrix* (114–33).

560 uxorem demus: though arranged marriage was the norm both at Athens (Vérilhac and Vial 1998: 210–14) and Rome (Dixon 1992: 62–6, Hersch 2010: 39–43), Simo's exhortation, as if Chremes' daughter were a commodity to provide or a medication to prescribe, seems particularly unfeeling. **consuetudine**: previously used to describe Pamphilus' association with Chrysis (110) and then Glycerium (279, 439). Simo speaks as if relationships can be easily established or substituted.

561 coniugo liberali, i.e. marriage with a social equal. At 122–3, Simo used the term more generally in describing Glycerium as *forma honesta ac liberali* (122–3).

564 neque ... neque: the double neg. reinforces rather than cancels the preceding *non* (*OLD* 7d). Don. thought the construction deliberately ambiguous: is *hanc*, presumably Chremes' daughter, subj. or obj. of *habere?*

Since Pamphilus' constancy is the point at issue, it is probably his ability to remain faithful to her rather than her ability to keep hold of him that is foremost in Chremes' mind, just as he, as a concerned father, thinks he could not endure the sight of his daughter trapped in what he will later call an *incertas nuptias* (830).   **perpetuo ... perpeti**: a traditional form of wordplay, particularly suited to Chremes' deep-seated conservatism. See 832n.

565 qui "how."   **periclum feceris** "put to the test."

566 periclum: Chremes sees clearly that what Simo called a test would for his daughter also be a risk.   **in** "in the case of" (*OLD* 42).

567 nempe "presumably." The particle acknowledges the concession implicit in the following statement (*OLD* 1c).   **incommoditas** "inconvenience." Simo puts the best possible spin on a potentially negative outcome.   **denique ... redit** "comes down in the end" (*OLD* s.v. *redeo* 14b). Cf. *Eun.* 158 *nempe omnia haec nunc uerba huc redeunt denique* ("so in the end all these words now come down to this").

568 si eueniat: an *ut*-clause might be expected after *huc redit*, e.g. *Hau.* 359 *in eum iam res rediit locum ut sit necessus* ("Matters have reached the point that it's essential"). Simo's substitution of a subjunc. condition stresses the remoteness of this possibility.   **discessio** "separation" (*OLD* 3), a euphemism for *diuortium* "divorce." (*discidium* is Pamphilus' word at 697.) Cairns 1969: 170 shows that the euphemism, along with the preceding apotropaic clause, finds an analogue in the language of Greek marriage contracts of the third century CE, e.g. P. Oxy. 1273 l. 52 καὶ ἐάν, ὃ μὴ εἴη, ἀπαλλαγὴ γένηται ("and if – may it never happen – a separation comes about . . ."). T. may thus be reproducing language found in his model, though the fact of six centuries between Menander and the papyri makes certainty impossible.

569 si corrigitur, sc. Pamphilus. The shift to an indic. reflects Simo's greater faith in this alternative possibility.

570 amico, sc. *mihi*. The first advantage Simo sees is for himself.   **restitueris**: since the fut. perf. is uncommon in a main clause, its use cannot be entirely explained as a metrically convenient alternative to the simple fut. In this case, what will be restored is represented as anterior to the two things that will be discovered. Cf. *ceperit* (213), *inuenerit* (381). See de Melo 2007: 35–50.

571 generum firmum: doubt on this score is, of course, the main reason for Chremes' hesitation. Simo represents as fact what is in reality only his hope.

572 quid istic? a common formula of concession, perhaps with a verb like *dicendum* understood, i.e. "What more is there to be said?" Cf. *Ad.* 133 *mihi sic uidetur.* :: *quid istic? si tibi istuc placet* . . . ("So it seems to me." :: "All right, then. If that's what you want . . ."). **animum induxti** "to convince yourself" (*OLD* s.v. *induco* 12b).

573 claudier: 203n. A rare verb appearing only three times in T. (never in Pl.) and only in this one archaic form. See Fantham 1972: 44–5.

574 maxumi: gen. of value.

575 With the central issue resolved, speech yields to song as the meter shifts to iambic septenarii.   **quid ais?** the quest. here introduces a new turn in the conversation that cannot, as at 137, be ignored (Barrios-Lech 2016: 173).

576 Dauos: 552n.   **intumst** = *intumus est.* The adj., "closest" (*OLD* 5), is constructed with gen. of the people and dat. of the thing.

577 nuptias . . . ut maturem: a logical inference from Davos' encouragement at 521–2.

578 censes: parenthetic.

579 tute adeo: doubly emphatic (162n.).   **heus!** Simo turns and orders Davos to be summoned from the house. Cf. Pl. *Mil.* 610 *euocabo. heus Periplectomene et Pleusicles, progredimini!*

580 eccum: 532n.   **foras:** adv. indicating motion from the house. Cf. loc. adv. *forīs* "outside" and n. *forīs*, pl. *fores* "door."

[III.iv] Davos, Simo, Chremes (580–606)

Davos preempts Simo's command by appearing of his own accord. The action is thus continuous, the division of line 580 between Simo and Davos being but one more indication of the artificiality of the scene divisions found in the MSS tradition. There are similar effects at *Hau.* 954, *Ph.* 795, and *Ad.* 81, 635, 958. (Pl. does not begin scenes in midline.) Shifting to the longer octonarius at 582 will facilitate the midline changes of speaker that come to characterize this scene and quicken its pace.

581 accersitur: 546n.   **aduesperascit:** so, too, *uesperascit* at *Hau.* 248. Inchoative verbs are not often built on nouns, though *lux* produces *lucisco* (*Hau.* 410, Pl. *Am.* 533, 543) as well as *luceo* (Pl. *Cur.* 9, *Mil.* 218, 709, etc.). For the formation, see Weiss 2020: 431–2. A wedding procession would normally begin in the early evening (362n.). Thus Cat. 62.1 *uesper adest, iuuenes, consurgite.*   **audin?** = *audisne?* Simo turns to Chremes, pointing to Davos' impatience as confirmation of his claim at 577–8. All but one tenth-century MS add the unmetrical *tu illum* to complete the sense, an intrusive gloss helpful to readers but unnecessary in performance, where the action would make the change of addressee clear.

582 dudum "previously" (*OLD* 1). Cf. Simo's expectation at 161–3.   **non nil** = *multum.*

583 uolgus seruorum "the common run of slaves," *uolgus* denoting members of a particular class or group (*OLD* 3). Cf. *Hec.* 600 *uolgus mulierum* "the whole class of women." Simo consistently thinks of Davos in terms recalling the comic slave stereotype, e.g. 159–60, 196–200, 471–80.

584 propterea quod: 38n.   **facerem**: a repudiating subjunc. (263n.) answering Simo's *faceres* (582).   **credidi**: the tense suggests that Simo has at long last put his suspicions aside.

586 fidem: 425n.   **qui** = *qualis* (*OLD* s.v. *qui*¹ 2).

587 quid? non? Davos feigns surprise on hearing what he had already surmised for himself (352–69).   **ea gratia**: 433n.

588 quid ais? here another expression of (feigned) surprise (137n.).   **uide!** exclamatory *uide* extends its meaning from quasi-literal "look," e.g. *Ph.* 986 *os opprime impurum: uide quantum ualet!* ("Shut his foul mouth: look how strong he is!") to emphatic "get this," e.g. Petr. 51.5 *uide modo.* Here it seems to mean something like "Fancy that!" or "Well, well!" Exx. in Hofmann 1951: 38.

589 numquam: Davos did of course recognize precisely this, but he will soon be brought up short by something he did not foresee.

590 ut "as soon as" (*OLD* 26).   **iussi**: as he did at 523. The aorist perf. establishes the following account in past time. Simo then slips into the pres. tense not, strictly speaking, a "historical" pres. to make the narrative more vivid as at 117 and 353, but because the conversation remains alive in his own mind. For the distinction between hist. pres. and past-referring pres., see Pinkster 1998: 71–6 and the exx. in *SEL* I 17–18.   **hic**, i.e. Chremes.   **hem!** a sign of alarm. Davos responds to the implications of Simo's *opportune.*

591 numnam: the particle serves as an intensifier, "are we really done for?" (234n.).   **perimus**: likely pres. though possibly perf. (= *periimus*), as often when *pereo* is an expression of despair (213n.). A contracted perf.

perīt also appears at *Eun.* 522.　　　**narro**: pres. for perf., "I've been telling him . . . "

592 audio: the MSS reading, but Don. knew fut. *audiam* as a variant and quotes Men. fr. 38 K–T τί ποτ' ἀκούσομαι; In this context, the difference between "What am I hearing?" and "What am I about to hear?" is slight.　　　**oro . . . exoro**: the *ex-* prefix indicates a successful action, the difference in this case being between asking and persuading. Cf. *pugno* "fight" and *expugno* "overcome." For the tense, cf. Pl. *Stich.* 528–9 *quam dudum in portum uĕnis?* :: *huc longissume postilla.* ("How long ago did you come into port?" :: "Not long at all after you."). 　　　**uixque** "with difficulty" (*OLD* 1).　　　**occidi!** Davos realizes that Chremes' assent makes the wedding once again a real possibility. This, along with his two previous short comments, are spoken aside to the audience and grow progressively louder in his distress until this one is partly overheard.

593 optume: the preceding hiatus at the change of speaker gives Davos a moment to recover and allows him to turn *occidi* into *optume*, another word of similar metrical shape beginning with "*o.*"　　　**per hunc**, i.e. *Chremetem.*

594 An exit line for Chremes, who has remained an acknowledged but silent witness to this conversation. In leaving, he confirms the truth of Simo's declaration. He will return at 740 after having given the promised instructions.　　　**modo** can indicate prospective action (*OLD* 5c), e.g. Pl. *Cas.* 526 *ego ad forum modo ibo.*　　　**apparetur**: impersonal.　　　**dicam**: here a verb of command, as the construction indicates. Cf. *Hau.* 340 *ibo obuiam, hinc dicam ut reuorantur domum.*　　　**renuntio**: pres. for fut., as often, esp. with verbs of motion (*SEL* I 18–21). The tense can sometimes be explained as equivalent to an Eng. pres. progressive, e.g. 732 *repudio quod consilium primum intenderam* ("I am abandoning the plan I had originally intended"), but it often refers to action thought to be entirely in the future, e.g. Pl. *Aul.* 400 *ego hinc artoptam ex proxumo utendam peto* ("I will request a baking pan to use from our neighbor here").

595 oro: the second such polite request to Davos (190, also accompanied by a voc.). Of its six other appearances, five are by Simo to Chremes (538, 556, 592, 823, 834), one by Chremes to Simo (548).　　　**mi**: Simo stresses his own interest in the wedding being arranged for his son.

596 solus "single-handed," an ironic aside. Davos recognizes that he has brought this new trouble upon himself.　　　**mihi corrigere gnatum**: Simo tacitly acknowledges Davos' influence over his son. The MSS read *corrigere mihi gnatum*, which to scan requires an awkward anceps before a diaeresis, i.e. *corrigeē.* Barsby's solution puts *mihi* in an emphatic position, which might suit Simo's focus throughout on himself. Brown prefers to read *gnatum mihi corrigere*.		**enitĕre**: imper. after *oro*, as at Pl. *Capt.* 1021 *sed <tu> dic oro. ut* + subjunc. might be expected, as at 556: Simo begins anew after the *quoniam*-clause interrupts his thought.

597 irritatus: Simo is thinking of the "quarrel" invented by Davos at 552.

598 quiescas "remain calm" (*OLD* 6b). The subjunc. suggesting advice rather than command is especially characteristic of slave speech (Barrios-Lech 2016: 64–6).		**age**: this intensifier in T. introduces questions as often as commands (Müller 1997: 53). It is used only by men.		**mirumni**: "I wouldn't be surprised if" (*OLD* s.v. *mirus* 3e). Davos surely knows that Pamphilus is at home because he just came from the house himself. Having at least temporarily lost the initiative, he seems reluctant to make a firm statement of any kind to Simo.

599 itidem "likewise" (*OLD* 2). Long-windedness, what Don. ad *Ad.* 68.3 called μακρολογία, commonly afflicts old men in comedy (Maltby 1979: 141–3). The redundancy of *eadem haec* and *itidem* may be examples of this trait in Simo.		**nullus sum!** like *occidi*, a stock expression of comic despair. Cf. Pl. *Cas.* 621 *nulla sum, nulla sum, tota, tota occidi*. Davos is again, as at 206, taken aback by Simo's action and finds himself momentarily at a loss.

600 in pistrinum: Davos would be saving Simo the trouble of making good on his threat at 196–9.		**rectā ... viā** "directly" (*OLD* s.v. *uia* 6c). At 442 the phrase is closer to its literal meaning.

601 preci: most often pl., as *Ph.* 498 *neque misericordia neque precibus molliri queas* ("you can be softened by neither pity nor prayers"), in the sing. only here in T. and at Pl. *Capt.* 244, *Cist.* 302 in the sense "entreaty."

602 erum fefelli: Davos may have in mind the claim that Pamphilus was resigned to the marriage (442–6, 519–20) and that the baby was part of a trick to deceive him (511–16).		**in nuptias conieci**: a colorful expression, as if Pamphilus were an animal in a snare or a prisoner in chains. It is repeated at 620 and 667.		**erilem filium**: 208n.

603 insperante: neg. *in-* attached to a pres. act. part. is familiar from coinages such as *insciens* (782) and *indicente* (*Ad.* 507), but the formation with *spero* is unusual.		**hoc**, i.e. Simo.

604 em astutias! 248n., with exclamatory acc. also at 785–6, 842. The pl., says Don., is ironic, *ut ei non una [astutia] sufficeret*.		**quod**: 289n. The action might certainly have taken a different turn had Davos not insisted that Pamphilus appear to agree to the marriage (386–98).

605 eccum ipsum, sc. *Pamphilum.* Davos responds to the sound of the opening door as Pamphilus emerges from the house. The shift from iambic to trochaic rhythm introduces a change of mood with the arrival of the new character.   **uideo**: hiatus creates the pause needed to give *occidi!* its full effect.

606 praecipitem: at 214 the imagined destination was the mill. Don. here imagines a sword or a noose. The word itself might suggest a cliff, the fate of Catullus' Mentula, as *Musae furcillis praecipitem eiciunt* (105.2).

[III.v] Pamphilus, Davos (607–24)

Pamphilus has met his father inside, learned that the marriage is once again in prospect, and realizes that Davos' scheme has backfired. As he vents his anger and dismay, Davos retreats to the side, commenting to the audience until noticed by Pamphilus at 616.

607 scelus: 317n.   **atque**: 225n.   **hoc**, i.e. the marriage. Subj. of *obtigisse.*

608 nulli: gen. of quality (*SEL* II 65–8, *NLS* §72 (6)). *nulli* for *nullius* also in Cato, *Orig.*, *FRHist* 153 (141P) *nulli rei sies* ("may you be of no account"). It is "corrected" to *nullius* in P. Oxy. 2401 and found in some MSS. For other irregular forms of the pronominal adjs., see Weiss 2020: 369.

609 seruon = *seruone.* For the exclamatory inf. clause, 245n.   **futtili** "useless" (*OLD* 3b). Derived from *fundo*, and not a common term of abuse. Don. refers to a sacrificial vessel that pours too easily and is thus not fit for purpose, perhaps like an unsuccessful *seruus callidus.* Pamphilus regrets having done precisely what the *adulescentes* of Pl. regularly do.

610 inultum numquam id aufert "he won't get away with it unpunished." For this idiomatic use of *aufero*, cf. *Ad.* 454 *haud sic auferent* ("they won't easily get away with it"). The admission of culpability does not keep Pamphilus from turning his anger on his slave.

611 malum: 431n. Don. quotes Men. fr. 39 K–T ἂν θεὸς θέλη, οὐκ ἂν ἀπολοίμην ("If god wills it, I won't die"), often taken to be T.'s original, though if so, he seems to have recast the thought significantly.

612 negabon: the fut. indic. is common in deliberative questions, e.g. Pl. *Capt.* 535 *quid loquar? quid fabulabor? quid negabo aut quid fatebor?* (*SEL* I 40).

613 ducere: taken with both *uelle* and *sum pollicitus.*   **qua audacia . . . audeam**: 242n. The same *figura etymologica* at *Eun.* 958–9 *qua audacia* |

tantum facinus audet? All MSS and Don. read *fiducia* "self-assurance" (*OLD* 4), congruent with the persistent emphasis on Pamphilus' *fides* (290, 296, 401, 425, 460, 643). OCT and most editors nevertheless print *audacia*, found in a medieval gloss, largely for stylistic reasons. The difference in meaning is slight.

614 nec quid . . . me faciam: a variant on the usual refrain of comic lovers (383n.). *me* (as also *mequidem*) is instrumental abl. (143n.).   **ago** "work at" (*OLD* 22).

615 aliquid me inuenturum: improvisation, or at least confidence in his ability to improvise, was a hallmark of the *seruus callidus*. Cf. Pl. *Ps.* 394–414 on the power of comic invention.   **producam** "produce" (*OLD* 5).

616 ehodum: 184n.   **bone uir**: ironic, as usual in T. (e.g. 846, *Eun.* 850, *Ad.* 556).   **uiden** = *uidesne*.

617 impeditum . . . expediam: an easy collocation, e.g. Pl. *Ep.* 86–7 *quo modo | me expeditum ex impedito faciam.*

618 nempe: ironic (*OLD* 1b).   **ut credam**: 263n.   **furcifer**: lit. "fork-bearer," a common, relatively mild term of abuse derived, says Don., from the practice of chastising a slave *ignominiae magis quam supplicii causa* by tying his hands to a wooden yoke (*furca*) set around his neck. For terms of abuse in comedy, see Duckworth 1952: 333–4 and, more broadly, Hofmann 1951: 85–9.

619 fretus sim: subjunc. in a cl. of characteristic. Cf. 335–6 *Dauom . . . quoius consilio fretus sum,* where the indic. makes this a statement of fact.

620 ex tranquillissuma re: Pamphilus' memory is highly subjective. His state of mind, not to mention his situation, has never been calm. Cf. the dilemma he acknowledges at 252–64.   **coniecisti**: 602n.

621 an non dixi: Pamphilus was hardly so definitive (399–400), but Davos is in no position to disagree.   **quid meritu's?** 202n. for the prodelision. Dacier, probably with the case of Socrates in mind (Pl. *Ap.* 36b), recalls the Athenian practice of asking a convicted defendant to propose a penalty, for which see Todd 1993: 133–5.   **crucem**: far graver a threat than the *furca*. The specter of crucifixion runs throughout comedy, either explicitly, e.g. Pl. *Mos.* 1133 (Theopropides to Tranio) *ego ferare faxo, ut meruisti, in crucem* ("I'll have you taken off to the cross, as you deserve") or by extension into vaguer phrases, e.g. [*abi*] *in malam crucem*, the functional equivalent of Eng. "Go to hell!" (e.g. *Ph.* 368). At 786, Davos will propose this punishment for Mysis. It is never a real threat in comedy (Parker 1989), but neither is it entirely a fiction. A (late Republican?) *lex* *libitinaria* from Puteoli (*AE* 1971.88, col. II 8–10), for example, specifies the equipment and personnel a public undertaker was obliged to provide (for a fee) to any private citizen wanting a slave crucified.

622 sine: 153n.   **ad me redeam** "recover myself" (*OLD* 5c), referring in this instance to mental recovery. Don. quotes Verg., *G.* 4.443–4 (Proteus returning to human shape) *uictus | in sese redit atque hominis tandem ore locutus.*   **ei mihi**: here an expression of frustration (73n.).

623 quom non habeo: for *quom* + indic. 96n.   **spatium** "time available for a purpose" (*OLD* 10), e.g. *Hec.* 130 *ubiquomque datum erat spatium solitudinis* ("whenever he'd been given time alone").

624 tempus "circumstances" (*OLD* 10).   **praecauere . . . ulcisci sinit**: the verb governs both inf., though it is appropriate only to the second. Don. calls this an ex. of syllepsis, a term more often reserved for a word used correctly but in different senses, e.g. "they covered themselves in dust and glory." When, as here, the word suits one context but not the other (*illud enim "cogit," hoc "sinit,"* Don.), the figure is more commonly called zeugma, e.g. Exodus 20.18: "And all the people saw the thunderings, and the lightnings, and the noise of the trumpet."

[IV.i] Charinus, Pamphilus, Davos (625–83)

At 374 Charinus left on a vaguely defined search for support in his hope of marrying Chremes' daughter. Now, having learned from Byrria of Pamphilus' apparent betrayal, he returns full of moral indignation but uncertain of how to proceed. His entrance mirrors Pamphilus' no less distraught entry at 236 (*hocinest humanum factu aut inceptu? hocin officium patris?*), though its differences prove on inspection more striking than its similarities. Pamphilus' outrage was specific from the outset: there is never doubt that the father he has in mind is Simo, and he expresses himself in the iambo-trochaic rhythms typical of T.'s metrical style. Charinus' song is at once more arresting and more traditional, arresting in large part *because* it is so outwardly traditional. Its precise metrical structure is a matter of conjecture since the medieval MS tradition preserves the text as prose and our oldest witness, P. Oxy. 2401 (iv/v cent. CE), is the work of a Greek-speaking scribe, who copied from an eclectic Latin text that was itself inconsistent in its colometry. The basic structure, however, is clear. The song opens with one dactylic line – the only dactylic tetrameter in extant Roman comedy – and then, having called attention in such dramatic fashion to the metrical change, it shifts to one of Pl.'s favorite lyric rhythms, the cretic (626–38). Only when

Charinus moves from moral generalities to his own immediate situation does the rhythm slip back into a more typically Terentian iambo-trochaic cadence (639).

Whether the inspiration for this song originated with Men. in *Perinthia* or some other source is unknown but ultimately less significant than T.'s willingness to appropriate an older Roman comic style to characterize his second young lover. Charinus' initial burst of moralizing before he comes to the matter at hand is traditional and thus, by Terentian standards, old-fashioned. Pl. often introduced monologues this way, e.g. *Epid.* 382–8, *Men.* 571–87, *Poen.* 210–15, but in his later plays, T. would, like Men. before him, either avoid such expansive introductions (e.g. *Hec.* 361–4) or keep them brief (e.g. *Ad.* 855–8: cf. Men. *Perik.* 532–6, *Sa.* 206–9). In both substance and manner, the ineffectual Charinus thus comes much closer to the Plautine *adulescens* than to most such characters in T.

What are Pamphilus and Davos doing in the interim? Charinus is too preoccupied to notice them until Pamphilus intrudes on his musings at 642, and Davos does not speak again until brought into the conversation at 665. It is easiest to imagine Pamphilus and Davos moving down to one end of the stage, continuing in dumb show their spirited discussion of punishment as Charinus enters from the opposite wing and addresses the audience. Something toward the end of his song then catches Pamphilus' attention and leads to their tense and awkward exchange. That misunderstanding finds some parallel at Pl. *Bac.* 534–60, where Mnesilochus feels betrayed by his friend Pistoclerus (*estne his meus sodalis?* :: *estne hic hostis quem aspicio meus?*) and, somewhat closer in characterization and moral tone, in the encounter of the friends Phaidimos and Nikeratos in an unidentified comic fragment that is tentatively dated to the third century BCE (*PCG* Adesp. 1017).

Charinus' *canticum* has attracted much discussion. For its colometry, see Questa 2007: 440–1 and for the testimony of the papyrus, Macedo 2018: 81–4. For its relation to older stylistic models, see Denzler 1968: 55–8, Lefèvre 2008: 115–17, Moore 2013: 105–8, Welsh 2014: 65–8. *PCG* Adesp. 1017 (no. 65 in Page 1962: 300–5) is discussed by Nesselrath 2011: 127–34.

625 memorabile "a thing to be proud of." Cf. Pl. *Cur.* 8 (Palinurus complaining of his lovesick master's conduct) *istuc quidem nec bellum nec memorabile.*

626 ut siet: an infin. cl. might be expected after the impersonal *est credibile*, e.g. Pl. *Mer.* 210–11 *neque credibile est forma eximia mulierem | eam me emisse ancillam matri* ("nor is it believable that I bought this very beautiful

woman as a maid for my mother"), but Charinus' overwrought expression
is hardly articulate. Two cls. of result then follow upon *tanta uecordia*. For
one *ut*-clause introducing another this way, a fairly frequent occurrence in
comedy, cf. Pl. *Bac.* 42–3, *Mil.* 1–4, *Ps.* 190–3; T. *Eun.* 220, 339–40, 501–2,
868–71, *Ph.* 733–4, 776–7, etc.

627 ut . . . gaudeant: the first of the two cls. of result. The sg. *quoiquam* is
followed by pl. verbs, a phenomenon that grammarians call *constructio ad
sensum*, but also an indication of the singer's agitation.   **atque**: introduces the second *ut*-clause.

628 alterius: to be understood with both *malis* and *incommodis*.   **com-
parent** "procure" (*OLD* s.v. *comparo*[1] 5).

629 uerum "morally right" (*OLD* 9).   **immo**: Charinus immediately
contradicts himself. He has thought of conduct even worse than what he
has just described.

630 modo "at one time" (*OLD* 6). The correlative will be not another
modo, but *post* "afterwards."   **quis** = *quibus* (dat. pl.).   **paullum**: adv.
"for a short while" (*OLD* 2c).

631 tempus, sc. *est.*

633 res premit: this ought to mean "the situation compels," but *premit* is
not normally used as a synonym for *cogit*. The oldest witness, P. Oxy. 2401
(iv/v cent.), did not clarify matters by reading the unmetrical *et timent et
tamen res eos pr{a}emit denegare* (Macedo 2018: 92). The line did not trouble Don., but some modern edd. bracket it as an intrusive gloss.

635 quor meam tibi? both a noun (e.g. *sponsam*) and a verb (e.g. *tradam*)
must be supplied, the ellipsis being another mark of Charinus' agitation.

636 proxumus = *carus, beniuolus* (Don.). A trochaic colon rounds off this
first part of the song.

637–8a The song ends with a brief coda as Charinus returns to his own
voice. The shift is marked by the use of shorter cretic cola and then a second trochaic climax.

637 si roges: generalizing subjunc. (66n.).

638 nil pudet: for the neut. noun with *pudet*, cf. Pl. *As.* 933 *nilne te pudet?*,
Men. 643 *quando nil pudet*. For similar constructions with normally impers.
verbs, see *SEL* II 90–1.   **hic . . . illi**: adv. of place, with a similar contrast
between *hic* and *illic* at 720.   **uerentur**: 323n. Dacier notes a similar
thought at Pl. *Epid.* 166–8 *plerique homines, quos quom nil refert pudet,* | *ubi*

pudendum est ibi eos deserit pudor, | *quom usust ut pudeat* ("most people, who feel shame when there's no need, when they should feel shame, their sense of shame deserts them, although there's need to feel shame"). The song ends with a short trochaic colon as a transition to recitative as Charinus moves from a generalized complaint to something more specific.

639 adeamne: Charinus is not one for decisive action. At 315 he posed a similar question to Byrria. Here Pamphilus will answer the question for him.

640 ingeram mala multa? the heaping of insults is again Plautine language: *Bac.* 875, *Men.* 717, *Ps.* 359. Don. hears this as a military metaphor, e.g. *tela ingerere* (Liv. 31.46.10, 37.41.9).   **aliquis dicat** "suppose someone says," a potential subjunc. (Palmer 1961: 314–15).   **promoueris**: intr. "to make headway" (*OLD* 5), a colloquial sense. P. Oxy. 2401, annotated for student use, glosses ἐργάσει "you'll earn [nothing]." For the fut. perf., cf. *Ad.* 842–3 *et istam psaltriam . . .* | *hinc abstraham.* :: *pugnaueris!* ("I'll pull that music-girl away . . . from here." :: "That will win the day!"). de Melo 2007: 42–3 calls this an "inbuilt consequence." So too the following *fuero* and *gessero*.

641 multum, sc. *promouero.*   **morem gessero** "gratify" (*OLD* s.v. *gero* 8d), here with *animo* standing for *mihi* as the thing gratified (*OLD* s.v. *animus* 2a). Charinus thus obscures his implicit contrast between *ei* in the first clause and himself in the second.

642 imprudens "unintentionally" (*OLD* 2).   **respiciunt** "show concern for" (*OLD* 8). Prosodic hiatus ensures that the prns. remain clearly articulated in delivery.

643 itane: the adv. introduces an indignant question (*OLD* s.v. *ita* 12).   **soluisti fidem** "you've kept your promise" (*OLD* s.v. *soluo* 20). Phaidimos adopts a similarly sarcastic tone when he thinks his friend Nikeratos has wronged him, *PCG* 1017.39 ὑπερεπιτηδείως διάκεισαι ("How wonderfully well-disposed you are!").

644 quid "tandem"? Pamphilus balks not at the charge that he has broken a promise but, as *tandem* ("at last") implies, that he has long sought an excuse for doing so.   **ducere** "lead on" (*OLD* 17). At 180, the meaning is completed by *falso gaudio*; here the verb carries that sense on its own.   **postulas** "expect" (*OLD* 4).

645 complacitast, sc. *Philumena*. T. uses this semi-deponent form again at *Hau.* 773 *eius sibi complacitam formam* ("her looks were attractive to him"). Pl. also uses an active form, e.g. *Rud.* 727 *si autem Veneri complacuerunt* ("if they were attractive to Venus").

646 heu me miserum: this exclamatory acc., so appropriate to the comic lover, is also found in tragedy (Enn. 78 *TrRF*, Pacuv. 294R, Accius 346R). **animum**: 164n. **spectaui** "judged" (*OLD* 6c).

647 hoc . . . gaudium, i.e. the prospective marriage to Philumena. Charinus feels he has been deliberately misled, and his emphasis on Pamphilus as the agent of his trouble complicates the word order. Understand *hoc solidum gaudium uisumst non tibi sat esse.*

648 lactasses "had led on," a very rare word, frequentative of the equally rare *lacio.* (The common form is *lacesso.*) In comedy, *lacto* appears only here and at 912 (restored by Don. from MSS nonsensical *iactas*), in Caecilius 91R, and Pl. *Cist.* 217 (by conjecture). It is slightly more frequent in tragedy, Pacuv. 211R, 241R; Accius 66R, 414R, and may add tragic color to Charinus' complaint.

649 habeas, sc. *eam.* Cf. Simo's equally bitter injunction at 889, though the obj. there is Glycerium. **uorser** "subject to" (*OLD* 12). Subjunc. in the ind. question, as very often after *nescio* (*SEL* I 336 counts 86 exx.), though Pamphilus reverts to the indic. in the next line. There are similar shifts of mood at 272–3 and 967–8.

650 hic: Pamphilus points to Davos. Having confessed his mistake (642), he quickly places responsibility for it on his slave. **conflauit**: a very colorful and versatile verb. Its original sense of kindling a fire (e.g. Pl. *Rud.* 765) expands to mean "arouse," "concoct," or "cause," usually with negative connotations. It was replaced here in all MSS by the anodyne gloss *confecit*; Don. preserves the correct reading.

651 carnufex: the generalized term (183n.) is made specific by addition of the adj., i.e. "my executioner." **de te**: placed before *si* (and immediately following the caesura) for emphasis. Charinus is not so ready to allow all blame to be shifted to Davos.

652 dicas, si cognoris: for the choice of tense, where classical Latin would say *diceres* and *cognouisses,* see 276n.

653 scio: Charinus continues his sarcastic tone. So, too, 658, 659. **altercasti**: active only here and Pacuv. 210R *mecum altercas? tace.* Perhaps another ex. of Charinus' pretentious diction. He is imagining what excuse Pamphilus might make. He knows, or thinks he knows, from Byrria's report of the conversation overheard at 418–25, that Pamphilus has agreed to the marriage.

655 immo etiam "just the opposite" (Thesleff 1960: 65–6). **quo**: abl. of degree of difference with *minus.* Pamphilus' earnestness is accentuated by the shift from song to speech, which continues (with one notable exception at 663–4) to 681.

660 destitit, sc. *Dauos*. The subj. should be evident from 650, but Charinus will require clarification as much for the audience's benefit as for his own. Cf. the emphasis on the name Stilpo at *Ph.* 356, 389–90, 740. The verb governs *instare* in the following line. *suadere* and *orare* in 662 may be hist. infin.

663–4 The text as printed creates a particularly lively exchange, but it has not gone unchallenged. The back-and-forth could be simplified by assigning one continuous response to Charinus: *Dauos interturbat? quam ob rem?* (Victor 1999: 271). More significantly, Bentley eliminated the musical intrusion by deleting *interturbat* and then *satis scio*, thus turning the lines into *senarii*. Neither change seems necessary or particularly desirable, but they well illustrate the inherent contingency of the extant text and its interpretation.

663 istuc, sc. *fecit*.   **interturbat**: the prefix works as an emphasizer. Don. quotes Pl. *Mer.* 833 *interemptus, interfectust* ("completely destroyed, done in").

664 nisi "except that" (*OLD* 5a).   **iratos qui auscultauerim**: for the construction, cf. *Ad.* 368 *mihi, qui id dedissem consilium, egit gratias* ("he thanked me for proposing that plan").

665 factum: hiatus at the change of speaker gives Charinus a moment to adjust to this admission.   **scelus**: 317n. The ease with which the two *adulescentes* shift all responsibility to Davos is as remarkable as his willingness to accept it.

666 duint: in origin an aor. optative, this archaic form of *dare* is reserved in T. for imprecations, as here, and wishes, e.g. *Ph.* 1005 *di melius duint* ("may the gods help us!"). For its etymology, see Weiss 2020: 444, 462; for its use in Pl. and T., de Melo 2007: 255–60.

667 eho: 88n.   **coniectum in nuptias**: the same expression at 602 and 620, each time used by a different speaker.

668 uellent . . . darent: in archaic Latin the imperf. subjunc. indicating an unreal condition could have either pres. or past reference (de Melo 2007: 72–7). Eng. usage thus requires a choice of tense that Latin need not make. A past reference is commonly assumed here.

669 deceptus sum "disappointed" (*OLD* 2) or "mistaken" (*OLD* 1)? T. uses the verb in both senses, the former at *Hau.* 725 and 728, the latter at *An.*

271, *Ph.* 469, 538, 927. Davos is being as euphemistic as he can, but as at 183, 209, and 600, he must acknowledge at least a momentary setback.

670 successit "turn out well" (*OLD* 7b), used impersonally.   **hac**, sc. *uia*, anticipating *alia uia*.   **aggrediemur** "approach," probably with overtones of hostile intent, e.g. Liv. 41.19.8 *pars deuio saltu circumdata ab tergo aggrederetur*. Don.'s text apparently read the more colorful *adoriemur*, which makes a military connotation explicit. Cf. 479 *adortus esset*, where Don. comments, *qui ex insidiis repente inuadit* and glosses *aggressus*. Some edd., e.g. OCT and Brown, therefore prefer it as the *lectio difficilior*, but unlike Don.'s *conflauit* at 650, which adds a sense missing from the MSS reading *confecit*, *adoriemur* only clarifies what the MSS already read and may thus itself be a gloss that found its way into Don.'s text.

671 nisi si: 249n.   **id**: anticipates the following inf. cl.   **processit**: indistinguishable in meaning from *successit* (and also impersonal). The variant gives Davos an impressive sequence of *p*-sounds.   **parum** "not too well." Cf. *Ph.* 735 *nisi . . . parum prospiciunt oculi* ("unless my eyes aren't seeing too well"). Davos is again being deliberately euphemistic.

673 immo etiam: Pamphilus assumes Charinus' ironic tone.

675 hoc tibi pro seruitio debeo: Davos reflects the master's view of a slave's responsibility, a frequent topic for slave monologues in Pl., e.g. *Aul.* 587–607, *Men.* 966–76, *Ps.* 1103–15. Since Davos' obligation is, strictly speaking, to Simo as *erus* (183) and not to Pamphilus as *erilis filius* (602), what he describes comes closer to the role of the comic *callidus* than to any actual master–slave relationship. For the Plautine topos, see Hunter 1985: 145–7, Fraenkel 2007: 167–6, 416, Richlin 2017: 342–9.

676 manibus pedibus: 161n.

677 capitis periclum: instances of self-sacrifice on behalf of a master become a staple of Roman moralizing. Val. Max. 6.8 *De fide seruorum* seems to draw upon a collection of such anecdotes. For *fides* and *obsequium* in the Roman ideology of slave behavior, see Bradley 1987: 33–40.   **dum** "provided that" (*OLD* 2).

678 tuomst, sc. *officium*.   **praeter spem**: another euphemism.   **euenit**: since the metrical beat falls on the first syllable, the likely scansion is *ēuĕnit*, i.e. pres. tense.

679 quod ago: subj. of *succedit*.

680 uel "or if you prefer" (*OLD* 1).   **me missum face** "fire me" (*OLD* s.v. *mitto* 3b). The phrase appears to be colloquial in T., e.g. *Eun.* 864 *missa haec faciamus* ("let's stop this nonsense"), *Ph.* 946 *missum te facimus* ("we'll let you off"). Both Pl. and T. retain the archaic imper. *face* primarily at line-end. Pl., not T., also uses *dice* or *duce*, though T. does have *abduce* (*Ad.* 482) and *transduce* (*Ad.* 917). For these forms, see Weiss 2020: 158.

681 cupio: Pamphilus would presumably like both to have a better plan and to dispense with Davos' assistance, but he will settle for having Davos get him out of his current predicament.   **restitue**: the full expression would be *restitue in locum in quem . . .* Cf. *Hec.* 21 *poetam restitui in locum* ("I restored the poet to his place").

682 The music resumes with the return of comic business as Davos sets out to devise a new plan.   **hoc**, i.e. the task Davos is promising to undertake. The meaning is unchanged whether the prn. is understood as abl., as 32 *nil istac opus est arte*, or nom., as *Ph.* 593 *argentum opus esse*. For Pamphilus, the emphatic word is in any case *iam*.   **em**: at Pl. *Mil.* 196–9 Palaestrio sets up an elaborate pantomime of deep thinking, with his successive poses witnessed and described in detail by Periplectomenus, 200–18. Davos may be affecting a similar posture here, but he is almost immediately interrupted by the sound of the opening door.   **concrepuit**: 226n.

683 nil ad te, sc. *attinet*. Pamphilus wants no excuse for Davos to stop thinking.   **nuncin** = *nuncne*, the contraction is built from the old form *nunce + ne*.   **hem!** here a mark of impatience tinged with annoyance. Cf. 882 *hem! modone id demum sensti, Pamphile?*   **inuentum dabo** = *inueniam*. The participle is predicative and serves to make the commitment to action more emphatic, e.g. *Eun.* 212 *effectum dabo* ("I'll get it done"), *Ph.* 944 *incensam dabo* ("I'll get her fired up"). See *SEL* I 437–9 for exx. of these and other verbs used this way.

[IV.ii] Mysis, Pamphilus, Charinus, Davos (684–715)

Mysis enters. Her first words, addressed back through the door, make clear that she comes in search of Pamphilus, but for reasons more closely aligned with the requirements of plot than with human nature. Glycerium has just given birth – Pamphilus last encountered Mysis on her way to fetch the midwife (300) – but he shows no particular concern for her physical condition and expresses no desire to see his newborn child. The focus will remain fixed on the failure of Davos' first plan to forestall the wedding and his need to devise an alternative. The rapid changes of speaker in lines 702–15 enhance the urgency of the situation.

684 ubiubi "wherever." Cf. *utut* "however," *quisquis* "whoever."   **inuentum . . . curabo**: the same construction as 683 with the same emphasis, though *curo* is not commonly used this way.

686 ehem: 417n. Mysis turns in response to Pamphilus' voice.

687 era, i.e. Glycerium. The subj. comes to her almost as an after-thought.   **ut . . . uenias**: the most common construction for a request following *oro*, though *ut* is sometimes omitted, e.g. *Ph.* 1020, *Hec.* 721.

688 hoc malum: the trouble in question is presumably the turmoil caused by reports about the marriage. Pamphilus is so wrapped up in his own problem that he apparently gives no thought to Glycerium's postpartum condition. The insouciance with which comedy represents childbirth and its attendant risks stands in marked contrast to the ancient reality, for which see Carroll 2018: 56–62.   **integrascit**: the inchoative form of *integro* appears only here in extant Latin.

689 sicin = *sicne*. Cf. *hocine* (186). *-ne* introduces an indignant statement with acc. + inf. addressed, as *tua opera* makes clear, to Davos. All MSS (and Don.) read the archaic *sollicitarier*, which makes the line an octonarius, but since Pamphilus' complaint extends to the following septenarius, there is no dramatic point to the momentary change. Edd. thus maintain the run of septenarii by emending to *sollicitari*. (Contrast 662–3, where the sudden burst of music signaled by the change of meter can be thought to have dramatic point.)

690 nuptias . . . apparari: obj. of *sensit*. The noun thrust ahead of its clause gains further emphasis from the characteristic diaeresis after the fourth foot of the iambic septenarius.

691 quibus, sc. *nuptiis*. Abl. of separation with *quiesci*, an unusual con-struction. Charinus plays on *quiesco* "to take no action" (*OLD* 4) and "to say nothing" (*OLD* 5), with an impersonal first clause and *hic* in the sec-ond referring to Davos. With the mixed condition, past contrary to fact leading to an unreal but conceptually certain result, compare the entirely contrary to fact 604, *quod si quiessem, nil euenisset mali*. Charinus is quick to join in transferring all blame to Davos. The sound play is again a tradi-tional effect.

692 hic = Pamphilus. Davos responds ironically to Charinus.   **edepol**: 229n.

693 ea res est "that's the reason," seizing on Pamphilus' statement at 690. At 268–70, Mysis cited three sources of anxiety, the pain of childbirth, knowledge of the proposed wedding, and fear of being abandoned by Pamphilus. Only the second now comes into play.

694–5 Pamphilus repeats the assurance he gave at 282–98, perhaps as much for Charinus' benefit as for Mysis'.

695 inimicos: predicative, with *omnis homines* answering *omnis deos* just above.

696 contigit "it's come about" (*OLD* 8c), impersonal where something more direct might be expected, e.g. "I won her" (Barsby).   **ualeant**: a formula of contemptuous dismissal (*OLD* 3d). Cf. *Ad.* 622 (thinking Aeschinus has abandoned Philumena for another) *ualeas, habeas illam quae placet!* ("Good riddance! Have the girl you prefer!"). The ill-wisher in question is of course Simo, but like all Terentian *adulescentes* in his position, Pamphilus is circumspect in his condemnation: *non dixit, quod intenderat, "pereant"* (Don.). Contrast Ctesipho's wish at *Ad.* 519–20 that his father Demea remain bedridden *quod cum salute eius fiat* with the willingness of young Plautine lovers to imagine their father dead (*Mos.* 233–4, *Truc.* 660–1).

698 resipisco "I breathe again," probably spoken aside since Pamphilus seems not to notice the interruption.   **Apollinis . . . responsum**: an allusion to the Delphic oracle, known to Romans at least since the days of the Tarquins (Cic. *Rep.* 2.44) and deeply embedded in Roman folklore, e.g. the story of Brutus the Liberator at Delphi with Tarquin's sons (Cic. *Brut.* 53, Liv. 1.56.7–13, Val. Max. 7.3.2). Cf. Pl. *Ps.* 480 *quod scibo Delphis tibi responsum dicito.*   **atque**: after the comparative = *quam* (*OLD* 15). Cf. Pl. *Mer.* 897 *amicior mihi nullus uiuit atque is est* ("nobody living is a closer friend to me than he is").

699 ut ne: 259n.   **per me stetisse** "that it's my fault" (*OLD* s.v. *sto* 22).

701 id: anticipates *ut credat.*   **in procliui**: lit. "downhill," i.e. "easy."

702 quis = *qualis* (*OLD* s.v. *qui*[1] 3b). Having made his noble declaration, Pamphilus waits for the inevitable praise – and is disappointed. Cf. the responsibility he eventually accepts at 896–8.   **atque**: 545n.   **forti's** = *fortis es.* For the prodelision, cf. *locutu's* (202n.).

703 scio quid conere: since Davos has not yet announced a new plan, this would have to be a general statement based on past experience, e.g. "I know your efforts" (Barsby), but who is speaking? *si Pamphili est persona, cum ironia dicitur,* says Don., *si Charini, simplex laudatio est.* Brown, following Victor 1993: 274–5, prints *coner* and assigns the entire line to Davos: "I know what I'm aiming for; I'll certainly sort this one out for you."

704 quin = *immo.* Davos has at last devised a new scheme.   **ne erres**: a command, i.e. "make no mistake." Cf. *Eun.* 16 *is ne erret moneo* ("I warn [him] not to misjudge").

705 sat habeo: as at 335, Charinus is easily satisfied. T. strives to make him an active participant in the dialogue, responding here to Davos' declaration even before Pamphilus does, but he remains little more than a spectator to the action.   **cedo**: 150n.   **ut satis sit**: *"ut" pro ne non* (Don.), with a similar note ad *Hec.* 101. A neg. fear cl. introduced by *ut* could apparently confuse even fourth-century students.

706 ad agendum . . . ad narrandum: the distinction between action and talk is particularly striking in this comic world, where action is largely a function of talk.   **uacuom** "having leisure" (*OLD* 11). Davos follows in a long line of comic slaves too preoccupied with their scheming to explain themselves to their masters. (Syrus at *Hau.* 332–44 continues the pattern.) See Sharrock 2009: 148–9, though whether T. "alludes" to his comic predecessors or simply exploits a traditional comic trope remains an open question.

707 amolimini "clear off" (*OLD* 1b), only here in T. but a common formula of dismissal in Pl., e.g. *Ps.* 557 *agite amolimini hinc uos intro nunciam.* It is not, however, a colloquialism limited to comic diction: Pac. 16R *nonne hinc uos propere <e> stabulis amolimini?*, 184R *non tu te e conspectu hinc amolire?*; Acc. 304R *age age amolire, amitte!*

708 Pamphilus exits into Glycerium's house. Davos turns to Charinus.   **uis dicam?** 388n.   **immo etiam**: an ironic reply to Charinus followed by a resigned aside to the audience.

709 narrationis . . . initium: Davos anticipates a lengthy explanation, which *immo etiam* has in fact forestalled.   **me**: abl. (614n.).

710 impudens: at 371, Davos' *ridiculum caput!* addressed to Charinus was good-natured banter, but *impudens*, a favorite term of abuse in Pl. directed toward social equals and inferiors, is much stronger and something of a surprise coming from a slave. Davos does not hesitate to assert himself at Charinus' expense.   **dieculam**: dimin. of *dies* (f.) "the passing of time" (*OLD* 10) = "a few hours," i.e. a delay.

711 quantum "to the extent that" (*OLD* s.v. *quantum*² 2).   **promoueo** "postpone" (*OLD* 3a), a sense difficult to parallel. Davos has made good on Charinus' previous request to Pamphilus, 327–9.

712 ut ducam: a wish (409n.).   **huc face**: Charinus gestures in the direction of his house. *fac ut uenias* (*facito . . . ut uenias* at Pl. *Men.* 437) recurs as an epistolary formula, e.g. Cic. *Att.* 2.14.1; *Fam.* 1.10, 14.4.3, and in the birthday invitation of Sulpicia Lepidina at Vindolanda (Tablet 291) *rogo libenter facias ut uenias* (http://vindolanda.csad.ox.ac.uk). For *face*, rare in mid-line, see 68on.

713 age: a signal of acquiescence (310n.). The exchange stresses the degree of Charinus' dependence.

714 Charinus leaves for his house. Davos turns to Mysis, who has been a silent presence throughout this exchange.   **dum** "until," often in this sense with pres. indic. (*SEL* I 98).

715 inquam: 409n.

[IV.iii] Mysis, Davos (716–39)

Mysis' primary function so far has been as a surrogate for her mistress, at 228 and again at 684 literally crossing the threshold between the female world hidden from view behind Glycerium's door and the male-dominated action on the stage. She has been a sounding board for Pamphilus' protestations and the personification of her mistress' anxieties. She now assumes a new role as foil to Davos as he works out his latest schemes to thwart the marriage to Chremes' daughter. The scene as it develops is by far the play's most metatheatrically brilliant episode, exploiting both the genre's improvisational impulses and its capacity for farce. The effect, as Don. notes, depends more on action than on speech, *haec scaena actuosa est, magis enim in gestu quam in oratione est constituta* (ad 722). Mysis begins with a direct address to the audience, then turns at 721 to open the conversation with Davos. Their scheme is set up and then unfolds in the play's second extended run of iambic senarii (716–819).

716 proprium: *perpetuum, non temporale et mutuum* (Don.). The mutability of the human condition, e.g. Men. 96 J βέβαιον οὐδέν ἐστιν ἐν θνητῷ βίῳ ("nothing is dependable in mortal life"), becomes a commonplace of Roman moralizing. Cf. Lucil. 701 M *cum sciam nihil esse in uita proprium mortali datum* ("since I know that nothing in life is given to a mortal forever"), with a similar idea in Acc. 422–3R, Hor. *Ep.* 2.2.170–4.   **di uostram fidem!** Plautine versions of this exclamation (*Am.* 455, 1130, *Cist.* 663, *Truc.* 805) include a verb, *obsecro*. For the formula and its variations, see Müller 1997: 144–6.

718 amicum, amatorem, uirum: Mysis echoes the late Chrysis' words as reported at 295 with the tricolon here adding emphasis to *uirum*.

720 laborem "distress" (*OLD* s.v. *labor²* 6). Cf. Pl. *Cur.* 219 *ualetudo decrescit, adcrescit labor* ("my health declines, my suffering increases").   **facile**: *ueteres "facile" dicebant pro certo* (Don.). The word in this sense is more common as an expression of agreement, e.g. Pl. *Poen.* 591–2 *hunc uos lenonem* |

Lycum nouistis? :: *facile*. Thus *OLD* 4, but cf. *Rud.* 1366 (Daemones doubts the sincerity of Labrax) *istuc facile non credo tibi* ("I'm not so sure I believe you about that."). **hic . . . illic**: contrasting circumstances "now" with those "then" (*OLD* s.v. *hic*² 5b).

721 mi homo . . . obsecro: both *mi* + voc. and the verb, the two often paired, are marks of entreaty most characteristic of female speech (Adams 1984: 55–8, 71; Barrios-Lech 2016: 118, 120–7).

722 puerum: 400n. The new-born infant, which Davos has somehow managed to extract from its mother's arms, is about to become a prop in his latest scheme. It would have been wrapped tightly in swaddling clothes (Sor. *Gyn.* 2.14–15, Plin. *Nat.* 7.2–3) and is thus a conveniently manageable bundle to pass on to Mysis. **opus est**: *tua* makes clear that nouns will follow to complete the sense. For the construction, see *SEL* II 358–9.

723 exprompta: "put to use" (*OLD* 2). Davos' scheme will require both the ability to follow elaborate instructions (e.g. 729) and a knack for improvisation. Some MSS, not understanding the role of *memoria* in what Davos proposes, read *malitia*, but Davos, not Mysis, is the one of *mala mens, malus animus* (164).

724 ocius "quickly." The adv. has a superlative, *ocissimus*, but no positive equivalent of Gk. ὠκύς (Weiss 2020: 385). It generally appears in commands.

726 humine? placing a new-born on the ground to elicit a cry was the first test of an infant's viability (Sor. *Gyn.* 2.6.10), but Mysis' objection to such treatment at this stage – the first indication that the child is anything more than an object – is both human and humane. **ex ara**: Don. *De com.* 8.3 mentions two altars by the stage, one to Bacchus (Liber) and another to the god of the specific festival. Plautine plays occasionally mention a single visible altar often associated with Apollo – Athenian houses had by the door a shrine to Apollo Agyieus ("of the Street") in the form of a pointed column – though the association is sometimes with other divinities, e.g. Diana (*Mil.* 411), Venus (*Cur.* 71, *Rud.* 688). For the convention and its uses, see Duckworth 1952: 83–4, Marshall 2006: 53–4. This is the only mention of such an altar in T. **uerbenas**: a general term for aromatic foliage of the sort placed around an altar on special occasions, such as a wedding. Serv. ad Verg. *A.* 12.120 says that Men. here specified myrtle (another example of T. substituting the general for the specific?), but he does not quote the verse. Don. does quote Gk. here (fr. 40 K–T), but the text is hopelessly corrupt.

727 tute: emphatic. Mysis does not like being ordered about by Davos.

728 ad erum: substituting the prep. phrase for *ero* avoids confusion with the following dat.   **iurato** "under oath." This is Bentley's emendation for the unmetrical *ius iurandum* of the MSS. OCT and Barsby print *iurandum*, which was Don.'s reading, an awkward substitution in itself, and *opus sit* + nom. is a rare construction (e.g. 337).

729 ut liquido possim, sc. *iurare*. Davos' improvisation (he is making up this reason on the spot) leads him to shift constructions halfway through.   **liquido** "unequivocally" (*OLD* 3).

730 religio: connotations of the Latin word extend from conscience to religious awe to punctiliousness in meeting obligations, and all come into play here as Mysis comments (ironically) on Davos' new-found scruples over violating an oath and misleading his master.   **incessit** "has come over" (*OLD* 6b). Cf. Liv. 29.24.4 *timorque in exercitum incederet*.   **cedo**: 150n. Mysis reaches out to take the baby from Davos.

731 porro: with *agam* = *acturus sim*.

732 pro Iuppiter! exclamatory particle + voc. Davos catches sight of Chremes, returning from his house, where he has again begun arranging for the wedding (594).

733 We never learn what the plan promised at 704 would have been. The ability to shift rapidly from one scheme to another in this way aligns Davos with Plautine *callidi* like Pseudolus, who was always capable of inventing new schemes on the fly (*Ps.* 601–2, 667–8). T. is sometimes thought to have expanded what he found in Men. to reflect this more traditional Roman style of intrigue (e.g. Lefèvre 2008: 64–8), but certainty is impossible.

734 ab dextera: Chremes' approach should be from the right, which is the direction of both his house and the forum (361). Since the forum is also the purported direction of Davos' return at 745, both characters must make their entries *ab dextera*. This means that to avoid Chremes now, Davos must exit to the *left* – so how does he manage to return in short order from the opposite wing? Various solutions have been proposed, the discussion inevitably complicated by lack of clarity in the text over the distinction, in modern terms, between stage right and left and audience right and left. The simplest solution is to have Davos indeed exit to the left, move behind the *scaenae frons*, and emerge again on the right. Returns like this from an unexpected direction are sometimes explained in the text by reference to an unseen alley or back street (*angiportum*), e.g. *Eun.* 840–7, Pl. *Most.* 1043–6, but a rationale is hardly required. For the feasibility of backstage movement (and the implicit elasticity of Roman stage space), see Marshall 2006: 106–8, and for the *angiportum* (a much-debated feature of Roman staging), Duckworth 1952: 87–8, Manuwald 2011: 70–1.

735 ut subseruias "lend support to" (*OLD* b). The indirect command depends on *uide*. Davos expects her to follow his lead in whatever charade he enacts for Chremes' benefit, thus her need for the *memoria atque astutia* of 723.

738 quod "for which," adv. acc. For the construction, as well as the traditional play on *opera / opus*, cf. *Ph.* 563 *num quid est quod opera mea uobis opus sit?*   **ut**: causal (*OLD* 21), e.g. *Ph.* 638–9 *ut est ille bonus uir, tria non commutabitis | uerba hodie inter uos* ("since he's a good man, you won't be exchanging three words today to close the deal").   **plus uides**: the idiom can also be reversed, e.g. *Ad.* 992–3 *quae uos propter adulescentiam | minus uidetis* ("what you see less clearly because of your youth").

[IV.iv] Chremes, Mysis, Davos (740–95)

Davos' new scheme exploits the truth for maximum effect: Chremes can hardly be blamed for reacting as he does to the claim that Pamphilus is the father of Glycerium's new-born child. Mysis, however, is caught flatfooted by Davos' suddenly aggressive questioning and shows none of the *memoria* or *astutia* he had hoped to find in her. She proves to be a bumbling and confused partner, and her frank efforts to understand his questions and frame her replies accordingly make for a richly comic scene. Working in counterpoint to the main dialogue they stage for Chremes' benefit are Davos' instructions and Mysis' bemused replies that he does not hear as well as his increasingly shocked response to these revelations, which he voices in asides of his own to the audience. There is also, of course, the inevitable stage business surrounding the infant, left so conspicuously on Simo's doorstep at the outset and eventually bundled off again in Mysis' arms.

The *iocularium malum* that Chremes thinks he has escaped in this scene (782) is *iocularium* in more ways than he realizes. Glycerium is not only an Athenian citizen but his long-lost daughter, and the infant, whose existence so outrages him, is thus his own grandchild. The audience, at least formally, is as unaware of these facts as Chremes is, though anyone with experience of the genre might well guess all or most of the truth. This lack of knowledge concentrates attention on the immediately farcical elements of the situation while obscuring its underlying ironies, an effect that may well be T.'s doing. Menander generally supplies his audience with the important information that his characters lack, producing as a result an anticipatory suspense and a sense of amused superiority as they watch the characters stumble toward a truth they have known from the outset. Divine prologues appear to have been his favored way to do this – those in *Aspis* (Tyche), *Perikeiromene* (Agnoia), and *Sikyonios* (Demeter?) are the extant exx. – so T.'s substitution of his polemical introduction shapes not only the audience's initial response to the play but their experience of the action to come.

740 quae opus fuere: 337n., and for the archaic perf. in *-ēre*, 13n. Chremes is prone to old-fashioned diction. See 832n.

741 accersi: 546n.   **sed quid hoc?** Chremes sees the curious bundle set by Simo's door, moves toward it, and then realizes what it is.

742 mulier: Chremes sees Mysis standing by the infant but does not know who she is.   **illic** = *ille* + deictic *-ce,* i.e. Davos. Left suddenly to her own devices, Mysis is unprepared for her part and looks around frantically for her director.

744 Davos returns as if from the forum and addresses the world at large about the activity he pretends to have seen there. He ignores Chremes but begins playing a role for his benefit (the *oratio* of 736) that Mysis proves so slow to understand.   **di uostram fidem!** 716n.

745 quid: followed in each instance by a part. gen. (*NLS* §77 (ii)). In the second instance, *quid hominum* = *quot homines*, which then generates the pl. verb.   **illi**: adv., corresponding to *apud forum.*

746 annona: the price of grain (*OLD* 4), as Pl. *St.* 179 *per annonam caram dixit me natum pater* ("My father said I was born when the price of grain was high"). Since grain was a dietary staple in both Athens and Rome, this would be a natural topic of conversation in either agora or forum. For general background, see Casson 1984: 70–95, Temin 2013: 97–113.   **quid dicam**: spoken aside to the audience, acknowledging the artificiality of the role he is playing.

747 solam, sc. *reliquisti.* Davos interrupts before she can give the game away.   **quae haec est fabula?** a set phrase that as a response to some comment or situation means something like "what's going on here?" or "what's this nonsense?" (*Eun.* 689; Pl. *Men.* 1077, *Mos.* 937, *Per.* 788, *Rud.* 355). It is difficult, however, not to hear metatheatrical overtones here, where Davos and Mysis are in fact playing roles within roles, Davos affecting the genuine shock of Simo at 468–77. Thus Brown, "What's this performance?" See also 224n.

748 quisue: the enclitic conj. *-ue* links questions to form a series (*OLD* 3).

749 satin = *satisne.*   **rogites**: the iterative form of *rogo* acknowledges the cumulative effect of Davos' questions. Mysis proves to be a poor improviser: his appeal to her *memoria* and *astutia* (723) must have been more wish than fact.

750 neminem: Davos makes a point of not seeing Chremes, whose presence will not be acknowledged until 783.   **miror unde sit**: directed to the audience. The use of asides, i.e. comments directed to the audience by Davos and by Chremes as well as Davos' directions to Mysis that Chremes does not hear, is particularly effective in playing up the farcical and deliberately artificial elements of this scene. In doing so, T. makes full use of the available stage space in positioning his characters and exploits the permeable boundary between spectators and actors.

751 au! a female expression of surprise or distress (Adams 1984: 54, Müller 1997: 119–20). Davos is probably holding her arm none too gently as he draws her aside.   **ad dexteram**: the stage movement here is complex. Chremes and Davos entered in succession from the right (734n.). In the course of this dialogue, then, Chremes must have moved upstage and crossed left toward Simo's door, if now by taking Mysis off to the right Davos can put distance between him and them.

752 deliras: Mysis does not yet grasp that Davos is playing a part. She must again be interrupted before she says too much within Chremes' hearing.

753 faxis: pres. subjunc. of *facio.* (For the sigmatic fut. *faxo,* see 854n.) The stem is thought to derive either from a subjunc. of the -*s*- present desiderative, the *s* that produces *quaeso* from *quaero* and *uiso* from *uideo* (Weiss 2020: 446–7), or a subjunc./optative of the -*s*- aorist (de Melo 2007: 306–14). This sigmatic subjunc., already infrequent in Pl., is still less common in T. (de Melo 2007: 192–215). Here it may add some heft to Davos' vague threat, which otherwise lacks the menace of Simo's words to Davos at 196–200. The threat is made out of Chremes' hearing. In the following line, Davos reverts to speaking "in character."

754 male dicis? Davos feigns offense at *deliras.*   **undest**, sc. *puer.* **a nobis**: Mysis speaks the truth, though it is not yet clear whether she does so out of confusion or because she has at last caught the drift of Davos' pose. In either case, the response suits his purpose.

755 mirum uero: spoken ironically, though the irony becomes clear only at the end, where the *mulier* in question is identified as a *meretrix.* That characterization, as Davos almost surely knows (274–5, 286–8), is untrue, but it is well calculated to confirm Chremes in his prejudice.

ab Andriast: Chremes makes the logical inference, the Andrian woman in question presumably being Glycerium (as at 215). At an earlier stage in the narrative, the reference was to Chrysis (73, 85). Here, at 758, 766, 775, 780, and 782 he comments to the audience on the charade being acted out for his benefit.

758 in quibus . . . illudatis: this is the only ex. anywhere of *in* + abl. with *illudo*. The acc. of the person deceived, either with or without the prep. *in*, is the regular construction in T., e.g. 822 *illusi uitam filiae, Eun.* 942 *in nos illuseris*. Only later does a dat. become the norm, e.g. Hor. *S.* 1.4.9, Tac. *Hist.* 2.90. Davos echoes Simo's complaint at 492–3.

759 adeo: 440n.

760 Another direction unheard by Chremes to counter the previous instruction and keep Mysis rooted to the spot.   **mane**: the following pause as Mysis pulls back from the doorstep keeps the second syllable heavy. The scansion *cauĕ* is then the result of iambic shortening.   **excessis**: like *faxis* (753), a sigmatic subjunc.

761 Mysis seems never quite to grasp the nature of Davos' charade, but he manages to turn her all-too-true responses to his advantage. Her bewilderment adds to the farcical humor of the scene.

763 cedo "tell me" (150n.).   **quoium** "whose" (*OLD* s.v. *cuius²*). This rel./interrog. adj., probably formed from the gen. of the prn. by analogy with *suus*, occurs six times in T. (772, 932, *Hau.* 8, 996, *Eun.* 321 are the other exx.), is fairly common in Pl., and is found occasionally in other early texts, e.g. CIL 1². 583, Cato *Agr.* 139. However, by the time of Verg. *Ecl.* 3.1 *dic mihi, Damoeta, cuium pecus?* it is a deliberate, highly conspicuous archaism variously explained as either subliterary *rusticitas* or an evocation of comic diction. (For the formation, see Palmer 1961: 255, Weiss 2020: 373, and for its use in Virgil, Wills 1993).

764 mitte "never mind" (*OLD* 5). Cf. *Ad.* 185 (Aeschinus dismisses Sannio's complaints) *mitte ista atque ad rem redi* ("Forget that and come back to the matter at hand"), *Ad.* 838 (Micio brushing aside Demea's moral objections) *mitte iam istaec* ("Forget all that for now").

765 uostri: 357n. Davos is anxious to elicit the actual name for Chremes' benefit, so he presses the interrogation.   **quoius**: 336n.

766 semper: Chremes conveniently forgets that the marriage was originally his idea (99–101), but his shorter-term recollection is certainly correct.

767 animaduortendum "deserving punishment" (*OLD* 8).

768 quemne: the rel. prn. with the antecedent *puer* understood. Cf. Pl. *Mil.* 13 *quemne ego seruaui in campis Curculioniis?* ("What of the one whom I rescued in the Weevil Field?").

769 o hominem audacem! spoken aside. Mysis is taken aback by Davos' facility in twisting the truth to his advantage.   **uerum**, sc. *est.*   **Cantharam**: a slave's name at *Ad.* 353, Pl. *Epid.* 567. It suggests *cantharus*, a large drinking vessel, perhaps alluding to the old joke about women and wine (228n.). The name may be invented for the occasion: no Canthara ever appears. The action suggested here is not completely consistent with the story spun for Simo at 513–15: Davos' powers of invention and embellishment are considerable.

770 suffarcinatam: lit. "to be stuffed underneath" (*sub* + *farcio*), specifically with objects bulging under one's clothes (a particularly useful word in a world without pockets). Thus Pl. *Cur.* 289 (of Greeks) *qui incedunt suffarcinati cum libris cum sportulis* ("who go about bulging with books, with snack baskets").

771 liberae: freeborn women might be thought more credible witnesses than a slave like Mysis, whose evidence (should the question ever come before a court) would be admissible only under torture. She might well, then, be grateful that the birth was well established and that she would not be faced with physical coercion. Don. thinks this a specifically Roman reference, but analogous limitations on the evidence of slaves (and of women) also operated at Athens (Thür 2005: 150–2). Who these women were and how anyone beyond Mysis and the midwife Lesbia came to be present at the birth is never explained, nor are they ever mentioned again.

772 ne: 324n.   **illa illum**, i.e. Glycerium (the supposed schemer) and Chremes (the anticipated victim).   **quoius**: 336n.

773–4 Davos imagines Glycerium giving voice to her purported scheme. Such mimicry, with or without *inquit* or some similar verb to signal the quotation, was an established comic technique (134n.). The indicative verbs reflect the confidence of her assumption, which accordingly elicits the vehemence of both Davos' response and its echo in Chremes' equally forceful contradiction.

775 adeo: the adv. emphasizing *nunc* = "immediately."   **sis sciens**: 508n.

776 tollis: Davos means, literally, to pick the baby up from the threshold (*OLD* 1), but the additional implication remains that doing so acknowledges the child as belonging to their household (*OLD* 2).

777 prouolam . . . peruolam: the distinction, if any, would be between the direction (*pro-*) and the intensity (*per-*) of the action, but the variation is probably more stylistic than substantive.

778 homo: pejorative. Cf. *Eun.* 357–8 (of Phaedria's eunuch) *illumne, obsecro, | inhonestum hominem, quem mercatus est heri?* ("do you mean that unsavory wretch he bought yesterday?").   **sobrius**: like its Eng. cognate, the adj. may suggest the opposite of drunkenness, e.g. Pl. *Truc.* 855 *si alia membra uino madeant, cor sit saltem sobrium* ("even if her other parts are soaked with wine, her heart at least is sober") but also a more general seriousness of mind, e.g. *Ad.* 95 *ruri esse parcum ac sobrium* ("to be frugal and serious in the country"). The sense here, since Davos otherwise shows no particularly hedonistic impulses, likely tends toward the latter. This is probably when Mysis picks up the baby as Davos instructed. We do not hear of it again, though she must be holding it at 818, when she escorts Crito into Glycerium's house.

779 trudit "follows after" (*OLD* 4). *prouerbium*, says Don., though the line is not quoted elsewhere. The repetition *alia aliam* does, however, employ a traditional pattern for proverbs (Taylor 1996). Davos follows the sequence of his earlier account (215–24), where he also dismissed the claim of Athenian citizenship as a fiction (*fabulae!* 224), though here he is deliberately vague about his source of information (*susurrari*). At 875 Pamphilus will be equally vague.

780 hem! Chremes might well be taken aback by this news. To declare Athenian citizenship was a serious business. Penalties for a false claim included loss of property and even enslavement and, if a marriage was involved, put both parties at risk. These were the stakes, for example, in the notorious case of Neaira ([Dem.] 59), the one surviving example of a fourth-century suit over citizenship, a *graphē xenias*. See Patterson 1994.   **coactus legibus**: not strictly true, as far as we know, although the idea recurs at *Ad.* 490 and Pl. *Aul.* 793. Private remedies were in most instances preferable in such cases, precisely because they avoided the public exposure of a legal action. Scafuro 1997: 193–231 examines the options for redress of sexual offenses that were available in Athenian and Roman law.

781 au: 751n. The interjection is restored from Don.'s note. The MSS read *eho*, which seems less appropriate here (88n.).   **an non ciuis?** Mysis has no reason to doubt the truth of what Davos believes is a *fabula* and *fallacia*. Whether she, as a member of the household, has substantive reasons for thinking so remains unclear.

782 iocularium "laughable." Only here: the regular form is *iocularis*, e.g. *Ph.* 134 *iocularem audaciam!* This final aside is at least partially overheard by Davos. Whether he also heard and simply ignored Chremes' previous comments is unspecified, though we might imagine he kept half an eye on Chremes' responses while speaking with Mysis.

783 quis hic loquitur? 267n. Having elicited from Mysis all that needed to be said and judging that the effect of that news is satisfactory, Davos now turns with affected innocence to acknowledge Chremes' presence.   **per tempus**: *in tempore* at 758. Contrast Davos' initial reaction to Chremes' appearance at 732. He has managed to turn a momentary setback to his advantage.

785 obsecro: generally a marker of female speech (232n.). When used by male characters in T., *obsecro* + question is most characteristic of young men currying favor (9 of 12 instances: Barrios-Lech 2016: 124–5). Coming here from Davos, it may be a sign of calculated subservience.   **em**: 248n.

786 scelera: for the exclamatory acc., cf. 604 *em astutias!*   **hanc**: the reference to Mysis is pejorative ("this woman").   **in cruciatum**: the casual threat of torture, even by a slave to another slave or by a slave offering himself to torture (*Ad.* 483), is a striking feature of comic speech (621n.).

787 Addressed to Mysis, indicating Chremes. Though he is announced at 732 and mentioned by name at 773–4, she will eventually need his identity spelled out for her (793–4).   **non credas**: *non* for *ne* in a prohibition is extremely rare. (A few MSS "correct" the anomaly by reading *credes*.) The one early parallel is Pl. fr. 147L *Venus uentura est mea, non hoc pulueret* ("my Venus will be coming: don't let the place be dusty"). Quint. 1.5.50 considered this substitution of *non* for *ne* a fault, *quia alterum negandi est, alterum uetandi*, but it would become common in late Latin. The self-deprecation is intended for Chremes' benefit. Mysis, who has not consciously attempted to fool anyone, has no idea what he means.

788 mi senex: 721n. Mysis is being carefully polite.

789 est: on learning that Simo is at home, Chremes abruptly leaves to confront him.   **ne me attigas** "Don't touch me!" Davos must be moving toward Mysis, perhaps for a hug in celebration of this successful encounter, but she keeps her distance. *attigas* is pres. subjunc. formed by -ā- added to the root rather than the pres. stem, i.e. *attingas*. Such extra-paradigmatic subjunc. occur with some frequency in Pl., but the only others in T. are *creduas* (*Ph.* 993) and *fuat* (*Hec.* 610). See de Melo 2007: 275–7, Weiss 2020: 445.

790 A verb of speaking, e.g. *narrabo*, is cut off by Davos' interruption.

791 inepta "silly," a term of good-natured reproach, e.g. *Eun.* 1007 (slave to slave) *quid est, inepta?*, *Ad.* 271 (brother to brother) *age, inepte.*   **qui** "how?" (adv.)

792 socer: Chremes is of course only a prospective father-in-law, but the point is clear enough.

793 praediceres: the jussive subjunc. in the imperf. represents what ought to have been done but was not (*NLS* §110), e.g. *Ph.* 297 *dotem daretis* ("you should have given a dowry"). Davos did warn her that she would need to follow his lead in the coming improvisation (722–3, 735–6), but his instruction was vague.

794 ex animo "enthusiastically."

795 natura . . . de industria: the contrast is between spontaneous and calculated action.   **facias**: probably a generalizing second pers. in a statement of principle. Its obj. is *omnia*. This was, says Don., a statement rather than a question in Men., but he does not preserve the original Greek.

[IV.v] Crito, Mysis, Davos (796–819)

Further conversation between Davos and Mysis is interrupted by the arrival of a stranger, who is quickly identified as Chrysis' relative from Andros. This Crito has come to claim her property, a plausible enough motive for his timely appearance, though he will soon take on a far more significant role. Andros was, by Athenian standards, something of a cultural backwater, and this countryman's dim view of Chrysis' chosen occupation stands in marked contrast to the more dispassionate account of her career offered by the urbane Simo (69–79). Crito's sympathy for Glycerium, however, appears to be genuine, and he will not be cowed by Simo's bluster (919–22). Though he exists primarily as a kind of *hospes ex machina* to cut the dramatic knot, T. nevertheless provides him with a deftly drawn personality.

796 platea: a Gk. loan word (ἡ πλατεῖα [ὁδός], lit. "broad way"), this is comedy's standard word for the street that was represented by the stage platform, e.g. *Eun.* 344, *Ph.* 215; Pl. *Cas.* 799, *Trin.* 1006, etc., while *uia* is a more general term for "street" (e.g. 776) or for a "route," e.g. *Hec.* 360 *non sciunt ipsi uiam domum qua ueniant?* ("Don't they know the way home themselves?").

797 ditias = *diuitias*. The contracted form is normal in T., required by the meter (though the MSS consistently read *diuitias*), but probably also the colloquial pronunciation. The hardness shown by Crito lends credence to Simo's claim that Chrysis was driven from Andros *inopia et cognatorum neglegentia* (71).

798 potius quam . . . uiueret: this alternative course of action is equivalent to a neg. purpose and thus requires an imperf. subjunc. Cf. Pl. *Aul.* 11–12 *inopemque optauit potius eum relinquere* | *quam eum thesaurum commonstraret filio* ("He chose to leave him destitute rather than show this treasure to his son").

799 lege: the vague reference to legal authority is sufficient since by either Athenian law (MacDowell 1978: 98–9) or by Roman law (Watson 1971: 97–9), Chrysis' property could be claimed by her closest male relative. Only when a plot turns on some more specific feature, e.g. *Ph.* 125–6 on the Athenian law of the *epikleros*, does T. explain the legal situation in some detail.   **redierunt**: the technical term for receiving an inheritance (*OLD* 12). Cf. *Hec.* 72 *ea ad hos redibat lege hereditas.*

800 quos perconter: rel. clause of purpose. Crito notices the pair and seeks directions to Chrysis' house. The verb suggests not simply asking, but making a specific inquiry, i.e. to find out. Cf. *Eun.* 294–5 (Chaerea searching for the girl he has seen) *ubi quaeram, ubi inuestigem, quem perconter, quam insistam uiam* | *incertus sum* ("I'm unsure where to look, where to search, whom to question, which way to take"). Since in ancient cities streets and houses were not systematically marked, esp. not in residential neighborhoods, directions would always be required. Cf. Syrus' (exaggerated) instructions to Demea at *Ad.* 573–84 and for material evidence of street markers (largely from Pompeii), Ling 1990: 61–5.   **obsecro**: here simply an expression of surprise as Mysis catches sight of Crito, e.g. "Good heavens!" vel sim.

801 Crito: Mysis unobtrusively adds this final bit of information required for the stranger's identification.   **sobrinus**: specifically, a second cousin, though more generally any fairly distant relation. Cf. Cic. *Off.* 1.54 (on degrees of kinship after parents and children) *sequuntur fratrum coniunctiones, post consobrinorum sobrinorumque.* Gk. makes a similar distinction been first cousins (ἀνεψιός) and cousins once removed (ἀνεψιαδοῦς); Men., says Don., specified the latter.

803 itan Chrysis—: Crito avoids using an ill-omened word like *mortua*.   **hem!** a groan, says Don., replaces the missing verb. Given his initial focus on Chrysis' property, the sincerity of Crito's regret could be doubted, though his further questions about the state of the household, however necessary for moving the plot along, seem sincere.   **nos . . .**

perdidit: Mysis means both "she has left us bereft" (*OLD* 3c) and, thinking of Glycerium's current state, "She has left us ruined" (*OLD* 1).

804 The brief questions (minus their easily supplied verbs) sound distinctly colloquial.   **sic**: Don. understood this adv. as a one-word reply, i.e. "so-so" (*OLD* 11c). Cf. *Hau.* 858–9 (Bacchis finding fault with the wine) *"sic hoc," dicens. "asperum, | pater, hoc est"* ("This one's so-so," she says. "This one's rough, father."). Elsewhere, however, *sic* is immediately explained, e.g. *Ph.* 145 (Davos being solicitous) *quid rei gerit? :: sic, tenuiter* ("How's he getting on?" :: "Well, barely."). Either sense fits the situation here.

805 quando "seeing that" (*OLD* 3). It is a proverbial expression, as *aiunt* shows. For the construction, cf. *Ph.* 419 *"actum" aiunt "ne agas"* ("What's done, as they say, you can't undo"), where Don. comments, *"aiunt" dicimus, cum prouerbium significamus.* Here he quotes a version of the proverb from Caecilius' *Plocium* (fr. 11R) *uiuas ut possis, quando nequit ut uelis.* A similar idea in Men., ζῶμεν γὰρ οὐχ ὡς θέλομεν, ἀλλ' ὡς δυνάμεθα ("we live not as we wish but as we can"), is sometimes assigned to *Andria* (fr. 45 K–T), though the similarity could be coincidental. Cf. Byrria's advice at 305–6 and an analogous sentiment in the *Plocium* fr. 10R *patiere quod dant, quando optata non danunt* ("put up with what they give, seeing that they don't give what you want").

806 suos parentis: a first indication that Glycerium's claim of Athenian citizenship is no mere *fabula*.

807 huc me appuli "I've landed here." The nautical term for beaching a ship can also be extended to apply to people (*OLD* 3b).

808 pol: 229n.   **tetulissem pedem**: Don., quoting Verg. *Aen.* 2.657 *mene efferre pedem* and *G.* 1.11 *ferte . . . pedem*, suggests that this is too elevated an expression for comedy. (It is also found at Enn. *Medea* fr. 89.8 *TrRF.*) In Pl. it is found in three passages that are in some sense stylistically marked, *Ba.* 423 (pedantic), *Capt.* 456–7 (solemn), *Mer.* 831 (emotionally charged), but it also occurs twice in unmarked passages (*Men.* 381, 630). The reduplicated perf. *tetulissem*, however, is a conspicuous archaism in T. (832n.), and the entire phrase may be intended to add a note of solemnity (or pomposity) to Crito's claim. So Maltby 1979: 138–9, Karakasis 2005: 95–6.

809 eius . . . soror: 124n. The truth about Glycerium's parentage was known on Andros (930–1), and Crito presumably made his journey on the assumption that it was known at Athens, too. How and when he learned from Athenian sources that this was not the case is not explained.

810 quae illius fuere, i.e. Chrysis' property.   **possidet**, sc. Glycerium. If recognized as Chrysis' sister, she could herself claim the estate, significantly complicating Crito's position. It is thus in his own interest to have the truth be recognized, a fact that will make Simo initially suspicious of his testimony (908–25).   **me hospitem** "that I, though a stranger" (*OLD* 4). An emphatic position: Crito's lack of legal standing is foremost in his mind.

811 litis: acc. pl. Athenian law mandated a court hearing to determine the rightful claimant of an estate lacking a direct male heir and then a trial if a claim was contested (MacDowell 1978: 102–3, Todd 1993: 220–1). Such a legal action would inevitably put a stranger like Crito at a disadvantage, which is why he speaks ironically. Cf. *Eun.* 759–60 *peregrinus est,* | *minus potens quam tu, minus notus, minus amicorum hic habens.* Thus the Carthaginian Hanno's reluctance to pursue a suit in Calydon, *in alieno oppido* (Pl. *Poen.* 1403). Crito's word order reflects the priorities of this bitter rumination. A more logical, prosaic order would be *aliorum exempla commonent quam facile atque utile mihi sit me hospitem litis hic sequi.* (For *hic*, Don. here and ad *Hec.* 647 reads *id*, i.e. *me litis sequi*, a reading that also has some MSS support, but *hic* is both syntactically easier and semantically more meaningful.)

812 simul "besides" (*OLD* 5b).

813 amicum et defensorem ei: a woman at Athens would require a male *kyrios* to represent her in legal proceedings (Todd 1993: 207–10). The legal capacity of a Roman woman was greater, but a *tutor* might still be called upon to safeguard her interests (Watson 1971: 39–41, Gardner 1986: 14–22, and more generally, Halbwachs 2016).

814 grandicula "almost grown," dimin. of *grandis*.   **illinc**, i.e. from Andros.   **clamitent**: 144n. Crito imagines what would happen should he proceed. The possibility is in effect the apodosis of a future hypothetical condition with the protasis suppressed (*SEL* I 197–8).

815 sycophantam: because Athenian law permitted "anyone who wished" (ὁ βουλόμενος) to initiate a public prosecution, manipulation of the system for personal gain through sharp practice, blackmail, and rhetorical excess became a significant social problem (MacDowell 1978: 62–6, Christ 1998: 48–71). The malicious, self-serving prosecutor, called a sycophant (συκοφάντης) by his opponents, came to be roundly condemned in oratory and comedy (testimonia in Harvey 1990: 119–21). In Roman comedy, *sycophanta* appears both as a general term of abuse and, more specifically, to describe a trickster (e.g. Pl. *Trin.* 843–990): T. *Hau.* 38 lists the *sycophanta* *inpudens* along with the *parasitus* and *leno* as a comic type (Lofberg 1920). Since money-grubbing was a common motive for sycophancy at Athens (Harvey 1990: 110–12), Crito's concern here may originate with Men., though Scafuro 1997: 466–7, citing Pl. *Pers.* 62–4 on false claims to inheritance, suspects T. of putting a Greek veneer on a Roman legal scenario. At 919, *sycophanta* is more straightforwardly a term of abuse.

816 mendicum: the noun, subj. of *persequi*, not (*pace OLD*, incorrectly citing this passage s.v. *mendicus*¹ 1b "destitute") the adj. Pl. *Men.* 76 includes the *mendicus* in a catalogue of comic types.   **tum** "besides," introducing a further consideration (*OLD* 9). Crito shows greater sympathy for Glycerium, whose condition is not of her own making, than he did for Chrysis.

817 Davos, who has remained silent throughout this exchange, recognizes that Crito's information promises a solution to his difficulties. Thus his enthusiastic response.   **antiquom obtines** "you're your old self" (*OLD* s.v. *obtineo* 2). Cf. *Hec.* 860 *tu ecastor morem antiquam atque ingenium obtines* ("You're certainly still your old self, with your old ways"). The MSS assign this entire line to Mysis, but as Brown notes, Crito is no *hospes* to her, while Davos refers to Crito again as *hospes* at 843, as does Pamphilus at 914.

818 quando: 805n. Crito's thoughts have turned entirely to Glycerium, no doubt in part because he understands that resolving her situation also furthers his own interests.   **maxume**: a colloquial expression of agreement (*OLD* 7).

819 Spoken to the audience.   **nolo . . . uideat**: acc. + inf. is the more common construction with *nolle* in T. (as also for *uelle*), but subjunc. also at *Hau.* 701 and *Eun.* 906.   **in tempore hoc** "at this moment."   **senex**, i.e. Simo. Davos, preferring to await developments from a safe distance and out of his master's sight, follows Mysis and Chremes into Glycerium's house.

The poets of New Comedy needed to clear the stage at strategic intervals to provide opportunities for the choral interludes that occupied their four act breaks. Since the Roman practice of continuous performance eliminated the need for such empty stages, *palliata* dramatists were free either to ignore or to write over these pauses in the action, though traces of them often remain and provide analytic scholars with useful clues to the structure of the lost Greek models. Davos' exit here creates the one indisputable example of an empty stage in *An.* (another is sometimes posited after 171), and it is a logical place for what would have been the break between Men.'s fourth and fifth acts. By making the action continuous, with Chremes and Simo about to enter hot on the heels of Davos' exit, T. creates a quite different effect by orchestrating a near miss and thus giving comic point to Davos' *in tempore hoc*. For the Roman treatment of act breaks, see Duckworth 1952: 98–101 and Goldberg 1990; for act breaks in Men., Zagagi 1995: 72–82.

[V.i] Chremes, Simo (820–41)

Chremes emerges from Simo's house followed by Simo, who is intent on continuing their conversation. Chremes' discoveries at 740–89 have convinced him that the marriage should be called off, while Simo is equally sure that the "revelation" of Pamphilus' child was staged for Chremes' benefit. Both men, of course, are correct in their beliefs.

The music resumes at this point to mark this latest turn in the action.

820 spectata . . . amicitiast mea "my friendship has been tested" (*OLD* s.v. *specto* 6b). In their earlier encounter, Simo appealed specifically to their *amicitia* (538), but that kind of argument has lost its power over Chremes.

821 orandi iam finem: the remark makes clear that a discussion begun in the house has been carried over into the street.   **face**: 680n.

822 paene illusi "I've nearly gambled away" (*OLD* 3). Chremes' concern for his daughter's welfare seems, even in this society where arranged marriages are expected, to be genuinely touching. It is also characteristically Roman, which raises the possibility that in these closing scenes T. departed from his model to align the character of Chremes more closely with Roman sensibilities. For Roman fathers and daughters, see Hallett 1984: 54–9, 97–9, and for other possible changes of characterization from Menander's Chremes, Lefèvre 2008: 165–6.

823 enim: 503n.   **nunc quom maxume** "now especially" (*OLD* s.v. *maxime* 6b).

824 beneficium . . . initum, i.e. Chremes' acquiescence to the marriage at 572–3.   **uerbls . . . re**: the contrast between words and deeds is a comic commonplace, e.g. *Hau.* 636, *Eun.* 741–2, *Hec.* 416–17, *Ad.* 164. Cf. Men. fr. 740 K–T ὁ μὲν λόγος ⟨σου⟩ συνέσεως πολλῆς γέμει, | τὰ δ' ἔργα σύνεσιν οὐκ ἔχοντα φαίνεται ("your speech is full of much good sense, but your deeds appear to have no sense").

825 prae "under pressure of" (*OLD* 2).

826 modum "the limit" (*OLD* 5).   **neque . . . cogitas**: Chremes identifies Simo's most significant failing, viz. his persistent tendency to see things in terms of his own immediate interest with scant regard for their effect on others. Yet Simo will soon prove no less astute in assessments of character. That ability to see the truth, even if not all the truth and rarely the truth about oneself, is a trait frequently found in T.'s characters and helps elevate even his notionally stock figures above simple caricature.

827 remittas "to leave off" (*OLD* 10c). Construction with an inf. is more common with *mittere* (873n.).   **iniuriis**: a very strong word, which is why Simo immediately questions it.

828 perpulisti: Chremes did in fact agree to the marriage (572–3), but his reluctance to do so is now foremost in his memory.   **homini adulescentulo**: the redundancy, esp. combined with the dimin., has pejorative overtones. Cf. *mulier meretrix* at 756–7.

830 ut: repeating for clarity the *ut* of 828. Cf. Pl. *Ps.* 579–83 *ita paraui copias . . . ut . . . facile ut uincam*.   **in seditionem atque in incertas nuptias**: Simo had talked around the possibility of *incommoditas* in a union with Pamphilus (567), but now the full import of what he agreed to has finally dawned on Chremes. *seditio* is a very strong word for marital discord, what T. will call *iurgium* at *Hec.* 513 and *discordia* at *Hec.* 693, a play with the problems of an estranged couple at its center, and Pamphilus' divided loyalties would clearly render any marriage *incertae*. That would be especially true if, as Chremes now believes, Glycerium was a citizen and could make a legal claim on Pamphilus.

831 eius, i.e. his daughter, who would be suffering the consequences of the *incertae nuptiae*.   **medicarer**: medical imagery comes easily to discussions of love and its consequences (Fantham 1972: 14–18).

832 A remarkable line, redolent of the older comic style. There is, besides the archaic perf. *tetulit* (Palmer 1961: 272), the play on *fero* "to suggest" (*OLD* 31) followed by *fero* "to put up with" (*OLD* 20), and the alliteration of *nunc non fert: feras*. Cf. *Ph.* 138 *quod fors feret feremus aequo animo*. T. uses such traditional diction sparingly, which makes its occasional appearance especially marked.

833 Chremes explains what has changed his mind about the marriage.   **hinc** = "from Athens." In stating the basis for her claim to citizenship, the adv. elides the idea of location, as 337 *fugin hinc?* with the idea of origin, e.g. 126 *hinc illae lacrimae* (*OLD* 7b).   **aiunt**: Chremes generalizes his source (which was Davos, 780), with the implication that these facts are now common knowledge.   **missos face**: 68on.

834 per ego . . . oro: the word order is largely formulaic (289n.).   **ut ne**: 259n.   **illis**, i.e. Davos and his putative accomplices. Where Chremes was general in expressing belief (*aiunt*), Simo is specific in expressing suspicion.   **animum inducas credere** "don't let yourself believe" (*OLD* s.v. *induco* 12a). The meaning shifts slightly when the verb is followed by an inf. cl., as at 572.

835 illum, sc. *Pamphilum*. The plan, thinks Simo, is to blacken his son's character, and since it was *fama* that initially led Chremes to propose the match (96–101), there is some logic to this idea.

836 haec . . . omnia, i.e. Glycerium's Attic citizenship and Pamphilus' responsibility for her child.

837 desinent: if the fathers remain committed to the marriage, says Simo, the conspirators will drop their claims and all this scandal will simply disappear.

838 scio: Chremes refers to the conversation he overheard between Davos and Mysis (747–81), which Simo did not witness and could only imagine in a general way (507–9), but Simo has a well-established tendency to claim greater command of a situation than the circumstances warrant.   **at**: Chremes introduces an objection. The elision at the change of speaker serves as a mark of his impatience. For the dramatic value of elision (and of hiatus), see Moore 2012: 227–9.

839 uero uoltu: *quasi dixerit Simo "simulabat ancilla"* (Don.). The fact of masked performance does not prevent dramatists from referring to facial expression, e.g. *Ph.* 210 *garris.* :: *uoltum contemplamini.* ("You're joking." :: "Look at my face."). For the expressivity of masks, see Marshall 2006: 127–9, and for the face as an indicator of character, cf. 856–7; Pl. *Aul.* 717 *bonum esse ex uoltu cognosco.*   **quom neuter tum praesenserat**: causal, explaining why Chremes thinks their expression was genuine. Cf. *Hau.* 842–4 *nunc me fortunatissumum | factum puto esse quom te, gnate, intellego | resipisse* ("Now I think I've become most fortunate, since I see that you've come to your senses, son"). He never understands that the "argument" he overheard was staged for his benefit. There is indirect testimony that Don. read pl. *praesenserant* here (printed by OCT, Brown), but since 3rd pers. verbs with *neuter* as subj. are in Pl. all sing. (*Cas.* 1011, *Men.* 537, *Stich.* 733) and there are no further exx. in T., the change is dubious.

840 facturas: Simo tacitly accepts Davos' claim that the women alone are responsible for this charade.   **dudum praedixit mihi**: the reference is to their conversation at 507–10. Each in his own way, Simo and Chremes are at this point both victims of Davos' schemes.

841 nescio qui "somehow or other," i.e. *OLD* s.v. *nescio* 7c + adv. *qui* (6n.).   **ac** "as" (*OLD* s.v. *atque* 14).

[V.ii] Davos, Chremes, Simo, Dromo (842–71)

The problem as the two fathers understand it is about to be overtaken by events, though neither of them is quick to grasp their import. Shocked to find Davos emerging from Glycerium's house, Simo's long-suppressed anger at last breaks free when confronted once again with the claim of Glycerium's Attic citizenship. The violence of his response is signaled by a shift from trochaic to iambic rhythm at 861 before the scene settles back into speech at 866 as Simo prepares to confront his son.

842 animo . . . otioso: abl. of description, as in the common expression of encouragement *animo bono es* (*Eun.* 84, *Hau.* 822, *Ad.* 284). The abl. describes either external characteristics or internal qualities that can be fleeting or permanent, where the gen. of quality is limited to permanent and inherent qualities, e.g. 608 *nulli consili sum* (*NLS* §83–4).   **impero**: the verb reflects Davos' (soon to be shaken) confidence in his control of the situation.   **em Davom tibi!** 604n. So much, thinks Chremes, for putting trust, as Simo did, in the slave's reliability (840).

843 meo praesidio: military language comes easily to the slaves of comedy, though more often in Pl. than in T. and most frequently in the characterization of trickery or deceit (Fraenkel 2007: 159–61). Here it is another mark of Davos' self-confidence.   **hospitis**, i.e. Crito. The gen. (with *praesidium* understood) corresponds to *meo*.

844 hominem aduentum tempus: three nouns in asyndeton, the equivalent of *hominis in tempore aduentum*. T. shares comedy's fondness for triadic structure (Duckworth 1952: 341–2, Leo 1960b) and makes ample use of such lists, e.g. 54, 319, 891, but they do not, as here, normally replace a syntactically connected phrase.   **scelus**: 317n.

845 in uado: metaphorically too at Pl. *Aul.* 803 *esse in uado salutis* and literally at *Rud.* 170 (of the shipwrecked Palaestra) *at in uadost, iam facile enabit* ("She's in the shallows; now she'll easily swim out"). The metaphor has a negative connotation at Cic. *Cael.* 51 *quoniam emersisse iam e uadis . . . uidetur oratio mea.*   **cesso alloqui?** 343n. Simo turns to make his presence known. His movement alone must be sufficient to attract Davos' notice, since there is no verbal cue in the text for what follows.

846 bone uir: 616n.   **ehem**: 417n.   **o noster Chremes!** an ingratiating form of address (Dickey 2002: 224–7).

847 At 253, Davos was sent off to supervise preparations for the wedding. Though now momentarily taken aback by Simo's unexpected appearance, he decides to proceed as if nothing has changed and affects the same air of impatience that had previously provided some respite from the consequences of his actions (580–600). Simo's responses to his protestations are (predictably) ironic.

848 id, i.e. the presence of the bride.   **hinc** "from this situation." Cf. *Eun.* 716 *quo modo hinc abeam nescio* ("How I'll get away from this situation I don't know"), *Ad.* 361 *Syrum ire uideo. iam hinc scibo ubi siet.* ("I see Syrus coming. Now I'll learn from that [i.e. Syrus' arrival] where he is").

849 etiam . . . respondes: an impatient command (Barrios-Lech 2016: 83–4). The pres. indic. is restored from Don. ad *Ad.* 550. The MSS, having lost awareness of the idiom, read *responde*. Simo now gets to the point.   **istic**, i.e. apud Glycerium.   **ita**: the closest Latin equivalent to "yes" (*OLD* 11a).

850 tibi ergo "Yes, you!" *ergo* creates an emphatic echo of the preceding *mihi* (*OLD* s.v. *ergo*² 3c).   **modo** "just now" (*OLD* 5). The text printed requires hiatus after *modo* in preparation for Simo's immediate rejoinder *quasi quam dudum*. Brown, modifying a suggestion by Bentley, prefers to avoid the hiatus by reading *ĭntrŏĭuī*.

851 cum tuo gnato una: the statement takes Simo aback, as Davos knew it would. Simo was, after all, under the impression that Pamphilus had ended his association with Glycerium (552–4).

853 sunt, sc. *inimicitiae*. Davos answers Simo's second question, leaving him to infer an answer to the first.   **illum**, sc. *hic esse*.

854 ĭmmŏ: Pl. and T. frequently treat the first syllable of *immo* as light, with the second syllable then lightened by iambic shortening.   **indignum . . . facinus**: 145n. It is the obj. of *audies*, though word order deliberately recalls the phrase *facinus facere*, a favorite *figura etymologica* in Pl. (thirteen examples), but only used once by T. (*Eun.* 644).   **faxo**: a sigmatic future (Weiss 2020: 446–7). For its use in this causal construction, which does not require *ut*, see de Melo 2007: 180–9. Davos at this stage thinks it advisable to feign skepticism about Crito's testimony.

855 nescioquis senex "some old man or other," a vaguely pejorative expression. Cf. Pl. *Rud.* 482 *muliercula hanc nescioquae huc ad me detulit*, Cic. *Flac.* 39 *o pastores nescioquos cupidos litterarum!* Neutral alternatives would be *quidam* (a certain someone) and *aliquis* (an indefinite someone).   **ellum** = *em* + *illum*, said with a gesture toward Glycerium's house, since Crito is not present onstage.   **confidens catus**: "bold [and] shrewd" or "presumptuous [and] crafty"? Davos intends Simo to hear the latter. The parasite Phormio is *confidens* (*Ph.* 123); Pl.'s slave Tranio is a *catus orator* (*Most.* 1142).

856 uideas: a generalizing subjunc. (66n.).   **quantiuis preti**: gen. of quality like *nulli* (608n.). For *pretium* = "esteem" (*OLD* 4c), cf. *Ad.* 891–2 *hominem maxumi preti*.

857 tristis seueritas "austere gravity." For a similar pairing of appearance and speech, cf. Cic. *Brut.* 265 (on the orator Valerius Triarius) *quanta seueritas in uultu! quantum pondus in uerbis!* Its balance and compression made the line a favorite of Dacier: "There is no finer verse in T. than this." The text, however, is not beyond suspicion. Serv. ad *G.* 3.37 (*amnem seuerum*) and *Aen.* 10.612 (*tristia dicta*), noting that *seuerus* = *tristis*, quotes this line with the variant *tristis ueritas* ("stern and sincere"), which is also found in a few MSS of T. and in Don.'s quotation of the line ad *Eun.* 839. Some edd., with an eye to Chremes' phrase *uero uoltu* (839), therefore prefer to read *ueritas* to avoid the seeming redundancy. *ueritas* "truthfulness" (*OLD* 6) is the quality that Sosia lamented was in short supply (68).

858 apportas: 73n.

859 hem! Simo has always been suspicious of Davos (159–64, 492–4, 582–6), and his lingering threat of violence (196–200) at last breaks to the surface. Why now? Simo first learned of Glycerium's claim of citizenship from Chremes and was at pains then to dismiss it as a ploy (833–41). Its return now not simply as an assertion (*aiunt*) but as a purported certainty (*se scire*) reveals the emptiness of that earlier dismissal and thus Simo's initial foolishness in having accepted Davos' story at face value. His suspicion of yet another scheme afoot only adds to the growing realization that he lacks control of the situation. All that is too much for Simo.

860 Dromo, Dromo! Simo calls impatiently for assistance, with Davos' attempts to explain himself serving to cover the time required for that help to emerge from Simo's house. Dromo is Simo's enforcer, what Gell. 10.3.19 says comedy called a *lorarius* (lit. "flogger"). He plays the intimidating heavy, much like Parmeno, who accompanies Pamphilus and beats the pimp Sannio in the slapstick scene at *Ad.* 155–95. It is not commonly a speaking part – when Sannio needs to be talked into compliance, Syrus (not Parmeno) is given the job – but T. assigns Dromo just a few words, perhaps to amplify his very dullness. (For the *lorarii* of Pl., see Richlin 2017: 452–4).   **si addideris**: Simo's similarly incomplete threat at 164 replaced one thought with another. Here it is a mark of impatience as he interrupts himself for one last shout into the house.

861 sublimem "aloft" (*OLD* 1b). Cf. Pl. *Mil.* 1394 *si non sequitur, rapite sublimem foras* ("If he doesn't follow, pick him up and throw him out"),

Ad. 316 *sublimem medium primum arriperem* "first I'd lift him up from the waist").   **quantum potest** "as quickly as possible" (*OLD* s.v. *quantum*[2] 3b). *potest* is impers.

863 quicquam: obj. of *mentitum*. Cf. *Eun.* 703 *iam satis credis sobriam esse me et nil mentitum tibi?* ("Are you satisfied now that I'm sober and haven't lied to you about anything?").   **occidito**: the fut. imper. here has the permissive sense discussed by Barrios-Lech 2017: 492–3, citing Pl. *Ps.* 513 (Pseudolus' confidence in his ability to bilk his master of 2,000 drachmae) *faciam.* :: *si non apstuleris?* :: *uirgis caedito.* ("I'll do it." :: "If you can't get it?" :: "Then you can beat me with a switch.").   **audio**: pres. with fut. sense is common in refusals (*SEL* I 21). Thus *Ph.* 486 *audi obsecro.* :: *non audio*, but Pl. *Capt.* 603 (Hegio reluctantly agrees to hear out Aristophontes) *istinc loquere . . . procul. tamen audiam.*

864 te commotum reddam "I'll shake you up" (*OLD* s.v. *commoueo* 12). The situation was reversed at 456, when Davos caught Simo off balance and remarked, *commoui.*

865 cura . . . constringito: the shift in tense could reflect a sequence of actions, the *cura* necessarily preceding the hog-tying, but the pres. imper. can itself have fut. force, e.g. *dic* (383, 394), *face* (680, 712). Since the *-to* imper. was fading from use in the second century (Barrios-Lech 2017: 488), the variation in this case may be largely a matter of metrical convenience.   **quadrupedem**: Simo adds a further cruelty almost as an afterthought. He wants Davos not only securely restrained, but with hands and feet tied together and carried off like an animal to market. Pl. *Capt.* 721–50 is the only other example in extant Roman comedy of a slave bound onstage and hauled off for punishment. The situation is different, but no less violent, in the main fragment of Men.'s *Perinthia* (P. Oxy. 855), where Daos is taunted for his trickery and attacked with fire as he clings for refuge at the stage altar.

866 As at 196, the music stops and Simo shifts to speech to bring home the force of his message.

867 erum: the emphatic prolepsis also creates a chiastic order with the second obj., *patrem*, at the end of the sentence. The effect is further enhanced by the fact that *erum* and *patrem* are the same person.

868 illi, i.e. *Pamphilo*. Simo's anger, as becomes clear in what follows, is directed primarily at his son. The brute force represented by Dromo is sufficient, he thinks, to bend Davos to his will, but he has no corresponding power over Pamphilus, which only adds to his anger. He thus takes out on his slave the frustration he cannot take out on his son. Cf.

Micio, the indulgent father of *Ad.*, whose leniency is meant to forestall such behavior: *nam qui mentiri aut fallere institerit patrem aut | audebit, tanto magis audebit ceteros* (55–6).   **ne saeui**: 384n. Scenes of beating and bullying are fairly common on the Roman stage (Richlin 2017: 90–104), which makes Chremes' protest esp. noteworthy. He evidently finds Simo's response disproportionate to its apparent cause.   **o Chremes**: 846n.

869 pietatem: the obligation of child toward parent (*OLD* 3a), a concept so fixed in the Roman moral vocabulary that *p(ietatis) c(ausa)* is a common formula on tombstones (e.g. *CIL* 10.1765, 1818; 11.1285) and generates frequent jokes in Pl. Thus, Calidorus proposes swindling his mother as well as his father *pietatis caussa* (*Ps.* 120–2). See the material assembled by Segal 1987: 15–21. *pietas* is a more serious matter in T. The only other references to it are at *Hec.* 301, 447, 481, 584, a play predicated on the complexity of family relationships.

870 capere: the acc. subj. *me* is understood in this exclamatory clause (246n.).

871 age ... exi: Simo peremptorily summons Pamphilus from Glycerium's house. Such a command is a traditional way to start a scene, e.g. Pl. *Aul.* 40 *exi, inquam, age exi*; *Eun.* 668 *exi foras, sceleste.*   **ecquid te pudet?** for the neut. prn. as subj., cf. *nil pudet* (638n.).

[V.iii] Pamphilus, Simo, Chremes (872–903)

Pamphilus answers the call, though unsure who has summoned him. As happened previously to Davos (175–205), the sudden encounter with Simo puts him at a disadvantage, but where the earlier scene led to traditional sparring between master and slave, this one carries a keen and perhaps unexpected emotional charge. The *palliata* tradition was built on character types, as the dramatists themselves freely acknowledge (Pl. *Capt.* 57–8, *Men.* 75–6; *Hau.* 37–9, *Eun.* 36–8), with an *iratus senex* and at least one *adulescens amans* usually put at the center of the action. So it is with *An.*, yet T. has a way of letting the mask slip from his characters in moments of heartfelt sentiment as recognizable human emotions emerge to hint at a reality behind the stereotypes. He did this before in a small way with Chremes, whose genuine concern for his daughter's welfare suddenly burst out in his challenge to Simo (828–32). In the present scene, both Simo and Pamphilus have such a moment: Simo states clearly and truthfully the nature (and the enormity) of Pamphilus' moral failing while revealing his own frustration at his inability to correct it (876–92), and Pamphilus, who has throughout been as sincere in expressing his feelings as he has been feckless in acting on them, acknowledges the tangle of his obligations as he grasps at the hope of rescue from his dilemma (896–900). The resulting confrontation is not the play's climax, but is certainly its emotional highpoint.

872 quid ais: 137n. Chremes cuts short what was shaping up to be a torrent of abuse from Simo rather than a question. The parasite Gnatho silences another Chremes in a similar way at *Eun.* 797 *ah, quid agis? tace.*

873 mitte "put aside" (*OLD* 4b). Cf. *Ad.* 795–6 *mitto maledicta omnia: | rem ipsam putemus. mitte* is again constructed with an inf. at 904.

875 ain = *aisne.* Simo wastes no time in getting to the point.   **ita praedicant**: like the equally vague *aiunt,* a way to avoid responsibility for the statement, though Pamphilus knows perfectly well what lies behind the claim (220–1, 945–6). His evasion proves to be too much for Simo.

876 confidentiam "audacity" (*OLD* 2).

877 cogitat: addressed either to Chremes or, more probably, to the world at large. Lapsing into the third pers. begins to put emotional distance between Simo and his son.

878 uide: 588n.   **color** "complexion" (*OLD* 3). Cf. the famous line of Micio, shaming his son into a confession at *Ad.* 643: *erubuit: salua res est.* Men. fr. 301 K–T makes the thought explicit: ⟨ἃ⟩πας ἐρυθριῶν χρηστὸς εἶναι μοι δοκεῖ ("anyone who blushes seems honorable to me"). Simo might hope for a similar sign in Pamphilus. Once again, masked performance does not preclude the expectation of facial expression (839n.).

879 impotenti "lacking in self-control" (*OLD* 3). Simo expands on this idea at 884–5.   **esse**: subj. *eum* is understood, modified by abl. *impotenti animo.* The exclamatory inf. clause is of a piece with 870, but followed here by a clause of result.

880 morem . . . legem . . . uoluntatem: what Pamphilus seeks certainly runs counter to his father's will, and if, as Simo continues to believe, Glycerium was not a citizen, a marriage would indeed run counter to Athenian law. (That was, e.g., the basis for the charge leveled against Stephanos and Neaera, 780n.). Whether Pamphilus would also be offending Athenian custom might, given the general acceptance of liaisons with non-citizen women, be more open to question, but Simo's moral case is strong. Cf. the scolding Micio administers to Aeschinus, who clearly violated the norms of Athenian sexual behavior, at *Ad.* 685–6 *in qua ciuitate tandem te arbitrare* *uiuere?* | *uirginem uitiasti quam te non ius fuerat tangere.* The similarity is noted by Scafuro 1997: 300–5.

882 me miserum! Pamphilus' cry of despair implicitly acknowledges the truth of his father's accusation, which encourages Simo to address him directly once more.   **sensti** = *sensisti.* So too *induxti* just below.

883 olim: anticipates *eodem die* (885).   **animum induxti**: 572n.

885 istuc uerbum, sc. *me miserum* (240n.).

886 sed quid ego? direct address does not come easily to Simo in his present emotional state, and he promptly lapses again into a dismissive third pers.   **macero** "vex" (*OLD* 4). Cf. 685 *noli te macerare*, addressed to Glycerium, the other victim of Pamphilus' indecision.

887 huius: not *tua.* The mild hyperbaton puts some emphasis on the word, in part perhaps for the contrast with *meam*, but certainly to mark the return to the third pers.

889 habeat ualeat uiuat: Simo simultaneously dismisses Pamphilus from his thoughts and from his responsibility. As Don. observes, *non irascitur ut pater, sed dissimulat ut alienus, quia uehementer dolet.*

890–1 Simo throws Pamphilus' words back at him, the effect amplified by the two lines end-stopped with *patris* and *patre.*

891 domus "household" (*OLD* 6).   **liberi**: readily understood as a rhetorical pl. (*inuidiosius*, says Don.), though *liberi* has no sing. form and can be used in specific reference to a single child, e.g. *Hau.* 151, *Hec.* 212.   **inuito patre**: a particularly serious matter in the Roman context, where as long as a father lives, a son remains *in patria potestate* (52n.). Don. notes that the serious tone of this line is original to T.: *mira grauitate sensus elatus est; nec de Menandro, sed proprius Terentii.*

892 adducti qui . . . dicant, i.e. Crito. Another rhetorical pl., as if a crowd of witnesses was being brought forward to support the claim.   **uiceris**: perf. subjunc. or fut. perf. indic.? Commentators differ. *SEL* I 176 understands this as a permissive subjunc., "have your way," or as Brown translates, "you've won," and thus the functional equivalent of Pl. *Per.* 215 *iam abi, uicisti* ("off with you now, you've won"). Simo on that reading imagines a legal proceeding already as good as lost. In contrast, the fut. perf. indic. imagines the outcome of an action still only in prospect, i.e. "You'll get your way." Cf. *nil promoueris* (640n.). The former may better suit his tone of bitter resignation.

893 licetne pauca? sc. *dicere.* A politely worded request, since Pamphilus recognizes the precariousness of his position. Simo's *ausculta pauca* (536) is more abrupt (Barrios-Lech 2016: 104–5).   **dices**: the fut. adds a note of scorn or skepticism to the response, which is why Chremes thinks it necessary to intervene. Cf. 617 *at iam expediam.* :: *expedies?*

894 audiam: a repudiating fut. Cf. Pl. *Men.* 197–8 *salta sic cum palla postea.* :: *ego saltabo? sanus hercle non es.* ("Then dance around with that cloak." :: "Me dance? You're not in your right mind.")

895 Chremē: hiatus at the change of speaker, assuming the Gk. vocative is correct (247n.).   **age**: 310n. Cf. 956 (also Simo) *age, fiat.* Simo's somewhat grudging acquiescence is, pointedly, directed to Chremes, not Pamphilus, while Pamphilus addresses his father directly.

896 The emotional impact of Pamphilus' declaration is heightened by the return of the music, which will continue until the end of the play.   **hanc**, i.e. Glycerium, last mentioned by name at 875. As at 881, the demonstr. prn. reflects the immediacy of her presence in the speaker's mind.

897 me dedo: so Clinia anticipating reconciliation with Menedemus at *Hau.* 681 *dedo patri me nunciam ut frugalior sim quam uolt.* Pamphilus' surrender is not so complete, but no less sincere. His moral situation is considerably more complex than Clinia's.   **oneris**: part. gen. with *quiduis.*

898 mittere = *amittere.*   **ut potero**: Pamphilus leaves himself a very large loophole, mindful both of his promises to Mysis (270–98, 693–701) and of his hope of rescue from his dilemma by Crito. He may also be hoping, as Don. notes, that his confession of enduring love for Glycerium may again turn Chremes against the proposed marriage.

899 ut ne: 259n.   **allegatum** "suborned" (*OLD* s.v. *allego*[1] 2). Pamphilus makes an adroit appeal, asking not that Crito's testimony be heard – Simo's response to such a request is too easily imagined – but that he be allowed to refute the accusation that Crito's opportune appearance was contrived as part of a scheme. That is a much more difficult request for Simo to deny.

900 sine: 153n. The construction without *ut* is normal, *Hec.* 590–1 *neque sinam ut . . . dicat* being the one exception.   **adducas?** a repudiating question (263n.).

901 da ueniam: *concede quod petitur* (Don. ad *Ad.* 942).   **hoc**: acc. Pamphilus must exit at this point to bring Crito from Glycerium's house.

902 quiduis cupio, sc. *sinere.*   **comperiar**: deponent. T. used the active form with the same construction at 90–1. Simo, ever suspicious, remains on his guard.

903 A notably sententious, if not entirely relevant response as Chremes seeks to placate his neighbor. Note the chiasm of *pro peccato . . . supplici*, the *supplicium* being (presumably) the threat of Simo's enduring displeasure and lack of support. As Don. observes, Chremes might well leave in disgust at this point but instead remains surprisingly unmoved by Pamphilus' enduring loyalty to Glycerium: his continued presence onstage is crucial for the coming encounter with Crito.

[V.iv] Crito, Chremes, Simo, Pamphilus (904–56)

It takes remarkably little time, essentially the two lines between 901 and 904, for Pamphilus to enter Glycerium's house, find Crito, and induce him to come out and meet his father. Dacier was troubled by this overly rapid sequence and imagined some kind of dumb show enacted between Chremes and Simo to fill the gap, but whether the Roman theater needed to mark the passage of time in so "realistic" a way is doubtful.

The resulting recognition of Glycerium as an Attic citizen has been carefully, if ironically foreshadowed by early reports of her claim (221–4, 778–81) followed by Crito's confirmation of the fact to Mysis (806) and Davos' final declaration to Simo (859). That she is revealed to be not just a citizen but Chremes' long-lost daughter is perhaps more surprising, though surely not entirely unexpected. What *is* unusual is for the recognition to be effected entirely by recounting a life history (923–45), unlike, for example, the rediscovery of a later Chremes' daughter that is confirmed by a narrative but set in motion by discovery of a ring (*Hau.* 614–67). As a plot device, however, the recovery of Glycerium's lost identity remains of a piece with many such recognitions in the tradition of New Comedy, and T. is careful to embrace rather than resist the essential artificiality of the scene. He heightens the effect of the revelation by shifting midway through from trochaic to iambic rhythm (928/9) and designs a sequence of comments and reactions spoken aside by Pamphilus (914, 918, then 937–8, 940–1, 943–5) to bring its significance directly to the audience. The conclusive moment of recognition as Pamphilus himself supplies the missing piece of the puzzle stands further apart from the rest in diction and quite possibly again in meter (945n.). Pamphilus is often taken to be T.'s addition to this scene – the use of four speakers means he has certainly added something – and if so, his role as witness and intercessor is T.'s way to shape the audience's response to this long-awaited recognition.

904 mitte orare: 873n. As at 820, a conversation begun indoors is carried over into the street.   **una harum quaeuis causa** "any one of these reasons." The reasons themselves are set out in the following line.

905 quod "the fact that" (*OLD* 4).   **cupio** "to be well disposed to" (*OLD* 3). This is, to judge by 806, an honest sentiment.

906 On catching sight of Crito, Chremes cuts short the formulaic pattern of recognition and greeting found at 801 and often expanded for comic effect by Pl., e.g. *Aul.* 811–18, *Bac.* 534–9, *Rud.* 331–6, etc. T.'s more restrained use of the device may align him more closely with Men.'s practice (Goldberg 1990: 198–201). How Chremes came to know Crito, a comparative stranger to Athens, is not explained. Of greater dramatic significance is whether he is speaking to himself at this point or addressing the audience and thus tacitly signaling the artificiality of the coming scene of recognition.

907 Athenas: a verb of motion is readily understood from the acc. of the goal (*SEL* II 236–7, *NLS* §8).   **insolens** "unaccustomed" (*OLD* 1).   **euenit** "it happened." Chremes is deliberately vague, reluctant (as Don. notes) to acknowledge that his reason for coming to Athens was to secure Chrysis' property for himself.   **hicinest**: 478n.

908 eho tu: 88n. The particle here suggests impatience, with perhaps even a touch of rudeness. Simo gets right to the point.

909 paratus "rehearsed" (*OLD* 6b). Simo returns to the idea that Crito's claim is part of a plot, while Crito's evasive answers only feed his suspicions and thus encourage his incipient rant.

910 hic, i.e. at Athens.   **homines adulescentulos**: the dimin. suggests vulnerability, while the rhetorical pl. implies that Crito has come to town specifically as a corrupter of youth.

911 libere: 330n.   **in fraudem illicis**: Simo now casts his son as a victim, not a co-conspirator. Cf. Pl. *Mil.* 1435 (Pyrgopolynices acknowledging Palaestrio's trickery) *is me in hanc inlexit fraudem* ("he lured me into this trap").

912 sollicitando et pollicitando: the deliberate jingle is a function of Simo's passion. Cf. *Ad.* 988 (how his brother curries favor) *ex assentando indulgendo et largiendo, Micio*. It is, in the traditional language of the *palliata*, a prized effect, e.g. Caecil. *Plocium* 149R *ita plorando, orando, instando atque obiurgando me obtudit*.   **lactas**: 648n.

913 Simo continues his rant, undeterred by Crito's astonishment at the vehemence of this verbal assault. As Don. notes, he moves from attacking

Crito to defending his son.   **meretricios amores**: it suits Simo now
to portray Glycerium as unfavorably as possible. At other times, she was
only *peregrina* (469) and *hospita* (439).   **conglutinas** "cement" (*OLD*
2b), i.e. to buttress the affair with the illusion of a legitimate marriage.
Though Cic. will write neutrally of having "cemented" an alliance (*Att.*
1.17.10 *a me conglutinam concordiam*) and of "cementing" friendships (*Att.*
7.8.1 *conglutinare amicitias*), the verb in comedy often suggests trickery. Cf.
Pl. *Bac.* 693–4 (Mnesilochus exhorts Chrysalus) *compara fabrica finge quod*
lubet conglutina | ut senem hodie doctum docte fallas aurumque auferas ("plan,
devise, invent, glue together whatever you like to trick the shrewd old man
shrewdly today and take away his money"). Fantham 1972: 47–8 surveys
the range of metaphoric meanings.

914 metuo: what does Pamphilus fear? Don. is unhelpful, noting (as often)
that *ut* introducing a fear-clause = *ne non*, but saying nothing about the
verb that follows. *ut substet* should mean "not stand firm," but does that
mean to wilt under Simo's attack or not to restrain himself from attack in
kind since, as soon becomes clear, Crito also has a temper? Commentators
generally understand the former. *An.*'s first translator, Niccolò Machiavelli,
found the expression unequal to the moment and rendered it with a distinctly non-Terentian, colloquial directness, *io ho paura, che questo forestiero*
non si pisci sotto ("I'm afraid this stranger will piss in his pants").   **noris**:
perf. subjunc. indicating an action preceding that of the main cl. (*arbitrere*),
which is pres. subjunc. A present tense in the protasis would instead indicate simultaneous action. These contracted forms are the norm in comedy
(10n.).

916 attemperate "opportunely." The adv. appears only here.   **euenit**:
an ironic echo of Crito's *euenit* (907). Simo is deeply suspicious of the
timing of Crito's appearance and makes that suspicion clear. As at 471–6,
his skepticism tacitly acknowledges the artificiality of a comic convention
(Introduction 3.2).

917 uero: ironic, as at 755 and often (*OLD* 3b).

918 ni metuam . . . habeo: pres. subjunc. for the unreal protasis (Pamphilus
is afraid) followed by pres. indic. for the reality of what he does in fact
have, the two ideas being essentially independent. Cf. *Hau.* 632 *id equidem*
ego, si tu neges, certo scio ("I know it perfectly well, even if you deny it").
Further exx. in SEL I 274–5. Contrast Pl. *Aul.* 523–4 *compellarem ego illum,*
ni metuam ne desinat | memorare mores mulierum ("I'd speak to him, if I wer-
en't afraid he'd stop talking about women's ways"), where the one action
is contingent upon the other. For the indic. in these unreal conditions,
see Ernout and Thomas 1953: 247–8, *NLS* §200.   **illum**, i.e. Crito (obj.

of *moneam*). The *res* in question, i.e. a suitable response to Simo's suspicions, is the fact that Simo had himself initiated schemes regarding the wedding.

919 sycophanta! 815n. Simo likely means "swindler" in the common Roman sense, since as far as he knows, neither an inheritance nor a prosecution is in prospect.   **hem!** 116n. Crito, who had feared just this, is angered by the accusation and must be calmed down by Chremes.   **sic . . . hic**: a literal trans. of the original, says Don., who quotes Men. (fr. 42 K–T) οὗτως αὐτός ἐστιν.   **mitte**: 764n. Contrast 904, where the meaning is like 873.   **uideat** "pay attention to" (*OLD* 16b). A warning for Simo to mind his manners.   **qui** = *qualis* (*OLD* s.v. *qui*¹ 2).

920 Behind Crito's threat is a Gk. commonplace. Closest to it is Alcaeus, *PLG* 341αἴ κ' εἴπῃς τὰ θέλῃς, ⟨καί κεν⟩ ἀκούσαις τά κ⟨εν⟩ οὐ θέλοις ("If you say what you like, you may hear what you do not like"), but also in Hes. *Op.* 721, Hom. *Il.* 20.250, Eur. *Alc.* 704–5. There was probably also a version in Men.

921 Crito now turns to Simo. Keen to refute the charge of sycophancy, he professes no interest in any of Simo's affairs.   **istaec**: 28n.   **moueo**: 516n.   **aequo animo**: 397n.   **feras**: best explained as a deliberative subjunc. Cf. *Hau.* 583 *nonne accedam ad illos?* ("Can't I approach them?") Exx. in *SEL* I 182–3. This is the reading of A, the ancient Codex Bembinus, whose full text of *An.* only begins at 889. It is the *lectio difficilior*: all other MSS (and Don.) read *feres*, which would have passed unquestioned without the testimony of A.

922 nam: Crito moves to the matter at hand (*OLD* 4).   **ego**: subj. of *dico*, emphatically placed to contrast with *tu* just above. *quae dico*, i.e. the following narrative, provides the subj. for *potest*.   **audierim**: since Crito's source was the shipwrecked Athenian himself (927), he has confidence in the truth of what he says.

923–30 Crito tells essentially the same story as Davos (221–4), only adding details that Glycerium, Davos' presumed informant, would not have known. In vocabulary and structure, the two accounts are much the same. Both focus first on the shipwrecked Athenian, then add the presence of an accompanying child. There is a similar alternation of end-stopped and enjambed lines and a preference for simple over complex syntax. The one noteworthy difference, abl. absolute *naui fracta* replacing Davos' *nauem is fregit* (222), reflects the stylistic shift in complexity often observed in moving from spoken to accompanied verse (Haffter 1934: 49–50).

923 ad Andrum "off the coast of Andros" (*OLD* s.v. *ad* 13d). This is again the reading of A. The other MSS all read *apud Andrum*, as at 222.

924 una: adv.   **tum** "then" (*OLD* 8c), used again by Crito at 926 and 936 to mark stages in his narrative.   **applicat**: hist. pres. The verb suggests an appeal for protection, as a shipwrecked stranger might well do (*OLD* 8). Dacier quotes Cic. *De or.* 1.177 on the rights of an exile at Rome *si se ad aliquem quasi patronum applicauisset*.

925 primum: adv.   **fabulam**: Simo responds to this account much as Davos did (224). The interjection is directed to Chremes, as his rejoinder *sine* ("Let it go!") makes clear.

927 ex illo: the shipwrecked merchant. Crito's eyewitness testimony – not the impersonal *aiunt* of hearsay – is crucial to the authority of his account.

928-9 The attribution of speakers in these two lines has been debated since antiquity. Don. records several possibilities, as does the MSS tradition. The text printed here reproduces the first hand in A, which has Crito struggling with some frustration to recall the merchant's name, overcoming his initial hesitation, and then continuing his account with growing confidence. Alternatives include making *Phania!* a prompt from Pamphilus or taking *hem! perii!* as his expression of dismay at Crito's hesitation or having *hem!* stand alone as Simo expresses growing annoyance as the tale unfolds.

928 ibi, i.e. at the house of Crito's relative.   **Phania**: Cic. may be alluding to this scene in a letter to Caelius Rufus when he refers to Phanias, the trusted freedman of Ap. Claudius (cos. 54), as appearing "like a witness in a comedy" (*iam* κωμικός μάρτυς, *ut opinor, accidit Phania, Fam.* 2.13.2). A Phanias was the title-figure of Men.'s *Kitharistes*; the name also appears at *Hau.* 169 and *Hec.* 458. Difficulty remembering a name, an effective device for impressing its significance on the audience, recurs at *Ph.* 386–90, where the repetition of "Stilpo" sets up a farcical moment of recognition at 740. Plautine variants on the routine include a guessing-game over an improvised name (*Trin.* 906–27) and a deft recovery when memory of a name fails (*Ps.* 984–91).

930 Rhamnusium "from Rhamnus," an Athenian coastal deme overlooking the Euboean Straits just north of Marathon. At *Hau.* 63, T. changed the deme-name Halae found in his model (fr. 127 K–T) to a vague *in his regionibus*, but the deme identification is essential here. It was part of an Athenian's legal name – so at Ar. *Nu.* 134, the identification "Pheidon's son Strepsiades from Kikynna" (Φείδωνος υἱός Στρεψίαδης Κικυννόθεν) is full and formal – and appearance in the deme register was an essential proof of citizenship (MacDowell 1978: 68–70, Todd 1993: 180–1). Thus Chremes' initial response comes not to the merchant's name, but to the mention of his deme, which is what confirms his identity.

931 multi alii: witnesses could be expected to strengthen the case, the number of witnesses probably counting for more in the Athenian system than at Rome, where their prestige was more important than their number. See Todd 1990: 23–31 (Athens); Meyer 2016: 275–7 (Rome).   **in Andro**: in early Latin the abl. of place required the prep. with the name of all islands, large or small (*SEL* II 376).   **audiuere**: 13n.   **utinam . . . spero!** Chremes voices his excitement in an aside to the audience. The exclamation at 930 is less certainly spoken aside, since Crito could be understood as responding to that surprised reaction, but T. is clearly using the device to highlight the formality – and by implication, the artificiality – of the recognition scene. With *eho*, Chremes turns back to address Crito (88n.).

932 eam: acc. subj. of the following *esse*. In his excitement, Chremes breaks into pieces what is logically a single thought, viz. *eamne aibat suam esse?*   **aibat**: but *aiebat* just above, 950 (534n.).   **fratris filiam**: Gk. has words for niece (ἀδελφιδῆ) and nephew (ἀδελφιδοῦς), but Lat., though it distinguishes between paternal (*patruus*) and maternal (*auunculus*) uncles, does not. Thus Pl. *Poen.* 1195–6 *o patrue, o patrue mi!* :: *quid est, fratris mei gnate, quid uis?* (A *nepos* is a grandchild or, more generally, a descendant.)

933 certe meast: Chremes' simple yet surprising revelation elicits an immediate response from each of the others.   **quid ais?** the formulaic expression of surprise (137n.) here is literally appropriate as Crito and then Simo take in the full implication of Chremes' statement. Simo's *tu* adds emphasis.

934 qui "how?" (53n.).   **illic**: 742n.   **noram et scio**: *ad personam* [*Phaniam*] *et ad rem* [*fratrem*] *rettulit*, Don.

935 bellum hinc fugiens: Men.'s career, which extended from ca. 321 to his death in 292/291, coincided with a long period of intermittent war and social unrest as Athens weathered the dynastic struggles that enmeshed the Greek world after the death of Alexander in 323 BCE (Habicht 1997: 36–97). What T. calls *bellum* could, in the original, have alluded to anything from the ill-fated Lamian War (323–322) to the campaigns against Athens by Cassander (307–304) to the domestic turmoil surrounding the tyrannies of Lachares (330) and then Demetrius (295). Though a Roman audience would not have known (or probably cared) to identify the precise reference, Romans would themselves certainly have understood what the upheavals of war can do to families. The very casualness of the reference here is perhaps its most telling feature.   **in Asiam**, i.e. Asia Minor. Andros, at the north end of the Cyclades, would indeed have been on his route.

936 illam relinquere hic: on setting out for Asia, Chremes evidently left his daughter behind at Athens in his brother's care. What happened to the girl's mother is unexplained; Chremes' present household seems to include no citizen women (364). Just as T. wrote Simo's wife out of the play (Appendix II.3.2), so here he passes over an opportunity to establish, even indirectly, a female presence in this second household.   **hoc primum**: the search for a lost relative could be difficult and perilous, especially in times of unrest, so Chremes' inability to acquire news of his brother is hardly surprising. Cf. the tribulations of Pl.'s Hanno (*Poen.*) and Sosicles (*Men.*), who were deeply committed to such quests, and Richlin 2017: 398–409 on the anxieties attendant on dislocation and reunion in Pl.

937 illo: instr. abl. (143n.).   **apud me**: 408n.

938 mirando: gerundive with *bono,* a somewhat ordinary noun after such an effusive build-up.

939 ne: 324n.   **tuam**: predicative. The remark is addressed to Chremes, though to judge from what follows, Pamphilus seems to think his father is speaking to him.   **credo**: the expected response to congratulations (*gaudeo*), e.g. *Eun.* 1051, *Ad.* 972 (*OLD* 8b).

940 scrupulus, lit. a small stone, but by extension, like a stone caught in one's sandal, to mean any source of discomfort or impediment, e.g. *Ph.* 954, 1019; *Ad.* 228.   **dignus** "deserve," sc. that discomfort. Thus Don. glosses, *qui male habearis.* Cf. *Hau.* 813 *is tu hinc quo dignus es?* ("Why don't you take off where you deserve?").

941 religione "scruples" (730n.).   **odium**: probably voc., like *scelus,* a mild term of abuse, e.g. Pl. *Poen.* 352–3 *ecce odium meum! quid me uis?* ("Look, my nuisance. What do you want from me?"). The alternative construction of *dignus* + acc. is limited to prns., e.g. *Ph.* 519 *di tibi omnes id quod es dignus duint!*   **nodum in scirpo**: a proverbial expression for looking for trouble where it does not exist (since bulrushes do not have knots). Also at Pl. *Men.* 247, Enn. *Sat.* 70V, Lucil. 36M.   **istud**, i.e. the *scrupulus* that troubles Chremes.

942 aliud, sc. *nomen.*

943 huius, subj. gen. (*NLS* §72(2)). Pamphilus does not want his future happiness compromised by Chremes' faulty memory.

944 quom ego possim: since *quom*-clauses in early Latin regularly take the indic. (96n.), exceptions are usually explained as instances of attraction (*NLS* §231). Some exx. of subjunc. verbs with causal *quom*, however, clearly prefigure the classical usage, e.g. *Hec.* 704–5 *nam puerum iniussu credo non tollent meo,* | *praesertim . . . quom sit mi adiutrix socrus* ("I don't think they will acknowledge the child against my wishes, especially since my mother-in-law is on my side").   **medicari**: 831n.

945 Pasibula: an unexceptionable, though unparalleled female name, but when and why did she abandon it? Name changes and aliases were common among *hetairai* (e.g. Athen. 13.567c–d), but Crito knew her as Glycerium even on Andros (806), so the change predated her life with Chrysis at Athens. It was perhaps a longstanding family nickname, though their reticence in calling women by name in public makes the Athenians' practice in female nomenclature difficult to document (Schaps 1977). A Roman audience would certainly have heard "Glycerium" as a meretrix' name (134n.), so the revelation here would come – at least notionally – as a surprise.

The first and third vowels of *Pasibula* should be long: to scan the line as an iambic octonarius requires lightening the first syllable. That is not impossible, as the scansion of *Niceratum* might suggest (87n.). The Bembine codex (A) omits *non patiar*, which interrupts the long run of octonarii by making this a single trochaic septenarius to mark the dramatic significance of Pamphilus' declaration. No less noteworthy (and present in both variants) is the echoing sound of *Pasibulast ipsast east*, a deliberately artificial effect. Dacier, praising this *jeu de Theatre* [sic], imagined the two excited old men responding in unison to the news, though this would entail shortening the line by a foot, an unlikely effect.

946 hoc: acc. Cf. 362 *iam id gaudeo.* The inf. clause is the obj. of *credere* in the next line.

947 te credo credere: Simo plays on the formulaic response to good news (939n.).   **ita me di ament**: a common formula of asseveration (Müller 1997: 146–7).   **pater**: whether Pamphilus pauses here to prompt a response or is interrupted before he can complete his thought depends on how one interprets the character of Simo.

948 iamdudum "for a long time now" (*OLD* s.v. *dudum* 2b). In fact, Simo's change of heart came only at 934 after it became clear that this was not one of the *meretricios amores* he had railed against (913).   **redduxit**

me . . . in gratiam "has reconciled me" (*OLD* s.v. *gratia* 2). The idiom recurs with *redigo* (*Ph.* 966) and *restituo* (*Hec.* 29).   **lepidum**, *est uenustas* (Don.), and often in comedy with connotations of indulgence, e.g. *Ad.* 910–11 (after Demea reveals his sudden change of heart) *placet,* | *pater lepidissime.* :: *euge! iam lepidus uocor.* So, too, Pl. *Cas.* 1008, *Mil.* 155, *Ps.* 435.

949 de uxore: Pamphilus' wish (273) is at last close to fulfillment, though with one remaining hurdle.   **possedi**: the verb is more naturally used in asserting legal ownership of property (810, *Hau.* 969), not wives. Contrast the more general language of Callicles, in a position much like Chremes, though responding with considerably less grace, at Pl. *Truc.* 843–4 *nam hau mansisti, dum ego darem illam: tute sumpsisti tibi.* | *nunc habeas ut nactu's* ("You didn't wait for me to give her to you: you took her for yourself. Now keep her as you've acquired her"). Pamphilus probably means simply that their union is a fait accompli: *possessio* as a legal concept is a development only of the later Republic (Watson 1971: 64 n. 8), while the *interdictum ut possidetis* sometimes read into this passage applied specifically to immoveable property, not to people (Festus 260.35L, Watson 1968: 87–90).   **causa optuma**: a formula of agreement answering the implied question *num quae causa est . . .?* Cf. Pl. *Aul.* 261–2 *sed nuptias* | *num quae causa est quin faciamus hodie?* :: *immo edepol optuma.* The corresponding negative reply is found at *Amph.* 852 *nulla causa est.*

950 nisi . . . pater: the permission of both fathers would be expected (Watson 1967: 41–7, Gardner 1986: 41–4).   **nempe id** "Certainly he agrees to it," the particle of agreement + the thing agreed to.

951 decem talenta: a large sum by any measure. The dowries in fourth-century Athens known from oratory and inscriptions range from 2,000 to 6,000 drachmas (6,000 drachmas = one talent). Those in New Comedy are significantly higher, from two talents (*Asp.* 321, *Mis.* 446, P. Oxy. 2533) to four talents (*Epitrep.* 134, P. Oxy. 4646 and 1824), while the husband of *Plokion* fr. 333.11 K–T mentions an exceptional ten talents as recompense for accepting an ugly wife. The twenty-talent dowry of Pl. *Cist.* 561–2 thus borders on the fantastic. The dowry is ten talents at *Merc.* 703, while the spiteful Callicles of *Truc.* 844–5 proposes *deducting* six talents from a dowry as punishment for Diniarchus' presumption. At *Hau.* 838 the dowry is a still generous two talents. Casson 1976: 58 may be right in suggesting that the difference between the Greek and Roman examples reflects new Roman definitions of wealth. See Casson 1976: 53–9, Vérilhac and Vial 1998: 172–6, Golden 2015: 112–14, 187–8 (Greek dowries) and Watson 1971: 24–7, Dixon 1992: 50–3 (Roman dowries).   **accipio**: Pamphilus' formal acceptance creates a legally binding agreement.   **eho**: as at 184, an imper. is readily understood with the particle.

952 illam me: subj. and obj. respectively of *nosse*. He wants Crito with him to facilitate the introduction. It may reflect a sense of paternal duty as well as dramaturgic efficiency that Chremes settles the terms of the marriage before hastening inside to meet his long-lost daughter.   **illam huc transferri**: the transfer will presumably be without a formal wedding procession (362n.), perhaps just as well since the new-born child must be included. Cf. *Ad.* 909 (a marriage under similar conditions) *hac transfer: unam fac domum.*

954 qui? adv. (53n.).   **magis ex sese** "more in accordance with his needs" (*OLD* s.v. *ex* 20). Simo shows some reluctance to admit what he has done to Davos.

955 ita, i.e. *recte*. Simo pretends to hear Pamphilus' *non recte* not as "not justly" but as "not thoroughly."   **obsecro**: Pamphilus is being elaborately polite (Barrios-Lech 2016: 124–5).

956 eo intro: Simo ignores Pamphilus' final, less carefully worded request. This is the last we see of him.

[V.v] Charinus, Pamphilus (957–64)

The scene division here is again entirely artificial. Pamphilus' exclamation *o faustum et felicem diem!* (956) begins a monologue that will continue without significant break until Davos enters at 963. Charinus, who was last seen heading for home at 714, makes his entrance at 957 and comments on what he overhears (963, 969, 971, 973), but he will not be recognized by the others until he steps forward to address Pamphilus at 974.

957 prouiso: 404n.   **Pamphilus**: hiatus at the diaeresis of the octonarius, a nice ex. of how a metrical feature coincides with a dramatic feature. Charinus' entry line is spoken to the audience. The momentary pause created by this hiatus is the time required for him to turn and see his friend across the stage.   **eccum**: 532n.

958 putet: potential subjunc.   **sic** "in this way." Cf. *Ad.* 68 *mea sic est ratio et sic animum induco meum…* ("this is my philosophy and this is my way of thinking…"). What so pleases Pamphilus is the realization that the present state of affairs (*hoc*) is true.

959–61 Pamphilus' philosophical turn is marked by the shift to a trochaic rhythm, which will continue to the end of the play. The thought here, says Don., is taken from Men.'s *Eunouchos*, and this lifting of material from one play for use in another is what critics meant by *contaminari non decere fabulas* (*An.* 16). He seems to have in mind *Eun.* 591–2 *nunc est profecto interfici quom perpeti me possum,* | *ne hoc gaudium contaminet uita aegritudine aliqua* ("surely now is when I could endure dying, so life would not spoil this joy with some distress"). Germany 2016: 167–9 discusses the relationship between the two passages.

That the gods' happiness and leisure are functions of their immortality is, as Don. also notes, an Epicurean idea, e.g. Lucr. 1.44–9/2.646–51, Cic. *Nat.* 1.45, Sen. *Ep.* 85.18. Men. is said to have served as an ephebe alongside Epicurus (Str. 14.638 = T 6 K–T), but the Epicurean sentiments often noticed in his plays are difficult to distinguish from commonplaces of contemporary popular philosophy. See Long 2006: 17–18, and for the idea of happiness in Epicurus more generally, Lobel 2017: 42–54.

959 sempiternam: a word for "everlasting," says Don., appropriate to the gods, as distinct from *perpetuus,* appropriate for mortals, though *amicum sempiternum* is found at Pl. *Most.* 247 and *Pers.* 35. Cic. *Att.* 5.20.3 calls a mountain range of Cilicia *hostium plenus sempiternorum.*

960 propriae: 716n.   **mi immortalitas**: Cf. *Hau.* 693 (Clinia) *deorum uitam apti sumus, Hec.* 843 (Pamphilus) *deus sum si hoc itast.* For the *topos,* see Flury 1968: 94–6.

961 partast "acquired" (*OLD* 5b).

962 potissimum: 454n.   **exoptem . . . dari**: potential subjunc. For the construction, cf. *Hau.* 758 *te mihi ipsum iamdudum optabam dari* ("You're the very one I've been hoping to run into for some time").

963 illud gaudist: 2n.   **mallem**, sc. *uidere.*

964 hunc . . . solum: Pamphilus expects Davos to share his joy, but he is remarkably unmindful of Charinus, whose language at 647 he unconsciously echoes. Alliteration (*solide solum*) and a *figura etymologica* (*gauisurum gaudia*) suggest his excitement by the use of strikingly traditional comic diction.

[V.vi] Charinus, Pamphilus, Davos (965–81)

The play moves swiftly to its conclusion as Pamphilus promises to share his good fortune by securing Charinus' happiness as well as his own.

965 Davos emerges from Simo's house slightly disoriented and probably still smarting from the physical manhandling he has received. He is thus slow to see and then to recognize Pamphilus.

966 certe: Davos agrees with Pamphilus' *nescis*. His own punishment is, not unreasonably, foremost in his mind. Note the chiastic balance of the line, *nescis . . . scio.*

967 quidem: an ex. of "extending quidem," where a second speaker supplements an earlier statement (Solodow 1978: 110–12).   **euēnit:** perf. Davos offers a specific ex. of a general truth, viz. *fama mali celerior est quam boni* (Don.). The earliest source of this proverbial idea in Eng. appears to be Elizabethan, Kydd's *The Spanish Tragedy* I.iii, "Nay, evil news fly faster still than good."

969 suos parentis: Crito, not knowing the domestic situation at Athens, spoke generally of Glycerium's "parents" (806). She has now, as far as we know, found only her father. Pamphilus is probably using a rhetorical plural rather than making a statement about Chremes' current marital status.   **factum bene!** 105n. Davos makes no mention of his former skepticism (220–4).

970 amicus summus "a great friend" (*OLD* s.v. *summus* 10). Cf. *Ph.* 35, 1049.

971 uxorem: predicative.   **num ille somniat:** Charinus has difficulty shaking his skepticism in the face of these developments. Don. recalls Verg. *Ecl.* 8.108 *credimus? an, qui amant, ipsi sibi somnia fingunt.* ("Can I believe it, or do those in love fashion their own dreams?").

973 solus est quem diligant di: the subjunc. is descriptive (*NLS* §155, *SEL* I 291–2). The line as a whole is problematic on levels of text, sense, and connotation. A few MSS, along with P. Oxy. 2401, read *es*, adopted by Ashmore, who compares *Ph.* 854 (on a lover's good fortune) *nam sine controuersia ab dis solus diligere* ("without argument, you are the one man loved by the gods"), and also by Brown, who understands it as a question directed to Pamphilus: "Are you the only one the gods love?" But why would Davos respond so grudgingly to Pamphilus' good fortune? If *est* is retained in a statement, is Davos speaking of the child (so Barsby: "He must be the darling of the gods"), or aside with reference to Pamphilus (so Shipp). And if the latter, what does Davos mean, and why is there no further mention of the child? The line poses an additional challenge to modern readers alive to patterns of echo and allusion in Latin poetry. Its closest parallel originates in Men. *Dis Exapaton* fr. 111 K–T ὅν οἱ θεοὶ φιλοῦσαν ἀποθνῄσκει νέος ("whom the gods love dies young"), a line widely quoted in antiquity. At Pl. *Bac.* 816–17 that became *quem di diligunt | adulescens moritur,* spoken by Chrysalus, another cheeky slave. The Plautine tag could possibly stand behind T.'s line. (The papyrus in fact reads *di diligant.*) Allusion and coincidence can be especially difficult to distinguish in as highly stylized a genre as *palliata* comedy.

974 quis homost? Pamphilus overhears Charinus' *colloquar* and turns to face him, much as Davos turned to face Pamphilus at 965.   **in tempore ipso** "at just the right time" (*OLD* 8d).

975 in tuis secundis, sc. *rebus.*   **respice**: 642n.

976 tuos "friendly to you" (*OLD* 6).

977 longumst "it would take too long (to)" (*OLD* 12). The pres. indic. is regular in this idiomatic construction.

978 hac, i.e. into Glycerium's house.

979 hinc: best taken with *auferant*. To bring Glycerium to Simo's house will require not only an escort but porters to carry her belongings.   **eo**: Davos' apparent slowness could be attributed to the lingering effects of his treatment, or simply be a function of Pamphilus' impatience and desire to assert his authority.

980–1 Who speaks these lines is uncertain. The Bembine codex (A) treats *eo* as Davos' exit cue and assigns what remains to Pamphilus. Most other MSS presume Pamphilus' exit together with Charinus at 979 and leave the rest to Davos. Whether it is thought more suitable for Pamphilus, who has just ordered Davos off on a final errand, to remain behind alone to assert this final touch of mastery over the situation, or for Davos to linger somewhat cheekily after his dismissal and declare an end to the action his own initiatives have kept in motion depends largely on the strength of character imagined for each. The finale of Pl. *Cist.* was signaled by a similar declaration that begins in a similar way: *ne exspectetis, spectatores, dum illi huc ad uos exeant. | nemo exibit. omnes intus conficient negotium.* ("Don't wait, spectators, for them to come out here to you. Nobody will come out. They will all finish the business inside.") That speech, however, continues with further jokes about acting and actors (784–7), an explicitly extra-dramatic appeal that MSS assign, after old Demipho and his slave Lampadio have left, to "the company" (*Caterua*). T. may be deliberately echoing these lines (so Sharrock 2009: 268–9), though the language could simply be thought traditional. Cf. 973n.

980 despondebitur: impers. pass.

981 quod restet: this would include, at the least, the kind of betrothal scene previously enacted for Pamphilus (947–56). T. avoids repeating what he has already dramatized.   **plaudite!** "Give us your applause!"

The curtainless stage requires some way to signal the play's end: here an actor steps out of character to provide the necessary indication. All six Terentian plays end with variants of this formula, which became something of a cliché. For Cic. *Sen.* 70 *usque ad "plaudite" ueniendum est* means, in effect, "until the final curtain." So Quint. 6.1.52 invokes the phrase *quo ueteres tragoediae comoediaeque cluduntur "plodite."* The extra-dramatic injunction is signaled somewhat mysteriously in the MSS by a lower-case omega, perhaps a remnant of the algebraic notation used to mark the actors' parts in ancient scripts (cf. Jory 1963, Gammacurta 2006: 7–32). The ascription to "Cantor" found in the OCT goes back to a suggestion by Bentley ad *An.* 981, citing Hor. *Ars* 155 *sessuri donec cantor "uos plaudite" dicat,* but the importation of such a figure makes little stage sense. The concluding address to the audience found in Pl. is sometimes fuller (and funnier), assigned to *grex* at *As., Bac., Epid.* and to *caterua* at *Capt.* and *Cist.* See Moore 2012: 73–5. The corresponding Greek convention found in Men. (*Dys., Mis., Sa., Sik.*), Posidippus (*PCG* 6.11–13) and P. Oxy. 1239 (*PCG* VI.2 fr. 903, Men.?) is a more solemn invocation of Victory (Νίκη).

APPENDIX I

ALTERNATIVE ENDING(S)

T.'s ending leaves Charinus hopeful but hanging, and in antiquity efforts were made to "improve" upon it by giving his situation a more explicit resolution. Some texts circulating in Don.'s time, though not (he says) the best ones, contained an alternative ending designed to give Charinus his due, though neither Don. (ad 978) nor the somewhat later commentator Eugraphius (ad 975) considered it authentic. Remnants of some such alteration survive. The Oxyrhynchus fragment, first published in 1957 (P. Oxy. 24.2401), breaks off after a version of line 977 that hints at an additional scene now lost (Macedo 2018: 85–7). A second, fuller version of an actual alternative ending is preserved in a group of inferior mediaeval MSS. The earliest of these dates from the eleventh century, with perhaps all of them deriving from a single ancient exemplar (Victor 1989: 64–8). The scene as it comes down to us from this source is probably not complete – it begins abruptly with Chremes' unannounced return and ends with no explicit mark of closure – but its intent is clear enough. Whether it represents changes made to the original script for some revival performance or is the work of an overly engaged reader remains unknown. Unlike Pl., whose texts include doublets and interpolations believed to reflect ancient performance variants (Goldberg 2004, Marshall 2006: 266–72), T.'s text shows fewer signs of such reworking, *Hau.* 48–50/*Hec.* 49–51 and *Hec.* 790–1 being the most likely instances. Nevertheless, though T.'s stage history becomes problematic after the first century BCE (Tansey 2001, Kragelund 2012), interest in the plays remained high throughout antiquity and inevitably gave the text a certain fluidity even while it rested largely in the hands of readers and teachers (Cain 2013). The author of this scene – "forger" makes unjustifiable assumptions about its intent – shows awareness of comic conventions and various features of early comic style, and while the versification can be clumsy, it is not inept. The scene may not, as it stands, be particularly satisfying or dramatically effective, but it remains a significant landmark in the history of T.'s reception.

The text of the papyrus printed here as (I) reproduces the transcription of Macedo 2018. The text found in the MS tradition follows as (II) and appears as established by Skutsch for the OCT. Its considerable difficulties were first explored in detail by Ritschl 1845b. See now Skutsch 1957 and Victor 1989. Lefèvre 2008: 80–1 and Sharrock 2009: 269–70 offer useful observations about its significance.

I.

Pamphilvs Charinvs

?tr[7]	PAM	memini adq(ue) a.[	977?
	CHA	.[..]o.[	978a
	CHA	[	979a

977? This fragmentary line looks to be a version of T.'s 977, which may have been rewritten to take the scene in what was evidently a new direction. Whatever followed would then have replaced the extant text from 978 to the end.

978a–9a The papyrus assigns the beginning of both these lines to Charinus, which means there was at least one change of speaker in 978 and thus represents something different from what is found in the standard text. A brief exchange with Pamphilus is the likely hypothesis. How (or if) their dialogue introduced the scene preserved in the mediaeval MSS cannot be determined: it is possible, though by no means certain, that the papyrus preserves traces of a different variant ending.

II.

Pamphilvs Charinvs Chremes Davos

?tr[7]	PAM	memini adq(ue adeo ut uolui commodum huc senex	
		exit foras.)	977a
tr[7]		te expectabam: est de tua re quod agere ego tecum uolo.	
		operam dedi ne me esse oblitum dicas tuae gnatae alterae.	
		tibi me opinor inuenisse dignum te atque illa uirum.	
	CHA	ah,	
		perii, Daue, de meo amore ac uita <nunc> sors tollitur.	
	CHR	non noua istaec mihi condicio est, si uoluissem, Pamphile.	5
	CHA	occidi, Dauē.	
	DAV	mane.	
	CHA	perii.	
	CHR	id quamobrem non uolui eloquar:	
		non idcirco quod eum omnino adfinem mihi nollem . . .	
	CHA	hem!	
	DAV	tace.	
	CHR	sed amicitia nostra quae est a patribus nostris tradita	
		nobis, aliquam partem studui adauctam tradi liberis.	
		nunc cum copia ac fortuna utrique ut obsequerer dedit,	10
		detur.	
	PAM	bene factum.	

Dav	adi atque age homini gratias.	
Cha		salue, Chremes,

ᵃ⁶   amicorum meorum omnium mihi †agissime.
quod mihi non minus est gaudio quam id <quod volo>
quod <abs te expecto et summo studio> abs te expeto:
me repperisse ut habitus antehac fui tibi.   15

Chr   animum, Charine, quod ad cumque applicaueris
studium, exinde ut erit tute existimaberis.
id ita esse facere coniecturam ex me licet:
alienus abs te tamen quis tu esses noueram.

Cha   ita res est.   gnatam tibi meam Philumenam   20

Chr   gnatam tibi meam Philumenam   20
uxorem et dotis sex talenta spondeo.

The author of this new ending was a careful reader of T.'s play. The scene
again puts Charinus to one side, expressing anxiety and momentary dismay at the conversation he overhears, although this time he has Davos to
reassure him. It draws on details, such as Chremes' appeal to the *amicitia*
between himself and Simo and the name of the daughter to be betrothed
to Charinus, that are lifted directly from earlier scenes (8–9 ~ 539–43,
820; 20 ~ 306). Diction and word order are mined from the authentic
Terentian text, a technique also found in the *argumentum* ascribed to
Sulpicius Apollinaris. The author may not have been as metrically adept as
T. (or Pl.), but that would be to judge by a very high standard. When and
why he wrote remain uncertain. Though clearly post-Terentian, anomalies of syntax and meter that might point to a late date – the archaizing
tendencies of the second century CE would make it a likely possibility –
are not definitive. The best discussion of the scene's language and meter
is by Skutsch 1957: 65–8, who left the question of date open. And so it
remains.

977a Ritschl 1845b 598 recognized that a transition was required to move
from T.'s established text to the later ending and suggested a revision of
T.'s 977 along these lines.

1 de tua re: antecedent of *quod*. In speaking to Chremes, Pamphilus takes
the initiative with greater self-assurance than he has previously shown.

2 operam do: 157n. A common Terentian idiom, e.g. 243, 307,
327.   **tŭaĕ gnatae**: verbs of remembering and forgetting more commonly take an acc. obj. in early Latin. This and *Eun.* 306 are the only exx.
of *obliuiscor* + gen. in Pl. and T. (*SEL* II 88, *NLS* §73.1). Here, as at 14 (*fŭĭ*)
and 18 (*tămĕn*), the author shows awareness of iambic shortening as a feature of dramatic prosody.   **alterae**: the expected gen. *alterius* appears

at 628, but gen. *aliae* at Cic. *Div.* 2.30 and Lucr. 3.918 provide some precedent for this variant form here (Weiss 2020: 369). Why Pamphilus feels
any responsibility for Chremes' second daughter or why Chremes might
think he should do so is not explained. It was a good deal more in character when Simo told Chremes, *tibi generum firmum et filiae inuenies uirum*
(571). This reminder of a second daughter is perhaps more for the audience's benefit than for Chremes.

5 condicio "marriage proposal" (*OLD* 2), e.g. *Ph.* 579 *nam hanc condicionem
si quoi tulero extrario . . .* ("if I offered the match to some outsider . . .").
si uoluissem, sc. *hanc condicionem.* The implication is that Charinus had
been proposed as a husband for his daughter once before and been
refused for the reason Chremes will now provide. Cf. 374n. Victor 1989:
68, noting that *eum* (7) will lack an explicit antecedent, posits a lacuna
between 4 and 5 and by way of example supplies, CHR *quaeso, quis is est?*
PA *is Charinus, iuuenis omnimodis probus.*

6 occidi . . . perii: Charinus' immediate response is probably colored by
his memory of that earlier refusal.   **Dauē**: *brevis in longo* at the change
of speaker (267n.).   **id,** i.e. the proposal.   **non uolui**: as often for
nolui, e.g. 920, *Hau.* 433, *Hec.* 560.

7 eum, i.e. Charinum.

8 amicitia: though logically the subj. of *tradi*, it stands alone here as a *nominativus pendens* introducing an idea that is kept syntactically independent
of the thought it will generate, e.g. Pl. *Poen.* 659 *tu, si te di amant, agere
tuam rem occasiost* ("You, if the gods love you, there's a chance to advance
your interests"). Cf. *Hec.* 286; Cato *Agr.* 34.2; Cic. *Fin.* 3.11, *Tusc.* 3.16 and
the discussion of Surbat 1991. Simo referred to their *amicitia* at 539–43.

9 aliquam partem "to some degree" (*OLD* 2b), an adverbial acc. with
adauctam. Cf. Pl. *Ps.* 1322 *nonne audes, quaesso, aliquam partem mihi gratiam facere hinc de argento?* ("Couldn't you please give me a bit of a break
over the money?"). The balance *nobis . . . liberis* is another effect in the
Terentian manner.

10 cum: the MSS spelling. The regular Republican spelling *quom* for the
conj. is elsewhere restored by modern editors, as also, apparently, at 623
by a corrector of P. Oxy. 2401. What this author actually wrote would probably have depended on when he wrote, though he does think to construct
cum here, as so often in comedy, with an indic. verb (944n.).   **copia
ac fortuna** "resources and good fortune." The sing. verb with compound
subj. is readily paralleled, e.g. *Hec.* 2 *interuenit uitium et calamitas* (other
exx. in *SEL* I 1–2), but *dedit + ut* less readily so. Skutsch 1957: 60 proposed

reading *copiam hanc* "this opportunity" (cf. *Eun.* 21 *inspiciundi copia*), which produces a more likely construction as well as excellent sense. **utrique**, i.e. Pamphilus and Charinus.

11 detur: 101n.   **bene factum**: also at 975 and also responding to good news.   **adi**: Davos now urges Charinus to approach Chremes.

12 Charinus' address to Chremes reverts to senarii, not a traditional practice in a final scene. Only the alternative endings of Pl.'s *Poen.* (1355–71, 1372–97) offer anything comparable.   †**agissime**: an impossible reading. Likely corrections include *carissime* (Ritschl), *amicissime* (Lindsay), and *antiquissime* (Skutsch), the last being less effusive than the others. Dickey 2002: 130–7 notes that in expressing affection and esteem, superlative forms are in practice weaker than positive forms, *carissime* being esp. common in addressing friends and acquaintances.

13 quod: anticipates *me repperisse* (15).   **gaudio**: pred. dat. (*NLS* §68). Cf. Pl. *Poen.* 1217 *gaudio ero uobis*.

13–15 Neither text nor thought is clear in what follows. As printed, Charinus is saying, "It's no less a joy to me than what I wish for, the thing I await from you and with utmost earnestness seek from you, that I've discovered how I previously appeared to you." He seems pleased to have learned from Chremes' statement (8–9) that his earlier suit was unsuccessful through no deficiency of his own.

15 ut "how." Cf. Pl. *Rud.* 924–5 *nam ego nunc mihi . . .* | *repperi ut piger si uelim siem* ("I've now discovered how to be lazy if I want to be").   **habitus . . . fui** "I appeared" (*OLD* 24). Cf. Pl. *Aul.* 123 *nos odiosas . . . haberi.* Indic. in the ind. quest., as often in comedy, e.g. *Ad.* 559 *uide ut discidit labrum!* (235n. and *SEL* I 121 for further exx.).

16 quod ad cumque: tmesis of *quodcumque* with *ad* postponed. Cf. 63 *cum quibus erat cumque*, 263 *quae meo quomque animo.* For the sense, Skutsch 1957: 63 points to 56 *ut animum ad aliquod studium adiungant.*

17 exinde ut "in the same measure as" (*OLD* 3).

18 id ita esse: obj. of *facere coniecturam.* For the expression, cf. 512 *coniecturam hanc nunc facio.*

19 alienus "aloof," and thus "unsympathetic" (*OLD* 7). The two ideas readily merge, e.g. *Ad.* 326 (alarmed by Aeschinus' apparent betrayal) *alienus est ab nostra familia.*   **tamen** "although." Chremes again stresses that his refusal of the original suit was no reflection on Charinus' character.   **quis** = *qualis* (702n.).

20 Philumenam: 306n. The author has clearly drawn his material with some care from T.'s text.

21 dotis sex talenta: the dowry offered Pamphilus was ten talents (951n.). Actual Athenian practice seems to have favored equal dowries when two daughters were to be provided for: Lys. 16.10, Is. 2.3.5, D. 40.24, 41.3.29. See Casson 1976: 54.   **spondeo**: a legal *sponsalia* was contracted by a formal sequence of question and answer (Gell. 4.4.2) as is found, e.g., at Pl. *Cur.* 674 *spondesne, miles, mihi hanc uxorem?* :: *spondeo.* So too *Aul.* 255–6, *Poen.* 1157, *Trin.* 1157–8, 1162–3, but at *Trin.* 569–73 *spondeo* is not preceded by the traditional question. See Watson 1971: 14–17.

The scene (and with it the play) ends quite abruptly here. Ritschl 1845b 599, sensing that some explicit closure was required, suggested by way of example *agatur intus, si quid restet. ω plaudite.*

APPENDIX II

THE GREEK MODELS

Menander fecit Andriam et Perinthiam.
qui utramuis recte norit ambas nouerit,
non ita dissimili sunt argumento, et tamen
dissimili oratione sunt factae ac stilo.
quae conuenere in Andriam ex Perinthia
fatetur transtulisse atque usum pro suis.   (*An.* 9–14)

Terence invites us almost from the outset to think about his sources, and
if we had them before us, we would doubtless learn a great deal not just
about his techniques of composition, but about his genre and his place
in it. Unfortunately, those models do not survive. Most of what we know
about Men.'s *Andria* and much that is relevant about his *Perinthia* comes
instead from Don., in some ways a problematic source. For Aulus Gellius
in the mid-second century CE, it was still possible, if not common, to compare a Roman comedy directly with its Greek model, but Don. some two
centuries later does not appear to have had that ability.[1] At least one of his
sources, however, did, and remnants of an earlier, detailed comparison
are thus preserved in the extant commentary. These include a few lines
and phrases of Greek together with intriguing observations about dramatic structure and characterization.

1. Menander's Andria

Aside from the testimony of Don., the Greek *Andria* otherwise made little
impression on the later tradition. No papyri have been identified, and
two of the three fragments drawn from other sources, a quotation by the
fifth-century anthologist Stobaeus (fr. 43) and a line found in Byzantine
lexica (fr. 45), are not easily matched to anything in the Latin text. The

---

[1] Gell. 2.23, comparing scenes of Caecilius' *Plocium* with its Menandrean model. For Don.'s use of Greek, see Barsby 2002: 255–9, Maltby 2019, Goldberg 2020.
The utility of comparing whole texts to fragments or to lost plays as reconstructed
from fragments is necessarily limited. For the history of the method, see Goldberg
1986: 61–75, Halporn 1993, and for discussion of its results, Danese 2002. Webster 1960: 77–83 uses T.'s play as a blueprint for reconstituting the *disiecta membra*
of the lost *Andria* and *Perinthia*.

fragments of this *Andria* as presented in K–T are as follows (*PCG*, vol. 6.2 numbers in parentheses):

fr. 33 (35) Don. ad 204: *sic Menander,*

νῦν δ᾽ οὐ λέληθάς με . . . as it is, you haven't escaped my notice

fr. 34 (37) Don. ad 406: *Menander,*

εὑρετικὸν εἶναί φασι τὴν ἐρημίαν highbrows say a deserted spot
οἱ τὰς ὀφρῦς αἴροντες is the place for solving problems.

fr. 35 (38) Don. ad 473: *obstetriciam hanc potestatem Iunoni attribuit, quamquam illam Menander Dianam appellet.*

Ἄρτεμι to Artemis

fr. 36 (39) Don. ad 483: *sic enim est Menander,*

λούσατ᾽ αὐτὴν αὐτίκα bathe her at once

fr. 37 (40) Phot. et Sud. s.v. νεόττος: the yolk of an egg . . . Menander in *Andria,*

καὶ τεττάρων and afterwards, dear, the yolk
ὠιῶν μετὰ τοῦτο, φιλτάτη, τὸ νεόττιον. of four eggs

fr. 38 (42) Don. ad 592: *legitur et "audiam;" Menander enim sic ait,*

τί ποτ᾽ ἀκούσομαι; What am I about to hear?

fr. 39 (43) Don. ad 611: *si hoc euasero, scio me postea non periclitaturum. Menander sic,*

ἂν θεὸς θέληι, if god wills it,
οὐκ ἂν ἀπολοίμην I won't die

fr. 40 (44) Don. ad 726: *"ex ara" Apollinis scilicet, quem* Λοξίαν *Menander uocat.* . . . *"uerbenae" autem dictae ueluti "herbenae." Menander sic,*

ἀ]πὸ Λοξίου σὺ μυρρίνας [take?] boughs of myrtle from Loxias

fr. 41 (45) Don. ad 794: *et haec sententia a Terentio* ἐρωτηματικῶς ["interrogatively"] *prolata est, quam Menander* ἀποδεικτικῶς ["demonstratively"] *posuit.*

fr. 42 (48) Don. ad 919: *hic Chremes traducit illum ab iracundia dicendo sic eum esse. Menander,*

οὕτως αὐτός ἐστιν that's how he is

fr. 43 (49) Stob. *Ecl.* 4.20.51: Μενάνδρου Ἀνδρίαι (*An.* 218?):

τὸ δ᾽ ἐρᾶν ἐπισκοτεῖ   being in love throws a shadow over
ἅπασιν, ὡς ἔοικε, **καὶ** τοῖς εὐβόλως everyone, it seems, both those far-
     ing well
καὶ τοῖς κακῶς ἔχουσιν   and those faring badly.

fr. 44 (41) Don. ad 543: τῶι ἑλληνισμῶι· [Menander?] μὴ λιτάνευε, μὴ
μάχου. ("don't entreat, don't wrangle.")

fr. 45 (47) Monost. 190 et Sud. (=*An.* 804?):

ζῶμεν γὰρ οὐκ ὡς θέλομεν, ἀλλ᾽ ὡς δυνάμεθα we live not as we wish, but
     as we can

2. MENANDER'S *PERINTHIA*

Perinthia is somewhat better attested. Ten fragments amounting to some
sixteen lines are preserved in quotations by later authors, and a whole
column of text survives in a third-century papyrus from Oxyrhynchus (P.
Oxy. 855).[2] The book fragments include references to the citizen-sponsor
of a metic (fr. 1 προστάτης), to "a very expensive corpse" (fr. 2 πολυτελῆ
νεκρόν), to a heavy-drinking old woman (fr. 4), and to a slave bringing tiny
fish (fr. 6 ἑψητούς) that can all, with a little imagination, be accommo-
dated in the general outline of T.'s play. The papyrus preserves a fragment
of a strikingly cruel scene as an old man named Laches supervises four of
his slaves (including a Pyrrhias and a Sosias) as they carry in firewood to
drive another slave from his refuge at an altar. This slave, another Daos, is
mocked angrily by his master as he clings to safety:

ΛΑ   νυνί ἐπ]ίδειξαι, Δᾶε, τὴν πανουργίαν,
         τέχνην τιν᾽ εὑρὼν διαφυγών τ᾽ ἐνθένδε με
ΔΑ   τέχνην ἐγώ;
ΛΑ   ναί, Δᾶε, τὸν μὲν ἀπράγμονα
         καὶ κοῦφον ἐξαπατᾶν γάρ ἐστι δεσπότην
         φλύαρος.

La   Now,] Daos, show off your trickery,
         invent some scheme to give me the slip from here.
Da   A scheme? Me?
La   Surely, Daos, it's a trifle
     to trick your easy-going and lightweight
     master.   (11–15)

---

[2] The evidence, along with helpful discussion, is readily available in Arnott
1996: 472–501.

The taunt is all the more bitter because we learn from another of the book fragments that Laches is actually throwing Daos' own words back at him, for Daos had at some earlier point claimed to someone that it was really no great achievement for a servant "endeavoring to trick an easy-going, lightweight master" (fr. 3 ὅστις παραλαβὼν δεσπότην ἀπράγμονα | καὶ κοῦφον ἐξαπατᾶι θεράπων). The violence just under the surface when T.'s Simo orders Davos hogtied and hauled off for punishment (*An.* 860–8) seems to break to the surface here in *Perinthia* with Men.'s Laches.

3. DONATUS ON THE GREEK MODELS

In addition to quotations, Don.'s commentary occasionally notes points of comparison and contrast between T.'s play and his models. These are discussed individually in the commentary, but it can also be helpful to consider them as a group.

1. ad *An.* 10.1 VTRAMVIS: *prima scaena Perinthiae fere isdem uerbis quibus Andria scripta est, cetera dissimilia sunt exceptis duobus locis, altero ad uersus XI, altero ad XX qui in utraque fabula positi sunt.* [10.2]. QVI ⟨VTRAMVIS RECTE NORIT AMBAS NOVERIT ID EST: QVI⟩ *norit unam, norit ambas et nouerit omnem rem.*

The first scene of *Perinthia* was written in almost the exact same words as *Andria.* The rest is different except for two passages, one of some eleven lines, the other of some twenty, which are found in each play. [10.2] ⟨who⟩ knows one, knows both and will have known the entire matter.

[NOTE: The two passages that the plays are said to have in common remain unidentified.]

2. ad *An.* 14 FATETUR TRANSTULISSE: *Quare ergo se onerat Terentius, cum possit uideri de una transtulisse? sic soluitur: quia conscius sibi est primam scaenam de Perinthia esse translatam, ubi senex ita cum uxore loquitur, ut apud Terentium cum liberto. ut in Andria Menandri solus est senex.*

Why does Terence thus burden himself, since it can be seen that he transferred from a common stock? This is the solution: since he was aware that the first scene was taken over from *Perinthia,* where the old man speaks in this way with his wife, as in Terence with his freedman. But in Menander's *Andria* the old man is alone.

3. ad *An.* 301.2 QUID AIS, BYRRIA: *has personas Terentius addidit fabulae (nam non sunt apud Menandrum) ne †ΟΠΙΘΕΛΤΟΝ† fieret Philumenam spretam relinquere †sancte† sine sponso Pamphilo aliam ducente.*

Terence added these characters to his play – for they are not in Menander – so it would not become <?> to leave Philumena rejected and without a husband when Pamphilus marries another woman.

[NOTE: Greek can be garbled beyond recognition in Don.'s text. The most likely possibilities for the obelized word are παθητικόν ("affecting," printed by Wessner) and ἀπίθανον ("unconvincing," endorsed by Fraenkel). Donatus does not indicate whether "not in Menander" means not in the Greek *Andria* (but taken by T. from his *Perinthia*) or not in either play by Men. and thus T.'s independent creation.]

4. ad *An.* 801 ESTNE HIC CRITO SOBRINUS CHRYSIDIS: *"sobrini" sunt consobrinorum filii – nam sic dicit Menander.*

"Sobrini" are the children of first cousins, for this is what Menander says.

5. ad *An.* 977 (ATQUE ADEO LONGUM EST ILLUM EXPECTARE): *quia et audacter et artificiosissime binos amores duorum adulescentium et binas nuptias in una fabula machinatus est (et id extra praescriptum Menandri, cuius comoediam transferebat), idcirco aliud in proscaenio, aliud post scaenam rettulit, ne uel iusto longior fieret uel in eandem propter rerum similitudinem cogerentur.*

He boldly and very ingeniously engineered the double love affairs of the two young men and the double marriages in the one play – this is outside the design of Menander, whose comedy he was adapting. For this reason, one is handled on stage, the other off stage, either so that the play not be made longer than is suitable or so that they not be forced into repetition due to the similarity of subject.

Perhaps also relevant …

6. ad *An.* 959 EGO DEORUM VITAM: *hanc sententiam totam Menandri de Eunucho transtulit. et hoc est quod dicitur (u. 16) "contaminari non decere fabulas."*

He has transferred this entire idea from Menander's *Eunuch*. And this is what is meant by "it is not right for plays to be contaminated" (*An.* 16).

[Note: There is no corresponding line in T.'s *Eunuchus*. The closest we can come, similar in sentiment if not in expression, is *Eun.* 551–2: "Now is surely a time when I could endure being put to death/rather than have life contaminate [*contaminet*, i.e. "spoil"] this joy with some anguish."

The obvious meaning of Don.'s comment is that T. appropriated this line for his *An.* from a third source, viz. Men.'s *Eunouchos*, and this sort of carry-over from play to play is what he means in the *An.* prologue by "contaminating" plays [i.e. "to spoil by mixing"?]. It is, however, no less possible that Don. is simply commenting on the sense of *contaminet* in *Eun.* 552 and that his quotation of *An.* 16 led to misallocation of the remark to the *An.* commentary.]

APPENDIX III

CICERO'S *ANDRIA*

tu quoque, qui solus lecto sermone, Terenti,
conuersum expressumque Latina uoce Menandrum
in medium nobis sedatis uersibus effers,
quiddam come loquens atque omnia dulcia dicens.

You too, who alone with precise diction, Terence,
brought Menander converted and rendered in Latin speech
into our midst with quiet verses,
speaking with true charm and saying everything sweetly.

Cic. Limo ap. Suet. VitaT 7

Though Cicero would on occasion acknowledge the dominant view of his time that Caecilius was the best of the *palliata* poets, his own preference was unquestionably for T., whom he particularly admired as a stylist.[1] As the first play in the corpus, *An.* figures most prominently among his many citations of T. and might even, not unreasonably, stand for the whole, e.g. *Fin.* 1.4 Synephebos *ego, inquit, potius Caecilii aut* Andriam *Terentii quam utramque Menandri legam?* As the following passages make clear, *An.*'s opening scene was read closely in the course of rhetorical education (1–5), tag lines from the play might readily spring to mind (6–8), and isolated features could linger in memory (9–10).[2]

1. Cic. *Inv.* 1.33, quoting *An.* 49–50, 51, 157, 168

Atque his de partitione praeceptis in omni dictione meminisse oportebit, ut et prima quaeque pars, ut exposita est in partitione, sic ordine transigatur et omnibus explicatis peroratum sit, ut ne quid posterius praeter conclusionem inferatur. partitur apud Terentium breuiter et commode senex in *Andria*, quae cognoscere libertum uelit:

---

[1] Cic. *Opt. gen.* 2 *itaque licet dicere et Ennium summum epicum poetam . . . ut Pacuuium tragicum et Caecilium fortasse comicum.* This was certainly the view of Volcacius ap. Gell. 15.24 (*Caecilio palmam Statio do*). Cf. Cic. *Att.* 7.3.10 contrasting Caecilius, *malus auctor Latinitatis,* with the *elegantia sermonis* of T. A second epigram Suet. attributes to Caesar similarly praises T. as *puri sermonis amator.* Wright 1931: 65–70 traces Cicero's fondness for T. See also Manuwald 2014.

[2] On *An.*'s place in rhetorical education, see Anderson 2003/2004, and more generally, Lefèvre 2008: 15–18.

> eo pacto et gnati uitam et consilium meum
> cognosces et quid facere in hac re te velim.   [49–50]
> itaque quem ad modum in partitione proposuit, ita narrat,
> primum nati uitam:
> > nam is postquam excessit ex ephebis . . .   [51]
> deinde suum consilium:
> > et nunc id operam do . . .   [157]
> deinde quid Sosiam uelit facere, id quod postremum posuit in
> partitione, postremum dicit:
> > nunc tuum est officium . . .   [168]
> quem ad modum igitur hic et ad primam quamque partem
> primum accessit et omnibus absolutis finem dicendi fecit, sic
> nobis placet et ad singulas partes accedere et omnibus absolutis
> perorare.

Now that the rules for partition have been fully stated, it is necessary to remember that throughout the speech the sections should be completed in order one after another as set out in the partition, and that after all have been completed, the speech is brought to a close so that nothing is introduced after the conclusion. Terence's old man in the *Andria* makes a brief and neat partition of what he wishes his freedman to know:

> In this way you'll learn my son's manner of life and my plan,
> and what I want you to do in the matter.

And his narrative follows the plan as set out in the partition: first, his son's manner of life,

> for after he had left his ephebeia . . .

then his plan:

> and now I am anxious . . .

then what he wants Sosia to do: what was put last in the partition is stated last:

> now your task is . . .

Just as he turned his attention first to each point as it arose and after finishing them all stopped speaking, so I favor turning attention to each topic and when all have been completed, bringing the speech to an end.

2. Cic. *Inv.* 1.27, quoting *An.* 51

Argumentum est ficta res, quae tamen fieri potuit. huiusmodi apud Terentium: "nam is postquam excessit ex ephebis . . .

An *argumentum* is a fictitious narrative which nevertheless could have occurred. An example from Terence: "For after he had left his ephebeia . . ."

3. Cic. *De or.* 2.326–7, quoting *An.* 51, 117 + 128, 129

Videant illa "nam is postquam excessi ex ephebis" [51] quam longa est narratio! mores adulescentis ipsius et seruilis percontatio, mors Chrysidis, uultus et forma et lamentatio sororis, reliqua peruarie iucundeque narrantur. quod si hanc breuitatem quaesisset:

> effertur, imus, ad sepulcrum uenimus, [117 + 128]
> in ignem imposita est, [129]

[fere] decem uersiculis totum conficere potuisset; quamquam hoc ipsum "effertur, imus," concisum est ita, ut non breuitati seruitum sit, sed magis uenustati. quod si nihil fuisset, nisi "in ignem imposita est," tamen res tota cognosci facile potuisset.

Just consider the passage beginning, "For ever since the day he left his ephebeia . . ." What a long narrative it is! The young man's own character, the slave's inquiry, the death of Chrysis, her sister's face and figure and mourning, and all the rest of it are pleasantly narrated with stylistic variety. But if he had sought brevity like this:

> She's brought out, we follow, we come to the tomb,
> the body is placed on the pyre—

he could have completed the whole thing in ten verses, although the actual phrase "she's brought out, we follow," though very concise, nevertheless achieves not brevity but rather stylistic grace. If he had done nothing but, "she was placed on the pyre," the whole matter could nevertheless have been easily understood.

4. Cic. *Am.* 89, quoting *An.* 68

Sed nescio quo modo uerum est, quod in *Andria* familiaris meus dicit, "obsequium amicos, ueritas odium parit." molesta ueritas, siquidem ex ea nascitur odium, quod est venenum amicitiae, sed obsequium multo molestius, quod peccatis indulgens praecipitem amicum ferri sinit.

It is somehow true, as my close associate said in his *Andria*, that "compliance produces friends, truth hatred." Truth is a troublesome thing if indeed it engenders hatred, which poisons friendship, but much more troublesome is compliance, which in indulging his faults allows a friend to be brought to ruin.

5. Cic. *De or.* 2.172, quoting *An.* 110–12

Maiora autem et minora et paria comparabimus sic: ex maiore: "si bona existimatio diuitiis praestat et pecunia tanto opere expetitur, quanto gloria magis est expetenda!" ex minore:

> hic paruae consuetudinis
> causa huius mortem tam fert familiariter:
> quid si ipse amasset? quid hic mihi faciet patri?

We will compare the greater, the lesser, and the equal in this way. Working from the greater: "If a good reputation is superior to riches and money is sought with great effort, by how much more should glory be sought!" Working from the lesser:

> On such small acquaintance
> he takes her death so much to heart:
> What if he himself had loved? What will he do for me, his father?

6. Cic. *Cael.* 61, quoting *An.* 126

Si manebat tanta illa consuetudo Caeli, tanta familiaritas cum Clodia, quid suspicionis esset si apud Caelium mulieris seruus uisus esset? sin autem iam suberat simultas, exstincta erat consuetudo, discidium exstiterat, hinc illae lacrimae [126] nimirum et haec causa est omnium horum scelerum atque criminum.

If Caelius was maintaining such a close connection, such familiarity with Clodia, what suspicion would there have been if the woman's slave were seen at Caelius' house? But if there was already a quarrel, the connection terminated, a separation created, that's the source of those tears and surely this is the cause of all these crimes and charges.

7. Cic. *Att.* 13.34, quoting *An.* 185

De quo [Cicero's divorce of Publilia] quae fama sit scribes. "id populus curat scilicet!" non mehercule arbitror; etenim haec decantata erat fabula. sed complere paginam uolui.

Let me know what the gossip about it is. "As if the public really cared!" No, I don't suppose they do. It was the old, old story. But I wanted to fill the page.

8. Cic. *Fam.* 12.25.5, quoting *An.* 189

"nunc hic dies aliam uitam adfert, alios mores postulat," ut ait Terentius. quam ob rem, mi Quinte [Q. Cornificius], conscende nobiscum et quidem ad puppim. una nauis est iam bonorum omnium, quam quidem nos damus operam ut rectam teneamus, utinam prospero cursu! sed quicumque uenti erunt, ars nostra certe non aberit.

"Now this day brings another life, demands another way of acting," as Terence says. For that reason, my dear Quintus, come on board with us and right up to the helm. All honest men are now in the same boat, which I am trying to keep on course. May we have a successful voyage! But whatever winds there be, my skill will certainly not be wanting.

[Some four hundred years later, Paulinus of Nola echoes this line in a poem defending his change of calling to Ausonius, his former teacher: *nunc alia mentem uis agit, maior deus,* | *aliosque mores postulat* (*Carm.* 10.29–30 "now another power moves my mind, a greater god, and demands another way of acting").]

In addition, two possible allusions:

9. Cic. *De or.* 2.206 (cf. *An.* 44)

Plusque proficit, si proponitur spes utilitatis futurae quam praeteriti benefici commemoratio.

It is more effective if an expectation of future utility is advanced rather than a recollection of past service.

10. Cic. *Fam.* 2.13.2 (cf. *An.* 928)

Nam et honorificus in me consul fuit [Ap. Claudius Pulcher, cos. 54] et suauis amicus et studiosus studiorum etiam meorum. mea uero officia ei non defuisse tu es testis, cui iam κωμικὸς μάρτυς, ut opinor, accedit Phania; et mehercule etiam pluris eum feci quod te amari ab eo sensi.

As Consul he was respectful toward me and a pleasant friend and interested in my literary activities. Friendliness was not wanting on my side, as you are a witness. To which now, I suppose, Phanias is added, like a witness in a comedy. And I certainly valued him even more because I saw you were esteemed by him.

BIBLIOGRAPHY

WORKS CITED

Abel, L. 1963. *Metatheatre*, New York

Adams, J. N. 1982. *The Latin Sexual Vocabulary*, Baltimore

——. 1983. "Words for 'prostitute' in Latin," *Rheinisches Museum* 126: 321–58

——. 1984. "Female Speech in Roman Comedy," *Antichthon* 18: 43–77

——. 1994. "Wackernagel's Law and the Position of Unstressed Personal Pronouns in Classical Latin," *Transactions of the Philological Society* 92: 103–78

——. 2003. *Bilingualism and the Latin Language*, Cambridge

Allen, W. S. 1973. *Accent and Rhythm. Prosodic Features of Latin and Greek. A Study in Theory and Reconstruction*, Cambridge

——. 1978. *Vox Latina. The Pronunciation of Classical Latin*, 2 ed., Cambridge

Anderson, W. S. 2003/2004. "Terence and the Roman Rhetorical Use of the *Andria*," *Leeds International Classical Studies* 3: 1–9

——. 2004. "The Invention of Sosia for Terence's First Comedy, the *Andria*," *Ramus* 33: 10–19

Arnott, W. G. 1979/1996/2000. *Menander*, 3 vols., Loeb Classical Library, Cambridge, MA

——. 1985. "Terence's Prologues," *Papers of the Leeds Latin Seminar* 5: 1–7

Augoustakis, A. and A. Traill, eds. 2013. *A Companion to Terence*, Malden, MA

Bader, B. 1971. "The Ψόφος of the House-Door in Greek New Comedy," *Antichthon* 5: 35–48

Bagordo, A. 2001. *Beobachtungen zur Sprache des Terenz*, Göttingen

Bailey, D. R. S. 1953. "*Num* in Direct Questions: A Rule Restated," *Classical Quarterly* 3: 120–5

Bain, D. 1977. *Actors and Audience. A Study of Asides and Related Conventions in Greek Drama*, Oxford

Bannon, C. J. 1997. *The Brothers of Romulus. Fraternal Pietas in Roman Law, Literature, and Society*, Princeton

Barrios-Lech, P. 2016. *Linguistic Interaction in Roman Comedy*, Cambridge

——. 2017. "The Imperative in -*to* in Plautus and Terence," *Classical Quarterly* 67: 485–506

Barsby, J., ed. 1999. *Terence: Eunuchus*, Cambridge

——. 2000. "Donatus on Terence: The *Eunuchus* Commentary," in E. Stärk and G. Vogt-Spira, eds. *Dramatische Wäldchen. Festschrift für Eckard Lefèvre zum 65. Geburtstag* (Hildesheim) 491–513

——. 2001. "Improvvisazione, metateatro, decostruzione: Approcci alle Bacchidi di Plauto," *Lecturae Plautinae Sarsinates IV: Bacchides* (Urbino) 51–70

——. 2002."Terence and his Greek models," in Questa and Raffaelli 2002: 251–77

——. 2007. "Native Roman Rhetoric: Plautus and Terence," in W. Dominik and J. Hall, eds. *A Companion to Roman Rhetoric* (Malden, MA) 38–53

——. 2013. "Terence in Translation," in Augoustakis and Traill 2013: 446–65

Batstone, W. W. 2005. "Plautine Farce and Plautine Freedom: An Essay on the Value of Metatheatre," in W. W. Batstone and G. Tissol, eds. *Defining Genre and Gender in Latin Literature: Essays Presented to William S. Anderson on his Seventy-fifth Birthday* (New York) 13–46

Bauer, C. F. 1933. "The Latin Perfect Endings -*ere* and -*erunt*," *Language* 9: 7–79

Beacham, R. 2007. "Playing Places: the Temporary and the Permanent," in McDonald and Walton 2007: 202–26

Beare, W. 1942. "The Life of Terence," *Hermathena* 59: 20–9

——. 1964. *The Roman Stage. A Short History of Latin Drama in the Time of the Republic,* London

Benz, L., E. Stärk, and G. Vogt-Spira, eds. 1995. *Plautus und die Tradition des Stegreifspiels.* ScriptOralia 75. Tübingen

Bernstein, F. 1998. *Ludi publici. Untersuchungen zur Entstehung und Entwicklung der öffenlichen Spiele im republikanischen Rom.* Historia Einzelschriften 119. Stuttgart

Bianco, O. 1962. *Terenzio: problemi e aspetti dell' originalità,* Rome

Bonner, S. F. 1977. *Education in Ancient Rome,* Berkeley

Borgmeier, R. 2001. "'The Gods' Messenger and Secretary'? Thornton Wilder and the Classical Tradition," *International Journal of the Classical Tradition* 7: 344–65

Bradley, K. R. 1987. *Slaves and Masters in the Roman Empire. A Study in Social Control,* Oxford

Braun, L. 1970. "Polymetrie bei Terenz und Plautus," *Wiener Studien* 4: 66–83

Brink, C. O. 1971. *Horace on Poetry. The* "Ars poetica," Cambridge

Brown, P. G. McC. 1987. "Masks, Names and Characters in New Comedy," *Hermes* 115: 181–202

——. 1993. "Love and Marriage in Greek New Comedy," *Classical Quarterly* 43: 189–205

——. 2002. "Actors and actor-managers at Rome," in Easterling and Hall 2002: 225–37

——. 2007. "Movements of Characters and Pace of Action in Terence's Plays," in Kruschwitz et al. 2007: 175–88

——. 2012. "Terence, *Andria* 236–300 and the Helpfulness of Donatus' Commentary," in R. López Gregoris, ed. *Estudios sobre teatro romano: el mundo de los sentimientos y su expresión* (Zaragoza) 23–45

——. 2014. "Interpretations and Adaptations of Terence's *Andria*, from the Tenth to the Twentieth Century," in Papaioannou 2014: 241–66

——. 2015. "Plautus and Terence in Tudor England," in T. F. Earle and C. Fouto, eds. *The Reinvention of Theatre in Sixteenth-Century Europe. Traditions, Texts and Performance* (London) 255–79

Cain, A. 2013. "Terence in Late Antiquity," in Augoustakis and Traill 2013: 380–96

Cairns, F. 1969. "Terence, *Andria* 567–8," *Classical Review* 19: 263–4

Cameron, A. 2011. *The Last Pagans of Rome*, Oxford

Carney, T. F., ed. 1963. *P. Terenti Afri* Hecyra, Pretoria

——. 1964. "The Words *sodes* and *quaeso* in Terentian Usage," *Acta Classica* 7: 57–63

Carroll, M. 2018. *Infancy and Earliest Childhood in the Roman World*, Oxford

Cartledge, P. et al., eds. 1990. *Nomos. Essays in Athenian Law, Politics and Society*, Cambridge

Casson, L. 1976. "The Athenian Upper Class and New Comedy," *Transactions of the American Philological Society* 106: 29–59

——. 1984. *Ancient Trade and Society*, Detroit

Caston, R. R. 2016. "Terence and Satire," in F. Montanari and A. Rengakos, eds. *Roman Drama and its Contexts*. Trends in Classics 34 (Berlin) 435–52

Ceccarelli, L. 1991. "Prosodia e metrica latina arcaica 1956–1990," *Lustrum* 33: 227–400

Chalmers, W. R. 1965. "Plautus and his Audience," in T. A. Dorey and D. R. Dudley, eds. *Roman Drama* (New York) 21–50

Christ, M. R. 1998. *The Litigious Athenian*, Baltimore

Cioffi, C., ed. 2017. *Aeli Donati quod fertur commentum ad Andriam Terenti*, Berlin

Clackson, J. and G. Horrocks. 2007. *The Blackwell History of the Latin Language*, Oxford

Coleman, R. G. G. 1999. "Poetic Diction, Poetic Discourse and the Poetic Register," in J. N. Adams and R. Mayer, eds. *Aspects of the Language of Latin Poetry*. Proceedings of the British Academy 93 (Oxford) 21–93

Courtney, E. 1993. *The Fragmentary Latin Poets*, Oxford

Croce, B. 1966 [1936]. *Philosophy Poetry History*, tr. C. Sprigge. London

Csapo, E. G. 1989. "Plautine Elements in the Running-Slave Entrance Monologues?" *Classical Quarterly* 39: 148–63

——. 1993. "A Case Study in the Use of Theatre Iconography as Evidence for Ancient Acting," *Antike Kunst* 36: 41–58

——. 2002. "Kallipides on the floor-sweepings: the limits of realism in classical acting and performance styles," in Easterling and Hall 2002: 127–47

Csapo, E. G. and W. Slater, eds. 1995. *The Context of Ancient Drama*, Ann Arbor

Dale, A. M. 1969. *Collected Papers*, Cambridge

Damen, M. L. 1992. "Translating Scenes: Plautus' Adaptation of Menander's *Dis Exapaton*," *Phoenix* 46: 205–31

Danese, R. M. 1989. "Revisione del P Vindob. L. 103 (Terenzio)," *Studi classici e orientali* 39: 133–57

——. 2002. "Modelli letterari e modelli culturali del teatro plautino," in Questa and Raffaelli 2002: 133–53

Davidson, J. 1997. *Courtesans and Fishcakes. The Consuming Passions of Classical Athens*, New York

Davis, C. B. 2003. "Distant Ventriloquism: Vocal Mimesis, Agency and Identity in Ancient Greek Performance," *Theatre Journal* 55: 45–65

Davis, J. E. 2014. "Terence Interrupted: Literary Biography and the Reception of the Terentian Canon," *American Journal of Philology* 135: 387–409

de Melo, W. D. C. 2007. *The Early Latin Verb System: Archaic Forms in Plautus, Terence, and Beyond*, Oxford

Demetriou, C. 2014. "Aelius Donatus and His Commentary on Terence's Comedies," in Fontaine and Scafuro 2014: 782–99

Denzler, B. 1968. *Der Monolog bei Terenz*, Zurich

Deufert, M. 2002. *Textgeschichte und Rezeption der plautinischen Komödien im Altertum*, Berlin

——. 2014. "Metrics and Music," in Fontaine and Scafuro 2014: 477–97

de Vaan, M. 2008. *Etymological Dictionary of Latin and the Other Italic Languages*, Leiden

Dickey, E. 2002. *Latin Forms of Address: From Plautus to Apuleius*, Oxford

Dixon, S. 1992. *The Roman Family*, Baltimore

Dodwell, C. R. 2000. *Anglo-Saxon Gestures and the Roman Stage*, Cambridge

Dohm, H. 1964. *Mageiros: die Rolle des Kochs in der griechisch-römischen Komödie*, Munich

Duckworth, G. 1936. "The dramatic function of the *servus currens* in Roman Comedy," in *Classical Studies Presented to Edward Capps* (Princeton) 93–102

——. 1952. *The Nature of Roman Comedy*, Princeton

Du Plessis, P. et al., eds. 2016. *The Oxford Handbook of Roman Law and Society*, Oxford

Dutsch, D. M. 2007. "Gestures in the Manuscripts of Terence and Late Revivals of Classical Drama," *Gesture* 7: 39–70

——. 2008. *Feminine Discourse in Roman Comedy. On Echoes and Voices*, Oxford

——. 2012. "Gender, Genre, and the Lover's Suicide Threats in Roman Comedy," *Classical World* 105: 187–98

Dziatzko, K., ed. 1884. P. *Terenti Afri Comoediae*, Leipzig

Easterling, P. and E. Hall, eds. 2002. *Greek and Roman Actors. Aspects of an Ancient Profession*, Cambridge

Ehrmann, R. K. 1985. "Terentian Prologues and the Parabases of Old Comedy," *Latomus* 44: 370–6

Ernout, A. 1953. *Morphologie historique du latin*, 3 edn., Paris

Ernout, A. and F. Thomas. 1953. *Syntaxe latine*, 2 edn., Paris

Ernout, A. and A. Meillet. 1994. *Dictionnaire étymologique de la langue latine: histoire des mots*, Paris

Erskine, A. 2012. "Polybius among the Romans: Life in the Cyclops' Cave," in Smith and Yarrow 2012: 17–32

Evans Grubbs, J. and T. Parkin, eds. 2013. *The Oxford Handbook of Childhood and Education in the Classical World*, Oxford

Fairweather, J. 1983. "Traditional Narrative, Inference and Truth in the *Lives* of the Greek Poets," *Papers of the Liverpool Latin Seminar* 4: 315–69

Fantham, E. 1972. *Comparative Studies in Republican Latin Imagery*, Toronto

——. 1981. "Plautus in Miniature. Compression and Distortion in the *Epidicus*," *Papers of the Liverpool Latin Seminar* 3: 1–28

——. 1982. "Quintilian on Performance," *Phoenix* 36: 243–63

——. 2000. "DOMINA-tricks, or How to Construct a Good Whore from a Bad One," in E. Stärk and G. Vogt-Spira, eds. *Dramatische Wäldchen. Festschrift für Eckard Lefèvre zum 65. Geburtstag.* Spudasmata 80 (Hildesheim) 287–99

——. 2002. "Orator and/et Actor," in Easterling and Hall 2002: 362–76

——. 2004. "Terence and the Familiarisation of Comedy," *Ramus* 33: 20–34

Fantham, E. et al. 1994. *Women in the Classical World*, Oxford

Farnham, F. 1976. *Madame Dacier. Scholar and Humanist*, Monterey, CA

Feeney, D. 2010. "Crediting Pseudolus: Trust, Belief, and the Credit Crunch in Plautus' *Pseudolus*," *Classical Philology* 105: 281–300

——. 2016. *Beyond Greek. The Beginnings of Latin Literature*, Cambridge, MA

Feldherr, A. 1998. *Spectacle and Society in Livy's History*, Berkeley, CA

Fitzgerald, W. 2019. "Slaves in Roman Comedy," in M. T. Dinter, ed. *The Cambridge Companion to Roman Comedy* (Cambridge) 188–99

Flury, P. 1968. *Liebe und Liebessprache bei Menander, Plautus und Terenz*, Heidelberg

Fontaine, M. 2010. *Funny Words in Plautus*, Oxford

Fontaine, M. and A. Scafuro, eds. 2014. *The Oxford Handbook of Greek and Roman Comedy*, Oxford

Fordyce, C. J. 1961. *Catullus. A Commentary*, Oxford

Fortson, B. W., IV. 2008. *Language and Rhythm in Plautus*, Berlin

Fraenkel, E. 1957. *Horace*, Oxford

——. 2007 (1960). *Plautine Elements in Plautus*, Oxford

Frangoulidis, S. A. 1996. "Food and Poetics in Plautus, *Captivi*," *Acta Classica* 65: 225–30

French, V. 1986. "Midwives and Maternity Care in the Roman World," *Helios* 13: 69–84

Frost, K. B. 1988. *Exits and Entrances in Menander*, Oxford

Gaiser, K. 1972. "Zur Eigenart der römischen Komödie: Plautus und Terenz gegenüber ihren griechischen Vorbildern," *Aufstieg und Niedergang der römischen Welt* I.2: 1027–113

Gammacurta, T. 2006. *Papyrologica Scaenica. I. Copioni teatrali nella tradizione papiracea*, Alessandria

Gardner, J. F. 1986. *Women in Roman Law and Society*, Bloomington, IN

Garton, C. 1972. *Personal Aspects of the Roman Theatre*, Toronto

Gehl, P. F. 2016. "Selling Terence in Renaissance Italy: The Marketing Power of Commentary," in C. S. Kraus and C. Stray, eds. *Classical Commentaries. Explorations in a Scholarly Genre* (Cambridge) 253–74

Gelhaus, H. 1972. *Die Prologe des Terenz. Eine Erklärung nach den Lehren der inventio und dispositio*, Heidelberg

Germany, R. 2016. *Mimetic Contagion. Art and Artifice in Terence's Eunuch*, Oxford

Gilula, D. 1989. "The First Realistic Roles in European Theatre: Terence's Prologues," *Quaderni Urbinati di Cultura Classica* 33: 95–106

——. 1996. "The Allocation of Seats to Senators in 194 BCE," in R. Katzoff, ed. *Classical Studies in Honor of David Sohlberg* (Ramat Gan) 235–44

Goldberg, S. M. 1977. "*The Woman of Andros*: Terence Made Wilder," *Helios* 5: 11–19

——. 1983. "Terence, Cato and the Rhetorical Prologue," *Classical Philology* 78: 198–211

——. 1986. *Understanding Terence*, Princeton

——. 1990. "Act to Action in Plautus' *Bacchides*," *Classical Philology* 85: 191–201

——. 1998. "Plautus on the Palatine," *Journal of Roman Studies* 88: 1–20

——. 2004. "Plautus and His Alternatives. Textual Doublets in *Cistellaria*," in R. Hartkamp and F. Hurka, eds. *Studien zu Plautus' Cistellaria* (Tübingen) 385–98

——. 2005. *Constructing Literature in the Roman Republic. Poetry and its Reception*, Cambridge

——. 2011. "Roman Comedy Gets Back to Basics," *Journal of Roman Studies* 101: 206–21

——. ed. 2013. *Terence:* Hecyra, Cambridge

——. 2018. "Theater Without Theaters: Seeing Plays the Roman Way," *TAPA* 148: 139–72

——. 2019. *Terence:* Andria. Bloomsbury Ancient Comedy Companions, London

——. 2020. "Donatus on Terence and the Greeks," *American Journal of Philology* 141: 83–102

Golden, M. 2015. *Children and Childhood in Classical Athens*, Baltimore

Goldhill, S. 1997. "The Audience of Athenian Tragedy," in P. E. Easterling, ed. *The Cambridge Companion to Greek Tragedy* (Cambridge) 54–68

Goth, M. 2014. "Exaggerating Terence's *Andria*: Steele's *The Conscious Lovers*, Bellamy's *The Perjur'd Devotee* and Terentian Criticism," in Olson 2014: 503–36

Gowers, E. 1993. *The Loaded Table. Representations of Food in Roman Literature*, Oxford

——. 2004. "The Plot Thickens: Hidden Outlines in Terence's Prologues," *Ramus* 33: 150–66

Grant, J. N. 1986. *Studies in the Textual Tradition of Terence*, Toronto

Gratwick, A. S. 1982. "Drama," in E. J. Kenney and W. V. Clausen, eds. *The Cambridge History of Classical Literature. Vol. II: Latin Literature* (Cambridge) 77–137

——, ed. 1993. *Plautus*, Menaechmi, Cambridge

Gruen, E. S. 1990. *Studies in Greek Culture and Roman Policy*, Leiden

——. 1992. *Culture and National Identity in Republican Rome*, Ithaca

Habicht, C. 1997. *Athens from Alexander to Antony*, Cambridge, MA

Haffter, H. 1934. *Untersuchungen zur altlateinischen Dichtersprache*, Berlin

——. 1953. "Terenz und seine künstlerische Eigenart," *Museum Helveticum* 10: 1–20, 73–102

Hagendahl, H. 1974. "Jerome and the Latin Classics," *Vigiliae Christianae* 28: 216–27

Halbwachs, V. 2016. "Women as Legal Actors," in P. J. Du Plessis and C. Ando, eds. *The Oxford Handbook of Roman Law and Society* (Oxford) 443–55

Halla-Aho, H. 2018. *Left-Dislocation in Latin: Topics and Syntax in Republican Texts*, Leiden

Hallett, J. P. 1984. *Fathers and Daughters in Roman Society. Women and the Elite Family*, Princeton

Halporn, J. W. 1993. "Roman Comedy and Greek Models," in R. Scodel, ed. *Theater and Society in the Classical World* (Ann Arbor) 191–213

Handley, E. W. 1965. *The* Dyskolos *of Menander*, Cambridge, MA

——. 2001. "Actoris opera: Words, Action and Acting in *Dis Exapaton* and *Bacchides,*" in R. Raffaelli and A. Tontioni, eds. *Lecturae plautinae sarsinates IV*: Bacchides (Urbino) 13–36

——. 2002. "Theme and variations," in Questa and Raffaelli 2002: 105–20

Hanses, M. 2013. "*Mulier inopia et cognatorum neglegentia coacta*: Thornton Wilder's Tragic Take on *The Woman of Andros,*" in Augoustakis and Traill 2013: 429–45

——. 2020a. "Men among Monuments: Roman Memory and Roman Topography in Plautus's *Curculio*," *Classical Philology*: 115: 630–58

——. 2020b. *The Life of Comedy after the Death of Plautus and Terence*, Ann Arbor

Harris, W. V. 1994. "Child-Exposure in the Roman Empire," *Journal of Roman Studies* 84: 1–22

Harvey, D. 1990. "The Sycophant and Sycophancy: Vexatious Redefinition?" in P. Cartledge et al., eds. *Nomos. Essays in Athenian Law, Politics and Society* (Cambridge) 103–21

Haugen, K. L. 2011. *Richard Bentley. Poetry and Enlightenment*, Boston

Hayes, J. C. 2009. *Translation, Subjectivity, and Culture in France and England, 1600–1800*, Stanford, CA

Hersch, K. K. 2010. *The Roman Wedding: Ritual and Meaning in Antiquity*, Cambridge

——. 2013/2014. "Introduction to the Roman Wedding: Two Case Studies," *Classical Journal* 109: 223–32

Hinds, S. 1998. *Allusion and Intertext. Dynamics of Appropriation in Roman Poetry*, Cambridge

Hofmann, J. B. 1951. *Lateinische Umgangssprache*, 3 ed., Heidelberg

Holford-Strevens, L. 2003. *Aulus Gellius: An Antonine Scholar and his Achievement*, Oxford

Hope, V. 2007. *Death in Ancient Rome: A Sourcebook*, London

Horsfall, N. M. 1976. "The Collegium poetarum," *Bulletin of the Institute of Classical Studies* 23: 79–95

Hunt, P. 2018. *Ancient Greek and Roman Slavery*, Chichester

Hunter, R. 1985. *The New Comedy of Greece and Rome*, Cambridge

——. 2006. *The Shadow of Callimachus. Studies in the Reception of Hellenistic Poetry at Rome*, Cambridge

——. 2014. "Some Dramatic Terminology," in F. Montanari and A. Rengakos, eds. *Roman Drama and its Contexts*. Trends in Classics 34 (Berlin) 13–24

Jachmann, G. 1924. *Die Geschichte des Terenztextes im Altertum*, Basel

———. 1929. *Terentius' Codex Vaticanus Latinus 3868 phototypice editus*, Basel

———. 1934. "P. Terentius Afer," *RE* V A.1: 598–650

Jakobi, R. 1996. *Die Kunst der Exegese im Terenzkommentar des Donat*, Berlin

Jocelyn, H. D. 1995. "The Life-style of the Ageing Bachelor and Theatrical Improvisation (Plaut. *Mil.* 596–812)," in Benz et al. 1995: 107–22

Johnston, M. 1933. *Exits and Entrances in Roman Comedy (Plautus and Terence)*, Geneva, NY

Jones, L. W. and C. R. Morey. 1930–1931. *The Miniatures of the Manuscripts of Terence Prior to the Thirteenth Century*, 2 vols., Princeton

Jory, E. J. 1963. "'Algebraic' Notation in Dramatic Texts," *Bulletin of the Institute of Classical Studies* 10: 65–78

———. 1970. "Associations of Actors at Rome," *Hermes* 98: 224–53

Jürgens, H. 1972. *Pompa diaboli. Die lateinischen Kirchenväter und das antike Theater.* Tübingen Beiträge 46. Stuttgart

Karakasis, E. 2005. *Terence and the Language of Roman Comedy*, Cambridge

Kaster, R. A. 1988. *Guardians of Language: The Grammarian and Society in Late Antiquity*, Berkeley

———. 1997. "The Shame of the Romans," *Transactions of the American Philological Association* 127: 1–19

Kaster, R. A., ed. 1995. *Suetonius*, De grammaticis et rhetoribus, Oxford

Keane, C. 2018. "Conversations about *sermo,*" in B. W. Breed et al., eds. *Lucilius and Satire in Second-Century BC Rome* (Cambridge) 217–35

Keefe, B. R. 2015. "Illustrating the Manuscripts of Terence," in Torello-Hill and Turner 2015: 36–66

Kennell, N. M. 2015. "The *Ephebeia* in the Hellenistic Period," in W. M. Bloomer, ed. *A Companion to Ancient Education* (Malden, MA) 172–83

Kenny, S. S. 1968. "Eighteenth-Century Editions of Steele's 'Conscious Lovers,'" *Studies in Bibliography* 21: 253–61

Klose, D. 1966. *Die Didaskalien und Prologe des Terenz*, Bamberg

Knorr, O. 2007. "Metatheatrical Humor in the Comedies of Terence," in Kruschwitz et al. 2007: 167–74

Kragelund, P. 2012. "Evidence for Performances of Republican Comedy in Fourth-Century Rome," *Classical Quarterly* 62: 415–22

Krause, J.-U. 2011. "Children in the Roman Family and Beyond," in Peachin 2011: 623–42

Kruschwitz, P. 2016. "*Ne cum poeta scriptura evanesceret.* Exploring the Protohistory of Terence's Dramatic Scripts," in Velaza 2016: 29–43

Kruschwitz, P. et al., eds. 2007. *Terentius poeta*. Zetemata 127. Munich

Laidlaw, W. A. 1938. *The Prosody of Terence*, London

Lambrecht, K. 2001. "Dislocation," in M. Haspelmath et al. *Language Typology and Language Universals*, vol. 2. (Berlin) 1050–78

Lateiner, D. 2004. "Gestures: The Imagined Journey from the Roman Stage to the Anglo-Saxon Manuscript." Rev. of Dodwell 2000. *International Journal of the Classical Tradition* 10: 454–64

Laughton, E. 1964. *The Participle in Cicero*, Oxford

Lebek, W. D. 1996. "Money-making on the Roman Stage," in W. J. Slater, ed. *Roman Theater and Society* (Ann Arbor) 29–48

Lefèvre, E. 2008. *Terenz' und Menanders Andria*. Zetemata 132. Munich

Leo, F. 1912. *Plautinische Forschungen zur Kritik und Geschichte der Komödie*, Berlin

——. 1913. *Geschichte der römischen Literatur*, Berlin

——. 1960a. *Ausgewählte kleine Schriften I. Zur römischen Literatur des Zeitalters der Republik*, ed. E. Fraenkel. Rome.

——. 1960a (1898). "Analecta plautina II. De figuris sermonis," in Leo 1960: 123–62

——. 1960b (1906). "Analecta plautina III. De figuris sermonis," in Leo 1960: 163–84

Leppin, H. 1992. *Histrionen. Untersuchungen zur sozialen Stellung von Bühnenkünstlern im Westen des römischen Reiches zur Zeit der Republik und des Principats*, Bonn

Leumann, M. 1977. *Lateinische Laut- und Formenlehre*, 6 ed. *Lateinische Grammatik*, 1 Bd. (Handbuch der Altertumswissenschaft II.2.), Munich

Lightfoot, J. L. 2002. "Nothing to do with the *technītai* of Dionysus?," in Easterling and Hall 2002: 209–24

Linderski, J. 1987. "The Aediles and the *didascaliae*," *Ancient History Bulletin* 1: 83–8

Lindsay, W. M. 1907. *The Syntax of Plautus*, Oxford

Ling, R. 1990. "Street Plaques at Pompeii," in M. Henig, ed. *Architecture and Architectural Sculpture in the Roman Empire* (Oxford) 51–66

Lobel, D. 2017. *Philosophies of Happiness*, New York

Lofberg, J. O. 1920. "The Sycophant-Parasite," *Classical Philology* 15: 61–72

Long, A. A. 2006. *From Epicurus to Epictetus. Studies in Hellenistic and Roman Philosophy*, Oxford

Lowe, J. C. B. 1985. "Cooks in Plautus," *Classical Antiquity* 4: 72–102

——. 1997. "Terence's Four-Speaker Scenes," *Phoenix* 51: 152–69

——. 2009. "Terence and the Running-Slave Routine," *Rheinisches Museum* 152: 225–34

Lucarini, C. M. 2016. "Playwrights, Actor-managers and the Plautine Text in Antiquity," in Velaza 2016: 9–27

Luck, G. 1964. *Über einige Interjektionen der lateinischen Umgangssprache*, Heidelberg

Ludwig, W. 1968. "The Originality of Terence and His Greek Models," *Greek, Roman and Byzantine Studies* 9: 169–82

MacDowell, D. 1978. *The Law in Classical Athens*, Ithaca

Macedo, G. N. 2018. "P. Oxy. 2401 and the History of Terence's Text in Antiquity," *Bulletin of the American Society of Papyrologists* 55: 71–117

Maltby, R. 1979. "Linguistic Characterization of Old Men in Terence," *Classical Philology* 74: 136–47

———. 1985. "The Distribution of Greek Loan-Words in Terence," *Classical Quarterly* 35: 110–23

———. 2019. "Greek in Donatus' Terence Commentaries," in N. Holem et al., eds. *Lemmata Linguistica Latina*. Vol. I: Words and Sounds (Berlin) 312–28

Manuwald, G. 2010. *Roman Drama: A Reader*, London

———. 2011. *Roman Republican Theatre*, Cambridge

———. 2014. "Cicero, an Interpreter of Terence," in Papaioannou 2014: 179–200

Marshall, C. W. 1999. "*Quis hic loquitur?* Plautine Delivery and the 'Double Aside,'" *Syllecta Classica* 10: 105–29

———. 2006. *The Stagecraft and Performance of Roman Comedy*, Cambridge

———. 2013. "Sex Slaves in New Comedy," in B. Akrigg and R. L. S. Tordoff, eds., *Slaves and Slavery in Ancient Greek Comic Drama* (Cambridge) 173–96

Marti, H. 1974. "Zeugnisse zur Nachwirkung des Dichters Terenz im Altertum," in U. Reinhardt and K. Sallmann, eds. *Musa Iocosa. Festschr. A. Thierfelder* (Hildesheim) 158–78

Martin, R. H. 1964. "Three Notes on Terence's *Andria*," *Classical Review* 14: 3–4

Mattingly, H. B. 1959. "The Terentian *didascaliae*," *Athenaeum* 37: 148–73

———. 1960. "The First Period of Plautine Revival," *Latomus* 19: 230–52

McCarthy, K. 2004. "The Joker in the Pack: Slaves in Terence," *Ramus* 33: 100–19

McDonald, M. and J. M. Walton, eds. 2007. *The Cambridge Companion to Greek and Roman Theatre*, Cambridge

McWilliam, J. 2013. "The Socialization of Roman Children," in Evans Grubbs and Parkin 2013: 264–85

Meiser, G. 1998. *Historische Laut- und Formenlehre der lateinischen Sprache*, Darmstadt

Meyer, E. 2016. "Evidence and Argument. The Truth of Prestige and its Performance," in Du Plessis et al. 2016: 270–82

Minarini, A. 1987. *Studi Terenziani*. Bologna

Momigliano, A. 1975. *Alien Wisdom. The Limits of Hellenization*, Cambridge
Moodie, E. K. 2009. "Old Men and Metatheatre in Terence: Terence's Dramatic Competition," *Ramus* 38: 145–73
Moore, T. J. 1995. "Seats and Social Status in the Plautine Theater," *Classical Journal* 90: 113–23
———. 1998. *The Theater of Plautus*, Austin
———. 2007. "Terence as Musical Innovator," in Kruschwitz et al. 2007: 93–109
———. 2008. "When did the *tibicen* Play? Meter and Musical Accompaniment in Roman Comedy," *Transactions of the American Philological Association* 138: 3–46
———. 2012. *Music in Roman Comedy*, Cambridge
———. 2013. "*Andria*: Terence's Musical Experiment," in T. J. Moore and W. Polleichtner, eds. *Form und Bedeutung im lateinischen Drama / Form and Meaning in Latin Drama* (Trier) 87–114
Morgan, L. 2010. *Musa Pedestris. Metre and Meaning in Roman Verse*, Oxford
Mouritsen, H. 2011. *The Freedman in the Roman World*, Cambridge
Müller, R. 1997. *Sprechen und Sprache. Dialoglinguistiche Studien zu Terenz*, Heidelberg
Nesselrath, H.-G. 2011. "Menander and his Rivals: New Light from the Comic Adespota?" in D. Obbink and R. Rutherford, eds. *Culture in Pieces. Essays on Ancient Texts in Honour of Peter Parsons* (Oxford) 119–37
Norwood, G. 1923. *The Art of Terence*, Oxford
Nünlist, R. 2002. "Speech within speech in Menander," in A. Willi, ed. *The Language of Greek Comedy* (Oxford) 219–59
Oakley, J. H. and R. H. Sinos. 1993. *The Wedding in Ancient Athens*, Madison
Oakley, S. P. 1998. *A Commentary on Livy. Books VI–X*, vol. II: Books VII–VIII, Oxford
Olson, S. D., ed. 2014. *Ancient Comedy and Reception. Essays in Honor of Jeffrey Henderson*. Berlin
Orgel, S. 1991. "What is a text?" in D. S. Kastan and P. Stallybrass, eds. *Staging the Renaissance* (London) 83–7
Orr, B. 2020. *British Enlightenment Theatre. Dramatizing Difference*, Cambridge
Otto, A. 1890. *Die Sprichwörter und sprichwörtlichen Redensarten der Römer*, Leipzig
Page, D. L. 1962. *Select Papyri III. Literary Papyri*. Loeb Classical Library 360, Cambridge, MA
Palmer, L. R. 1961. *The Latin Language*, London
Papaioannou, S. 2014. "The Innovator's Poetic Self-Presentation: Terence's Prologues as Interpretative Texts of Programmatic Poetics," in Papaioannou 2014: 25–58

Papaioannou, S., ed. 2014. *Terence and Interpretation*, Newcastle

Parker, H. 1989. "Crucially Funny, or Tranio on the Couch: The *Servus Callidus* and Jokes about Torture," *Transactions of the American Philological Association* 119: 233–46

——. 1996. "Plautus v. Terence: Audience and Popularity Re-examined," *American Journal of Philology* 117: 585–617

Parkin, T. 2013. "The Demography of Infancy and Early Childhood in the Ancient World," in Evans Grubbs and Parkin 2013: 40–61

Patterson, C. 1985. "'Not worth the rearing': The causes of infant exposure in ancient Greece," *Transactions of the American Philological Association* 115: 103–23

——. 1994. "The Case Against Neaira and the Public Ideology of the Athenian Family," in A. Boegehold and A. Scafuro, eds. *Athenian Identity and Civic Ideology* (Baltimore) 199–216

Peachin, M. 2011. *The Oxford Handbook of Social Relations in the Roman World*, Oxford

Pezzini, G. 2015. *Terence and the Verb "To Be" in Latin*, Oxford

Pinkster, H. 1998. "Is the Latin present tense the unmarked, neutral tense in the system?" in R. Risselada, ed. *Latin in Use*. Amsterdam Studies in the Pragmatics of Latin (Amsterdam) 63–83

Prescott, H. W. 1939. "Link monologues in Roman comedy," *Classical Philology* 34: 1–23, 116–26

Prete, S. 1970. *Il codice di Terenzio vaticano latino 3226*, Vatican City

Questa, C. 1965. *T. Maccius Plautus* Bacchides, Florence

——. 2001. "Per un'edizione di Plauto," *Giornate filologiche 'Francesco della Corte' II* (Genoa) 61–83

——. 2007. *La metrica di Plauto e di Terenzio*, Urbino

Questa, C. and R. Raffaelli, eds. 2002. *Due seminari plautini. La tradizione del testo. I modelli*, Urbino

Rawson, E. 1987. "*Discrimina ordinum*: the *lex Julia theatralis*," *Papers of the British School at Rome* 55: 83–114

——. 1993. "Freedmen in Roman Comedy," in Scodel 1993: 215–33

Redard, G. 1956. "Le rajeunissement du texte de Plaute," in *Hommages à Max Niedermann*. Collection Latomus XXIII (Brussels) 296–306

Reeve, M. D. 1983a. "Aelius Donatus, *Commentary on Terence*," in Reynolds 1983: 153–6

——. 1983b. "Terence," in Reynolds 1983: 412–20

Rehm, R. 2007. "Festivals and Audiences in Athens and Rome," in McDonald and Walton 2007: 184–201

Reynolds, L. D., ed. 1983. *Texts and Transmission. A Survey of the Latin Classics*, Oxford

Richlin, A. 2017. *Slave Theater in the Roman Republic. Plautus and Popular Comedy*, Cambridge

——. 2019. "Blackface and Drag in the *palliata*," in S. Matzner and S. Harrison, eds. *Complex Inferiorities. The Poetics of the Weaker Voice in Latin Literature* (Oxford) 49–72

Ritschl, F. 1845. *Parerga zu Plautus und Terenz I.* Berlin

——. 1845a. "De actae *Trinummi* tempore," in Ritschl 1845: 339–54

——. 1845b. "De gemino exitu *Andriae* terentianae," in Ritschl 1845: 583–602

Rosenmeyer, T. G. 2002. "'Metatheater': An Essay in Overload," *Arion* 10: 87–119

Rostagni, A., ed. 1954. *Suetonius. De Poetis e biografi minori; restituzione e commento,* Turin

Rous, S. A. 2020. "*Homo sum*: John Adams Reads Terence," *Classical World* 113: 299–334

Russell, A. 2012. "Aemilius Paullus Sees Greece: Travel, Vision, and Power in Polybius," in Smith and Yarrow 2012: 152–67

——. 2016. *The Politics of Public Space in Republican Rome.* Cambridge

Scafuro, A. 1997. *The Forensic Stage. Settling Disputes in Greco-Roman Comedy,* Cambridge

Schaaf, L. 1977. *Der Miles Gloriosus des Plautus und sein griechisches Original,* Munich

Schaps, D. 1977. "The Woman Least Mentioned: Etiquette and Women's Names," *Classical Quarterly* 27: 323–30

Schmidt, P. L. 1989. "*Postquam ludus in artem paulatim uerterat.* Varro und die Frühgeschichte des römischen Theaters," in G. Vogt-Spira, ed. *Studien zur vorliterarischen Periode im frühen Rom.* ScriptOralia 12 (Tübingen) 77–133

Scodel, R., ed. 1993. *Theater and Society in the Classical World,* Ann Arbor

Sear, F. 2006. *Roman Theatres. An Architectural Study,* Oxford

Segal, E. 1987. *Roman Laughter. The Comedy of Plautus,* 2 ed. Oxford

Shapiro, J. 2010. *Contested Will. Who Wrote Shakespeare?,* New York

Sharrock, A. 2009. *Reading Roman Comedy. Poetics and Playfulness in Plautus and Terence,* Cambridge

——. 2014. "Reading Plautus' *Trinummus*: Who'd Bother?," in I. N. Perysinakis and E. Karakasis, eds. *Plautine Trends. Studies in Plautine Comedy and its Reception.* Trends in Classics 29 (Berlin) 167–95

Shatzman, I. 1975. *Senatorial Wealth and Roman Politics.* Collection Latomus 142, Brussels

Skutsch, O. 1957. "Der zweite Schluss der *Andria*," *Rheinisches Museum für Philologie* 100: 53–68

Slater, N. W. 1985. *Plautus in Performance. The Theatre of the Mind,* Princeton

Smith, C. and L. M. Yarrow, eds. 2012. *Imperialism, Cultural Politics, and Polybius,* Oxford

Solodow, J. B. 1978. *The Latin Particle quidem,* Boulder, CO

Soubiran, J. 1988. *Essai sur la versification dramatique des romains: sénaire iambique et septénaire trochaïque*, Paris

Spengel, A., ed. 1888. *Die Komödien des P. Terentius*, I: *Andria*, 2 ed., Berlin

Stephens, L. 1985. "Indirect Questions in Old Latin: Syntactic and Pragmatic Factors Conditioning Modal Shift," *Illinois Classical Studies* 10: 195–214

Stürner, F. 2011. *Monologe bei Plautus. Ein Beitrag zur Dramaturgie der hellenistisch-römischen Komödie*. Hermes Einzelschriften 103, Stuttgart

Suerbaum, W., ed. 2002. *Handbuch der lateinischen Literatur der Antike. Erster Band: Die archaische Literatur*, Munich

Surbat, G. 1991. "Intégration à la phrase latine d'un groupe nominal sans fonction syntaxique (le 'nominativus pendens')," *Langages* 104: 22–32

Sutton, D. F. 1987. "The Theatrical Families of Athens," *American Journal of Philology* 108: 9–26

Tansey, P. 2001. "New Light on the Roman Stage. A Revival of Terence's *Phormio* Rediscovered," *Rheinisches Museum für Philologie* 144: 22–43

Taplin, O. 1977. *The Stagecraft of Aeschylus. The Dramatic Use of Exits and Entrances in Greek Tragedy*, Oxford

———. 1993. *Comic Angels and Other Approaches to Greek Drama through Vase-painting*, Oxford

Taylor, A. 1996. "The History of a Proverbial Pattern," *De Prouerbio* 2

Taylor, L. R. 1937. "The Opportunities for Dramatic Performances in the Time of Plautus and Terence," *Transactions of the American Philological Association* 68: 284–304

Temin, P. 2013. *The Roman Market Economy*, Princeton

Teramura, M. 2018. "Black Comedy: Shakespeare, Terence, and *Titus Andronicus*," *ELH* 85: 877–908

Thesleff, H. 1960. *Yes and No in Plautus and Terence*, Helsingfors

Thomadaki, M. 1989. "La mise en scène du théâtre de Térence dans les commentaires de Donat," *Dioniso* 59: 365–72

Thumiger, C. 2009. "On Ancient and Modern (Meta)theatres: Definitions and Practices," *Materiali e discussioni* 63: 9–58

Thür, G. 2005. "The Role of the Witness in Athenian Law," in M. Gagarin and D. Cohen, eds. *The Cambridge Companion to Ancient Greek Law* (Cambridge) 146–69

Todd, S. C. 1990. "The Purpose of Evidence in Athenian Courts," in Cartledge et al. 1990, 19–39

———. 1993. *The Shape of Athenian Law*, Oxford

Torello-Hill, G. and A. J. Turner. 2015. *Terence between Late Antiquity and the Age of Printing. Illustration, Commentary and Performance*. Metaforms, Vol. 4, Leiden

——. 2020. *The Lyon Terence. Its Tradition and Legacy,* Leiden

Traina, A. 1968. "Terenzio 'traduttore,'" *Belfagor* 23: 431–8

Treggiari, S. 1969. *Roman Freedmen During the Late Republic,* Oxford

——. 1991. *Roman Marriage,* Oxford

Trümper, M. 2012. "Gender and Space, 'Public' and 'Private,'" in S. L. James and S. Dillon, eds. *A Companion to Women in the Ancient World* (Chichester) 288–303

Umbrico, A. 2010. *Terenzio e i suoi nobiles. Invenzione e realtà di un controverso legame,* Pisa

Velaza, J., ed. 2016. *From the Protohistory to the History of the Text.* Studien zur klassischen Philologie, Bd. 173. Frankfurt

Vérilhac, A.-M. and C. Vial. 1998. *Le Mariage grec du VIe siècle av. J.-C. à l'époque d'Auguste,* Athens

Vickers, B. 2002. *Shakespeare, Co-author. A Historical Study of Five Collaborative Plays,* Oxford

Victor, B. 1989. "The 'alter exitus Andriae,'" *Latomus* 48: 63–74

——. 1993. "Remarks on the *Andria* of Terence," *Harvard Studies in Classical Philology* 95: 273–9

——. 1996a. "A Problem of Method in the History of Texts and its Implications for the Manuscript Tradition of Terence," *Revue d'histoire des textes* 26: 269–87

——. 1996b. "Four Passages in the *Andria* of Terence," *Echos du monde classique: Classical Views* 40: 371–7

——. 1999. "Further Remarks on the *Andria* of Terence," *Harvard Studies in Classical Philology* 99: 269–73

——. 2013. "History of the Text and Scholia," in Augoustakis and Traill 2013: 343–62

——. 2014. "The Transmission of Terence," in Fontaine and Scafuro 2014: 699–716

Watson, A. 1967. *The Law of Persons in the Later Roman Republic,* Oxford

——. 1968. *The Law of Property in the Later Roman Republic,* Oxford

——. 1971. *Roman Private Law Around 200 BC,* Edinburgh

Webster, T. B. L. 1960. *Studies in Menander,* 2 ed., Manchester

——. 1995. *Monuments Illustrating New Comedy,* 3 ed. rev. and enlarged by J. R. Green and A. Seeberg, 2 vols. London

Weiss, M. 2020. *Outline of the Historical and Comparative Grammar of Latin,* 2 ed., Ann Arbor

Welsh, J. T. 2011. "Accius, Porcius Licinus, and the Beginning of Latin Literature," *Journal of Roman Studies* 101: 31–50

——. 2014. "Singing the *Sermo Comicus* with Terence," in Papaioannou 2014: 59–74

Wessner, P., ed. 1902–1908. *Aeli Donati Commentum Terenti,* 3 vols., Leipzig

West, M. L. 1982. *Greek Metre*, Oxford

Wilkins, J. 2000. *The Boastful Chef. The Discourse of Food in Ancient Greek Comedy*, Oxford

Williams, G. 1958. "Some Aspects of Roman Marriage Ceremonies and Ideals," *Journal of Roman Studies* 48: 16–29

———. 1968. *Tradition and Originality in Roman Poetry*, Oxford

Wills, J. 1993. "Virgil's *CUIUM*," *Vergilius* 39: 3–11

———. 1996. *Repetition in Latin Poetry: Figures of Allusion*, Oxford

Wilson, B. D. 2012. "Bevil's Eyes: Or, How Crying at 'The Conscious Lovers' Could Save Britain," *Eighteenth-Century Studies* 45: 497–518

Wilson, P. 2000. *The Athenian Institution of the* khoregia, Cambridge

Wiseman, T. P. 1995. *Remus. A Roman Myth*, Cambridge

———. 1998. *Roman Drama and Roman History*, Exeter

———. 2008. *"Praetextae, togatae* and Other Unhelpful Categories," in *Unwritten Rome* (Exeter) 194–9

Wolfram, N. 2012. "'I am my master's servant for hire': Contract and Identity in Richard Steele's 'The Conscious Lovers,'" *The Eighteenth Century* 53: 455–72

Wright, D. H. 2006. *The Lost Late Antique Illustrated Terence*, Vatican City

Wright, F. W. 1931. *Cicero and the Theater*, Northampton, MA

Wright, J. 1974. *Dancing in Chains: The Stylistic Unity of the comoedia palliata*, Rome

Wyles, R. 2016. "Ménage's Learned Ladies. Anne Dacier (1647–1720) and Anna Maria van Schurman (1607–1678)," in R. Wyles and E. Hall, eds. *Women Classical Scholars. Unsealing the Fountain from the Renaissance to Jacqueline de Romilly* (Oxford) 61–77

Zagagi, N. 1995. *The Comedy of Menander*, Bloomington, IN

Zelnick-Abramovitz, R. 2005. *Not Wholly Free: The Concept of Manumission and the Status of Manumitted Slaves in the Ancient Greek World*, Leiden

Zetzel, J. E. G. 1974. "*Andria* 403 (II 3,29)," *Hermes* 102: 372–6

———. 1981. *Latin Textual Criticism in Antiquity*, New York

———. 2018. *Critics, Compilers, and Commentators. An Introduction to Roman Philology, 200 BCE–800 CE*, Oxford

INDEX

Numbers prefixed by p. or pp. refer to pages. All other references are to line numbers in the Commentary. For further guidance, consult the headings and subheadings in the Introduction and Appendices.